Lecture Notes in Artificial Intelligence 587

Subseries of Lecture Notes in Computer Science
Edited by J. Siekmann

Lecture Notes in Computer Science
Edited by G. Goos and J. Hartmanis

R. Dale   E. Hovy
D. Rösner   O. Stock   (Eds.)

Aspects
of Automated Natural
Language Generation

6th International Workshop
on Natural Language Generation
Trento, Italy, April 5-7, 1992
Proceedings

Springer-Verlag
Berlin Heidelberg New York
London Paris Tokyo
Hong Kong Barcelona
Budapest

Series Editor

Jörg Siekmann
Universität des Saarlandes, DFKI, Gebäude 43.2
Stuhlsatzenhausweg 3, W-6600 Saarbrücken, FRG

Volume Editors

Robert Dale
Centre for Cognitive Science, University of Edinburgh
2 Buccleuch Place, Edinburgh EH8 9LW, Scotland, UK

Eduard Hovy
USC/Information Sciences Institute
4676 Admiralty Way, Marina del Rey, CA 90292, USA

Dietmar Rösner
Forschungsinstitut für anwendungsorientierte Wissensverarbeitung (FAW)
Universität Ulm, Postfach 2060, W-7900 Ulm, FRG

Oliviero Stock
Instituto per la Ricerca Scientifica e Tecnologica (IRST)
38050 Povo, Trento, Italy

CR Subject Classification (1991): I.2.1, I.2.7, J.5

ISBN 3-540-55399-1 Springer-Verlag Berlin Heidelberg New York
ISBN 0-387-55399-1 Springer-Verlag New York Berlin Heidelberg

© Springer-Verlag Berlin Heidelberg 1992
Printed in Germany

Typesetting: Camera ready by author
Printing and binding: Druckhaus Beltz, Hemsbach/Bergstr.
45/3140-543210 - Printed on acid-free paper

Preface

This book comprises the papers selected for presentation at the Sixth International Workshop on Natural Language Generation held in Castel Ivano, Trento, Italy, April 5 – 7, 1992. The five previous international workshops on natural language generation were held in Stettenfels, near Stuttgart (Germany) in 1983; Stanford, California (USA) in 1984; Nijmegen (Netherlands) in 1986; Santa Catalina Island near Los Angeles (USA) in 1988 and Dawson, Pennsylvania (USA) in 1990.

Some of these previous workshops have resulted in published proceedings, e.g., G. Kempen (Ed.) *Natural Language Generation*, NATO ASI Series E 135, Martinus Nijhoff Publishers, 1987, and Cécile L. Paris, William R. Swartout and William C. Mann (Ed.), *Natural Language Generation in Artificial Intelligence and Computational Linguistics*, Kluwer Academic Publishers, 1991. On this occasion the organizers adopted the approach of having a published version of the proceedings ready in time for the workshop. This sacrifices the possibility of papers being revised on the basis of workshop discussions, but has the benefit of producing a more timely snapshot of the state of the art in a rapidly consolidating field, avoiding the usual lengthy publishing delays.

The papers submitted were reviewed by an international programme committee; based on their judgement and criticism the 17 papers included in this book were selected.

In addition to the organisers the following colleagues acted as reviewers:

Hans Ulrich Block — SIEMENS, Munich, Germany
Koenraad De Smedt — University of Leiden, Leiden, The Netherlands
Helmut Horacek — University of Bielefeld, Bielefeld, Germany
Kathy McCoy — University of Delaware, Newark, USA
David McDonald — Cambridge, USA
Kathy McKeown — Columbia University, New York, USA
Johanna Moore — University of Pittsburgh, Pittsburgh, USA
Henk Schotel — University of Amsterdam, Amsterdam, The Netherlands
Donia Scott — Brighton Polytechnic, Brighton, England
Patrick St Dizier — INRIA, Toulouse, France

In addition to the paper presentations, the workshop included an invited lecture and two panel discussions. In order to broaden our own perspective, we chose to invite Professor Nadia Magnenat-Thalmann, University of Geneva (Switzerland), a well-known researcher in computer animation and author of several books and numerous papers on this topic, to present her views of the two fields and their potential for collaborative research in the future.

The two panels are organized around the topics of "Multilinguality and Generation" and "Extending Language Generation to Multiple Media". The majority of the panelists' statements are included in this book, although some were unfortunately not available in time for the publication deadline.

As on previous occasions, this workshop has been organized on a volunteer basis. The workshop would not have been possible without the help and efforts of numerous people: We have to thank all researchers who submitted papers, and all those who took part in the workshop presentations and discussions. We have to thank the international programme committee for their timely and thorough reviewing work. We have to thank the secretarial staff of our institutes, i.e., the Information Sciences Institute (ISI) in Marina del Rey, Los Angeles, the Centre for Cognitive Science, University of Edinburgh, the Forschungsinstitut für anwendungsorientierte Wissensverarbeitung (FAW) in Ulm, the Istituto per la Ricerca Scientifica e Tecnologica (IRST) in Trento, and – last but not least – the staff and management of Castel Ivano who made available to us the marvellous site of the workshop.

We also have to thank the co-sponsoring organizations for their support: The special interest group on generation of the Association for Computational Linguistics (ACL SIGGEN), and the ESPRIT Basic Research Actions. A very special thanks goes to Harry Schoett, a diploma student of economics, mathematics and computer science at the University of Ulm and research assistant at the FAW who managed to get all contributions into the book in order to have it published in time by Springer-Verlag.

February 1992

Robert Dale
Eduard Hovy
Dietmar Rösner
Oliviero Stock

Table of Contents

A Model for Creating and Visualizing Speech and Emotion

Nadia Magnenat-Thalmann and Prem Kalra

MIRALab, CUI
University of Geneva
12 rue du Lac
CH 1207 Geneva
Switzerland

Abstract

This paper presents a methodology of specifying, controlling and synchronizing the temporal and spatial characteristics for 3D animation of facial expressions. The proposed approach consists of hierarchical levels of controls. The top level requires direct animator input of global abstract actions and their durations, which correspond to intuitive and natural specifications for facial animation. These actions are then decomposed to less abstract entities and transmitted to lower levels of control. At the lowest level, muscle actions are integrated with their respective intensities to cause the appropriate movement of points in the 3D facial model. This multi-level system encapsulates facial movements linked to both emotion and conversation.

1 Introduction

It is difficult to create a model for facial animation that is both physically realistic and easy to use. We use a multi-level approach, which divides the facial animation problem into a hierarchy of independent levels. The upper levels use higher degrees of abstraction for defining entities such as emotions and phrases of speech, allowing animators to manipulate these entities in a natural and intuitive way. From the highest to the lowest, the levels of abstraction in our system are illustrated in Figure 1. A synchronization mechanism is provided at the top level that requires animators to specify the highest level entities: emotions, sentences and head movement with their durations. The system provides default values for durations in case they are not specified. These entities are then decomposed into lower level entities and sent through the pipeline of control at the lower levels of the hierarchy. The temporal characteristics of animation are generally controlled at higher levels and the spatial characteristics are controlled at lower levels in our multi-level system.

1.1 Overview

The paper is divided into sections. Section 2 puts our approach in perspective with previous work in facial animation, focussing on the control mechanism for the dynamics of facial animation. After this brief review, we describe our facial model in

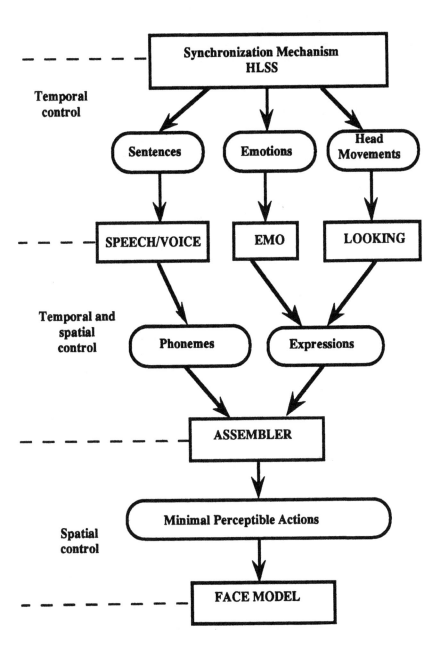

Fig. 1. Hierarchical Structure of the Multi-level Facial Animation System

Section 3. The creation and specification of expressions and phonemes are given in Section 4. Definition of emotions and sentences used for conversation are given in the subsequent section. The synchronization mechanism is presented in Section 5. Finally, we conclude with a brief discussion for the proposed approach and its limitations.

2 Background and Review

There has been extensive research done on basic facial animation and several models have been proposed. Early models proposed by Parke (1975, 1982), used a combination of digitized expressions and linear interpolation of features such as eyelids and eyebrows, and rotations for jaw. Motions are described as a pair of numeric tuples that identify the initial frame, final frame, and interpolation.

Platt and Badler (1981) based their facial animation system on the Facial Action Coding System (FACS) developed by Ekman and Friesen (1975). In the FACS, facial expression is specified in terms of Action Units (AU) that are single muscles or clusters of muscles. In their model, skin is outermost level represented by a set of 3D points defining a surface that can move. Bones, on the other hand represent an internal level that cannot be moved. Muscles are groups of points with elastic arcs between the two levels.

In the model of Waters (1987), muscles are geometric deformation operators which the user places on the face to simulate the contraction of real muscles. Two types of muscles are created linear and parallel muscles that pull, and sphincter muscles that squeeze. These muscles are independent of the underlying bone structure, which makes the muscle model independent of specific face topology. The control parameters are based on FACS.

Nahas et al. (1988) proposed a method based on B-splines. A digitizing system is used to register the position of certain points on the face that are organized in a matrix. The matrix is used as a set of control points for a 5-dimensional bicubic B-spline surface. Motion of the face is obtained by moving these control points.

Magnenat-Thalmann et al. (1988) have provided another approach to simulate a muscle action by using a procedure called an Abstract Muscle Action (AMA) procedure. Each AMA has an associated procedure with a set of parameters that can be used to control the motion of vertices composing the face. By combining the facial parameters obtained by the AMA procedures in different ways, complex entities corresponding to the concept of facial expressions can be constructed.

Terzopoulos and Waters (1990) have extended the Waters model, using three layered deformable lattice structures for facial tissues. The three layers correspond to the skin, the subcutaneous fatty tissue, and the muscles. The bottom surface of the muscle layer is attached to the underlying bone. The model uses a physically-based technique.

Parke (1991) reviews different parameterization mechanism used in different previously proposed models and introduces future guidelines for ideal control parameterization and interface. Ideal parameterization is a universal parameterization that would enable all possible individual faces with all possible expressions and expression transitions.

Recently several authors have provided new facial animation techniques based on the information derived from human performances (deGraf 1989, Williams 1990, Terzopoulos and Waters 1991). The information extracted is used for controlling the facial animation. These performance-driven techniques provide very realistic rendering and motion of the face. Kurihara and Arai (1991) introduced a new transformation method for modeling and animating the face using photographs of an individual face. This transformation method enables the movement of points in the skin mesh to be determined by the movement of some selected control points. Texture mapping is used to render the final image.

Efforts for lip synchronization and automated speech initiated with the first study of Lewis and Parke (1987). In their approach, the desired speech is spoken and recorded. The recording is then sampled and analyzed to produce a timed sequence of pauses and phonemes. Hill et al. (1988) have introduced an automatic approach to animate speech using speech synthesized by rules. Magnenat-Thalmann et al. (1987) have used lip synchronization based on AMA procedures. A collection of multiple tracks is used, where each track is a chronological sequence of keyframes for a given facial parameter. Tracks are independent but can be mixed in the same way as sound is mixed in a sound studio. This approach was used in the film *Rendez-vous à Montréal* (1987). However, the process of synchronization is manual and must be performed by the animator.

3 Facial Model

3.1 Simulation of Muscle Actions

In our model the skin surface of a human face, an irregular structure, is considered as a polygonal mesh. Muscular activity is simulated using free form deformations (Sederberg and Parry 1986). We employ rational basis functions for the trivariate tensor product of Bernstein polynomials. The inclusion of weights for each control point provides an extra degree of freedom for controlling and manipulating the deformations. To simulate the muscle actions on the skin of a human face, we define regions on the facial mesh corresponding to the anatomical description of the regions of face where a muscle action is desired. A region is a set of selected polygons in the mesh. A parallelepiped control unit then can be defined on the region of interest. The deformations obtained by actuating muscles to stretch, squash, expand and compress the inside volumes of the facial geometry are simulated by displacing the control points of the control unit. The region inside the control unit deforms like a flexible volume, according to the displacement and the weight at each control point.

The system provides convenient interactive facilities to specify regions, displacements and weights of control points. We use what we call the "Ball and Mouse" metaphor (LeBlanc et al. 1991) employing a six degree freedom device, the Spaceball and a mouse for easy access of various geometric 3D entities in different orientations.

3.2 Minimum Perceptible Action (MPA)

A Minimal Perceptible Action is a basic facial motion parameter. Each MPA has a corresponding set of visible features such as movement of eyebrows, jaw, or mouth and others occurring as a result of muscles contracting and pulling. MPAs also include non-facial muscle actions such as nodding and turning of head and movement of eyes. Each MPA is specified with a normalized intensity between 0 and 1 or -1 and 1. An MPA can be considered as an atomic action unit similar to the AU of FACS, execution of which results in a visible and perceptible variation of a face.

The calculation of MPAs from higher level entities is completely independent of the facial model. However, the type of control offered by MPAs is at lower level from animators point of view; specification of MPAs is analogous to programming in assembly language.

4 Expressions and Phonemes

Expressions and phonemes in our system are considered as facial snapshots, i.e., a particular position of the face at a given time. For phonemes, only the lips are considered during the emission of sound. A facial snapshot consists of one or more MPAs with their intensity specified. The set of MPAs included is general enough to account for most possible facial expressions. A generic expression can be represented as follows:

```
[expression <name>
        [mpa <name-1> intensity   <i-1>]
        [mpa <name-1> intensity   <i-1>]
        ...
]
```

Example of an expression

```
[expression surprise
        [mpa openjaw intensity  0.17]
        [mpa puffcheeks intensity   -0.41]
        [mpa stretch_cornerlips intensity   -0.50]
        [mpa raise_eyebrows intensity  0.40]
        [mpa close_lower_eyelids intensity   -0.54]
        [mpa close_upper_eyelids intensity   -0.20]
]
```

Example of a phoneme

```
[phoneme ee
        [mpa stretch_cornerlips intensity   -0.29]
        [mpa openjaw intensity  0.50]
        [mpa lower_cornerlips intensity   -0.57]
        [mpa raise_upperlips intensity   -0.20]
]
```

The specification of expressions and phonemes is analogous to macros used in a program. The intensity of expression is directly influenced by the intensity of contained MPAs. A strong or feeble expression can be created by appropriately changing the intensities of the associated MPAs. This helps the spatial control of facial animation.

These facial snapshots representing expressions and phonemes can be built up in an interactive expression editor provided inside the system. Users can construct, edit and save the static expressions and thus build a library of pre defined expressions. This library can then become available for a later sequence of animation. By design, the expression editor is independent of the low level realization of muscles and their actions. This scheme of independence makes it plausible to use entirely different simulation models for each MPA separately without affecting the high level control.

The system also allows composition or blending of two or more expressions. This is attained by integrating the MPAs in the respective expressions. This can be interpreted as summing up two or more signals of MPAs where the resulting intensity is the normalized sum of the individual intensities (see Figure 2)

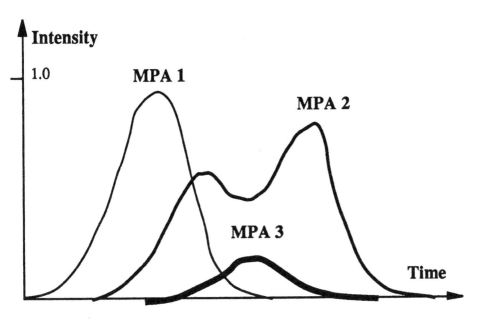

Fig. 2. MPAs' curves

All facial expressions do not necessarily correspond to emotions and phonemes. Some expressions are exhibited as secondary expressions that differentiate one expressive mode from the others. For example, raised eyebrows may signify termination of a sequence of a speech and may not be a signal of surprise. Similarly a turn of the head may symbolize negation of an issue. The animation can thus incorporate such expressions once created and defined in the expression editor. In Figure 3, the first row illustrates the instances of the expression "surprise" and the second row shows the snapshot for phonemes "ow", "aa", "bb" and "ee", respectively.

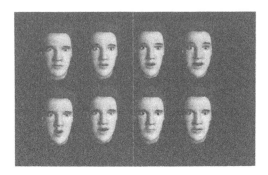

Fig. 3. Some expressions and phonemes

5 Emotions, Sentences and Head Movements

5.1 Emotions

An emotion is considered as an expressive episode of a face over a period. It can be interpreted as evolution of a face over time. For example, when starting from a neutral or background state, an emotion would include all the sequence of visible changes involved in returning to the same neutral or background state. A generic emotion is an envelope consisting of four stages attack, decay, sustain, and release (Ekman and Friesen 1978). Figure 4 shows a hypothetical example of emotion illustrating the four stages.

The duration (temporal characteristics) and intensity (spatial characteristics) are context dependent. For example, intensity and duration of a 'smile' in a normal situation and in a laughable situation are different. In addition, each stage of emotion is not equally sensitive to the expansion of time. Attack and release stages do not expand proportionally to the scale of expansion for the entire duration. To preserve this non- proportionality of expansion for each stage we incorporate a sensitivity factor associated with each stage of emotion. At any instance the duration for each stage is given as

$$t' = \alpha s_i t_i$$

where

α: scaling factor the entire duration

s_i: sensitivity factor for each stage i, with $\sum s_i = 1$

t_i: average duration for each stage i

The intensity of emotion is determined by the intensities of the sequence of expressions attached to the intermediate stages of emotion. We give as an example the emotion "surprise" that uses three different instances of expression surprise.

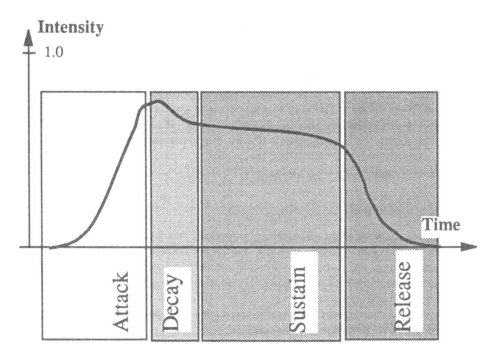

Fig. 4. Hypothetical example of emotion showing four stages

```
[emotion surprise
    [attack duration 12 sensitivity 0.15] [expression surprise1 intensity 0.7]
    [decay duration 12 sensitivity 0.35] [expression surprise2 intensity 0.8]
    [sustain duration 12 sensitivity 0.35] [expression surprise3 intensity 0.7]
    [release duration 12 sensitivity 0.15]
]
```

This parameterization mechanism for both temporal and spatial characteristics also enables us to differentiate and identify what are called "spontaneous" and "deliberate" emotional expressions. The spontaneous or elicited emotions are unmodulated expressions congruent with an underlying emotional state, while deliberate expressions are those intentionally employed by the sender for some purpose. For example, felt (spontaneous) and false (deliberate) smiles can be differentiated both in temporal and spatial nature. For false smiles the attack stage is shorter and the sustain stage is longer than of felt smile. Furthermore false smiles exhibit no orbiculi activity. These facts help us to add behavioural attributes to emotions.

5.2 Sentences

Delivery of a sentence or word with proper lip-synchronization needs several issues to be addressed. In our system we provide mechanisms to control the intensity, duration and emphasis of each word. Pauses (punctuators) are added to control the rhythm and intonation of the sentence. A word is specified as sequence of phonemes. A dictionary table is used which consists of decomposition of each word in use as phonemes. The relative duration of each phoneme in a word is determined according to its placement and its neighboring phonemes and syllables in the given word. The system also allows the decomposition of a word into phonemes and their durations from a recorded voice. For each word the sequence of phonemes is considered as a list of relative expressions with normalized duration (between 0 and 1).

5.3 Head Movement

Movement of the head plays an extremely important role for a natural facial animation. While talking in addition to using lips for emission of sounds, a person may turn or roll his head and move his eyes simultaneously to accentuate and regulate the emphasis for the conversational signals. We consider head movement as a separate entity involving non-muscular actions such as a turning of the head and movement of the eyeballs. The sequence of expressions during the span of head movement is represented as list of relative expressions.

6 Synchronization

We need a mechanism of synchronization to ensure smooth flow of emotions and sentences with head movements. A language HLSS (High Level Script Scheduler) (Kalra et al. 1991) is used to specify the synchronization in terms of an action and its duration. From the action dependence the starting time and the terminating time of an action can be deduced. The general format of specifying an action is as follows: while <duration> do <action>.

The duration of an action can be a default duration, a relative percentage of the default duration, an absolute duration in seconds or a deduced duration from the other actions preceding or succeeding the present action.

The starting time of each action can be specified in different ways, for example, sequentially or parallel using the normal concepts of "fork" and "end fork" employed in a scheduling problem. Figure 5 shows some examples of how starting time can be specified in the system.

Figures 6(a) and (b) show some of the frames in an animation with emotion and speech for two different actors.

7 Discussion

A multi-level approach is proposed to control the temporal and spatial attributes in human facial animation. In this approach, from the lowest to the highest level,

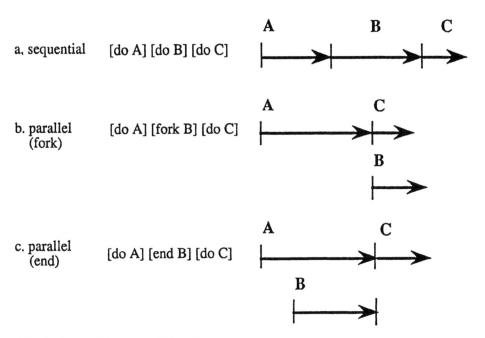

Fig. 5. Sequential and parallel actions

the degree of abstraction increases. For the animator, this essentially reduces the complexity of the specification of entities. The defined entities correspond to intuitive concepts such as phonemes, expressions, emotions, and sentences which make it easy and natural to manipulate. The animator provides the system with "what to do" and system configures "how to do" at each level in its hierarchy. The system is extensible; each layer is independent of the others. A goal with such a system would be to create a behavior-driven system that will allow the animator to specify facial actions in terms of high level behaviors.

Acknowledgment

The research was supported by le Fonds National Suisse pour la Recherche Scientifique. The authors are grateful to Martin Hans Werner for reviewing the English of the text.

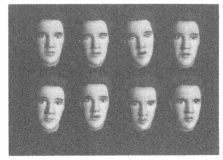

Fig. 6. Facial animation with emotion and speech

References

deGraf, B. (1989): In: State of the Art in Facial Animation. SIGGRAPH '89 Course Notes, No. 26, pp. 10–20.

Ekman, P; Friesen, WV. (1975): *Unmasking the Face: A Guide to Recognizing Emotions from Facial Clues*. Printice-Hall.

Ekman, P.; Friesen, WV. (1978): *Facial Action Coding System*. Investigator's Guide Part 2. Consulting Psychologists Press Inc.

Hill, DR; Pearce, A.; Wyvill, B. (1988): *Animating Speech: An Automated Approach Using Speech Synthesised by Rules*. The Visual Computer, Vol. 3, No. 5. Pages 277–289.

Kalra, P.; Mangili, A.; Magnenat-Thalmann, N.; Thalmann, D. (1991): *SMILE: A Multi-layered Facial Animation System*. Proceedings IFIP WG 5.10. Tokyo, Japan (Ed Kunii Tosiyasu L). Pages 189–198.

Kurihara, T.; Arai, K. (1991): *A Transformation Method for Modeling and Animation of the Human Face from Photographs*. Proceedings Computer Animation '91. Geneva, Switzerland (Eds Magnenat-Thalmann, N. and Thalmann, D.). Pages 45–57.

LeBlanc, A.; Kalra, P.; Magnenat-Thalmann, N.; Thalmann, D. (1991): *Sculpting with the "Ball & Mouse" Metaphor*. Proceedings Graphics Interface '91. Calgary, Canada. Pages 152–159.

Lewis, JP.; Parke, FI. (1987): *Automated Lipsynch and Speech Synthesis for Character Animation*. Proceedings CHI '87 and Graphics Interface '87. Toronto. Pages 143–147.

Magnenat-Thalmann, N.; Primeau, E.; Thalmann, D. (1988): *Abstract Muscle Action Procedures for Human Face Animation*. The Visual Computer, Vol. 3, No. 5. Pages 290–297.

Magnenat-Thalmann, N.; Thalmann, D. (1987): *The Direction of Synthetic Actors in the film Rendez-vous Montral*. IEEE Computer Graphics and Applications, Vol. 7, No. 12. Pages 9–19.

Nahas, M.; Huitric, H.; Saintourens, M. (1988): *Animation of a B-Spline Figure*. The Visual Computer, Vol. 3, No. 5. Pages 272–276.

Parke, FI. (1975): *A Model for Human Faces that allows Speech Synchronized Animation*. Computer and Graphics. Pregamon Press. Vol. 1, No. 1. Pages 1–4.

Parke, FI. (1982): *Parametrized Models for Facial Animation*. IEEE Computer Graphics and Applications, Vol. 2, No. 9. Pages 61–68.

Parke, FI. (1991): *Control Parameterization for Facial Animation*. Proceedings Computer Animation '91. Geneva, Switzerland (Eds Magnenat-Thalmann, N. and Thalmann, D.). Pages 3–13.

Platt, S.; Badler, N. (1981): *Animating Facial Expressions.* Proceedings SIGGRAPH '81. Pages 245–252.

Sederberg, TW.; Parry, SR. (1986): *Free Form Deformation of Solid Geometric Models.* Proceedings SIGGRAPH '86. Pages 151–160.

Terzopoulos, D.; Waters, K. (1990): *Physically Based Facial Modeling, Analysis and Animation.* Visualization and Computer Animation, Vol. 1, No. 2. Pages 73–80.

Terzopoulos, D.; Waters, K. (1991): *Techniques for Realistic Facial Modeling and Animation.* Proceedings Computer Animation '91. Geneva, Switzerland (Eds Magnenat-Thalmann, N. and Thalmann, D.). Pages 59–74.

Waters, K. (1987): *A Muscle Model for Animating Three Dimensional Facial Expression.* Proceedings SIGGRAPH '87, Vol. 21, No. 4. Pages 17–24.

Williams, L. (1990): *Performance Driven Facial Animation.* Proceedings SIGGRAPH '90. Pages 235–242.

Integrated Natural Language Generation Systems*

Mark Kantrowitz and Joseph Bates

School of Computer Science, Carnegie Mellon University,
5000 Forbes Avenue, Pittsburgh, PA 15213

Abstract

Many existing natural language generation systems can be characterized according to their modularization as either *pipelined* or *interleaved*. In these *separated* systems, the generator is divided into several modules (e.g., planning and realization), with control and information passing between the modules during the generation process. This paper proposes a third type of generator, which we call *integrated*, that unifies the modules into a single mechanism. The mechanism uses a small set of orthogonal basic operations to produce planned and grammatical language output.

Integrated systems are conceptually attractive and may support generation of pragmatic effects more effectively than other systems. After discussing the advantages of the integrated approach, we summarize GLINDA, an integrated generator currently under development at Carnegie Mellon. GLINDA is the generator used for narration and intercharacter communication in the Oz Interactive Fiction and Virtual Reality Project.

1 Introduction

This paper distinguishes two classes of natural language generation (NLG) systems, which we call *separated* and *integrated*. A separated system divides the generator into several specialized modules, with each module having different representations and processes, corresponding to one or more hierarchically organized linguistic levels [6, 11]. Separated systems often include a *planning* component, which is responsible for selecting and organizing the conceptual content of the message to be expressed, and a *realization* component, which is responsible for executing the text plan and producing grammatical natural language output. These modules are also known by the names deep and surface generation, strategic and tactical generation, text planning and plan execution, message and form levels, functional and positional levels, and conceptual and grammatical levels. Some systems further subdivide the

---

* This work was supported in part by Fujitsu Laboratories, Ltd., and in part by a National Science Foundation (NSF) Graduate Fellowship. The views and conclusions contained in this document are those of the authors and should not be interpreted as representing the official policies, either expressed or implied, of Fujitsu Laboratories or the NSF.

realization component into modules that parallel linguistic levels such as phonology, morphology, lexical selection, and phrase, clause, and sentence structure.

Besides using distinct representations and processing mechanisms in each module, separated systems often define sharply constrained module interfaces which restrict cross-level information flow. However, motivated in part by our application's demand for more flexible communication between levels (see also [12, 36]), we have tried to identify commonalities in the operations and representations used at each linguistic level and to generalize them into a simple framework that can be used for all aspects of generation. The resulting *integrated* generator has a single engine, with any modularization of the generator appearing solely in the organization of its rules.

In this paper we argue in favor of integrated systems, describing the motivation, characteristics, and benefits of such systems, and suggest that they may be feasible to build. Our initial architectural ideas are embodied in a program called GLINDA which is beginning to be used for narration and intercharacter communication in the Oz Interactive Fiction and Virtual Reality Project at Carnegie Mellon. The generation rules which drive GLINDA also are under active development.

1.1 Types of Natural Language Generators

The three types of generation systems are illustrated in Fig. 1.

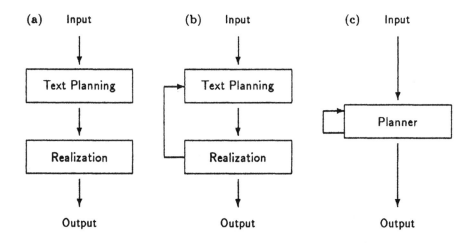

Fig. 1. Generator Organizations: (a) Pipelined, (b) Interleaved, and (c) Integrated

Separated systems can be roughly divided into *pipelined* systems and *interleaved* systems [17, 19, 27]. In a pipelined generator, all text planning decisions must be completed before any surface realization may begin. The planning stage produces a fully specified and ordered message which is then translated into natural language text by the realization stage. The text planner is completely free of any linguistic knowledge and the realizer has only linguistic knowledge available to it. There is no communication from the realization module back to the planning module. Examples of such systems include McKeown's TEXT [28, 29] and Jacob's PHRED [20, 21].[2]

Pipelined generators are conceptually simple. They seem to separate concerns, as demanded by the principles of software engineering. Unfortunately, in generating even modestly sophisticated texts the planning stage is not independent of the realization stage. In particular, since the planner isn't aware of syntax, it can't take into account opportunities and inadequacies that arise during the realization stage. For example, constraints during realization could preclude the effective expression of a concept, causing the generator to "talk itself into a corner". In this case the text plan cannot be realized, and the generator is not able to replan the utterance. Likewise, if the realization module can achieve more than one communicative goal at once — say, the word it chose encompasses two concepts — there is no way for it to tell the planner to eliminate the extraneous plan segment. This may lead to repetitive and stilted text. The context in which a sentence is realized can also affect how it is expressed. Thus the planner in pipelined systems is more or less limited to choosing the topics, establishing the sentence order, and hoping realization is successful.

Hovy argued that to avoid some of the problems of pipelined systems the planner should make only enough commitments to allow it to begin the realization process, and then pass the control and information back and forth between the modules, interleaving their execution [19]. He demonstrated the particular usefulness of this approach for generating pragmatic (non-literal) effects in text [18]. The pragmatic rules in Hovy's PAULINE were limited to coloring the text based on the interlocutors' personal characteristics, their interpersonal goals and the conversational setting, but it seems reasonable to expect that any generator which needs to achieve pragmatic effects should be capable of evaluating the effects of its speech acts. In Hovy's words, "Generators must be able to reason about *why* they say what they say," [18, p. 156].

Other examples of interleaved systems besides Hovy's PAULINE include McDonald's MUMBLE [26, 27], Kempen's IPG [11, 23], Colby's PARRY [8], Clippinger's ERMA [7], and Davey's PROTEUS [10].

Although one could, in theory, use a pipelined system to generate the same output text as an interleaved system, by taking matters of syntax and lexical selection into account, one would pay a huge computational price. Exactly the same kinds of arguments as are made in recent planning literature about the benefits of reactive planning and emergent behavior apply to text planning in natural language generation. Like a reactive planner, an interleaved generator can respond opportunistically to changes in the state of its goals and its available choices, and makes only those decisions which are directly relevant to the message it is trying to express. The interleaved architecture also permits the incremental production of output, although not all interleaved generators do so.

---

[2] Unless a researcher has published flow charts or descriptions of a generation algorithm, it may be difficult to decide whether a generator is pipelined, interleaved or integrated. It is our hope that this paper will popularize the use of this terminology for the description and discussion of NLG systems. We regret if we've inadvertently misclassified a generator.

In our study of existing interleaved generators we began to notice that the operations used for text planning appeared similar in many ways to the operations used for surface realization, and thus wondered whether one might be able to use the same operations to accomplish both tasks. Decomposing these existing operations into primitives that distill the essence which is common to both levels yields a finer-grained set of orthogonal operations. The planning engine that processes this finer basis of factored operations unifies the modules into a single mechanism which does the work of both modules using the same set of operations.

For example, the goal ordering rules of text planning and the precedence relations of a realization grammar are both instances of "serialization". That is, they both assign a linear order, one to communicative goals and the other to syntactic constituents. Even the realization of a word involves the linear ordering of its morphemes. Thus, serialization is one operator in our unified basis.

Similarly, selection of content and selection of words are both restricted by constraints imposed during past generation. The decision of what content should be explicitly included and what should be inferred is similar to the decision whether to realize a representation in full or to use anaphora, deixis and ellipsis. The aggregation of information into paragraph and sentence groups parallels the expression of groups of content as words and phrases. Thus, "transformation" rules are another kind of primitive operation in our model.

Following this line of reasoning leads to the integrated style of generator, in which all text planning, surface realization, and other processes are accounted for within a single formalism. The generator uses a uniform representation for all the linguistic levels, and the single engine applies the same set of basic operations at each level. The levels communicate by the two-way flow of information across the boundaries between levels. The only difference between levels is isolated in the rule definitions.

To our knowledge, Appelt's KAMP system [2] comes the closest of any previously discussed generator to being integrated, at least in spirit, although it seems more like a homogeneous interleaved system in which all of the levels happen to use the same planner. For example, earlier versions of KAMP had the grammatical knowledge spread throughout the rules and operated in a semi-pipelined fashion, with critics providing limited feedback between adjacent levels. Later versions isolated surface realization into a separate component called TELEGRAM that could invoke the planner at choice points during realization to help it make a decision [1]. Nevertheless, Appelt presented the view that all generation processes, even realization, involve planning, and used a planner based on NOAH [32] to control the generation.

Certain blackboard systems, such as DIOGENES [30], while viewable as interleaved systems with more than two modules, nonetheless have much of the flavor of integrated systems. For example, the modules in DIOGENES all use the same representation language because they must communicate by posting messages to the blackboard and triggering off of the messages found on the blackboard.

We have completed a brief look at the potential benefits of integrated generation systems, and turn now to GLINDA, the integrated generator we are developing for Oz. This work is in its early stages, and both the architecture and rules are under active development. We present GLINDA here as concrete, if unfinished, example of how one might organize an integrated generator.

2 The GLINDA Integrated Natural Language Generator

In this section we survey GLINDA, presenting it as an example of an integrated generation system. We do not intend this as an in-depth description, but as a concrete illustration of the ideas discussed above. To date, work on GLINDA has focussed on implementing surface realization using operators derived from text planning systems. We believe the framework is general enough to do arbitrary text planning, given appropriately defined rules, but have not yet done so.

The Oz system is intended to let human users participate in dramatically interesting simulated microworlds that are inhabited by moderately intelligent and emotional agents. Oz is intended as the technical framework for a new interactive art form [3, 35]. GLINDA is used both for narration of interaction with an Oz world, describing locations, objects, actions, and events, and to allow computer simulated agents to communicate with each other and with human players [4, 5, 22, ?, 31].

2.1 Motivation

Oz presents a novel set of requirements for generation. Most generators are successful if they produce well-formed and lucid text. For narration, however, Oz needs to be able to tune the generation to engender subtle emotional reactions in and exert influences on the human player, and to present a variety of vivid views of the simulated world [35]. Characters must occasionally make some of the same errors and have the same idiosyncrasies in speech as human beings. The coverage of language phenomena should be broad but not necessarily deep.

Several items on our "wish list" for generation could best be characterized as multi-level linguistic phenomena with cross-level information flow and feedback. Pragmatic effects, such as those implemented in PAULINE, involve many individual local effects contributing to create a global effect. To produce drunken speech the generator needs to simultaneously make grammatical errors and apply rules that lengthen sibilants to produce slurred speech. Rhyme, alliteration, and poetry involve rewriting and editing with multi-level constraints on form. The ability to talk oneself into a syntactic corner and restart requires that the generator detect errors and backtrack across the levels to a choice point where it can begin anew.

Cross-level influences can occur even during straightforward generation. For example, the morphology of certain words depends on their syntactic category. The word "loaf+s" is realized as "loaves" as a noun or as "loafs" as a verb. Various kinds of agreement, including subject-verb agreement and coordinated clause tense agreement, can also be characterized as the cross-level propagation of information [22]. Producing these varied effects was the primary motivation for developing GLINDA.

We are experimenting with explicit feature propagation as a means to producing such output. For example, a pragmatic goal feature propagates throughout the generation process, causing different local effects at each level. The total effect of the many individual changes yields the desired global pragmatic effect. The integrated nature of the generator makes it easy to share knowledge between levels because the information at each level is represented using a single language and is subject to the same kinds of operators.

2.2 Representation: Groups and Features

A representation that is suited to all levels of generation must be very flexible. We use a generalized feature representation called groups. A *group* is an unordered set of items, where an *item* is a group or a feature. A *feature* is a pair consisting of a property name and a property value, (name value). Features are often referred to by name. See Fig. 2 for an example of a group.

```
((type sentence) (role sentence) (mood declarative)
 ((type relation) (role matrix)
  ((type parameter) (role predicate)
   ((type word) ((type morph) (cat verb) (root die))))
  ((type parameter) (role agent)
   ((type word) (age 1)
    ((type morph) (cat noun) (root cat-1)
     (person 3) (number singular) (gender male)))))))
```

Fig. 2. An Example of a Group

A group inside another is called a subgroup of the containing parent group. Each group must contain a role feature which specifies the overall function of the group within its parent. A group can have at most one role, and every subgroup of a group must have a distinct role. Every group should also contain a type feature to indicate the structure of the group. The type determines the roles of the group's subgroups. It also specifies the level of the group in the linguistic hierarchy (e.g., phoneme, syllable, morpheme, word, phrase, clause (relation), sentence (multi-relation) and paragraph). If no role feature is present, it defaults to the value of the type feature.

For each type of group there is a particular role which when contained in a subgroup identifies that subgroup as the *head* or *local projector* of the group. If one repeatedly selects head subgroups of a group, one eventually reaches a group that contains only features. The head feature of this group is known as the *projector* of the containing groups, and forms the core of the concept represented by the containing groups. The form (define-group-head <type> <role>) defines a new head.

All of the projectors used in GLINDA are arranged into an inheritance hierarchy, and all rules are suspended from constraint-tries (discrimination nets) attached to categories in the hierarchy. On occasion, the immediate parent of a projector in the hierarchy can instead be specified by including a cat feature in the group.

Often one may summarize a group by specifying the value of its role feature and the value of the projector feature, as if it were the feature (<role> <projector>). For example, the agent subgroup of the group shown in Fig. 2 could be abbreviated as the feature (AGENT CAT-1). The full meaning of a group is the composition of the meanings of its subgroups and features, with the subgroups corresponding to elements of the representation and the features describing the relationship between the subgroups and properties of the group as a whole.

2.3 Constraints

A GLINDA rule fires when the *constraint set* on its left hand side matches a group under consideration. Matching is similar to unification, except that instead of comparing two ordered representations element by element, constraints in the pattern are tagged with roles and must match against the corresponding items of the group. If there is no constraint for a particular subgroup's role, the subgroup is ignored.

Each *constraint* in the constraint set matches against either a group or a feature. The shorthand representation for groups as a (role projector) pair makes them look like features, allowing groups and features to be interchangeable from the point of view of the matcher. This is the sense in which a group is just a generalized feature. Note that if a projector is specified in a constraint, it matches any projector below it in the projector hierarchy. The same is true for the role specifiers.

Constraints have the general format of (name value), where name can either be the name of a property, if the constraint is to match against a feature, or the value of a role feature, if the constraint is to match against a subgroup. The value of the constraint can specify the value of the feature or the value of the projector, and may be a string, symbol, number or wildcard, or a range of values formed with disjunctions, conjunctions, and negations. Values can also be constraint sets, in which case they recursively match against the contents of the subgroup. If the value is a variable, it gets bound to either the feature value or group projector or the contents of the group, depending on the type of the variable. (The latter is useful for anaphora generation and the splicing operator described below.) The only restriction is that the binding of all variables in the constraint set must be consistent for the match to succeed.

Because GLINDA is a forward-chaining reactive system, constraints are always matched against groups, and never against expressions containing variables. In fact, each constraint is matched against a single group, so there is at most one valid set of bindings for the variables in the constraint set. This yields a match algorithm that avoids the combinatorial explosion in processing time often found in unification-based generators. Matching a constraint set against a group runs in time linear in the size of the constraint set.

2.4 Rule Formats

All rules in GLINDA have the same general format, with three distinct parts:

- CONSTRAINTS: Preconditions on the input which permit the rule to run.
- ACTIONS: Generic atomic actions, ranging from output to side-effecting the generator mechanism.
- RESULTS: Result features that are returned after running the rule to report the effects of executing the rule and impose constraints on further processing. If generation was unsuccessful, this may result in backtracking.

A rule's input specification is a conjunction of a set of constraints. The constraint sets are represented as trees, which are attached to rule-specified projectors in the class hierarchy. Because constraints are priority-ordered and occurrences in multiple rules are shared, the most significant constraints are tested first and once only. This use of structure sharing was inspired by the RETE algorithm, and yields a rule selection time which is not affected by the size of the grammar. If several rules match, the current conflict resolution strategy is to choose randomly among the most specific rules, and keep track of the other rules for possible backtracking.

2.5 Types of Operators

In examining the operations which occur at the different levels of a separated generator, we identified five distinct kinds of functions. GLINDA's grammar consists of a set of five basic types of rules corresponding to the five different kinds of operations. Each type of rule performs a single function and may be applied to any group.[3] The five basic kinds of operations are:

1. Transformation of Representation.[4]
2. Control of Information Flow.
3. Side-effecting of the Generation Mechanism.
   - Goal Ordering (serial ordered goals and parallel unordered goals).
   - Parameter Setting.
4. External Actions.
   - Text Output.
   - Generic Actions.
5. Reviewing and Repairing (Critics).

Transformation of representation rules include *mapping* rules and *splicing* rules. A mapping rule may add, delete or replace some of a group's items. For example, the phenomenon of do-support in English is implemented by a mapping rule which adds a modal emphatic to a group if the group contains a negative feature and an active voice feature but no modal, perfect, or progressive features:

```
(define-maprule
  :constraints ((type relation) (truth negative) (voice active)
                (modal (not *))(perfect (not *))(progressive (not *)))
  :return ((modal emphatic)))
```

Mapping rules may also be used to expand "macrofeatures" into sets of simpler features. This allows a "global" feature to have different effects in different contexts. For example, a feature describing the focus of a sentence could be operationalized by changing the voice feature of the sentence.

```
(define-maprule :constraints ((focus ?a) (agent ?a)) :return ((voice active)))
```

Mapping rules can also control the expression of general features. Because English doesn't have a morphologically realized future, the future tense feature is replaced

---

[3] Although it is possible for a specific rule to be general enough to operate on any group, no matter what its structural (linguistic) level, often the rule constraints will restrict a rule to operating on a specific level.

[4] No relation to transformational grammar.

with an r-time not-past feature and an intent modal. A splicing rule may modify some of a group's items by inserting one group within another, grouping two groups into a subgroup, or merging some groups together. Typical uses include subordination and conjunction, and the aggregation of groups into paragraphs and sentences.

Control of information flow rules are similar to mapping rules in many ways. When the generator finishes operating on a group it returns some features to provide feedback on the effects of the generation. When the generator operates on a group, it has access not only to the group but also to features passed in from the parent group and to the returns from its left sibling groups. Information flow rules specify which of these features will actually be provided to a group during its generation. For example, subject-verb agreement is accomplished in GLINDA by propagating the **number** and **person** features from the subject group to the verb group. Tenses are coordinated by propagating **r-time** features (values **past** and **not-past**) and blocking modal **future** features. Case-marking features are added to the flow based on the relative order of the items of a group after the group has been serialized by the goal-ordering rules. Information about recent references can be propagated to enable lexical selection rules to decide whether to use anaphora. For example, the following rules illustrate case marking, subject-verb agreement, and tense coordination:

```
(define-flow-rule noun :constraints ((role agent)(voice active))
  :pass-down ((case nominative) mood form))
(define-flow-rule noun :constraints ((case nominative))
  :pass-up (person number))
(define-flow-rule verb :constraints ((role matrix)) :pass-up (r-time))
```

The side-effecting rules come in two varieties. The first controls the goal ordering of the generator, where the items of a group are considered to be communicative goals. Usually these are *serialization* or *organization* rules, which order the items of a group according to their roles. Sometimes they are *parallelization* or *coordination* rules, which cause the group's items to be generated concurrently. Parallelization rules could be used to coordinate speech acts with other kinds of actions, such as producing sounds, gestures, winks and pauses. The second set of rules controls various parameters of the generator. For example, they can control line width, indentation, and the level of caching.

The goal-ordering process may be efficiently implemented by maintaining a tree of active serialization and parallelization rules and the corresponding local and global state of the generator.[5] To do the next operation, the generator finds its way from the root to a leaf by traversing serialization rules in a depth-first manner (expanding the head of the ordering until it completes before operating on the rest of the ordering) and the parallelization rules in a breadth-first manner (expanding each unordered goal in turn, one level at a time). Features are propagated and transformed and a rule is selected to operate on the leaf. If the rule is a primitive action, it is executed; otherwise the rule is used to continue the expansion of the tree. When the rule execution finishes or the expansion completes and the tree collapses, features are

---

[5] If the generator only needed serialization rules, it could execute them by recursively traversing the ordering, as was done in an earlier version of GLINDA [22]. The introduction of parallelization rules requires some form of concurrency, such as that provided by the iterative traversal of an active plan tree [25].

returned up the tree to update the local and global state. If we add success tests to the rules, those tests could be checked along every pass from the root to a leaf, augmenting the reactivity provided by the feature-returns.

Several serialization rules are shown below. The first realizes the agent role as the word "by" in objective case. The next two rules are default rules for the class of verbs in the projector hierarchy, and handle the organization of a clause in the active voice and the conjugation of regular verbs. These may be locally overridden by placing more specific rules lower in the hierarchy, as the next two rules demonstrate. The first generates the past tense of an irregular verb. The second illustrates how slang can be generated by substituting groups in the serialization instead of just copying subgroups. For example, if the group in Fig. 2 is generated with the (voice active), (idiom slang) and (time past) features, it will be realized as the sentence "The kitten kicked the bucket." Finally, the last three rules show how progressives can be generated. The progressive feature is realized as a group representing the verb begin. The realization of the progressive feature also passes up an inflection feature, which serves as the suffix for the realization of the verbal group to the right. This inflection feature will be realized as the suffix "ing".

```
(define-organization-rule (role agent)
  :constraints ((case objective)) :order ("by"))

(define-organization-rule verb :constraints ((type relation)(voice active))
  :order (role agent r-time truth modal perfect progressive voice
              predicate object iobject))
(define-organization-rule verb :constraints ((type morph))
  :order (root suffix))

(define-organization-rule go :constraints ((type morph)(inflection past))
  :order ("went"))
(define-organization-rule die :constraints ((type relation)(idiom slang))
  :order (agent r-time truth modal perfect progressive
              ((type parameter) (role predicate)
               ((type word) ((type morph) (cat verb) (root kick))))
              ((type parameter) (role object) (case objective)
               ((type word) ((type morph) (cat noun) (root bucket))
               (number singular) (person 3) (gender neuter)(form lexical)
               (reference definite)))))

(define-organization-rule (progressive begin)
  :order (((type word) (cat verb) (root begin))))
(define-flow-rule progressive :pass-up ((inflection pres-part)))
(define-organization-rule (inflection pres-part) :order ("ing"))
```

The operation of organization rules is similar to the scan-copy device proposed by Shattuck-Hufnagel [34]. The rules constitute a skeletal framework for the group, and the items of the group are "inserted" into the slots of the framework as the serialization operator processes the elements of the group. Organization rules can specify the order of communicative goals for textual structuring or the precedence relations in a sentence, and they can also specify the structure of words in the lexicon. In particular, a word in the lexicon is simply an organization rule with the slots already filled in with the word's morphemes.

Note that any kind of "selection" operation can be implicitly incorporated into the organization rules by the presence of constraints and the deliberate omission of a role from the ordering. Alternatively, we could define transformation rules to delete the "unselected" items from the group.

The external action rules may be used to produce output and execute actions. These rules produce text as a side-effect of the "evaluation" of the group by the generator. These rules can add a string to the cache, print the contents of the cache, or print a string without first saving it in the cache. Strings are temporarily saved in the cache before being output in order to give the reviewing and repairing rules a chance to modify them based on the next string generated.

The reviewing and repairing rules, also known as *combination* rules, are used to monitor output as it is added to the cache, and possibly modify it where the cached output and new strings are combined. The main uses of these rules have been for morphological modification of words when suffixes are added and for producing interword spacing. Two combination rules which demonstrate I-replacement and Elision are illustrated below:

```
(define-char-variable vowel "aeiou")
(define-morph-rule :name "I-Replacement"
  :left ((#\i #\y) (#\e :null)) :right ((#\i :as-self)))
(define-morph-rule :name "Elision"
  :left (((:not vowel) :as-self) (vowel :as-self) (#\e :null))
  :right ((#\e :as-self)))
```

2.6 Generation Process: Control Flow and Information Propagation

The generation process in GLINDA proceeds as follows: A particular group G is about to be processed. The generator has access to the contents of the group, the feature returns from the processing of its siblings, and some features of the group's parent, including any global features which have flowed down from the top.

1. Information flow rules are selected and used to decide what features from the parent group and what features returned by the siblings will be used during the generation of the current group G.
2. Transformation rules are selected and used to modify the features and the group.
3. An organization rule is selected and used to control the recursive generation of the subgroups of the group G. The recursive generation reinvokes this whole process on the embedded subgroups.
4. External action rules are executed to produce (cached) text and other actions.
5. Combination rules are used at leaf nodes to merge the new text into the cache and incrementally output the contents of the cache.
6. Information flow rules are selected and used to decide what features will be returned for this group, based on the original features of the group and on the features returned by the recursive generation of the subgroups of the group.

Thus GLINDA uses a forward-chaining reactive style of planning which responds directly to the generator's current communication goals. This process is illustrated in Fig. 3.

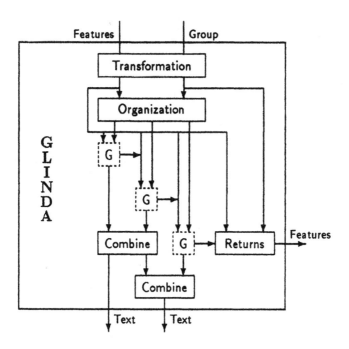

Fig. 3. The GLINDA Generation Process

2.7 An Example of Generation

Let us consider generation for a group representing a bad act by a good actor, such as George kicking the cat named Lyotard. A possible pragmatic goal feature might be to try to minimize the badness of George's actions. A transformation rule would implement this by introducing a feature that deemphasized (defocused) the actor. This feature would be propagated to the clausal level, where another transformation rule would introduce a passive voice feature because the actor is defocused and the actor is the agent of the clause. If the action can be cast in the passive voice, an organization rule which generates the subgroups of the clause in the order OBJECT ACTION AGENT would be selected. The object is realized as "Lyotard",[6] returning its person and number features. Those features are then used during the realization

---

[6] A different pragmatic rule might decide to emphasize the cat's tender age in order to cause sympathy, and hence generate "The kitten" instead.

of the action to ensure that the verb agrees with the subject of the sentence. When realizing the action, the voice feature, which was passed down from the parent group, is realized as "was", a form of the BE verb, and returns a past-participle inflection feature. This feature is used during the generation of the predicate, and is generated as the string "ed" after the generation of the verb "kick". The generator continues with the generation of the agent. Since the agent is marked with an objective case feature, the agent role feature is realized as the preposition "by". Next the actual agent is realized as the string "George". Finally, an end-of-sentence feature is realized as a period. The full sentence generated is then "Lyotard was kicked by George."

The generation of the voice feature before the verb, the verb root before the inflection feature, and the agent role before the agent were all accomplished by organization rules. If the verb were irregular, instead of using rules attached to the **verb** class in the projector hierarchy, it would use rules attached closer to the word, either executing different inflection rules as in the case of throw/threw/thrown and hit/hit, or using rote retrieval as in the case of go/went/gone. The same mechanism of rule retrieval accounts for both regular and irregular verb inflections. Although we've glossed over a lot of details, this example should give a bit of the flavor of the generation process in GLINDA.

2.8 Performance

Our initial implementation of GLINDA yields adequate performance for our needs. The generator itself is small, approximately 10 pages of Lisp code. The current grammar contains about 600 rules, expressed as roughly 20 pages of Lisp code. In this configuration, running in CMU Common Lisp on an IBM RT-APC, a 3-MIPS machine with a good Lisp implementation, GLINDA generates 2 clauses per second (about 500 words per minute). The speed did not decrease as the rule base grew.

3 Psycholinguistic Plausibility of Integrated Systems

This section very briefly presents evidence which suggests the psycholinguistic plausibility of integrated generation systems as models of human language production behavior. The evidence — from studies of speech errors — assumes that the human language production system is a mechanism which exhibits characteristic breakdown. When the system fails, it does so in ways that show how it is put together.

Inspection of speech-error corpii such as the UCLA corpus [13, 14] and the MIT-CU corpus [15, 16, 34] readily demonstrates that speech errors are highly regular phenomena. Each constraint on the structure of spontaneous speech errors has implications for models of human language processing. In particular, a parsimonious explanation for this data may be that the array of errors is caused by the failure of a single mechanism.

For example, speech errors involve either movement of fragments, such as shifts and exchanges, or changes in fragments, such as additions, omissions, and substitutions. Shattuck-Hufnagel observes that errors of all five basic types occur for every level of representation from phoneme through sentence constituent [34]. While one could claim that the same flaws appear in each level's independent processing module, it is simpler to suppose that the similarity of errors is caused by the flaws in a single engine which processes every level of representation.

The existence of anticipatory errors, often with several words intervening, implies that the speaker's internal representations span more than just the next word of the utterance [24]. The fragments which change, move, or are omitted in speech errors correspond to linguistically motivated units such as phonetic features, single consonants and vowels, syllables, words, phrases and clauses [13].[7] Together this suggests that language production involves planning, and that this planning employs the same units as are proposed by linguists and grammarians. Moreover, the exchanged elements must be similar and such exchanges occur within levels but not across levels, suggesting that planning operates at distinct levels of processing [34]. Because NLG researchers often cite this as evidence for distinct modules operating at each level, we will note that this evidence is consistent with a single-mechanism model in which the mechanism operates only on one kind of data at a time.

Other kinds of speech errors, such as spoonerisms, intentional distortions and tongue twisters, obey the same constraints as spontaneous speech errors. Tongue twisters, in particular, exhibit these constraints both in their inherent structure and in the errors produced when people say them. Most tongue twisters are constructed by mixing regular alternating stress patterns with irregular patterns in a way that overloads the human language production system [33]. When people stress the language production system by saying tongue twisters fast, they often regularize the patterns. Although the patterns often are phonetic, phonemic and syllabic, they can occasionally involve words and phrases,[8] suggesting again that the problems at each level are caused by the failure of a single mechanism.

4 Conclusions

The traditional view of natural language generation regards language processing as if it were separated into distinct modules, with each module responsible for the processing of the rules and representations corresponding to one or more linguistic levels. We have suggested that the modularization of the generation process does not require distinct kinds of rules and representations at each level, and indeed that there are advantages to using a single framework across all levels.

We have also described GLINDA, an integrated generator which attempts to address a wide range of natural language problems under this paradigm. GLINDA uses a uniform computational framework with explicit feature propagation and cross-level feedback to achieve multi-level textual effects. We hope to extend GLINDA to produce multi-modal output as well. While the work reported here is preliminary, we see some signs of the approach yielding a simple, elegant, and efficient generator, which is especially suited to producing pragmatic shadings in its output.

---

[7] In some sense this generalizes the notion of complementary distribution in linguistics.

[8] For example, "A lump of red lead, a red lead lump."; "Knee deep, deep knee."; "A fine field of wheat, a field of fine wheat."; and the famous "Peter Piper picked a peck of pickled peppers; how many pickled peppers did Peter Piper pick?".

5 Acknowledgments

We'd like to thank Eduard H. Hovy for providing the inspiration behind the design of GLINDA and for commenting on a draft of this paper. Sergei Nirenburg and Bryan Loyall also provided useful comments on the draft. We'd also like to thank Robert C. Berwick for discussions of the separation of descriptions of rules and representations from the processing of the same.

References

1. D. E. Appelt. TELEGRAM: A grammar formalism for language planning. In *Proceedings of the 8th IJCAI*, pages 595–599, Karlsruhe, West Germany, August 1983.
2. D. E. Appelt. *Planning English Sentences*. Cambridge University Press, Cambridge, UK, 1985. Based on Stanford PhD thesis, SRI Tech Note 259, March 1982.
3. Joseph Bates. Virtual reality, art, and entertainment. *Presence: The Journal of Teleoperators and Virtual Environments*, 1, 1992. MIT Press, Cambridge, MA. This is a revised version of *Deep Structure for Virtual Reality*, CMU-CS-91-133, School of Computer Science, Carnegie Mellon University, May 1991.
4. Joseph Bates, A. Bryan Loyall, and W. Scott Reilly. Broad agents. In *Proceedings of AAAI Spring Symposium on Integrated Intelligent Architectures*, Stanford, CA, March 1991. Available as *SIGART Bulletin* 2(4):38-40, August 1991.
5. Joseph Bates, A. Bryan Loyall, and W. Scott Reilly. Integrating Reactivity, Goals, and Emotion in a Broad Agent. Submitted to AAAI-92, San Jose, CA, January 1992.
6. Kathryn Bock. Exploring levels of processing in sentence production. In Gerard Kempen, editor, *Natural Language Generation: New Results in AI, Psychology, and Linguistics*. Martinus Nijhoff Publ., Boston, 1987.
7. J. H. Clippinger. *A Discourse Speaking Program as a Preliminary Theory of Discourse Behavior and a Limited Theory of Psychoanalytic Discourse*. PhD thesis, University of Pennsylvania, Philadelphia, PA, 1974.
8. K. M. Colby. *Artificial Paranoia: A Computer Simulation of Paranoid Processes*. Pergamon Press, Oxford, 1975.
9. Joseph H. Danks. Producing ideas and sentences. In Sheldon Rosenberg, editor, *Sentence Production: Developments in Research and Theory*. Lawrence Erlbaum Associates, Hillsdale, NJ, 1977.
10. A. Davey. *Discourse Production*. Edinburgh University Press, Edinburgh, 1979.
11. Koenraad De Smedt and Gerard Kempen. Incremental sentence production, self-correction and coordination. In Gerard Kempen, editor, *Natural Language Generation: New Results in AI, Psychology, and Ling*. Martinus Nijhoff Publ., Boston, 1987.
12. G. S. Dell and P. A. Reich. Stages in sentence production: An analysis of speech-error data. *Journal of Verbal Learning and Verbal Behavior*, 20:611–629, 1981.
13. Victoria Fromkin. The non-anomalous nature of anomalous utterances. *Language*, 47:27-52, 1971.
14. Victoria Fromkin. *Speech Errors as Linguistic Evidence*. The Hague, Mouton, 1973.
15. Merrill F. Garret. The analysis of sentence production. In G. H. Bower, editor, *The psychology of learning and motivation: Advances in research and theory*, volume 9, pages 133-177. Academic Press, New York, 1975.
16. Merrill F. Garret. Levels of processing in sentence production. In B. Butterworth, editor, *Language Production*, volume 1. Academic Press, New York, 1980.

17. Eduard Hovy. Integrating text planning and production in generation. In *Proceedings of the 9th IJCAI*, Los Angeles, CA, 1985.
18. Eduard Hovy. *Generating Natural Language under Pragmatic Constraints*. Lawrence Erlbaum Associates, Hillsdale, NJ, 1988.
19. Eduard Hovy. Two types of planning in language generation. In *Proceedings of the 26th Meeting of the ACL*, Buffalo, New York, April 1988.
20. P. S. Jacobs. *A Knowledge-Based Approach to Language Production*. PhD thesis, University of California at Berkeley, Berkeley, CA, 1985.
21. P. S. Jacobs. PHRED: A generator for natural language interfaces. *Computational Linguistics*, 11(4):219–242, October-December 1985.
22. Mark Kantrowitz. GLINDA: Natural language text generation in the Oz interactive fiction project. Technical Report CMU-CS-90-158, School of Computer Science, Carnegie Mellon University, Pittsburgh, PA, 1990.
23. Gerard Kempen and Edward Hoenkamp. An incremental procedural grammar for sentence formulation. *Cognitive Science*, 11:201–258, 1987.
24. Karl S. Lashley. The problem of serial order in behavior. In Lloyd A. Jeffress, editor, *Cerebral Mechanisms in Behavior*, pages 112–146. John Wiley, New York, 1951.
25. A. Bryan Loyall and Joseph Bates. Hap: A reactive, adaptive architecture for agents. Technical Report CMU-CS-91-147, School of Computer Science, Carnegie Mellon University, Pittsburgh, PA, June 1991.
26. D. D. McDonald. *Natural Language Production as a Process of Decision Making under Constraint*. PhD thesis, MIT, Cambridge, MA, 1980.
27. D. D. McDonald and J. D. Pustejovsky. Description-directed natural language generation. In *Proceedings of the 9th IJCAI*, pages 799–805, Los Angeles, CA, 1985.
28. Kathleen R. McKeown. Discourse strategies for generating natural-language text. *Artificial Intelligence*, 27:1–42, 1985.
29. Kathleen R. McKeown. *Text Generation: Using Discourse Strategies and Focus Constraints to Generate Natural Language Text*. Cambridge University Press, Cambridge, 1985. Based on PhD thesis (Univ. of Penn., May 1982), Tech Report MS-CIS-82-5.
30. Sergei Nirenburg, Victor Lesser, and Eric Nyberg. Controlling a language generation planner. In *Proceedings of the 11th IJCAI*, pages 1524–1530, Detroit, MI, August 1989.
31. W. Scott Reilly and Joseph Bates. Building Emotional Agents. Submitted to AAAI-92, San Jose, CA, January 1992.
32. E. D. Sacerdoti. *A Structure for Plans and Behavior*. North Holland/American Elsevier, 1977. Based on PhD thesis, SRI Tech Note 109, August 1975.
33. L. Schourup. Unique new york unique new york unique new york. In *Papers from the 9th Regional Meeting, Chicago Linguistic Society*, pages 587–596, 1973.
34. Stefanie Shattuck-Hufnagel. Speech errors as evidence for a serial-ordering mechanism in sentence production. In W. Cooper and E. Walker, editors, *Sentence Processing: Psycholinguistic Studies Presented to Merrill Garrett*, pages 295–342. Lawrence Erlbaum Associates, Hillsdale, NJ, 1979.
35. Sean Smith and Joseph Bates. Toward a theory of narrative for interactive fiction. Technical Report CMU-CS-89-121, School of Computer Science, Carnegie Mellon University, Pittsburgh, PA, 1989.
36. J. P. Stemberger. An interactive activation model of language production. In Andrew W. Ellis, editor, *Progress in the Psychology of Language*, volume 1. Lawrence Erlbaum and Associates, 1985.

An Integrated View of Text Planning

Helmut Horacek

Universität Bielefeld
Fakultät für Linguistik und Literaturwissenschaft
Postfach 8640, D-4800 Bielefeld 1, Deutschland
Tel.: (+49-521)-106-3678, Fax: (+49-521)-106-5844
Email: horacek@techfak.uni-bielefeld.de

Abstract

Augmenting the currently dominating view of text planning, which is essentially understood as planning the organization of a text's structure, this paper presents an approach that integrates this part of the generation process into a broader context. The influences of various conceptual and linguistic phenomena on a text's structure are examined: exploitation of conversational implicature, performing aggregation of propositions with common parts, and impacts on the text structure caused by the repertoire of expressing conceptual specifications in terms of lexical items. Their integration is supported by adopting the view of handling several versions of text structures. They range from a concise, redundancy-free, and entirely explicit version, termed as argumentative structure to a version of the more usual kind of text structures, which widely mirrors the surface text finally produced. The approach is demonstrated by the generation of an explanation of medium complexity, and the impacts on the text structure in each processing step are illustrated.

1 Motivation

In its early days, research in natural language generation has been dominated by single sentence generators, which concentrate on syntactic phenomena or use simple pattern matching techniques. Over the last decade, the research goals have significantly expanded: they moved even towards the most ambitious enterprises of generating multi-sentence text in multiple languages augmented by multi-modal techniques. Although the power to be ultimately exhibited by the systems under development should occasionally surpass that of many humans, especially when capabilities incorporating multi-linguality and multi-modality are addressed, today's theories of natural language processing still suffer from many unresolved (and more basic) problems. These deficits manifest themselves in limited capabilities achieved in implemented systems so far: their linguistic and conceptual coverage is relatively poor, their expressiveness is rather inflexible in comparison to that of humans, and their applicability typically holds for a couple of specialized genres only.

It seems to us that a reason for these shortcomings lies in the yet underdeveloped methodologies applied. A common strategy is to study a certain subset of phenomena only - which is a perfectly justified approach - but the potential for integration with others is usually neglected. A reason for this situation may be that there is practically no agreement about how a communicative intention, which constitutes the initial specifications text generation is based on, looks in more concrete terms - this makes integration of subsystems a hard task. Moreover, there hardly seem to be systematic relations between the conceptual elements which constitute the source of a text to be generated (in particular, if these elements are not linguistically motivated) and the linguistic means to express these conceptual specifications.

These considerations motivate the purpose of this paper, which is to present an integrated view comprising a good deal of generation issues illustrated from the point of view of text planning. Text planning is examined in a broader context by featuring the relations to other areas involved in the production of natural language utterances: the interrelations to phenomena of conversational implicature, performing aggregation of propositions with common parts, and impacts on the text structure caused by the repertoire of expressing conceptual specifications in terms of lexical items and features are examined. It is shown how decisions concerning the way of expressing certain conceptual specifications in a given context and perspective influence a text's structure. As a consequence, several versions of text structures, ranging from an explicit argumentative structure to a text structure of the usual kind are used. A processing model is presented which carries out changes from one version to the other. In addition, an example is presented how the interior structure of a communicative intention (the argumentative structure) is built in a systematic way from elements of an expert system's model that constitute arguments for an explanation.

2 Text Planning Reviewed

Some early approaches in the area of text planning have pursued planning methods in the sense known from AI to satisfy the communicative goals of a speaker [1, 19]. Whereas these approaches have been very ambitious and without compromise, they have a rather limited scope, and a good deal of linguistic concepts is missing or underrepresented: for instance, the textual coherence and the repertoire for building object descriptions. Moreover, these approaches are unsatisfactorily inefficient because the level on which the basic operations are defined is mostly inadequate.

Over the last years there are two dominating approaches applied to text planning: text schemas (introduced in [17]), which describe conventional text structures in terms of patterns, and rhetorical relations (best known in form of the Rhetorical Structure Theory - RST [16]), which state the relationships between individual elements of a text. Since their origin text schemas, which have been attributed the disadvantage of being rigid and inflexible, have been augmented by additional schemas [21] and have been generalized further across domains [18], which results in a hierarchical schema library useful for a wider range of application. Rhetorical relations, whose original form is purely descriptive, are operationalized by [12] and others allowing for incremental structure building. Increased flexibility of textual realizations is focussed on in [14], for instance. Despite there is a significant distinction between these two principal approaches, they constitute two end points on a scale rather than entirely distinct methods - a view also elaborated in [12].

In the early approaches content selection and text organization (though the latter was much less developed yet) are fairly intertwined. In the original realization of text schemas and in the first operationalization of rhetorical relations, an apparent concentration on determining the order of text units can be observed. Organization of text structure dominates the selection of content in TEXT [17], and the content is already selected prior to consideration of structuring text units in [11]. In more recent approaches (e.g., [20]) content planning and organization are more interrelated and influence each other, which is considered more natural and better extendible.

In most of these approaches text structuring operations expect clause-sized chunks as elementary units. Only recently this restriction has been relaxed slightly (e.g., in [14]), also allowing noun phrases - adjuncts, in particular - as realizations of basic elements in the structuring process. This measurement is plausibly motivated by the evident fact that (non-linguistic) propositions derived from a computer system and intended to be communicated can hardly be expected to correspond to clause-sized information packages in general. Moreover, the expressive potential of natural languages is so rich that more variations than clauses (or phrases) can be thought as candidates to express a certain fact under given perspectives. Hence, current approaches to text generation have some serious limitations, and they are confronted with certain problems. In our view, these problems have two major sources:

- It is an unsolved problem how the selection process determining the information to be included in a response can be described in a systematic way independent from concrete applications. Further evidence for this problem is constituted by the missing agreement about the ontology of rhetorical relations.
- It is almost impossible to anticipate the consequences of text plan specifications on potential surface realizations. Moreover, it has been occasionally impossible to carry out the consequences of text plan specifications because the repertoire for lexicalization did not provide adequate means for the particular situation.

In this paper, we focus our considerations on demonstrating that the widely accepted view of propositional content to be expressed as a set of composable facts is too much simplified. By means of examples from our domain of application, which is giving explanations for solutions to room assignment in offices done by the expert system OFFICE-PLAN [13], we introduce the usage of multiple relations that hold between individual facts (more than just rhetorical relations) for issues of text planning. Together with optionality associated with elements of conceptual specifications, they build the basis for expressing the same content with different degree of precision according to the concrete environment and the actual perspectives.

3 Text Planning in a Broader Context

In most approaches to text planning, the genre and domain are skillfully chosen insofar, that conceptual specifications widely correspond to clause-size chunks. Meeting this requirement is favored by several characteristics of the underlying content:

- it mostly consists of individual facts,

- which are expressed on comparable levels of granularity and view, and
- the terms originally present remain widely the same.

In general, these restrictions cannot be expected to hold for long. In applications which entail more complexity and variety, for instance when providing explanations for selected aspects of a solution to an assignment problem like in our case, propositional specifications, their interrelations, and their potential exploitation for adequate and concise presentation introduce further issues to be coped with:

- Similar assertions referring to individuals and sets of objects imply the relevance of various phenomena of quantification for suitable presentation techniques.
- Assertions may come from different levels of representation and view; they may refer to referential or generic levels, to domain objects or processing descriptions, which may have several consequences on presentation and text organization.
- The inference potential that arises in the context of causal relations and associated knowledge has consequences on the presentation of the underlying content. Among others, this raises the choice of mentioning facts explicitly or leaving their relevance implicit by trusting the addressee's inferential capabilities.

Augmented by the potential of lexical realizations, we discuss these features in more detail. According to the underlying reasons the phenomena addressed are:

- choices in the presentation motivated by conversational implicature, i.e. exploiting inferential power, knowledge, and the particular context,
- taking structural similarities into account, which is already known from other approaches under the term of grouping (or aggregation) phenomena, and
- the impacts of the lexical repertoire on text organization structures.

In the following, we consider each of these influences on text organization in turn.

3.1 Conversational Implicature

The phenomenon of conversational implicature goes back to Grice [4] and is a consequence of the maxims of conversation he has proposed. The effects occur in a variety of constellations, and both the speaker and the hearer in a discourse situation rely on the other's conversational skill. In the field of natural language generation, selected aspects of conversational implicature have been addressed by [22] who aims at avoiding unwanted inferences, and by [8] who exploits conversational implicature for producing concise utterances. Since conversational implicature is rather a typical dialog than a text phenomenon, this may constitute a reason for the little attraction is has imposed on researchers concerned with text planning so far. However, we believe that its consideration is fairly important, since this phenomenon is also relevant for texts. Additionally, dialog contributions may occasionally convey so much information that issues of text structure are also relevant for this genre.

For our purposes we distinguish between three types of conversational implicature motivated by the source of the inferential task which the implicature exploits:

- The inference is supposed to be drawn by **the hearer** due to **world knowledge** attributed to him/her. For instance, if a system wishes to inform the user that a flight lands at LaGuardia airport, it has, in addition to stating this fact explicitly, the option of simply calling the flight a shuttle, thereby relying on the user's knowledge about the default landing place for shuttles to New York. In general, if a system wants to convey some properties about an object which all follow from giving a more accurate classification of this object, this technique seems to be superior to explicitly uttering statements about each of the properties. Hence, if the task is to communicate that a certain computer runs the EDT text editor and the RUNOFF text formatter, it is usually preferable to describe the computer as a VMS VAX, provided evidence that the user has the world knowledge to draw the necessary inferences (the examples are taken from [22]).

- The inference is carried out by **the speaker**. This strategy is usually applied if a system wants to elicit knowledge from its dialog partner. As an alternative to asking directly for a certain information, another question may be asked, the answer of which makes it possible to infer the information originally required. For instance, if an advisory system in the domain of financial investment [5] needs to know whether the user wants to buy an asset with high or with low liquidity, it may alternatively ask the question 'Do you want to have access to your money during the term of the investment?' The underlying inference is realized by terminological transformations (as described in [2]). The motivation behind not asking directly for the information wanted may go back to knowledge attributed or not to the user, or the alternative formulation may just be simpler.

- The inference is justified by **the context** (and the hearer is supposed to be able to draw it). In the course of a dialog, this applies to newly established common knowledge and to matters of coherence. Consider, for instance, explanations in the office planning domain (concerning the assignment of rooms to persons). In such an environment, it is perfectly adequate to answer a question like 'Why is Smith assigned to room 1?' by 'Group leaders have to be assigned to single rooms' or by 'Smith is a group leader' instead of citing the generic condition and the class membership of each of the entities involved (see [8]). The adequacy of this concise message is also supported by the (generally known) types of relations between generic assertions and the referential entities they apply to.

To summarize, the generated utterances may either express the underlying facts in an entirely explicit way, or only parts of these facts are actually mirrored by the surface expressions derived. In some cases, the underlying facts bear a certain kind of redundancy in view of the proper communicative intention (a subset of the facts follows from another one), which offers alternatives for the propositional content to be expressed. As for the impacts on text structure, it seems to be desirable to establish relations between text structure elements and the explicit arguments underlying a text portion. This has the benefit of providing a source which a text's structure is derived from, and of yielding more evidence in cases where parts of conceptual specifications are left implicit.

Therefore, we introduce several versions of text structures, which range from a concise, redundancy-free, and entirely explicit version, termed *argumentative struc-*

ture, ultimately to a version of the more usual kind of *text structures,* which widely mirrors the surface text finally produced. The argumentative structure reflects the original and internal content of a system's communicative intention. First, it is partially augmented by adding (possibly redundant) supporting arguments to provide a source of variability in presenting the conceptual specifications, thus reaching its richest version. The text structure is derived from the argumentative structure by successively modifying it according to the decisions made in the course of the generation process, which usually results in much shorter expressions (by leaving some parts implicit). Thus, the task of text planning is not restricted to an environment where conceptual specifications are more or less considered as a set of composable facts, from which relevant ones are to be selected and structured adequately.

We demonstrate the derivation of alternative text structures and the modifications applied to them for the examples given in this section (in Fig. 1). They essentially result from reductions of the (partially expanded) argumentative structure. It is due to the small size of the examples that the resulting text structures consist of single nodes only (with the exception of (1b)). Furthermore, apart from (1d), the argumentative structures that constitute the content of the communicative intention are first expanded by applying relevant rules of various kinds (justified by defaults, plausible inferences, and domain knowledge).

So far, we do not yet know how these types of rules can be used in a systematic way; if the repertoire of rules is limited, the problem does not seem to be too severe, but there must be restrictions imposed on the application of such rules in the general case. For the time being, we contend ourselves by showing the results of applying these rules, which manifest themselves in expansions impose on the argumentative structure. In addition, the effects on possible text structures are illustrated, which are obtained by applying tree reduction operations - for instance, the deletion of a branch and the replacements of a node by a successor node, which became the only one due to prior deletions. We only introduce these procedures informally by means of the examples given in Fig. 1. Additional advantages of these structures are the provided control over feasible alternatives and the increased evidence usable for determining the focus of attention and for justifying reference generation.

3.2 Grouping Phenomena

Grouping phenomena have been mentioned several times in the literature (e.g., [15, 3]), and their relevance for text structure has already been discussed in [12], among others. According to Hovy's view, there are arguments for both, performing grouping operations prior to text structuring (which imposes more effort on grouping, but may lead to better results - our conjecture), and for applying these processes in the opposite order (which imposes more effort on text structuring, since the number of elements is bigger - our conjecture). In our approach, we integrate the treatment of grouping phenomena into text planning by performing text structure modifications that reflect the effect of decisions concerning grouping variants selected.

Usually, a distinction is made between structurally motivated and content based groupings, which we basically maintain, but we divide structurally motivated group-

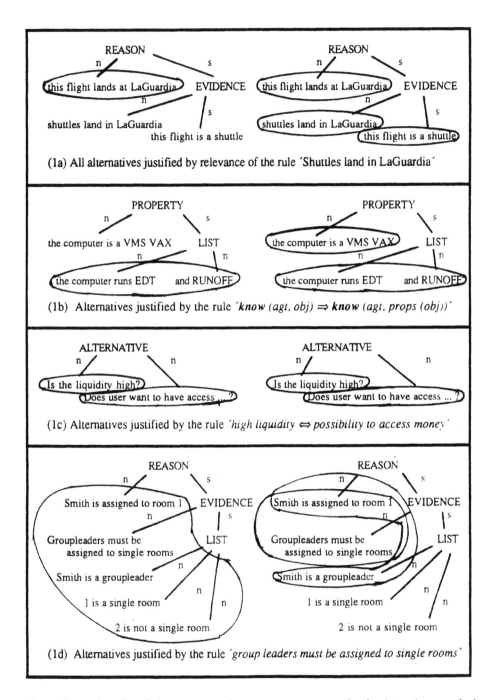

(1a) All alternatives justified by relevance of the rule 'Shuttles land in LaGuardia'

(1b) Alternatives justified by the rule 'know (agt, obj) ⇒ know (agt, props (obj))'

(1c) Alternatives justified by the rule 'high liquidity ⇔ possibility to access money'

(1d) Alternatives justified by the rule 'group leaders must be assigned to single rooms'

Fig. 1. Examples of explicit argumentative structures: communicative intentions marked on the left side and (alternatives for) text structures marked on the right side

ings further. Apart form those involving propositional assertions only, we have introduced others involving quantifications. We discuss each of these types in turn.

- **Content** based groupings: this type of aggregation is based on world knowledge. A typical example is 'John hits Peter' and 'Peter hits John back' (Fig. 2a), which can be expressed by 'John and Peter fight' by aggregating over the actions involved. Furthermore, related object transfers like 'John gives Peter a book' and 'Peter gives John a record' can alternatively be expressed by an exchange. However, it is remarkable that the compact alternatives tend to cause a loss of the degree of precision in which the underlying facts can be expressed. In the example of fighting, for instance, the information about who actually started the fight gets lost. Moreover, when stating the underlying events explicitly, it is always possible to mention the associated circumstances as well, even if they are different from each other. This possibility gets lost in the case of mentioning the aggregated version. Hence, building aggregations is not only a matter of achieving conciseness, but it involves a real decision concerning the accuracy in which the information to be conveyed can be presented.
- **Structurally** motivated, purely **propositional** groupings. Fig. 2b entails a slight enhancement of the usual aggregation of this type. It starts with a summarizing fact that involves an abstraction of individual objects yielding their common type, and it is followed by an enumeration. In a certain sense, this example is a combination of structurally motivated and content based grouping. A further, somehow related possibility consists in breaking up long sequences of lists into sublists, thereby introducing a more pronounced structure. In general, it would be desirable that the actual kind of breaking up long enumerations can be motivated by certain properties holding among their elements (we demonstrate an example in the next section). However, if there are no evident ones, it is more colloquial to present a list of smaller lists each of which is expressed in a slightly different way instead of producing a long and boring enumeration, although the latter might even be preferable for technical texts.
- **Structurally** motivated groupings involving **quantifications**: when aggregation is not done on the basis of knowledge about the objects involved, but on their cardinality, a new flavor is introduced. Fig. reffig2c gives a non-trivial example, which additionally presupposes that the three rooms mentioned constitute the entire set of rooms in the focus of attention. If a vague quantifier is generated, considerations similar to those mentioned for content based groupings apply concerning a potential loss of degree of precision.

3.3 Lexicalization

Finally, the repertoire for expressing conceptual specifications in lexical terms may effect the simple correspondence between text structure elements and clauses in a good deal of instances. However, there seems to be a considerable overlap to content based groupings, and we doubt whether a clear definition of the difference is possible at all - at least we do not believe so. As far as our approach is concerned,

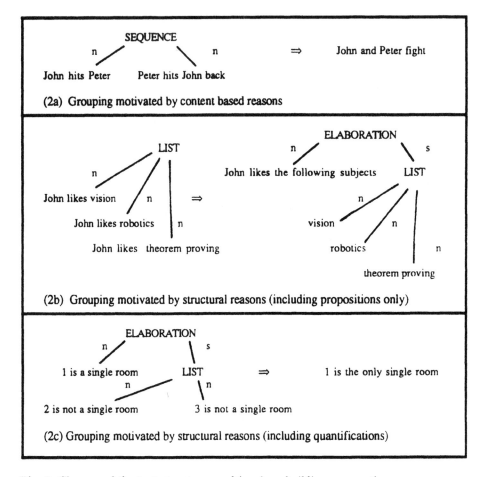

Fig. 2. Changes of the text structure resulting from building aggregations

the distinction is made according to the method applied for achieving the intended restructuring process. In case of groupings, this is done by terminological transformations (as described in [2] and in [7]) which are applied to introduce **new** predications (on a purely **conceptual** level) on the basis of terminological definitions in a KL-ONE like style (i.e., hierarchical relations, roles of entities, and mappings between their fillers). As for lexicalization the restructuring process is carried out by applying a small set of composable schemata as introduced in [6], which are used to express **given** predicates in different degrees of granularity and explicitness. Unfortunately, conceptual specifications are already replaced by linguistic expressions in the Figures for the sake of readability, hence the difference cannot be made explicit.

Augmenting the variation of expressing one of these elements by a noun phrase instead of a clause, Fig. 3a gives a simple example for expressing a temporal circumstance by a tense feature. However, its applicability seems to be broader than

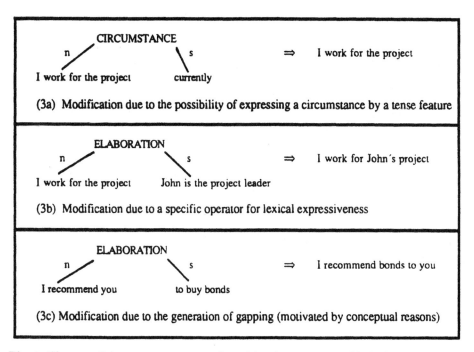

Fig. 3. Changes of the text structure motivated by the repertoire of lexical expressiveness

for vague circumstances like 'currently' in the actual instance. In principle, circumstances should be provided for all events involved in the argumentative structure, especially in certain genres like narratives. However, if there is no change of circumstance over a series of facts mentioned, it is, for all but the first fact, possible to leave the circumstance out, since it can be inferred to remain unchanged. In such cases, expressing a circumstance by a tense feature is perfectly adequate.

Furthermore, Fig. 3b gives an example where a state holding between two entities is simply expressed by a grammatical feature instead of an entire clause. Again, this choice is accompanied by a decrease in the accuracy exhibited when expressing the underlying state this way - John could be the leader of the project or he could simply work for it (compare also the considerations on groupings in the previous section).

Lastly, two propositions connected by a rhetorical relation may melt into a single surface expression in which some parts of the original specification are gapped. In Fig. 3c, we present a special gapping phenomenon which arises due to the particularities of the lexeme 'recommend'. The underlying explicit constellation, which is expressed by an elaboration relation, states that the action of buying bonds is the thing that is recommended. However, since it is perfectly evident that the action to be applied to the bonds is buying and not any other procedure, mentioning it explicitly can be omitted, which is enabled by the lexical properties of the verb 'recommend' - it alternatively allows bearing a direct object or an infinitive group.

4 Text Planning in Generating an Explanation

We illustrate our integrated approach to text planning by demonstrating the generation of a text structure for an explanation to a problem solution obtained by the expert system OFFICE-PLAN [13]. The system is applied to solve room assignment problems in offices, which are represented as constraint-satisfaction problems. Given a partial assignment of rooms to a certain set of employees, the system attempts to find adequate rooms for another set of employees while satisfying requirements concerned with supporting communication, providing the necessary resources, avoiding social conflicts, etc. One after the other, employees are assigned to the set of rooms still consistent with the constraints evaluated so far and with those constraints derived from the requirements associated with the employee integrated actually. At the end, this procedure results in sets of assignments which constitute all solutions.

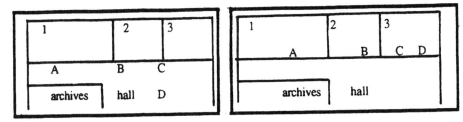

Fig. 4. (a) An office-planning problem (b) The solution to the associated problem

Constraints:	Associated justifications:
1 A must be in a big single room,	because he/she is a group leader
2 B must be in a room different from C´s room,	because C does not tolerate smokers (B is a smoker)
3 B must be in a room different from D´s room,	because D does not tolerate smokers (B is a smoker)

Fig. 5. The relevant set of constraints and justifications for a particular saspect

Components integrated and constraints associated:		Sets of feasible assignments:
A	A must be in a big single room	{(A/1)}
B		{(A/1,B/2), (A/1,B/3)}
C	C must be in a room different from B´s room	{(A/1,B/2,C/3), (A/1,B/3,C/2)}
D	D must be in a room different from B´s room	{(A/1,B/2,C/3,D/3)}

Fig. 6. The trace of the process solving the office-planning problem

A constraint is derived from a requirement by reducing it to the restriction imposed and leaving out the associated justification. For instance, the requirement 'if an employee is a group leader, he/she must be in a single room' breaks down into a constraint 'the employee must be in a single room' and into a justification '(because) he/she is a group leader'. For the problem solving process, only the constraints are of relevance, while the associated justifications become important for explanations.

We demonstrate the functionality of the system by the following example. The employees A, B, C, and D are to be assigned to the rooms 1, 2, and 3 (1 is a big and, 2 a small single room, 3 is a double room). Fig. 4a shows the topological relations of this office-planning problem. Fig. 4b represents the only possible solution in view of the set of constraints and associated justifications listed in Fig. 5 (constraints and justifications. The entire process of solving this problem is illustrated in Fig. 6 by the aid of an abbreviated trace. It contains the employees and the constraints associated with them in the order these employees are assigned to rooms. In addition, the sets of feasible room assignments resulting after integration of the employee assigned most recently are included. Explanations to be considered here refer to questions of the type: Why is <set1 of person/room assignment> feasible (and not <set2 of person/room assignment>) ?

The conceptual specifications for appropriate answers consist of a set of responsible constraints and associated requirements. The algorithm described in [9] performs the determination of a set of responsible constraints by verifying the relevance of each constraint selected. In addition, the set of constraints is structured (partitioned into subsets) in such a way that each subset of constraints represents a reason for the exclusion of at least one room from the set of assignments feasible otherwise. Thus, the composition of all these subsets constitutes the complete explanation.

Let us consider the example: 'Why are C and D together in room 3?' The assignment problem presented is simplified in such a way that all constraints are relevant for restricting the feasible assignments to a unique solution. Also for the question considered, all constraints are relevant: constraint 1 for exclusion of the assignment of either C or D to room 1 (partition 1), and constraints 2 and 3 together for the exclusion of room 2 from being a feasible place for either of them (partition 2).

After their separation into two partitions, the constraints and the associated justifications are transduced into the argumentative structure for the explanation to be generated. This structure is further enhanced by the location specific properties referred to by the constraints. This transduction is performed in the following way:

- descriptions of all partitions are connected by a LIST relation,
- the description of a partition breaks down into an assertion stating the set of rooms excluded (which becomes the nucleus) and the constraints responsible for this (which become satellites); they are connected by a REASON relation,
- if several constraints belong to a partition, they are connected by a LIST relation,
- a JUSTIFICATION relation is used to link a constraint (the nucleus) and the associated justification (the satellite),
- a justification breaks down into a generic domain rule (which becomes the nucleus), and it is linked to statements about the class memberships of the entities involved (which become the satellite) by an ELABORATION relation.

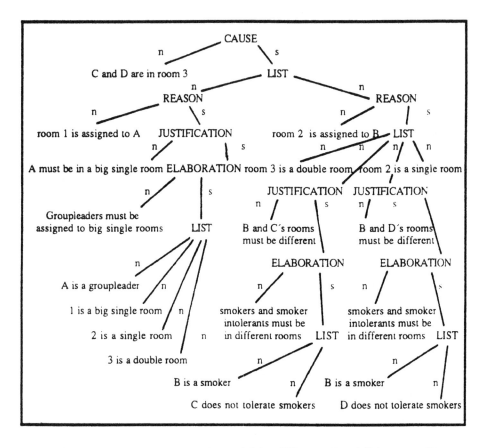

Fig. 7. The argumentative structure for explaining 'Why are C and D in room 3?'

If a room type is referred to by a constraint 'directly' (e.g., by 'single room'), an appropriate statement is linked to the justification. Otherwise, it becomes the nucleus of an ELABORATION expanding the REASON of the partition that explains its exclusion; the types of the rooms that represent feasible locations are added to the last partition. An example for an argumentative structure is presented in Fig. 7.

It is assumed that the addressee knows only the set of rooms and the set of employees, but nothing about their properties. First, rules expressing conversational implicature are applied (see [9]), whose results are illustrated in Fig. 8. From the fact that A is a group leader and from the assertion 'A must be assigned to a big single room' follows the corresponding rule. As for the rule about smoker intolerance, the user is assumed to be familiar with it due to common sense knowledge. Hence, stating one of the facts — B is a smoker or C (D) does not tolerate smokers — triggers the relevance of that rule and the truth of the other fact as well, since only these two employees are in the focus of attention due to the constraint forcing them to be in different rooms. Note, that it is insufficient to state the rule instead of one of the facts, since this does not make clear which employee is the smoker and who is the smoker intolerant person. Classifying B as a smoker is preferred to noting that the others are smoker intolerant, because this alternative can be exploited better for performing aggregation. The uppermost relation is eliminated, because it is subject to elliptification later on. Also, the categorization of room 3 is left out, because the question states that the two employees are assigned to the same room.

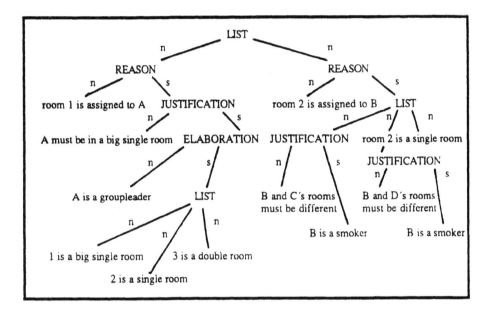

Fig. 8. Text structure modified accordingly after exploiting conversational implicature

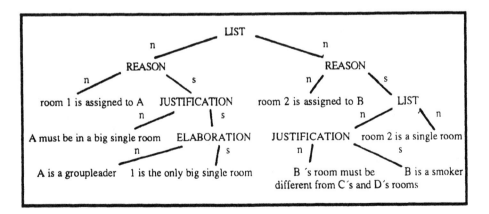

Fig. 9. The final text structure obtained after modifications by exploiting aggregation

Next, the potential for aggregation is explored, which leads to simplifications in two parts of the tree. First, a quantifier is generated for the assertions about the class membership of big single rooms. Then, the two reasons for the exclusion of room 2 can be grouped into a single one, since also their justifications are identical. The result is then shown in Fig. 9.

From the text structure obtained finally, there are several possibilities to generate a surface text. In this paper we do not address the question involved in finding out a good alternative, which includes considerations of order if given a choice, reference generation, and appropriate realization of the rhetorical relations. We just present a rather elaborated verbalization for purposes of illustration:

'Room 1 is assigned to A, because A as a group leader must be assigned to the only big single room, 1. Room 2 is assigned to B, because it is a single room and because B's room must be different from C's and D's room since B is a smoker.'

So far, very little has been said about suitable control structures for that approach. In the presentation of the example we have assumed the selection of the best (or, at least, of a very reasonable) alternative without detailed considerations of how the underlying criteria are obtained, what problems are posed by the associated dependencies, and how they can be mastered. In [10] we have outlined various strategies of how decisions can be made intelligently, also discussing impacts on the degree of quality and the effort involved. However, if the repertoire of alternatives a system has at its disposal becomes larger, one can also expect an increase of the dependencies among criteria on alternatives to be chosen from, which may make local decisions and giving up other alternatives at an early stage of processing an increasingly dominating strategy (in a sequential approach). Thus, we favor the integration of our approach with incremental and parallel control structures (like that proposed in [23]), which seems to be a promising topic for future research.

5 Conclusion

The contribution of this paper is to advocate for and to outline an integrated strategy in the area of text planning. A major aspect lies in the combination of text (structure) planning with the exploitation of conversational implicature; the integration is further supported by taking into account slightly enhanced capabilities concerned with aggregation of propositions with common parts, and by considering the impacts on a text's structure caused by an increased flexibility in expressing conceptual specifications in terms of lexical items and features.

At the end, we have to point out that it is occasionally hard to establish well-justified preferences among the alternatives available, because dependencies among criteria involved as well as among the choices themselves may arise, which would cause severe control problems. For further progress, it will be necessary to solve these problems to a certain extent, to increase the coverage of this method to more rhetorical relations and to test its suitability across domains.

References

1. D. Appelt. *Planning Natural Language Utterances to Satisfy Multiple Goals.* PhD

thesis, Stanford University, 1981.

2. H. Bergmann. Short Description of FTRANSLATE. WISBER Memo Nr. 30, University of Hamburg, 1987.

3. R. Dale. *Generating Referring Expressions in a Domain of Objects and Processes.* PhD Thesis, Centre for Cognitive Science, University of Edinburgh, 1989.

4. H. Grice. Logic and Conversation. In *Syntax and Semantics.* Vol 3, Speech Acts, pp. 43-58, Academic Press, 1975.

5. H. Horacek et al. From Meaning to Meaning — A Walk Through WISBER's Semantic-Pragmatic Processing. In GWAI-88, W. Hoeppner (ed.), pp. 118-129, Geseke, 1988.

6. H. Horacek, C. Pyka. Towards Bridging Two Levels of Representation Linking the Syntactic Functional and Object-Oriented Paradigms. In Int. Comp. Sci. Conf. '88 — AI: Theory and Appl., Hong Kong, J.-L. Lassez, F. Chin (eds.), pp. 281-288, 1988.

7. H. Horacek. The Architecture of a Generation Component in a Natural Language Dialog System. In *Current Issues in Natural Language Generation,* R. Dale, C. Mellish, M. Zock (eds.), pp. 193-227, Academic Press, 1990.

8. H. Horacek. Exploiting Conversational Implicature For Generating Concise Explanations. In EACL-91, J. Kunze, D. Reimann (eds.), Vol. 1, pp. 191-193, Berlin, 1991.

9. H. Horacek. Towards Finding the Reasons Behind — Generating the Content of Explanations. In GWAI-91, T. Christaller (ed.), pp. 96-105, Bonn, 1991.

10. H. Horacek. Decision Making in the Systems WISBER and DIAMOD. In Workshop on Decision Making in NLG at IJCAI-91, M. Meteer, I. Zukerman (eds.), 1991.

11. E. Hovy. Planning Coherent Multisentential Text. In ACL-88, pp. 163-169, 1988.

12. E. Hovy. Unresolved Issues in Paragraph Planning. In *Current Issues in Nat. Language Generation,* R. Dale, C. Mellish, M. Zock (eds.), pp. 17-45, Academic Press, 1990.

13. W. Karbach, M. Linster, A. Voß. OFFICE-PLAN: Tackling the Synthesis Frontier. In GWAI-89, D. Metzing (ed.), pp. 379-387, Geseke, 1989.

14. J. Kreyß, H.-J. Novak. The Textplanning Component PIT of the LILOG System. In COLING-90, H. Karlgren (ed.), pp. 431-433, Helsinki, 1990.

15. W. Mann, J. Moore. Computer Generation of Multiparagraph English Text. In AJCL 7(1), pp. 27-29, 1981.

16. W. Mann, S. Thompson. Rhetorical Structure Theory: A Theory of Text Organization. In L. Polanyi (ed.), *The Structure of Discourse,* Norwood, Ablex, 1987.

17. K. McKeown. *Text Generation: Using Discourse Strategies and Focus Constraints to Generate Natural Language Text.* Cambridge University Press, Cambridge, 1985.

18. K. McKeown et al.. Natural Language Generation in COMET. In *Current Issues in Natural Language Generation,* R. Dale, C. Mellish, M. Zock (eds.), pp. 103-139, Academic Press, 1990.

19. J. Meehan. TALE-SPIN: An Interactive Program that Writes Stories. In IJCAI-77, pp. 91-98, 1977.

20. J. Moore, W. Swartout. A Reactive Approach to Explanation. In IJCAI-89, Detroit, pp. 1504-1510, 1989.

21. C. Paris. Description Strategies for Naive and Expert Users. In ACL-85, pp. 238-245, 1985.

22. E. Reiter. Generating Descriptions that Exploit a User's Domain Knowledge. In *Current Issues in Natural Language Generation,* R. Dale, C. Mellish, M. Zock (eds.), pp. 257-285, Academic Press, 1990.

23. N. Reithinger. Eine parallele Architektur zur inkrementellen Generierung multimodaler Dialogbeiträge Dissertation, Universität des Saarlandes, 1991.

Integrating Text Planning and Linguistic Choice by Annotating Linguistic Structures

Robert Rubinoff

Institute for Research in Cognitive Science
3401-4C Walnut St.
University of Pennsylvania
Philadelphia, PA 19104
rubinoff@linc.cis.upenn.edu

Abstract

Research into natural language generation has often divided the processing into separate text planning and linguistic realization components. Despite this division's intuitive plausibility and practical utility, it ultimately interferes with some of the decisions necessary in the generation process. The IGEN generator, described here, implements a solution to this dilemma by having the linguistic component provide feedback to the planner. This feedback is in the form of annotations that describe the effects and consequences of particular linguistic decisions. The planner can then ratify or override the decisions of the linguistic component, without needing any direct access to purely linguistic information. This allows the two components to interact fully while retaining the strict separation of the levels of processing.

1 Introduction: The Relation of Text Planning to Linguistic Choice

Research into natural language generation has often divided the processing into two largely independent components [Th1, MK1, MD1, Re1]. One of these (the "strategic" component or "text planner") selects and structures the information to be expressed. The other one (the "tactical" or "linguistic" component or "realizer") converts the structured information into grammatical sentences of some natural language. While this division seems quite natural and has proved useful, it cannot handle decisions that depend on both informational and purely linguistic factors. The work described here is an attempt to overcome this limitation while retaining the advantages of the division into separate planning and realization components.

The division into planning and linguistic components seems a natural one because the two components deal with different kinds of data and involve different kinds of reasoning. The planning component's data is primarily the information to be expressed and knowledge about how various kinds of information can relate to each other and fit together to make a coherent discourse. Its reasoning involves general reasoning, to characterize and relate the information to be expressed, and planning, to determine what arrangements of what information will clearly and appropriately express the intended information. The linguistic component, on the other hand, deals primarily with the lexical elements and syntactic constructions available in some language, the rules and/or constraints on using them, and mappings between these linguistic elements and the information they express. Its reasoning primarily involves building up compound structures and checking constraints on and across them.

Thus natural language generation seems to divide naturally into one component that uses fairly general reasoning methods about information and how to organize it and another that uses fairly specialized constraints and rules to organize specific types of linguistic structures. This approach has in fact served to simplify the generation task and even to allow research to be done on each component independently. For example, work on MUMBLE [MD1] and PENMAN [Pe1] has concentrated on the linguistic component, while work on TEXT [MK1] and the Moore and Paris's work [MP1] has concentrated on the planner. The successful use of MUMBLE as a linguistic component for the independently developed text planners in TEXT and ROMPER [Ru1, Ka1] provides even stronger evidence for the apparent independence of the two parts of the generation process.

The independence of the text planner and the linguistic component, though, depends crucially on the lack of interaction between decisions within each component. If some decisions can only be made on the basis of both text planning and purely linguistic information, there will be no way to handle them without allowing one or both of the components to know (and understand) what the other is doing. Unfortunately, natural language generation does involve this sort of decision.

Consider, for example, the decision between (1)a and (1)b:[1]

(1) a. John killed him with a gun.
    b. John shot him dead.

On the one hand, the decision between these two ways of expressing the same information seems like it should be made by the planner; the two sentences vary in dramatic force and in what they emphasize. Furthermore, they allow for different information to be left out; (1)a can be shortened to "John killed him", while (1)b can be shortened to "John shot him". Obviously the decision between the various full and shortened versions cannot be made on linguistic grounds. On the other hand, the decision depends on linguistic issues. Contrast (1) with (2) and (3), in which only one of the corresponding alternatives is possible:

(2) a. John infected him with a virus.
    b. **John virused him sick.
(3) a. **John homed him with an order.
    b. John ordered him home.

The planner can't choose between these alternatives because it doesn't know what it can choose from. Only the linguistic component knows, for each particular meaning, which of the alternative forms can be expressed in English.

The same kind of interaction can be seen in lexical choices such as the ones in:[2]

---

[1] These examples and others are discussed in more detail in Sects. 2.1.1 and 3.1 of [Ru2].

[2] These sentences are taken from a (randomly chosen) newspaper article discussing highway construction on top of an alleged Indian burial site/ground [Ro1].

(4) a. If the archaeologists suspect there is a *burial site*, the state notifies one of its officially recognized Indian chiefs.

    b. He added that "if it were a *burial ground*, I would be there."

Here the same place is described as either a "burial place" or a "burial ground"; this choice obviously must be made somewhere. On the one hand, it must be made by the planner, since it depends on the context in which and the purpose for which it is being discussed. On the other hand, it must be made by the linguistic component, since it's only because of the existence of the particular lexical items in English that the choice is possible. Thus only the planner knows how to choose between the alternatives, but only the linguistic component knows that there are alternatives to choose from.

For both the syntactic choices in (1)–(3) and the lexical choice in (4), neither the planner nor the linguistic component has enough information to make the decision. It thus appears that, despite its advantages, the rigid division into planning and linguistic components will ultimately have to be abandoned.[3]

The work described here resolves this dilemma by having the linguistic component provide feedback to the planner describing what it has done. The planner can then detect and respond to situations where linguistic choices interact with its own decisions. In order to do this, though, the linguistic component must be able to tell the planner what it has done without requiring the planner to understand and reason over linguistic structures. This is the central idea implemented in this work: the linguistic component provides feedback via a set of annotations that describe the various structures built by the linguistic component, indicating the properties that are relevant to the planner. The annotations abstract away from the details of what the linguistic component is doing, describing only the consequences of particular choices, not the choices themselves. Thus the linguistic component doesn't have to know anything about what the planner is doing, only what sorts of things the planner might care about. Conversely, the planner doesn't need to deal with or understand any linguistic issues; it only needs to understand what sorts of things language can be used for. The annotations mediate between the two components, allowing their decisions to be made separately but still interact when necessary.

2 Annotations for Linguistic Options

The **IGEN** generator handles interactions between the planner and the linguistic component via annotations that provide feedback from the linguistic component to the planner. The basic structure of this process is shown in Fig. 1. As in many systems, the planner is invoked with a description of what the generator needs to do (expressed in **IGEN** as a goal to be achieved) and responds by arranging a plan of information to be expressed; the elements of this plan are then passed on to the linguistic component. Rather than simply converting these into English sentences, the

---

[3] Danlos in fact argues for abandoning the distinction entirely and presents a generator that works simultaneously at multiple levels [Dal]. Her generator, however, starts with a specification of the information to be expressed. Much of the work of the text planner is still done by an (implicit) separate component.

linguistic component generates a series of possible ways of expressing each element of the plan. These options include annotations that indicate various relevant aspects of the option. The planner uses these annotations to evaluate the options (as they are produced) and indicate which it prefers. The preferred options are then assembled, subject to syntactic constraints and time pressure, to produce the English output.[4]

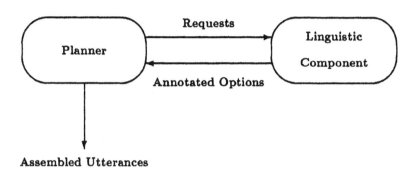

Fig. 1. Architecture of the IGEN generator

The annotations are predicates that apply (implicitly) to the option they annotate. Most of them also take an explicit argument indicating a semantic expression that the annotation relates to the option. The annotation predicates indicate several kinds of information:

The relationship between the meaning of an option and the information the planner wanted to express. Annotations can indicate how directly the option expresses the planner's request via **makes-explicit, makes-implicit,** and **indirectly-suggests** annotations. For example, the word "temperature" explicitly mentions the notion of temperature, and the word "drizzles" expresses the concept of rain implicitly without actually mentioning it. The word "weather" doesn't actually express the concept of temperature, but it does suggest it indirectly. Other annotations indicate **missing-info** that the option leaves out or **extra-info** that the option adds to what was requested. Also, **covers-other-entry** annotations indicate when an option expresses other parts of the planner's request in addition to the one it was suggested for. (There is one "entry" for each piece of information the planner requests options for.)

The effects on and dependencies on the presence and status of elements in the discourse context. This is not simply a question of what is available for anaphoric or definite reference. **Activates-in-context** annotations can also indicate effects on how various elements in the discourse context or the sentence(s) under construction

---

[4] For a more complete description of IGEN, see [Ru2].

will be perceived, since they can indicate properties of those elements. For example, using the phrase "the 15th" to describe a particular day suggests thinking of it within the sequence of days of the month, as opposed to thinking of its position within the week or year. If the planner is trying to tell the user that he's facing a deadline, this effect would be important, since the planner would want to describe the day within the smallest possible time-frame. Of course, these annotations could also be used to set up subsequent anaphoric reference. The current implementation of **IGEN** doesn't have a context model, though, so the annotations are not used this way.[5]

Pragmatic and stylistic features of the option. These annotations indicate the option's tone and register and interpersonal features such as politeness or deference. They are used to ensure appropriateness and consistency of these features. **IGEN** currently only uses one annotation of this type: concise-construction, used to mark constructions that are particularly concise. A global parameter controls whether **IGEN** prefers to be concise or verbose (or doesn't care), and the planner uses these annotations to enforce that preference.[6]

3 Using the Annotations to Generate Text

3.1 Example 1: The Basic Machinery

In this example, the generator is given the goal #<KNOW(HEARER,TOS-BUNCH)>, where #<TOS-BUNCH> is a collection of facts about the weather over a three day span starting on what the generator thinks is the current day. The planner then draws on its library of plans to construct an initial plan indicating what information to include and how to structure it to achieve this goal:

1. Overall Goal: #<KNOW(HEARER,TOS-BUNCH)>
2. Achieve (1) by sequencing information based on the #<SEQUENCE> of the three days involved
3. Support (2) with information about #<SEPT-25-1990>
4. Support (2) with information about #<SEPT-26-1990>
5. Support (2) with information about #<SEPT-27-1990>

Requests to express the information about each day's weather are then passed on to the linguistic component. In particular, the planner carries out step 4 of the plan by sending to the linguistic component the semantic expression:

#<OVER-TIME-SPAN(#<WITHIN-RANGE(TEMPERATURE,56DEG-75DEG-F)>,SEPT-26-1990)>

---

[5] The use of activates-in-context and from-context annotations to handle subsequent reference is discussed in [Ru2].

[6] The question of how to set such a preference was explored in PAULINE [Ho1]; the issue here is how to implement the preference.

Next, the linguistic component produces annotated options for each term of this request, along with an initial evaluation of the option based solely on the match between the option and the request. Each option is a (possibly partial) linguistic structure. These structures can be feature-values, words, phrases, phrase orderings, or (in principle) discourse structures, although most of the options in these examples are individual words. Once the options are placed in the work, the planner performs a fuller evaluation of them, and the preferred options for each term are assembled into an English sentence. The process proceeds as follows:

For #<TEMPERATURE>, the options are:[7]

- "weather": MEDIUM
  (MAKES-EXPLICIT #<WEATHER>)
  (INDIRECTLY-SUGGESTS #<TEMPERATURE>)
- "temperature": VERY-HIGH
  (MAKES-EXPLICIT #<TEMPERATURE>)
- "it": VERY-HIGH
  (MAKES-EXPLICIT #<TEMPERATURE>)
  (CONCISE-CONSTRUCTION)

Here both "temperature" and "it" get the highest rating, but "it" is marked as a concise instruction. The preference thus depends on the verbosity parameter; assuming here that it's set for conciseness, the preferred option will be "it".

The only acceptable option produced for the #<WITHIN-RANGE> relation:

- "be": HIGH
  (MAKES-EXPLICIT #<BE-LOCATED>)
  (MAKES-IMPLICIT #<WITHIN-RANGE>)

so this option is used.

For #<56DEG-75DEG-F>, the options produced are:

- "warm": HIGH
  (MAKES-EXPLICIT #<WARM>)
  (MAKES-IMPLICIT #<56DEG-75DEG-F>)
- "temperature": MEDIUM
  (MAKES-EXPLICIT #<TEMPERATURE>)
  (INDIRECTLY-SUGGESTS #<56DEG-75DEG-F>)

Here "warm" is the preferred option, because it does a reasonable job of describing the requested temperature range. The "temperature" option is not as good, but it at least gives a sense of what is being talked about, so it gets a more moderate evaluation.[8]

---

[7] The linguistic component actually produces several other options that are immediately ruled out as being completely inappropriate, e.g. the word "temperature" as an option for #<SEPT-26-1990>. Throughout these examples, such options will simply be ignored in the interests of brevity.

[8] This evaluation actually seems too high. Certainly, using "temperature" here is less appropriate than using "weather" for #<TEMPERATURE>, despite the two options having the same evaluation. A more subtle set of rankings would help; the set used here, though, seems to adequately determine the relative appropriateness of options in the examples.

In the cases considered so far, the planner has simply accepted the evaluations suggested by the planner. This is not always the case, though, as can be seen in the treatment of the options for #<OVER-TIME-SPAN>:

- [TENSE = FUTURE]: HIGH
  (MAKES-EXPLICIT #<OVER-TIME-SPAN>)
  (MAKES-EXPLICIT #<FUTURE>)
  (COVERS-OTHER-ENTRY entry for:#<SEPT-26-1990>)
  (MAKES-IMPLICIT #<SEPT-26-1990>)
- "over": VERY-HIGH
  (MAKES-EXPLICIT #<OVER-TIME-SPAN>)
  (ACTIVATES-IN-CONTEXT #<INSTANCE(SEPT-26-1990,LINEAR-SPAN)>)
- "on": HIGH
  (MAKES-EXPLICIT #<ON>)
  (MAKES-IMPLICIT #<OVER-TIME-SPAN>)
  (ACTIVATES-IN-CONTEXT #<INSTANCE(SEPT-26-1990,LINEAR-POS)>)

The **activates-in-context** annotations for "over" and "on" indicate that these options affect how the system (and the hearer) perceive the time span being talked about. Since the central organizing principle of the plan is the sequencing of the information by days, the planner wants to maintain the perception of the day as a point within the span of the next three days. Thus the planner doesn't accept the linguistic component's evaluations. Instead "on", which supports this perception, has its rating increased to VERY-HIGH. "Over", on the other hand, supports the perception of #<SEPT-26-1990> as a linear span, which conflicts with looking at it as a point. The option's rating is therefore reduced to HIGH, leaving "on" as the preferred option.

This case also shows how the use of annotations allows the planner to remain ignorant of purely linguistic issues. Here the planner has no way to distinguish between realizing #<OVER-TIME-SPAN> as a lexical item or as the value of some feature of another option. Its decision is based solely on the contextual effects of the available options.

The last piece of the request is #<SEPT-26-1990>, for which the linguistic component produces the following options:

- "tomorrow": HIGH
  (MAKES-EXPLICIT #<TOMORROW>)
  (MAKES-IMPLICIT #<SEPT-26-1990>)
  (ACTIVATES-IN-CONTEXT #<FEW-DAYS>)
- "Monday": HIGH
  (MAKES-EXPLICIT #<MONDAY>)
  (MAKES-IMPLICIT #<SEPT-26-1990>)
  (ACTIVATES-IN-CONTEXT #<WEEK>)

These options appear equally appropriate to the linguistic component, since they match the planner's request equally well. The planner, though, can distinguish between them on the basis of the concepts that they activate. Since both "tomorrow"

and "Monday" activate time scales, the planner prefers the one that is more similar
to the #<SEQUENCE> that is the basis for the plan structure. Accordingly, "Monday"
is downgraded to MEDIUM and "tomorrow" is the preferred option.

As these options are produced and evaluated, the preferred options are assembled
into an utterance and printed out. Here the preferred options combine to form "It
will be warm on tomorrow". Unfortunately, this sentence is not acceptable, since
"on tomorrow" is not grammatical. So instead the next best combination of options
is used, resulting in the output of:

"It will be warm on Monday".[9]

This simple example illustrates how the annotations allow **IGEN** to maintain
the traditional division into two independent components while still handling interactions between decisions at the planning and linguistic levels. The planner never
has to deal with linguistic structures, and the linguistic component never has to deal
with plans or information structures. For example, the planner can't distinguish between lexical items and feature values; conversely the linguistic component has no
access to the goals driving the planner or the plans it builds. Nevertheless, when
there are decisions that depend on both informational and linguistic structures, the
annotations allow **IGEN** to handle the interactions between the different levels.
The effects of these interactions are relatively minor in this example, but subsequent
examples will show how they can be more dramatic.

3.2 Example 2: Using the Feedback

This example demonstrates how **IGEN** can respond to interactions between particular linguistic choices and both other parts of the utterance and higher-level actions
in the plan driving the utterance. The construction of the plan in this example
(and in Example 3) is admittedly ad hoc; **IGEN** certainly doesn't have a complete
model of human psychological states. What's important here, though, is how the
plan and the annotations fit together to produce the kind of subtle effects that can't
be produced by the linguistic component or the planner alone.

In this example, the planner is given the goal "make the user happy", and responds with a plan to do so by discussing the weather:

1. Overall goal: #<BE-STATE(HEARER,HAPPY)>
2. Achieve (1) by achieving subgoals:
   (a) Goal: Downplay unpleasant information
   (b) Goal: Emphasize pleasant information
3. Achieve (2a) by expressing:
   #<MINIMAL-SIGNIFICANCE(#<CONSIST-OF(PRECIPITATION,RAIN)>)>

---

[9] Actually, "It will be warm tomorrow" would probably be a better choice. The final assembly of options is done on a left-to-right basis, though, so the choice between expressing
#<OVER-TIME-SPAN> via "on" or via future tense is made before the choice between
"Monday" and "tomorrow". This is purely an implementation issue; there would be no
fundamental difficulty in modifying the assembly process to consider all the choices at
once.

4. Achieve (2b) by expressing:
   #<WITHIN-RANGE(TEMPERATURE,60-80-DEG-F)>
5. Achieve (2b) by expressing:
   #<AT-TIME(NO-PRECIPITATION,THIS-AFTERNOON)>

The final result for this plan is:

   "It is only drizzling. It is warm. It will be clear soon." [10]

Most of this output is produced straightforwardly in a manner similar to the previous example. Some of the choices, however, are the result of interactions of a sort beyond what was seen there.

Consider the options for #<CONSIST-OF(PRECIPITATION,RAIN)> in step (3) of the plan; these include:

- "raining": VERY-HIGH
  (MAKES-EXPLICIT #<CONSIST-OF>)
  (MAKES-EXPLICIT #<PRECIPITATION>)
  (MAKES-EXPLICIT #<RAIN>)
  (COVERS-OTHER-ENTRY entry for:#<PRECIPITATION>)
  (COVERS-OTHER-ENTRY entry for:#<RAIN>)
- "drizzling": HIGH
  (MAKES-EXPLICIT #<CONSIST-OF>)
  (MAKES-EXPLICIT #<PRECIPITATION>)
  (MAKES-IMPLICIT #<RAIN>)
  (MAKES-EXPLICIT #<DRIZZLE>)
  (COVERS-OTHER-ENTRY entry for:#<PRECIPITATION>)
  (COVERS-OTHER-ENTRY entry for:#<RAIN>)
  (EXTRA-INFO #<STRENGTH(RAIN,WEAK)>)
- "pouring": HIGH
  (MAKES-EXPLICIT #<CONSIST-OF>)
  (MAKES-EXPLICIT #<PRECIPITATION>)
  (MAKES-IMPLICIT #<RAIN>)
  (MAKES-EXPLICIT #<POUR>)
  (COVERS-OTHER-ENTRY entry for:#<PRECIPITATION>)
  (COVERS-OTHER-ENTRY entry for:#<RAIN>)
  (EXTRA-INFO #<STRENGTH(RAIN,STRONG)>)

The linguistic component considers "raining" to be the best of these options, since it captures the intended meaning precisely. "Drizzling" and "pouring" are the next best options, since they capture the basic meaning, and are equally appropriate, since the linguistic component can't evaluate the significance of the extra information they present. The planner, however, sees the **extra-info** annotations and notices that

---

[10] The first sentence actually comes out as "It is drizzling only". This is a limitation of the implementation; the mechanism for handling adjuncts was set up assuming that they would always be phrase-final. Fixing this would be straightforward but tedious, and nothing important depends on it.

the extra information included in "drizzling" implies another part of the requested information (the #<MINIMAL-SIGNIFICANCE> relation), so "drizzling" becomes the preferred option.

The decision here to say "drizzling" instead of "raining" could not have been made by either the planner of the linguistic component alone. The decision depends on both the planner's knowledge that the concept #<DRIZZLE> supports another piece of the plan and the linguistic component's knowledge that there is a way to express #<DRIZZLE> without making explicit its distortion of the actual information that it's raining. It's only the interaction between the two components provided by the annotations that makes saying "drizzling" instead of "raining" possible.

In step (5) of the plan, #<AT-TIME(CONSIST-OF,THIS-AFTERNOON)> produces options including:

- "later": MEDIUM
  (MAKES-EXPLICIT #<LATER>)
  (MAKES-EXPLICIT #<AT-TIME>)
  (MAKES-IMPLICIT #<THIS-AFTERNOON>)
  (COVERS-OTHER-ENTRY entry for:#<THIS-AFTERNOON>)
  (EXTRA-INFO #<CLOSE(THIS-AFTERNOON,NOW)>)
- "soon": MEDIUM
  (MAKES-EXPLICIT #<SOON>)
  (MAKES-EXPLICIT #<AT-TIME>)
  (MAKES-IMPLICIT #<THIS-AFTERNOON>)
  (COVERS-OTHER-ENTRY entry for:#<THIS-AFTERNOON>)
  (EXTRA-INFO #<AFTER(THIS-AFTERNOON,NOW)>)

Here the planner prefers "soon" over "later" (and all other options), since it indicates that the pleasant event (the lack of rain) is not far away. This helps accomplish the action in step (2b) of the plan (which this utterance is part of). "Later", in contrast, emphasizes the *difference* between #<THIS-AFTERNOON> and the present, thus minimizing the utterance's ability to carry out its intended function.

This example shows two kinds of interactions that IGEN can handle: between two separate parts of an utterance and between linguistic choices and higher-level actions in the plan. IGEN chooses "drizzling" over "raining" because it reinforces another part of the utterance, and it chooses "soon" over "later" because it helps achieve a higher-level action in the plan.

3.3 Example 3: Varying the Plan Structure

The previous examples demonstrate how IGEN uses annotations on the linguistic options to handle interactions between the planner and the linguistic component. The point of using the annotations, though, was not just to enable these kinds of interactions, but more importantly to do so without compromising the principled separation of the two components. As a result, IGEN can generate different sentences to express the same information based solely on differences in the plan. If the purely linguistic issues are the same, the linguistic component will do exactly the same work, even though the differences in the output may depend in part on that work.

As an example, consider the goal "get the user to take his umbrella", for which the planner constructs the following plan:

1. Goal: #<TAKE(HEARER,UMBRELLA)>
2. Achieve (1) by achieving subgoal:
   #<WANT(HEARER,#<TAKE(HEARER,UMBRELLA)>)>
3. Achieve (2) by achieving subgoal:
   #<KNOW(HEARER,#<CONSIST-OF(PRECIPITATION,RAIN)>)>
4. Achieve (3) by expressing:
   #<CONSIST-OF(PRECIPITATION,RAIN)>

The information to be expressed here is the same as the information in step (4) of Example 2. Since the linguistic component doesn't have access to the plan, it necessarily produces the same options as in the previous example. The planner, though, uses these options differently, since it is using them to carry out a different plan.

#<PRECIPITATION> and #<CONSIST-OF> are handled as in Example 2. The options for #<RAIN>, however, are evaluated differently. Achieving subgoal (3) depends on the hearer believing that the rain is something he needs protection from. Thus "drizzling", which minimizes the danger from the rain, undercuts the plan and has its rating decreased. "Pouring", on the other hand, emphasizes the danger and thus becomes the preferred option. The final result is then:

"It is pouring".

4 Conclusion: Annotations and Feedback in the Generation Process

The examples above demonstrates how **IGEN** generator uses annotated linguistic options to express feedback from the linguistic component to the planner. This approach allows the bulk of the planning and linguistic decisions to go on independently, while the annotations let the planner detect linguistic choices that interact with issues at the planning level. Thus linguistic choices can be sensitive to other parts of the utterance, to higher level goals and actions within the plan, and to the basic organization of the plan. Furthermore, only the interactions that actually come up need be examined. The planner doesn't need to anticipate the entire (potentially unbounded) set of possible ways that the plan might interact with linguistic choices. Instead it merely has to check for interactions between the specific options constructed by the linguistic component and the pieces of the plan.

The technique of using feedback via annotations is not entirely without disadvantages, of course. For one thing, it requires a clear specification of the meaning and effects of any word, phrase, or construction the generator uses. There's no way to constrain the use of an option to a particular special case; if it's available in one case, it's available at all times and in situations that may not have been anticipated. Also, structures that require coordination between different parts of the utterance are problematic. For instance, in Example 2, the three sentences are fine individually, but they don't flow together well as a sequence of utterances. Neither the planner nor the linguistic component has the necessary information to smooth out the sentences into a more fluent text.

These are not necessarily problems, though. After all, since generation is a real-time activity, a generator can't always anticipate correctly what it should say in order to set up the next utterance. Furthermore, with a fuller understanding of the linguistic basis for phenomena such as discourse coherence, it should be possible for the linguistic component to identify the relevant effects for the planner, and for the planner take advantage of large-scale linguistic structures. Thus the limitations are not so much limitations of this approach to generation as limitations of the linguistic sophistication of the generator. In fact, since the use of annotations allows **IGEN** to preserve the the separation of the linguistic and planning levels, it should help focus further work on a fuller and more precise characterization of the function and role of both levels.

References

[Da1] Laurence Danlos. *The Linguistic Basis of Text Generation. Studies in Natural Language Processing*, Cambridge University Press, Cambridge, England, English translation edition, 1987. Translated by Dominique Debize and Colin Henderson.

[Ho1] Eduard H. Hovy. *Generating Natural Language Under Pragmatic Constraints.* Lawrence Erlbaum, Hillsdale, NJ, 1988.

[Ka1] Robin Karlin. *Romper Mumbles.* Technical Report MS-CIS-85-41, CIS Department, University of Pennsylvania, Philadelphia, PA, 1985.

[MD1] David D. McDonald. Natural language generation as a computational problem. In M. Brady and Robert Berwick, editors, *Computational Models of Discourse*, pages 209–265, MIT Press, 1983.

[MK1] Kathleen R. McKeown. *TEXT GENERATION: Using Discourse Strategies and Focus Constraints to Generate Natural Language.* Cambridge University Press, 1985.

[MP1] Johanna D. Moore and Cécile Paris. Planning text for advisory dialogues. In *Proceedings of the 27th Annual Meeting of the ACL*, pages 203–211, Association for Computational Linguistics, Vancouver, BC, June 1989.

[Pe1] The PenMan Project. *The Penman Documentation.* Technical Report, USC–Information Sciences Institute, Marina del Rey, CA, 1989.

[Re1] Norbert Reithinger. Popel — a parallel and incremental natural language generation system. In Cécile Paris, William Swartout, and William Mann, editors, *Natural Language Generation in Artificial Intelligence and Computational Linguistics*, Kluwer Academic Publishers, 1990.

[Ro1] Frank Rossi. The curse of route 55. *The Philadelphia Inquirer Magazine*, 38–45, October 4 1987.

[Ru1] Robert Rubinoff. Adapting mumble: experience with natural language generation. In *AAAI-86*, pages 1063–1068, American Association for Artificial Intelligence, Morgan Kauffman, Philadelphia, August 1986.

[Ru2] Robert Rubinoff. *Natural Language Generation as an Intelligent Activity: Proposal for Dissertation Research.* Technical Report MS-CIS-90-32, CIS Department, University of Pennsylvania, Philadelphia, PA, May 1990.

[Th1] Henry Thompson. Strategy and tactics: a model for language production. In *Papers from the Thirteenth Regional Meeting*, pages 651–668, Chicago Literary Society, 1977.

Employing Knowledge Resources in a New Text Planner Architecture

Eduard Hovy,[1] *Julia Lavid,*[2] *Elisabeth Maier,*[3] *Vibhu Mittal,*[1,4] *Cécile Paris*[1]

[1] USC/Information Sciences Institute
4676 Admiralty Way
Marina del Rey, CA 90292. U.S.A.

[2] Departaménto de Filologia Inglesa
Universidad Complutense de Madrid
280040 Madrid, Spain

[3] Projekt KOMET, GMD-IPSI
Dolivostr. 15
D-6100 Darmstadt, Germany

[4] Department of Computer Science
University of Southern California
Los Angeles, CA 90089. U.S.A.

Abstract

We describe in this paper a new text planner that has been designed to address several problems we had encountered in previous systems. Motivating factors include a clearer and more explicit separation of the declarative and procedural knowledge used in a text generation system as well as the identification of the distinct types of knowledge necessary to generate coherent discourse, such as communicative goals, text types, schemas, discourse structure relations, and theme development patterns. This knowledge is encoded as separate resources and integrated under a flexible planning process that draws from appropriate resources whatever knowledge is needed to construct a text. We describe the resources and the planning process and illustrate the ideas with an example.

1 Introduction

When generating a multisentential text, one has to perform several different types of tasks, such as selecting the material to be included, organizing this material into a coherent message, choosing words, and generating grammatical sentences. We describe in this paper a new text planner being built jointly at USC/ISI and GMD-IPSI that performs portions of the generation process. It is based on theoretical studies and experiments in text coherence, e.g., Rhetorical Structure Theory (Mann and Thompson 88), Conjunctive Relations (Martin 92), theories of discourse, e.g., (Grosz and Sidner 86, Polanyi 88), and text planning, e.g., (Hovy 88, Moore and Paris 89), advancing on those ideas and handling several new aspects of the problem.

Authors are listed in alphabetical order.

This new text planner was designed to address several problems that we had encountered in our own systems and had observed in other, similar enterprises. An important motivation was a clearer separation of declarative and procedural knowledge in a generation system, as well as the identification of the distinct types of knowledge necessary to generate a text (for e.g., Paris and Maier 91). We had noticed in our current systems that, as the planners' plan libraries grew, the same information (e.g., requirements of use and other preconditions) had to be represented several times, and it became harder to add new plans and to modify existing plans because of their interrelationships. Furthermore, existing planning systems often mix information regarding the planning process and information necessary for linguistic realization in one single plan operator. Finally, some of the linguistic knowledge necessary to plan a text is sometimes encoded in the planner itself, rendering the process more opaque. To address these problems, we attempt to make as clear as possible the distinction between procedural and declarative information, and to identify precisely and separate out the different types of knowledge required for creating a discourse structure.

We first present the knowledge sources that we have so far identified. The planning process is then described, followed by an example of text planning.

2 Knowledge Resources Required for a Text Planner

Our text planner embodies an attempt to isolate and use some of the major knowledge resources required to plan multisentential text.[2] In this section, we present the major knowledge resources that we have so far identified, namely: *text types, communicative goals, schemas, discourse structure relations*, and, finally, a resource to handle *theme development and focus shift*.

In some cases, the knowledge resources embody information about the order of some planning operations. Such resources we have implemented as systemic networks; they are the discourse relations and theme patterns. In other cases, the knowledge resources provide information which the planner uses to make decisions. Such resources we have implemented as property-inheritance networks; they are the text types, communicative goals, and schemas. Both types of representation are declarative, enable us to capture inherent commonalities within the resource, and promote notational clarity and simplicity of processing.

Each node in either type of network may contain one or more *realization operators* which indicate the effects of choosing the node, such as making additions to the discourse structure, choosing subsequent nodes to visit, setting requirements

---

[2] We consider discourse to be a structured collection of clauses. This structure is expressed by the nesting of segments of the discourse; a discourse can thus be represented as a tree structure, in which each node of the tree governs the segment (subtree) beneath it. At the top level, the discourse is governed by a single root node; at the leaves, the basic segments are single grammatical clauses. Each discourse segment has an associated purpose, which, following Grosz and Sidner (1986), we call the Discourse Segment Purpose, i.e., a communicative goal. Each adjacent pair of such purposes is related in the discourse structure by one or more discourse structure relations, as described in Section 2.4.

upon subsequent grammatical realization, etc. Knowledge resources co-constrain each other via these realization operators. In Section 3, we describe how the property-inheritance networks are used and the systemic networks are traversed during the planning process, and how a text structure is built during the traversal.

This planner is far from complete. Motivations for various choices have not been fully identified and several important text planning functions, such as noun phrase planning, lexical choice, lexical cohesion, and sentence structure planning are lacking altogether. We intend to investigate these issues in future work. In the remainder of this section we describe the various knowledge resources of the planner.

2.1 Text Type Hierarchy

It has long been observed that certain types of linguistic phenomena (e.g., the rhetorical structure, lexical types, grammatical features) closely reflect the genre of the text (e.g., scientific papers, financial reports). A text generation system that contains a rich set of expressive possibilities requires some representation of genres or text types in order to constrain its options, since no other resource will provide the necessary information, and the system will be unable to choose between alternative formulations.

Several text typologies have been proposed by linguists. To mention only a few: Biber (1989) identified eight basic types of texts based on statistically derived grammatical and lexical commonalities. The Washington School proposed a detailed classification of different genres of written scientific and technical English (Trimble 85), additionally pointing out typical relationships within and between rhetorical/textual units. de Beaugrande (1980) proposed a general classification of text types, also arguing that text types determine the types of discourse structure relations used.

Given its generality, we decided to base our text planner's hierarchy of text types on that of De Beaugrande, with extensions as needed to handle the text types we are addressing. The hierarchy (partially shown in Fig. 1) is represented as a property-inheritance network in the knowledge representation system Loom (MacGregor 88). Each text type in this hierarchy has associated with it the constraints it imposes on other resources, such as which communicative goals it entails, which discourse relations it favors, any appropriate grammatical constraints, etc. As a result, once a type has been established for the text to be generated, the selection of other parameters used during the generation process can be constrained appropriately (for instance, interpersonal discourse relations almost never appear in objective scientific reports, while love letters tend to contain mainly those relations). Thus our planner's predefined text types help pre-select or de-activate certain options in the generation process.

2.2 Communicative Goal Hierarchy

Communicative goals have been used in many generation systems to describe the discourse purpose(s) of the speaker. Our planner contains a rudimentary taxonomization of communicative goals, starting at the topmost level with some very general goals, such as INFORM, DESCRIBE, REQUEST, and ORDER, which are eventually refined

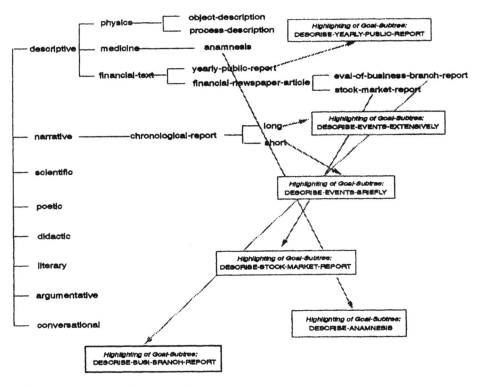

Fig. 1. A part of the Text Type Hierarchy.

into specific goals to describe specific types of information for specific contexts (see Fig. 2). Our taxonomy, which is implemented as a property-inheritance network, resembles the one being derived from speech acts by Allen and his colleagues (e.g., Allen 91).

Planning for a communicative goal results in a discourse segment (a sub-tree of the discourse structure for the generated text). Each communicative goal contains one or more realization operators — instructions for the planner to perform specific actions (see Section 3). We call our planner's lowest clause-level goals *planner primitive speech acts*; these primitive speech acts form the leaves of the discourse structure tree. During the planning process, they signal that the next step is grammatical realization.

2.3 Schemas

In many circumstances, texts exhibit a stereotypical structure. In text planning systems, such structure is usually represented in schemas, which specify the topics of discussion that appear in the text as well as their ordering (e.g., McKeown 85).

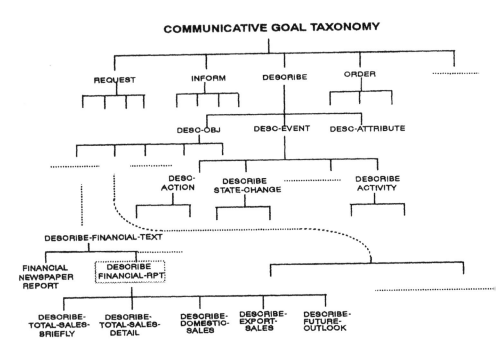

Fig. 2. A part of the Communicative Goal Hierarchy.

The stages of structural stereotypes can be defined at the clausal level (indicating the type of process of each sentence to be included and its position), but can equally well be defined at a more general level (indicating the sequence of general topics to be included). Linguists have proposed several schema-like approaches to model such structure: e.g., macrostructures (Van Dijk and Kintsch 83), holistic structures (Mann and Thompson 88), and the Generic Structure Potential (Halliday and Hasan 85). Recognizing the utility of such structures, we include them in our planner. We represent them as property-inheritance networks.[3]

A schema can be composed of several communicative goals: As an example, a schema to generate financial reports could contain the following communicative goals in the dictated order (see Fig. 2): (1) **describe-total-sales-briefly** (heading); (2)

---

[3] We believe that, in spite of the frozen nature of schemas that capture frequently occurring patterns of text structure in specific situations, there still exist rhetorical relationships among the different parts of each schema. Given sufficient knowledge, a system should be able to plan out the same text without using a schema. However, lacking a complete specification of all the resources required in generation, a planner can use schemas as a useful source of 'compiled knowledge' and so avoid the need to re-derive structures over and over again.

describe-total-sales-detail; (3) describe-domestic-sales; (4) describe-export-sales and (5) describe-future-outlook. We show in Section 4 how this schema is used in our planner to generate a particular text.

Just as the previous two resources co-constrain the other resources (e.g., the choice of text type can influence the selection of a schema), the instantiation of a schema can highlight or suppress different discourse relations, or the various stages of a schema can favor particular theme development patterns.

2.4 Discourse Structure Relations

Many linguists and computational linguists have studied the relationships that hold between sentences or segments of text, identifying relations that they claim need to hold in order for a text to be coherent; e.g., (Grimes 75, Mann 84, Hobbs 78, Mann and Thompson 88, Sanders *et al.* 91, Redeker 90). These relations can be used in a generation system in order to guide the selection and organization of the information to be included when other structuring guidance is lacking, such as when a schema stage calls for more material than can fit into a single clause. The necessity and use of discourse structure relations in text planners to ensure coherence has been amply discussed, as in (Hovy 88, Moore and Paris 89, Cawsey 90, Maybury 90).

Our text planner contains three networks of discourse relations, implemented as systemic networks. As a basis for the networks, we drew on several main sources: the relations defined in Rhetorical Structure Theory (Mann and Thompson 88), which were extended in Hovy's taxonomization of a collection of the relations proposed by over thirty researchers from various fields, later reorganized with Maier; see (Hovy 90, Maier and Hovy 91), and Martin's taxonomization of the conjunctive relations (Martin 92). We divided the relations into three major portions, according to the three major functions of language according to systemic linguistics (Halliday 85): semantic/ideational, interpersonal, and presentational/textual. Portions of the networks appear in Fig. 3. When organizing material, the planner is free in the general case to establish several discourse relations (typically, one for each of the major functions) between the existing discourse structure and the new piece of material; as shown in the networks, the selection of ideational, interpersonal, and textual relations is not exclusive.

As with the other resources, the discourse relation networks co-constrain the other knowledge resources, by, for example, preselecting theme patterns, posting communicative goals, or specifying aspects of grammatical realization.

2.5 Theme Development Information

Careful linguistic and computational studies have shown the need for a resource describing the potential theme developments and shifts of focus, in order to signal the introduction of a new topic of discussion and to provide its thematic relationship to previous topics (e.g., Halliday 85, Quirk *et al.* 72). Except for efforts such as Sidner (1983) and McCoy and Cheng (1988), these concerns have not been the subject of much computational work in text generation; they have generally taken the form of

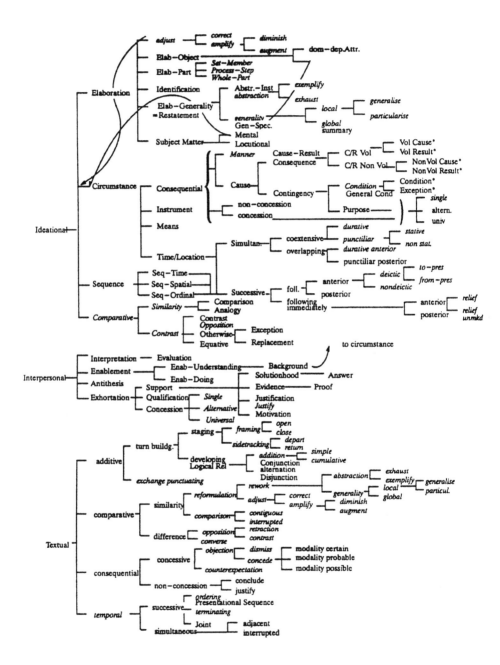

Fig. 3. Discourse structure relation networks.

focus shift rules (McKeown 85, McCoy and Cheng 88, Hovy and McCoy 89). Unfortunately, these rules have usually been implemented procedurally and the complexity of the issues underlying them have not been fully studied. In the new text planner, we represent the potentialities of theme development declaratively in a systemic network (see Fig. 4).

Although the study of theme has traditionally been restricted to the sentence level, it also plays a role at the clause-complex and discourse levels. This should be taken into consideration by a text generation system. Given a text to be generated, the system must establish how theme development may proceed and how themes are to be marked in each clause. The following three concerns arise:

- the type of theme to select: following Halliday (1985), there can be three different and simultaneous themes in each clause: the ideational (or topical; expressing processes, participants, or circumstances), the interpersonal (expressing modal meanings such as probability, usuality, or opinion), and the textual (such as expressed by the continuatives "yes,", "well,", "oh,", and similar conjunctions). The first type is semantically required.
- the theme progression pattern involved: the new theme can be the same as the theme of the previous clause; it may be part of the rheme of the previous clause; or it may be an element of what is called the "hypertheme," or general discourse segment topic (Daneš 74); Note that this is similar to the focus shift rules of Sidner and McKeown.
- the linguistic degree of markedness of the theme: realization depends on the type of clause.

The motivations behind each choice follow pragmatic principles of information processing, including:

- *the topic-comment constraint* (Werth 84, Giora 88), also known as the *graded informativeness requirement*: a message is maximally effective if information which is presumed or given in the context is presented before information which is new;
- *the processibility principle* (Leech 83): a text should be constructed so that it is easy to process in real time, by placing the focus tone group at the end of the clause (the *maxim of end-focus*) and the "heavy" constituents in final position (the *maxim of end-weight*);
- *discourse relation requirements* (Mann and Thompson 88): some discourse relations have a canonical (unmarked) order of surface realization.

3 The Planning Process

Planning with the networks proceeds analogously to the generation of single sentences with Penman (Penman 88, Mann 83, Mann and Matthiessen 85): in both cases, the traversal mechanism proceeds through the network, causing traversal choices to be made at nodes (systems), and building a tree-like structure as a result. We implemented the networks in Penman's internal notation so as to be able to reuse some of its traversal code.

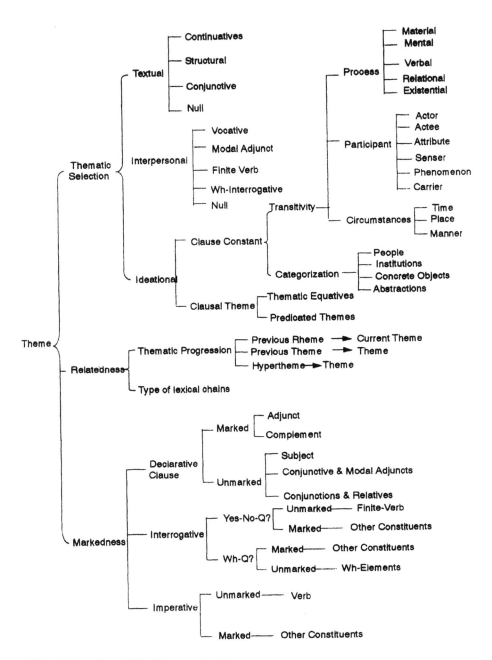

Fig. 4. A portion of the theme network.

Associated with each node in the networks is an inquiry function which queries the environment in order to determine which branch to follow, and a set of realization operators that instruct the planner what to do next.

The planning operation is very simple. After an initial setup phase, the system simply executes a basic planning cycle over and over again until planning is complete. In the setup phase, the user activates the planner with a communicative goal, as described in Section 2.2, which causes the selection of a desired text type, and is then posted on the goal stack and simultaneously on the Discourse Structure Tree. Then the basic planning cycle begins. Essentially, this cycle proceeds as follows: First, the planner checks whether there is a realization on the agenda. If so, it performs the realization by applying its action to its parameters. If there are no realizations left, the planner checks whether there is a discourse goal on the goal-stack. If there is, the planner finds the realizations associated with the goal and loads them onto the agenda; if no discourse goals remain, the planning is done.

Clearly, the action of the system lies in the realizations. Each realization is an instruction to be performed. At present, the system uses the following realizations:

1. (ACTIVATE-SCHEMA <schema-name>): Find the schema and load its realizations onto the agenda.
2. (ADD-TO-D-STRUC <goal> <concept> <parentpos>): Add the given communicative goal into the discourse structure tree at the given position.
3. (CHANGE-HYPERTHEME <chain-of-roles>): Change the topic under discussion to the filler of the given chain of roles, starting from the current topic.
4. (HIGHLIGHT-COMM-GOALS <goals>): Highlight the given goals so that only they will be considered for future planning.
5. (HIGHLIGHT-RELATION <relations>): Start traversal of the discourse relations network(s) at the given relations, using the current topic of discussion.
6. (BLOCK-RELATION <relations>): Mark the given discourse structure relations so that they cannot be traversed for the remainder of the current sentence.
7. (PREFER-THEME <concept-role>): Add instructions for the realization component that the given role of the topic under discussion should be thematized in the clause.
8. (SET-MACROTHEME <concept>): Change the overall topic of discussion.
9. (SET-UP-DISCOURSE-GOAL <goal>): Activate the given goal: load it onto the goal stack and into the discourse structure tree at the current growth point and add its realizations to the agenda.
10. (TRAV-ONE-NETWORK-NODE <node-name>): Locate the given node in the knowledge resource networks, apply its inquiry function, record the result (the inquiry choice), and load the realizations associated with the result onto the agenda.

4 An Example of the Planner in Action

In this section we provide a brief trace in order to show how the various linguistic resources interact to guide the construction of the discourse structure. As example we take a fragment of a text from a bank's annual report:

(1) Declines in Total Sales of the Swiss Cheese Union

(2) In the business year 1986/87 (ending July 31), the 40 cheese trading firms associated in the Swiss Cheese Union sold 79,035 tons of cheese altogether, (3) equal to a 2.6% decline. (4) Domestic sales of table cheeses enjoyed a relatively positive trend, (5) with Swiss households buying 22,100 tons of their preferred cheeses, (6) a gain of 3.9% from one year earlier.

We represented the semantic information in this text in the Loom knowledge representation system.

Given the communicative goal GENERATE-YEARLY-PUBLIC-REPORT and the topic of discussion CHEESE-UNION-SALES-86, the schema mentioned in Section 2.3 is activated, and the planner goes through the stages indicated in the schema. Let us assume now that the first two clauses – the headline and the first clause – have already been generated. The state of the discourse structure appears in Fig. 5.

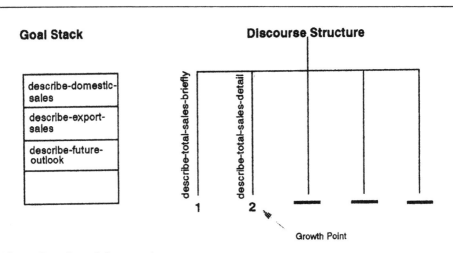

Fig. 5. Snapshot of the text planner state.

In generating (2), the goal DESCRIBE-TOTAL-SALES-DETAIL is popped off the goal stack, and its definition in the goal hierarchy is checked. This new information is now incorporated in the discourse structure, and the realization statements for the goal are loaded onto the agenda, including the one to highlight the discourse structure relation interpretation.

In the next cycle, the planner checks the agenda and finds the just-loaded realization. It performs the realization by highlighting interpretation in the interpersonal relations network, which causes the planner to check whether any topic material with that relation to the current topic of discussion can be brought into the discourse. This check is performed by an inquiry function that accesses the planner environment with a question that can be paraphrased as:

Interpretation-Q-Code:
"Was a numerical value mentioned in the last proposition and can it be
expressed in relation to other values?"

From the information about the topic (as contained in the knowledge representation system), a possible candidate for such a relation is the value of the role
weight-ascription. The inquiry code retrieves a role and a value which fulfills the
above condition: the role **weight-change-relative** represents the weight ascription
relative to that of the preceding year. The relevant segment of the domain model
appears in Fig. 6.

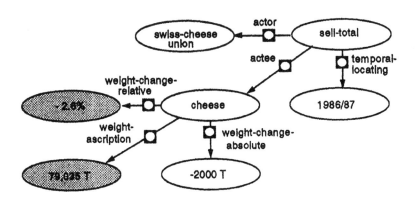

Fig. 6. Fragment of the Domain Model.

The successful finding of this material signals the applicability of the relation
interpretation. The planner then activates the realization statements associated
with this relation, in this case:

1. **knowledge selection:** Each relation contains specifications of the material it
   relates. The realization associated with **interpretation** selects both the absolute and the relative ascriptions for the weight, and calls for incorporating this
   new information.
2. **discourse structure growth:** This realization calls for the addition of the
   interpretation relation at the current growth point in the discourse structure
   tree of Fig. 5.
3. **theme determination:** This realization calls for traversal of the theme network
   in order to determine the thematization pattern of the new clause or clauses.
4. **operations on relations:** To prevent the repetitive use of the interpretation relation, which would lead to a monotonous text, this realization calls for
   interpretation to be blocked for further use until the end of the next sentence.

The planner loads these four realizations onto the agenda and thereby completes its cycle.

In the next cycle, the planner runs the knowledge selection realization listed above and selects the new material. In the following cycle, it adds the interpretation relation to the discourse structure tree. This relation indicates that clause (3) is related to clause (2) by the rhetorical relation **interpretation**. The resulting form of the discourse structure after these realizations appears in Fig. 7. In the following cycles, the remaining realization statements are executed.

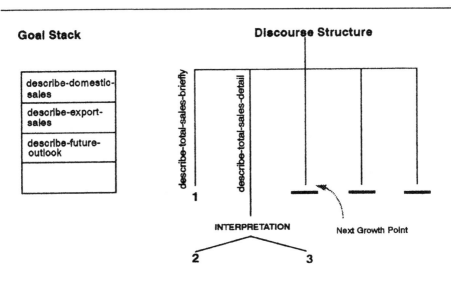

Fig. 7. Discourse structure after the new relation has been planned.

We cannot describe the rest of the planning in detail here. In essence, the planning cycle keeps repeating, first handling all the realizations on the agenda and then all the goals on the goal stack, until no more remain.

5 Conclusion

We have presented in this paper a new text planner currently being developed jointly at USC/ISI and GMD-IPSI. It is based on the idea that the linguistic resources needed to generate coherent text (as well as their interrelationships) should be represented explicitly, separately, and distinct from the procedural knowledge required for text planning.

We do not claim to have identified all the knowledge sources required to produce coherent discourse. We are only starting to study the issues of lexical choice and lexical cohesion in depth (Wanner and Maier 91), and the planning of noun groups (and referring expressions in general), the problem of sentence delimitation are all unaddressed in our planner. We do, however, believe that the architecture of our planner lends itself well to the incorporation of additional knowledge resources when they become available. The representational power of systemic networks — interlocking options that capture the potentialities of expression — and the clear and simple planning cycle offer, we hope, sufficient scaffolding for the needs of text planning of the future.

Other issues of course remain to be addressed as well. For example, will we be able to keep the complexity of the procedural aspect of the system to a minimum? As the inquiry operators are implemented procedurally, we clearly need to limit how much can be done in these operators, or, at least, we need to apply clear constraints to be used when writing these operators lest their complexity becomes such that they are hard to understand and modify. We also need to study how the architecture addresses some of the concerns raised by some researchers regarding top-down planners (e.g., Suthers (1991) and Mooney, Carberry and McCoy (1990)) . It is too early to discuss these issues. We will address them once the system has been more fully implemented and used to generate a greater variety of texts.

6 Acknowledgments

This planner was designed mainly during a period when both Lavid and Maier were visiting USC/ISI. In addition, many people have contributed, directly or indirectly, to the ideas embodied in this planner. While it is impossible to thank them all, we wish to acknowledge Béatrice Cahour (INRIA, France), Giuseppe Carenini (IRST, Italy) and Richard Whitney (USC/ISI) for their participation in the design.

In addition, we wish to thank the following sponsors: Hovy was supported by the Rome Air Development Center (now Rome Laboratories) under RADC contract FQ7619-89-03326-0001. Paris and Mittal were supported by NASA-Ames grant NCC 2-520 and under DARPA contract DABT63-91-C-0025. During her one-year visit to USC/ISI, Lavid was supported by the Spanish Ministry of Education under the PROEX program. During the 5 months Maier visited USC/ISI, she was supported under RADC contract FQ7619-89-03326-0001.

References

Allen, J.F. Discourse Structure in the TRAINS Project. In *Proceedings of the DARPA Speech and Natural Language Workshop*, Morgan Kaufmann, San Mateo, 1991.

Biber D. A Typology of English Texts. *Linguistics*, 27, 1989, pp. 3–43.

Cawsey, A. Generating Communicative Discourse. In *Current Research in Natural Language Generation*, Dale, R., Mellish, C., and Zock, M. (eds), Academic Press, Boston, 1990, pp. 75-102.

Clark, H.H. and Clark, E.V. Semantic distinctions and memory for complex sentences. *Quarterly Journal of Experimental Psychology*, 20, 1968, pp. 129-138.

Daneš, F. Functional sentence perspective and the organization of the text. In F.Daneš (ed.) *Papers on Functional Sentence Perspective*. Mouton, The Hague, 1974.

de Beaugrande, R. *Text, Discourse and Process*. Ablex Publishing Corporation, Norwood, N.J., 1980.

Giora, R. On the Informativeness Requirement. *Journal of Pragmatics* 12, 1988, pp. 547-565.

Grimes, J.E. *The Thread of Discourse*. Mouton, The Hague 1975.

Grosz, B.J. and Sidner, C.L. Attention, Intentions, and the Structure of Discourse. In *Journal of Computational Linguistics* 12(3), 1986, pp. 175-204.

Halliday, M.A.K. *An Introduction to Functional Grammar*. Edward Arnold Press, Baltimore, 1985.

Halliday, M.A.K. and Hasan, R. *Language, Context and Text: Aspects of Language in a Social-Semiotic Perspective*. Deakin University Press, 1985.

Hobbs, J.R. Why is Discourse Coherent? Technical Note no.176, SRI International, Menlo Park CA, 1978.

Hovy, E.H. Planning coherent multisentence text. *Proceedings of the ACL*, Buffalo, 1988.

Hovy, E.H. Parsimonious and Profligate Approaches to the Question of Discourse Structure Relations. In *Proceedings of the 5th International Workshop on Text Generation*, Pittsburgh, 1990.

Hovy, E.H. and McCoy, K.F. Focusing your RST: A step toward generating coherent multisentential text. In *Proceedings of the 11th Cognitive Science Conference*, Ann Arbor, 1989, pp. 667-674.

Leech, G.N. *Principles of Pragmatics*. Longman, London, 1983.

MacGregor, R. A Deductive Pattern Matcher. In *Proceedings of the 6th National Conference on Artificial Intelligence*, 1988, pp. 696-701.

Maier, E. and Hovy, E.H. A Metafunctionally Motivated Taxonomy for Discourse Structure Relations. In *Proceedings of the 3rd European Workshop on Language Generation*, Judenstein, Austria, March 1991, pp. 38-45.

Mann, W.C. and Matthiessen, C.M.I.M. Nigel: A Systemic Grammar for Text Generation. Research Report RR-83-105, USC/ISI. 1983.

Mann, W.C. An Overview of the Penman Text Generation System", Research Report ISI/RR-83-114, USC/ISI, 1983.

Mann, W.C. Discourse Structures for Text Generation. In *Proceedings of the COLING Conference*, Stanford, 1984.

Mann, W.C. and Matthiessen, C.M.I.M. Nigel: A Systemic Grammar for Text Generation. In R.Benson and J.Greaves, (eds), *Systemic Perspectives on Discourse: Selected Papers Papers from the 9th International Systemics Workshop*. Ablex, London, 1985.

Mann, W.C. and Matthiessen, C.M.I.M. and Thompson, S.A. Rhetorical Structure Theory and Text Analysis. Research Report ISI/RR-89-242, USC/ISI, 1989.

Mann, W.C. and Thompson, S.A. Rhetorical Structure Theory: Toward a Functional Theory of Text Organization. *Text* 8(3), 1988, pp. 243-281. Also available as USC/ISI Research Report RR-87-190.

Martin, J.R. 1992. *English Text: System and Structure*. Benjamins, Amsterdam. Forthcoming.

Maybury, M.T. *Planning Multisentential English Text Using Communicative Acts*. Ph.D.dissertation, Cambridge University, 1990. Also available as RADC Technical Report 90-411, 1990.

McCoy, K.F. and Cheng, J. Focus of attention: Constraining what can be said next. In *Natural Language in Artificial Intelligence and Computational Linguistics*, Paris, C.L., Swartout, W.R.and Mann, W.C.(eds), Kluwer, Boston, 1990, pp. 103-124.

McDonald, D.D. and Pustejovsky, J. Description-directed natural language generation. In *Proceedings of the 9th IJCAI*, Los Angeles, 1985.

McKeown, K.R. *Text Generation: Using Discourse Strategies and Focus Constraints to Generate Natural Language Text*. Cambridge University Press, Cambridge, 1985.

Mooney, D.J., Carberry, S. and McCoy, K.F. The Basic Block Model of Extended Explanations. In *Proceedings of the AAAI Workshop on Explanations*, Boston, 1990.

Moore, J.D. and Paris, C.L. Planning Text for Advisory Dialogues. In *Proceedings of the 27th ACL Conference*, Vancouver, 1989, pp. 67-75.

Paris, C.L. and Maier, E. Knowledge Sources or Decisions? *Proceedings of the Workshop on Decisions in Natural Language Generation*, IJCAI 1991, Sydney.

The Penman Documentation. 5 unpublished volumes, USC/ISI.

Polanyi, L. A Formal Model of the Structure of Discourse. *Journal of Pragmatics*, 12, 1988, pp. 601-638.

Prideaux, G.D. Text data as evidence for language processing principles: The grammar of ordered events. In *Language Sciences*, 11, 1989, pp. 27-42.

Prideaux, G.D. Syntactic form and textual rhetoric: The cognitive basis for certain pragmatic principles. *Journal of Pragmatics*, 16, 1991, pp. 113-129.

Quirk, R., Greenbaum, S., Leech, G. and Svartvik, J. *A Grammar of Contemporary English.* Seminar Press, New York, 1972.

Redeker, G. Ideational and Pragmatic Markers of Discourse Structure. *Journal of Pragmatics* 14, 1990, pp. 367-381.

Sanders, T.J.M., Spooren, W.P.M.S., and Noordman, L.G.M. Towards a Taxonomy of Coherence Relations. In *Discourse Processes*, 1992 (forthcoming)

Sidner, C.L. Focusing and Discourse. *Discourse Processes* 6, 1983, pp. 107-130.

Suthers, D.D. A Task Appropriate Hybrid Architecture for Explanation. *Computational Intelligence*, 7(4), 1991.

Trimble, L. *English for Science and Technology. A Discourse Approach.* Cambridge University Press, Cambridge, 1985.

Van Dijk, T.A. and Kintsch, W. *Strategies of Discourse Comprehension.* Academic Press, New York, 1983.

Wanner, L. and Maier E. Lexical Choice as an Integrated Component of Situated Text Planning, *Proceedings of the 3rd European Natural Language Generation Workshop*, Innsbruck, March, 1991.

Werth, P. *Focus, Coherence and Emphasis.* Croom Helm, London. 1984.

Type-Driven Suppression of Redundancy in the Generation of Inference-Rich Reports

David D. McDonald

14 Brantwood Road, Arlington MA 02174, USA
email: mcdonald@brandeis.edu

Abstract

We present a general solution to a common tactical problem, the context-sensitive suppression of redundant information. This solution is sensitive to unplanned, domain-specific inferences in the prior text. It employs a new, lexically grounded, conceptual representation for communicable information, which is part of a reversible model of how surface structures communicate information in naturally occurring reports.

The technique requires an extension to the kinds of syntactic knowledge we associate with relational lexical items and provides additional motivations for syntactic choices, and it assumes an architecture for text planning that keeps a careful, synchronized record of what information the surface structure communicates so that redundancy decisions can be made incrementally without explicit planning. The technique is most applicable in genres where texts communicate much of their information inferentially rather than literally.

1 Generating from the Output of a Parser

Over the course of the last year I have been studying a large corpus of articles from a single, specialized news source, the "Who's News" column of the Wall Street Journal. The corpus contains approximately 1100 articles, each anywhere from fifty to two thousand words long, taken from the Dow Jones News Retrieval online wire service.

The original purpose of this study was to develop a sublanguage grammar for a parser.[1] The current focus of this language understanding research (the task is now called "information extraction") is on the parser's target semantic representation. This representation supports a rule-by-rule compositional semantics that provides denotations for the syntactic structures that can occur in a text, including prepositional phrases and adjuncts. The end result of understanding a text is a universe of individuals of various types, including partial relations and complex variables.

---

[1] This effort has been reasonably successful, achieving a competence of 80% recall with 80% precision in a recent blind test extracting specific relational information from the articles to populate tuples in a database (see McDonald 1992). The parser, which I developed by myself, is called SPARSER.

The representation is essentially an object-oriented implementation of the lambda calculus; it is written in lisp.

Recently I have turned attention to generating the Who's News articles, starting from the model constructed by the parser for an individual article and working backwards. This methodology, while not providing for a motivated speaker with intentions, has the advantage of permitting a vast number of example texts to be generated, and invites experimentation with the structure of the controlling conceptual model and the rules of inference. A goal of the work is to make the conceptual and linguistic information it employs genuinely reversible in practice (see McDonald 1991b). This paper reports on the first results from this work, a technique for suppressing information that is trivially available to the reader by inference.

The articles in the Who's News corpus are reports. They announce executive level personnel changes such as appointments, confirmations, retirements, etc., and are representative of a genre that can be found in the trade publications of any field. The most frequent kind of article in the corpus is relatively short, describing events in a single company and focusing on one change and its coordinated changes. The example below is typical.

FAIRCHILD Corp. (Chantilly, Va.) – Donald E. Miller was named senior vice president and general counsel, succeeding Dominic A. Petito, who resigned in November, at this aerospace business. Mr. Miller, 43 years old, was previously principal attorney for Temkin & Miller Ltd., Providence, R.I.

2 Redundancy in Inference-Rich Genres of Text

Notice what was not said in the example article. We are not expressly told what company Mr. Miller was named to his position in; we are not told what position Mr. Petito resigned from. This information is not included in the literal text, yet any experienced reader of these articles knows it perfectly well because of the inferences they draw from the information that was given explicitly.

Such omissions are normal and extremely frequent in this genre. Indeed, inferentially available information is virtually never included except when it can do other duty: we would not have been told about the company in the article's body except that it provides a vehicle for saying what area of business Fairchild is in (". . . *at this aerospace business*").

We can characterize this genre as *inference-rich* one where as many propositions are conveyed implicitly through simple, conventional inferences as there are explicitly through the clauses and predications of the actual text. Another example of an inference-rich domain is story telling, where we assume a great many intermediary events interpolated between the salient or unpredictable events that we are explicitly told about. In stories, however, the omissions are largely of entire events, while my focus here is on the omission of optional arguments under the control of, lexically-triggered inferences.

The mechanisms within the generator that support this capability are interesting because of what they must be able to do.[2] The omissions cannot be specified a priori, for instance as annotations on a fixed schema, because they are strictly dependent on the actual prior context, including information that appears in datelines (as above), or which is buried deep within subordinate contexts. In a different context, say one where the company of the naming event was different from the one in the dateline (e.g. a subsidiary of it), or one where the person resigning had held only one of the two positions the new person was taking on, then the information would not have been omitted because it would have been informative rather than redundant.

Looking ahead, the procedure I shall propose for avoiding redundancy involves keeping track of the total set of facts, both explicit and inferred, that have been communicated up to the point where the next event is to appear, then making the realization of that event sensitive to the accumulated information. Semantically, an event is a relation with a certain set of arguments: a "resignation", for example, necessarily involves a person, their former title, and the company they are leaving, and like all events involves a time, a place, etc. Grammatically, the realization of the event by a given verb in a clause will require the inclusion of some of those arguments and make others optional (compare "resign" with "leave"). Together with the verb, these required and optional syntactic arguments communicate a set of facts, some of which, however, may already be available by inference from the facts that the generator knows have already been communicated. In such cases, if the redundant fact involves an optional argument that argument should be omitted, or if a required argument it should be marked for reduction to a pronoun or a definite reference. The issue, of course, is how to represent the rules of inference and the process that tracks them and controls the inclusion of optional arguments in an efficient manner.

The rest of this paper will lay out my proposal for how this efficiency can be achieved. The solution will require adopting a source representation for the information to be communicated that has some unusual, though not unreasonable properties, as well as a technique within the planning process that uses rules originally developed for my parser to track the inferences being conveyed by what is said.

3 The Framework for the Technique

The framework into which this work fits was set out in McDonald, Pustejovsky and Meteer (1987) (see also Meteer 1991, McDonald 1991a, and Conklin 1983). It aims for a theoretically maximal efficiency in the generation process, and is oriented towards psycholinguistic claims and explanations. We will begin by laying out in general terms what we take the problem of generation to be, and then present our particular approach as it stands today.

---

[2] It is important to distinguish the omission of redundant information from other phenomena that are the responsibility, I believe, of different kinds of mechanisms. In the example article these include the use of a subsequent reference to carry supplemental information ("*Mr. Miller, 43 years old*"), and conventional, default judgements such as that we do not need to be told who did the naming of Mr. Miller hence the clause is realized in the passive voice.

3.1 Generation as a task

Generation starts in the mind of the speaker as she acts upon an intention to say something – to achieve some goal through the use of language. The experimental analog to a human speaker is concretely here the execution state of a computer program: the one that would provide the explanations, tell the story, etc. In the present instance it is issuing a report.

Once the process is initiated, generation proper involves at least four interleaved steps, regardless of the approach taken.

(A) Information must be *selected* for inclusion in the utterance. Depending on how this information is reified into representational units (a property of the speaker's mental model), parts of the units may have to be omitted, other units added in by default, or perspectives taken on the units to reflect the speaker's attitude towards them.

(B) The information must be given a textual organization, a process we like to call *orchestration*. It must be ordered, both sequentially and in terms of specifically linguistic relations such as modification or subordination. The coherence relationships among the units of the information must be reflected in this organization so that the reasons why the information was included will be apparent to the audience.

(C) *Linguistic resources* must be chosen to support the information's realization. Ultimately these resources will come down to choices of particular words, idioms, syntactic constructions, productive morphological variations, etc., but the form they take at the first moment they are associated with the selected information will vary greatly between approaches. Note that to choose a resource is not ipso facto to simultaneously deploy it in its final form – a fact that is not always appreciated.

(D) The selected and organized resources must be *realized* as an actual text or voice output. This stage can itself involve several levels of representation and interleaved processes.

Processes A and B, the selection of information and its organization as a text, are usually lumped together and referred to as *text planning*. Process C, the selection of the words and other linguistic resources that will realize the selected information is usually lumped in with the process of linguistic realization (D) as part of a "linguistic component"; this is a serious mistake, however – one that has been responsible for a great deal on unnecessary confusion and paradox in recent years.[3]

Resource selection, in particular the choice of open-class lexical heads, is the single greatest source of constraints on the generator's choices. Given our framework of assumptions then, it should happen very early in the generation process so that later choices can reflect those constraints and not lead to backtracking. Indeed, we do lexical selection as each unit of information is selected,[4] allowing lexical constraints

---

[3] For an example of the paradoxes, see Danlos (1984). For a general discussion of the issue of component boundaries, see the proceedings of the AAAI Workshop on Text Planning and Realization (1988, summarized in Hovy et al. 1989).

[4] As already noted, one can select a word without simultaneously deploying it. In particular, one can pick a lexeme (Kempen and Huijbers 1983) and position it in a representational level without yet committing to the tense or number it will have when it is ultimately uttered, or even committing to its basic semantic type, e.g. "*decide*" versus

to influence both the unit's orchestration and the selection of later units.

Putting this in terms of the conventional nomenclature, we have made lexical choice an early and central part of text planning. We do not see any alternatives – we see no way by which a speaker can speak fluently (i.e. formulate consistently expressible text plans in the sense of Meteer 1991), other than to reason with units that are at least consistent with the lexical possibilities for their realization, if not actually based on lexical items as their primitives. Certainly this is an effective design for a purely conventional domain, such as this one, where the words that people use in naming events and states are precise descriptions of the actual state of affairs. Judging its psycholinguistic validity waits on the right kind of experiments.

3.2 An architecture for generation

As presently conceived, our architecture for natural language generation involves six successive levels of representation. Generation proceeds by mapping terms from early (high) levels to their corresponding terms or configurations of terms at the next level down, assembling that level in the process. These mapping operations are governed by declarative statements of the alternatives for each term or class of terms and the constraints on their use, which we refer to as *decision classes*; there are occasional exceptions for expediency where the mapping is done by procedurally-stated templates (McDonald and Meteer 1988).

To facilitate incremental generation, the processes that link the levels and carry out the mapping are in principle all active simultaneously and asynchronously (obviously, on serial hardware this is only simulated), such that only minimal units need to be in place at higher levels before their terms can be mapped into lower levels and eventually spoken (McDonald and Meteer 1990).

The earliest representational level is actually within the mind of the speaker: a model of its domain and current state, consisting of a universe of individuals, categories and relations. The first process in the generator, selection, operates over this level to form the second level, a representation of what units of information have been selected for inclusion, partially ordered according to their salience. This is a *staging level* from which the orchestration process takes units and positions them the in the third level – Meteer's *Text Structure* (1991, 1992). At Text Structure there is a commitment to the semantic type by which the unit will be expressed. This type reflects the unitUs function in the text and the particular perspective that has been taken on it. Text Structure is also the first level at which there is any commitment

---

"decision". Words do not belong in a "linguistic component" just because they are ostensibly linguistic entities – not if putting them there creates more problems than it solves. By contrast, grammatical affixes, stress patterns, spelling forms and phonetic structure appear to be purely linguistic entities that are unlikely to have a place in generation outside of a linguistic component. On the other hand, there is no obvious reason why the identity of a word – as distinct from its realization – shouldn't be taken as the name of a concept and act as a central part of the concept's semantic representation. Certainly that is the de facto policy in most generators, where the names of "concepts" are ordinary words and the issues of lexical choice are trivial.

to sentential structure, which may reflect the influence of a text style dictating the choice of syntactic relations between units.

Meteer's Text Structure is a tree structure with the units selected from the speaker's model as its constituents. It is a carefully considered abstraction of the structural relations at surface structure, representing structure at all levels from complex noun phrases to paragraphs. Like the surface structure two levels below it, Text Structure is processed by traversing it, topdown and left-to-right, expanding and reading out its elements as they are reached.

Just below the Text Structure is the *linguistic specification*, a representation comparable to the derivation structure in a Tree Adjoining Grammar (TAG). This *Lspec* is built as units are read out from the Text Structure under the control of their semantic types and their role. The units are projected onto TAG tree families of the appropriate arity and syntactic category, and augmented with the purely surface linguistic resources such as determination, plural, or gerundive.

In the Lspec, all of linguistic elements of the ultimate text are present and indelibly fixed. The specification is executed to create the surface structure representation of the text, which includes selecting syntactic trees from their tree families according to the constraints on the syntactic context and the context in the specification, linearizing and interleaving the trees, and introducing the grammatical relations among them. Execution of the surface structure produces the stream of words with their surface morphology. The processing of the Lspec and the surface structure is done by Mumble-86 (Meteer et al. 1987).

Since we have done no work ourselves on the production of speech, our architecture stops at this point; however a group at the University of Pennsylvania has produced actual speech using MumbleUs surface structure representation. They used the prosodic theory developed by Pierrehumbolt (1980) and a DecTalk.

4 Conceptual source and timing

To move this discussion of architecture to the problem of controlling redundancy, we should start by considering how entities in the speaker's model are represented. Much hinges on the choice of representation, since the whole notion of "omitting" redundant information presupposes that the information is present at some early stage and that some positive action must be taken to keep it from appearing in the final text. If the information isn't present in the source, then there is no work to be done.

What can we observe in these inference-rich texts that bears on this question of whether the redundant information is present in the speaker's source? A key fact is the strong dependency on the precise prior context. Consider the "resign" clause in the earlier example. The inferences available from the two prior clauses make it appropriate to say only " *who resigned in November*", and the reader fills in the facts about Mr. Petito's former title and company without needing to be told. If that same fact had been positioned at the very beginning of the article all of the particulars would have been spelled out: " *Bruce Hagstad resigned as president and a director of . . .*"; if the new person had been named to several positions and the old person had only held one of them the title would have been given: "... *succeeding Kenneth Dalton, who retired as chairman and chief executive, and Clive Brown who retired as President*".

These examples, taken from actual Wall Street Journal articles, indicate that not only is the order of the event important (i.e. before or after other events involving the same position), but also the specific details of those events (e.g. exactly what titles were involved in the earlier events). From this we can arguably conclude that the source of the events, as they are selected from the speaker's mental state, is the entire relation, i.e. all of the arguments that are semantically necessary. This allows the act of selection to be independent of the ultimate choice of position and context, since there is sufficient information in the source unit to accommodate any of the circumstances just illustrated.

The dependency on context also suggests that the timing of the redundancy check is relatively late: certainly after the selected information has been entered into the Text Structure, and probably as late as the point when everything to the left of the affected material has been readout from the structure and possibly even uttered. Given this, what we have here is a problem for syntax, one that must be accommodated by any candidate grammar and system for linguistic structure and realization, namely how to regulate the presence or absence of optional arguments given the information that happens to have appeared in a clause's (or other relational phrase's) left context.

At the same time, it is a problem for the text planner (and, arguably, for the choice of representation for the information that is the source of what the generator says). The text planner (selection and orchestration) must not only select the information that will be said explicitly, but must also track the information that is implied by that information, given the particular words it chooses. The planner must regulate the process by which it orchestrates its selections for the Text Structure, and by which it presents that structure for surface realization, so that this total body of information, literal and implied, is easily accessible to the "redundancy-checking process" without undue search or reasoning.

5 A mechanism for suppressing redundant information

In our approach, the ultimate order of one unit with respect to its neighbors is not fixed until it has been reached in the process of traversing the Text Structure and reading it out to form the Lspec. (Units never change their position in Text Structure once they have been introduced; however additional units can be added within the existing structure, extending it and modifying the ultimate linear order of the text segments that realize the units.) When the unit that the traversal reaches is a composite object, it is *expanded*, i.e. abstract linguistic resources and subunits of the unit are selected to provide its realization. The result is a new subtree of the Text Structure at the unit's position, which will be traversed recursively and its own leaves expanded until primitives are reached and are mapped to the linguistic specification.

It is at this point – when a composite unit is reached and expanded in the course

of the traversal of the Text Structure – that the possibility of redundancy is checked
for.

5.1 The source representation

To make this concrete, consider the object that I use as the representation of
Mr. Petito's resignation, shown in Fig. 1. This object is the one that my parser
will produce from a parse of the example paragraph once the inference rules fill in
the information that is missing from the literal text (i.e. the title and company,
conceptualized here as a composite individual of category 'position').

```
#<composite
  :type ( #<category resign>
          #<category leave-position>
          #<category transition>
          #<category event>   )
  :bindings
    ( ( #<variable person>
        #<person  Petito, Dominic>)
      ( #<variable position>
        #<composite
          :type ( #<category position> )
          :bindings
            ( ( #<variable title>
                #<composite
                  :type ( #<category collection> #<category title> )
                  :bindings
                    ( #<variable set>
                    ( ( #<title "vice president">
                        #<title "general counsel"> ))) >)
              ( #<variable company>
                #<company Fairchild corporation>)) >)
      ( #<variable time-of-event>
        #<month-of-a-year 11/90>) )>
```

Fig. 1. P the conceptual source of "who resigned in November"

This notation is interpreted as follows. Expressions in angle brackets with sharp
signs, $\#< \ldots >$, denote reified objects in the speaker's model. The first term inside
the brackets is the category of the object (a.k.a. 'type', 'sort'). '*Composite*' is a
structural category, essentially equivalent to a frame or a concept in a KL-ONE-
style structured inheritance lattice. The '*type*' attribute of a composite gives the
object's inheritance chain, a list of successively more general categories.

The '*bindings*' attribute is similar to the notion of slots or fields in a record, but its
underlying principles are actually those of variables in the lambda calculus. Following

Pustejovsky (1991), the definition of the category 'resign' is based on a relation of two arguments, 'person' and 'position', plus additional implicit arguments inherited from its super-categories. The verb *resign* in isolation thus denotes a function:

λperson. λposition. Resign(person, position)

Viewed in this way, the fully populated relation in Fig. 1 has bound these two open variables (and the 'time-of-event variable', inherited from 'event') to specific values, according to what appeared in the text as it was parsed using a rule-by-rule semantics and binary rules (see §1). The bindings attribute of a composite object represents this association between variable and value explicitly; bindings are reified, first-class objects in their own right.

5.2 The function of the optional arguments

To understand the redundancy checking mechanism, we must first appreciate that texts in the specialized genre of "Who's News" reports consist primarily of events such as this resignation or the naming and succession events that precede it. By inference, however, the mention of these events will also communicate facts about the state of the people and their positions before and after the events occurred. For example the succession event ("... [Miller] succeeding Dominic A. Petito") implicitly tells the reader that Mr. Petito used to hold the position that Mr. Miller has just been named to.

Similarly, a 'resign' event carries the inference that the person resigning used to hold the position they have resigned from. Conveying this inference, I claim, is the function of the optional "position" adjunct in a *resign* clause: The verb *resign* is intransitive, and the only purpose for including the optional prepositional phrase is to communicate this fact about the person's previous position – if it is not already known!

This, then, is the mechanism of the redundancy check. As the event (or any other sort of relational object) is expanded and its realization determined, any grammatically optional arguments to the event are passed through a filter before they can be added. This filter looks up the function that including the argument would serve, and if the function has already been satisfied by earlier parts of the text, it prevents the argument from being included in the event's expansion.

To establish that the check is done in the most efficient manner, we now have to look at the representation of these 'functions', and at the flow of information through the relevant parts of the generation process. This entails a small digression to look at the larger conceptual model for this domain, the complex object types it introduces, and at the reversible rules of inference that are used both by the selection process and SPARSER.

5.3 A shared model

The authors of the articles in this corpus assume that they and their readers share a common model of the typical 'job-turnover' relation: a person gets a new position, which used to be held by another person, who now holds a different position. Included in the model are commonsense assumptions such as that only one person can hold a given position at a time or that a person always has a position.

Key to the design of this shared model, as I have construed it, is that it is stated in terms of a set of domain-specific role variables – variables that we could gloss in English as "the new person" (i.e. the one who get the position and that the article is principally about), "the position the new person gets", "the person the new person displaces", etc. These variables are arguments to the posited job-turnover relation. They can be used to specialize the types of regular objects that form the content of the texts, and can acts as guides and cross-indexes that expedite the processing done in selection and orchestration.

To expedite the reasoning, we can generalize all the individual types of job-changes (appointments, elections, namings, retirement, deaths, etc.) as one of the two event types 'get-position' or 'leave-position'. (They all have essentially the same arguments and their pragmatic differences do not affect the inferences that follow from them.) You can see this in Fig. 1, where the list of inherited types for the object includes 'leave-position' as its first super-type.

Just above, I glossed the function of the optional position adjunct (i.e. "*[Mr. Petito] resigned as vice president and general counsel last November*") as being to communicate what position Mr. Petito used to hold before he resigned. Under this design, we can formalize that function as the binding of a particular variable. This looks as follows, with the binding object shown explicitly and the representation of the other objects substantially abbreviated.

#<binding
            :variable λposition. leave-position(#<Petito>, position)
            :value #<position vp&gs of Fairchild>>

Notice that the variable is a lambda expression. Formally it is a specialization of the usual 'position' variable (as in Fig. 1), where the relation that owns the variable has now been partially instantiated, recording Mr. Petito as the person who did the leaving. That partial relation would be the proximal representation of a phrase like "*Mr. Petito's resignation*". The source representation, on the other hand, would be the fully populated relation, where it is known what position he had, when the event took place, etc. Alternatively, the source object might be open in some of those variables, perhaps because the article is about what will happen when he retires and some of the specific values are as yet undefined or irrelevant.

The redundancy filter will know to omit the adjunct if it can establish that this binding, or its logical equivalent, has already been communicated by an earlier part of the text.[5] The question then is how it will know that, which takes us to the

---

[5] Of course when this system is mature, we will also have to pay attention to scope and to a rhetorical model of the reader's comprehension processes. If the fact about Mr. Petito's position was mentioned too long ago then we should not assume that it will necessarily be remembered. Similarly when information is very new or unexpected we should not automatically assume that it will be appreciated, in which case deliberate redundancy may be an appropriate strategy. However neither of these possibilities is realistic in these very short articles in this quite specialized genre, and in any event we would always want to know that we were being redundant so that our choice of what to do could be deliberate.

strategy that this generator will use and the rules of inference.

5.4 The selection process for Who's News articles

The procedure used for the selection process is suggested by a striking feature of the articles in the corpus, namely that they show no consistent regularity in the details that they present. Once one gets below the coarse generalization of 'gets-position', the particulars of what information is given or how it is organized have resisted any attempts to fashion a schema for this genre, because there appear to be many more pragmatic conditions then there are ordering and inclusion statements to be conditioned – the schema structure would just be too complex to be practical.

I have instead elected to have the selection of what to say be directed by the actual event data, as construed by the shared model of job-turnovers. Selection is done by navigating through the semantic net that the data forms, following some simple rules and subject to some general rhetorical requirements specific to this genre. This makes it a data directed selection process, in the sense of Swartout (1977), Conklin (1983), or my own early work.

Two general rules appear to be sufficient to reproduce the very simple Who's News articles such as the example: (1) Present the information in salience order,[6] and (2) present everything that is out of the ordinary. Salience order usually means putting the new personUs get-position event first, though occasionally a leave-position event will be first if it is what the journalist sees as the "news". The ancillary events dictated by the particular get-position will then follow, along with information about the position that the new person held before he or she got their new position, which is information that has appeared in every article and so is taken as one of the conventions of the genre.

Information out of the ordinary consists of deviations from the standard script of "new person gets position, displacing the old person who previously held that position, who now gets a new position of their own". This includes the new person taking on several positions, not all of which were previously held by the same person, the position being a new one and so there is no old-person to be displaced, and the like.

The key design issue here is how is this "navigation through the semantic net" to be done? What will indicate the possible paths if the data varies so much that no schema can reasonably be written for it? It is here that a set of domain-specific rules of inference come into play, rules that were developed initially for deducing the values of the text's omitted, redundant information during the parsing process, and now are inverted to guide selection and feed the filter that does the omission in the first place.

---

[6] To talk about salience order when reproducing a corpus of existing articles is something of an oxymoron, since the judgement as to what is salient will be taken directly from the article as the journalist wrote it and will then be reproduced. However, it is at least a hook in the algorithm for an independent motivation for salience that could be introduced at some later point, and manipulation of the apparent salience might lead to interesting effects.

5.5 Reversible rules of inference

When parsing, the presence a job-turnover relation in the text is recognized by the completion of rules over pairs of surface events. These rules impose an interpretation on the individuals in those events, binding them to the role variables of the turnover relation. The parser uses these variables as its hooks for drawing inferencesQthe generator will now use them to know what inferences have followed from what it has already said.

The rule that will apply in this case is shown in Fig. 2. (Only a small number of rules have been written at the time this paper goes to press, and they are open-code and do not yet have any user-level syntactic notation. For expository purposes though, we can gloss them as shown.) Besides binding the job-turnover variables, this rule concludes that the old-person left the position that the 'new person' has gotten. This conclusion is stated in terms of variables, rather than doing the substitution there and then, in order to allow for the condition where multiple positions and multiple old people are involved. The actual values have to only be subsumed by these types; they don't have to be identical.

```
#<get-position person1 position>   +   #<succeed person1 person2>
|= instantiate a job-turnover
   with    person1 = new-person
           person2 = old-person
           position = position-turned-over.
   conclude:  #<binding
                  :variable lposition. leave-position(old-person, position)
                  :value lposition. get-position(new-person, position)
```

Fig. 2. A reversible rule of inference

For parsing, this rule is triggered when text segments instantiating the get-position and the succession have both been parsed and those units entered into the accumulating semantic model of the paragraph. (Think of it as being done by a chart parser operating at a semantic level.) The rule's completion instantiates the turnover event, and binds the event's variables to the specific individuals mentioned in the text. It also adds the newly inferred fact into the model, creating a concrete individual to fit the schema indicated in the ruleUs conclusion. Abbreviating freely, this new object will be as follows:

```
#<leave-position #<Petito> #<vp&gc of Fairchild>>
```

If we expanded these abbreviations to present a full composite, we would have a subset of the object in Fig. 1: The 'leave-position' relation here subsumes the 'resign' there, and the binding objects for the person and position variables would in the state of the program be – literally identical, i.e. this object and the resign object would both point to the same bindings.

It is this identity property that both the parsing and generation architectures depend upon for their efficiency; it is implemented by an extensive cross-index and key-based lookup mechanism. On the parsing side it facilitates filling in incomplete information, and for generation it facilitates the work of the redundancy filter, as we shall see in the next section, where the above rule is inverted to supply a path for navigating through the network of job-change data.

6 Stepping through an example

For the example article, we can assume that the first event, "*Donald E. Miller was named senior vice president and general counsel*" is ipso facto the most salient.[7] Accordingly, this event is selected from the speaker's model and placed in the "staging" level of representation: the set of information units to be included in the text (see §3.2). The orchestrator can then enter it directly into the text structure as a full sentence, reflecting its importance as the topic of the article and the fact that nothing is already pending at that level that would have to be taken into consideration.

If we like, we could then have the unit passed all the way through the rest of the processes and levels and its text produced, though that would preclude the possibility of introducing any information into the middle of the unit's Text Structure expansion, such as an appositive giving the position that Mr. Miller held before this one. These are all issues for style, however, and at this point we are only experimenting with the possibilities and not in a position to make any definitive claims.

Having presented a get-position event, the rhetorical conventions of the genre now require the planner to say what has happened to the previous holder of that position, or if there has been no previous holder then to explicitly say that the position is a new one. In this example this will come to selecting the 'resign' unit of Fig. 1 and introducing it into the staging level.

We can imagine that selection could find out whether there was a 'old-person' by searching through the employment database in the speakerUs model, but a more efficient means is available here by leveraging the fact that we are navigating through a very rich semantic model that uses task-specific characterizations in its object types. This richness is reflected here by the 'naming' being not simply a get-position relation, but a sub-type of that relation where the position variable has been specialized and instantiated. The position Mr. Miller was named to is in this case a "position that was previously held by someone else", specifically

λposition. leave-position(#<Petito>, position) [8]

To know whether the position had been previously held, all selection has to do is look at the type of the event and dispatch accordingly. The specialized type also

---

[7] For lack of space I will ignore the question of how the generator knows that it would be redundant to mention the company where Mr. Miller holds his position. It involves a genre-specific rule that appreciates that the name of the company was given in the article's dateline.

[8] Recall that these reports are written by professional journalists who are accustomed to writing literally dozens of them per day. In modeling this task in a computer program it is quite reasonable to make the representations quite specific as a way to capture this expertise. The model is, needless to say, very carefully hand-coded.

expedites the actual access to the "person who has left the position", since it directly encodes that person in the representation of its position variable as shown.

With the resign event now pending on the staging level, the orchestration process must decide whether it can add it to the Text Structure immediately, making it the next text segment after the 'naming', or whether there must be some introduction. In this case an introduction is necessary since Mr. Petito is not already in the discourse.[9]

The necessary bridging relation can be found by inverting the rule shown in Fig. 2. Recall that that rule said that given a 'get-position' followed by a 'succeed' that one could infer the existence of a 'leave-position' event (i.e. within the inferred binding object). The orchestrator can find this rule by indexing from the 'naming' already in the Text Structure and the 'resign' pending at the staging level; at which point it can construct the needed 'succeed' relation and enter it into the Text Structure just after the 'naming' event, and enter the 'resign' just after it, thereby replicating the pattern that the parsing rule specified.

We of course not only want to ensure that fluency of the text by including appropriate linking relations, but we also want to track the inferences that follow implicitly from what is said explicitly. The rule of Fig. 2 serves this function as well: With the Text Structure now instantiating the rule's pattern, we are entitled to include as communicated information the unit that is the ruleUs "conclusion", namely the binding object that identifies the position Mr. Petito left with the position to which Mr. Miller has just been named. As we are generating and already know all the relevant information, the binding can now be given a concrete value rather than the variable used when parsing.

This binding is precisely the object that the redundancy filter will be looking for a moment from now when the 'resign' event is being expanded (see §5.3), meaning that the filter will be satisfied and the event will be passed to the linguistic specification without its position argument.

7 Summary

What I have attempted to illustrate in this all too short paper is a technique whereby information that would be redundant if it were included in the text can be noticed and omitted. The check for redundancy is necessary if we make the reasonable assumption that the input to the generator consists of full relations, relations that in other contexts would have all of their arguments expressed. The technique is sensitive to the information actually conveyed by a specific context rather than requiring complete, predefined schemas, and it can be done very efficiently given the representation for conceptual information that I have adopted.

---

[9] One can imagine that the needed cohesion could be achieved by linking off of the shared position, saying something like "..., *a position previously held by Dominic A. Petito, who resigned*". However, I have never yet seen such a phrasing, and my reference corpus is now in excess of a thousand articles. I conjecture that the reason it does not occur is that it would give the position undue prominence in the text, but in any event there is much to be said for scrupulously holding to the usage that has actually been observed in this genre, even if only as an exercise in maintaining a stipulated textual style.

This representation is lexically based, in that the most specific categories in the model employ abstract (unrealized) lexical items as their primitives. This design makes it possible to reverse lexically anchored inference rules originally developed for the parser and use them to track what additional information is communicated implicitly as the explicit text is produced.

The redundancy check is very precisely located at the point in our generation architecture where composite information units selected from the speaker's mental model have been situated in the Text Structure and are expanded to determine how they will be realized. Doing the check at this point in the process takes a burden off the planner. It has to only select and orchestrate the information, in its natural units, and does not itself have to worry about the possibility of redundancy within the content of the units it selects, since the check is carried out transparently by an independent mechanism operating later. This point is also logical because when a unit is reached in the traversal of the Text Structure its left context is definitive – nothing more can be added before this current point of speech.

The mechanics of accessing units and navigating through the speaker's representation of a job turnover is expedited by the fact that the representation supports partially populated relations and represents the association of a relation's arguments with their values using independent, first-class objects known as bindings. The type system that the representation employs is also important because it supports markedly more specific types than is customary; which allows the procedure for searching the model to be done by simple dispatches rather than actual search. This representation is not crucial to the redundancy-suppressing procedure; it only makes it more efficient.

This treatment of the suppression of redundancy is general. It presumes only that the function of any optional argument to a surface-level relational head (e.g. verb or nominalization) can be construed as the communication of certain information, and that it is possible to keep track of whether this information has been conveyed, implicitly or explicitly, by earlier portions of the text. If it has, then the argument is omitted ("suppressed"); if it has not then the argument is included.

References

Conklin, E. Jeffery (1983): *Data-driven Indelible Planning of Discourse Generation Using Salience.* Ph.D. dissertation. University of Massachusetts at Amherst. Department of Computer & Information Science.

Dale, Robert (1990): *Generating Recipes: An Overview of Epicure.* In: Dale et al. 1990. Pages 229–255.

Dale, Robert; Mellish, Chris; Zock, Michael (Eds) (1990): *Current Research in Natural Language Generation.* Academic Press, London.

Hovy, Eduard (1988): *Planning Coherent Multisentential Text.* In the Proceedings of the 26th Annual Meeting of the Association for Computational Linguistics. SUNY Buffalo. June 7-10, 1988. Pages 163–169.

Hovy, Eduard; McDonald, David; Young, Sheryl (1989): *Current Issues in Natural Language Generation: An overview of the AAAI Workshop on Text Planning and Realization.* AI Magazine 10(3), Fall 1989. Pages 27–29.

Joshi, Aravind (1987): *The relevance of Tree Adjoining Grammar to generation.* In: Kempen 1987. Pages 233–252.

Kempen, Gerard (Ed.) (1987): *Natural Language Generation.* Martinus Nijhoff, Dordrecht.

Kempen, Gerard; Huijbers, P. (1983): *The lexicalization process in sentence production and naming: Indirect election of words.* Cognition, 14. Pages 185–209.

Kukich, Karen (1988): *Fluency in Natural Language Reports.* In: McDonald and Bolc (Eds) 1988. Pages 280–311.

McDonald, David (1991a): *On the Place of Words in the Generation Process.* In: Paris et al. 1991. Pages 229–247.

McDonald, David (1991b): *Reversible NLP by Deriving the Grammars from the Knowledge Base.* In the Proceedings of the Workshop on Reversible Grammar in Natural Language Processing. June 17, 1991. ACL. Pages 40–44.

McDonald, David (1992): *An Efficient Chart-based Algorithm for Partial-Parsing of Unrestricted Texts.* In the Proceedings of the Conference on Applied Natural Language Processing. Trento, Italy, April 1-3, 1992.

McDonald, David; Meteer, Marie (Vaughan) (1988): *From Water to Wine: generating natural language texts from today's applications programs.* Conference on Applied Natural Language Processing. Austin, Texas. February 9-12, 1988. Pages 41–48.

McDonald, David; Meteer, Marie (1990): *The Implications of Tree Adjoining Grammar for Generation.* In the Proceedings of the 1st International Workshop on Tree Adjoining Grammar: Formal Theory and Application. Dagstuhl Castle International Conference and Research Center for Computer Science. August 15-17, 1990. Pages 71–79. Organized by Wahlster and Harbusch, DFKI, Stuhlsatzenausweg 3, D-6600 Saarbruchen 11, Germany.

McDonald, David; Meteer, Marie; Pustejovsky, James (1987): *Factors Contributing to Efficiency in Natural Language Generation.* In: Kempen 1987. Pages 159–181.

McDonald, David; Bolc, Leonard (Eds) (1988): *Natural Language Generation Systems.* Springer-Verlag. New York.

Meteer, Marie (1991): *Bridging the 'Generation Gap' between Text Planning and Linguistic Realization.* Computational Intelligence 7(4).

Meteer, Marie (1992): *Expressibility: The Problem of Efficient Text Planning.* Pinter. London.

Meteer, Marie; McDonald, David; Anderson, Scott; Forster, David; Gay, Linda; Huettner, Alison; Sibun, Penelope (1987): *Mumble-86: Design and Implementation.* TR #87-87. Dept. Computer and Information Science, University of Massachusetts at Amherst.

Mellish, Chris (1988): *Natural language generation from plans.* In: Zock and Sabah 1988. Pages 131–145.

Paris, Cecile; McKeown, Kathleen (1987): *Discourse strategies for describing complex physical objects.* In: Kempen 1987. Pages 97–115.

Paris, Cecile; Swartout, William; Mann, William (Eds) (1991): *Natural Language Generation in Artificial Intelligence and Computational Linguistics.* Kluwer Academic. Boston.

Pustejovsky, James (1991): *The Generative Lexicon.* Computational Linguistics 17(4).

Rösner, Dietmar (1987): *The automated news agency: SEMTEX P a text generator for German.* In: Kempen 1987. Pages 133–148.

Swartout, William (1977): *A Digitalis Therapy Advisor with Explanations.* Technical Report. Laboratory for Computer Science, MIT.

Zoch, Michael; Sabah, Gerard (1988): *Advances in Natural Language Generation.* Pinter. London.

Controlling Content Realization with Functional Unification Grammars

Michael Elhadad and Jacques Robin

Department of Computer Science
Columbia University
New York, NY 10027

Abstract

Standard Functional Unification Grammars (FUGs) provide a structurally guided top-down control regime for sentence generation. When using FUGs to perform content realization as a whole, including lexical choice, this regime is no longer appropriate for two reasons: (1) the unification of non-lexicalized semantic input with an integrated lexico-grammar requires mapping "floating" semantic elements which can trigger extensive backtracking and (2) lexical choice requires accessing external constraint sources on demand to preserve the modularity between conceptual and linguistic knowledge.

We introduce two control tools that we have implemented for FUGs to address these limitations: bk-class, a form of dependency-directed backtracking to efficiently process "floating" constraints and external, a co-routine mechanism allowing a FUG to cooperate with external constraint sources during unification. We show how these tools complement the top-down regime of FUGs to control the whole content realization process.

1 Introduction

Unification-based formalisms (Shieber 1986) and Functional Unification Grammars (FUGs) in particular, have proved popular in text generation. In previous work (Kay 1979, McKeown 1985, Appelt 1985, Paris 1987), the input to FUGs was a fully lexicalized specification. In recent work, however, the functionality of FUGs has been extended to encompass all of content realization, including lexical choice (McKeown et al 1990, Elhadad 1991b, Smadja 1991b, Robin 1992). In this framework, content realization is viewed as the process of unifying a purely semantic input with an integrated *lexico*-grammar, in the systemic sense (Matthiessen 1991).

When a non-lexicalized semantic structure is accepted as input, the FUG has the burden of mapping this structure onto a syntactic structure. This additional task increases the complexity of the unification process because semantic and syntactic structures are not isomorphic:

- Several elements in the semantic structure can be realized by a single syntactic constituent (*e.g.,* in a sports report, the verbal pattern *"X stunned Y"* expresses both that X is the winner of a game and that Y was the favorite).

- The same semantic element can be realized by linguistic constituents at different linguistic ranks (*e.g.*, the surprise expressed by *"X stunned Y"* can alternatively be conveyed by an adverbial phrase, as in *"against all odds, X defeated Y"* or an adjectival phrase *"X defeated the highly favored Y"*).

In FUGs, unification was traditionally controlled by a top-down regime guided by the input structure. When accepting a semantic input containing "floating" elements that can be realized by constituents at different levels of the syntactic tree, such a top-down regime can trigger expensive backtracking.

Moreover, lexical choice is constrained by many different factors: encyclopedic, interlexical, grammatical, discursive and interpersonal (Robin 1990). All of these constraints cannot be integrated in a single FUG. In a modular architecture, they must be provided by independent knowledge sources. To perform lexical choice, the FUG must interact with these various knowledge sources during unification.

To address these new needs, we propose to integrate explicit control annotations within FUGs. Specifically, we present two control tools that we have implemented in FUF (Functional Unification Formalism), our extended version of FUGs (Elhadad 1991a, 1990):

- **bk-class**, a form of dependency directed backtracking, used to handle floating constraints efficiently.
- **external**, a co-routine interface used to query external constraint sources from the FUG.

In this paper, we first describe the standard control regime used in FUF. We then introduce the **bk-class** construct and we quantitatively evaluate how it reduces backtracking for the realization of floating constraints. We then present the **external** tool and illustrate its use to query a domain knowledge base at unification time.

2 Standard Control in FUF

FUG relies on the primitive operation of unification of Functional Descriptions (FDs) (Kay 1979). FDs are sets of pairs (a v), called features, where a is an attribute and v is a value. A value is either : (1) an atom, (2) recursively an FD or (3) a path to another feature in the FD.[1] A given attribute a is allowed to appear at most once in a given FD. Two simple FDs are compatible if they do not include a contradictory value for the same attribute.[2] When they are compatible, the unification of two FDs merges the features from both to produce a more specific FD, the *total FD*.

There are four constructs of FUF that are of importance in this paper: alt, cset, **any** and **given**. The alt keyword expresses disjunction in FUG. The value of the

---

[1] Value paths are used to specify that two features share the same value. In FUF, a path is a list of embedded attributes surrounded by curly braces. This list can be prefixed by a number of carets, making the path *relative* to the level of embedding of the feature. An attribute is generally an atom. However, it can also be a path to allow for the specification of its value at various embedding levels in the recursive structure of an FD.

[2] There is no notion of variable in functional unification. Failure can only occur at the leaf of a feature structure when trying to unify two different atoms for the same attribute.

alt keyword is a list of FDs, each one called a *branch*. When unifying an input FD with such a disjunction, the unifier non-deterministically selects one branch that is compatible with the input. Disjunctions encode the available choice points of a system and introduce backtracking in the unification process.

During sentence generation, unification is used to add linguistic information from a functional unification grammar (FUG) to a semantic input, both represented as FDs. Figure 1 shows the input to generate the sentence *"Robinson scored 32 points"* and a FUG (grammar G1) specifying the mapping from semantic categories to syntactic categories. When unifying this semantic input I1 with G1 the following operations are performed: FUF picks branch 2 of the **alt** and merges it with the input. During the merging, the features uppercased in Fig. 1 get added to the result.

Semantic input I1:

```
((sem-cat action) (concept c-score) (tense past)  ;; Predicate
 (agent ((sem-cat individual) (concept c-player)  ;; Argument 1
        (name Robinson))))
 (medium ((sem-cat set) (concept c-stat)          ;; Argument 2
        (unit c-point) (cardinal 32)))))
```

Grammar G1:

```
( ...
 (alt
  (((sem-cat individual) (synt-cat proper-name))             ;; Branch 1
   ((sem-cat action) (synt-cat clause) (cset (agent medium))) ;; Branch 2
   ((sem-cat set) (synt-cat np))))                           ;; Branch 3
  ... )
```

Total FD after a single (top-level) unification:

```
((sem-cat action) (concept c-score) (tense past)
 (SYNT-CAT CLAUSE) (CSET (AGENT MEDIUM))
 (agent ((sem-cat individual) (concept c-player) (name Robinson)))
 (medium ((sem-cat set) (concept c-stat) (unit c-point) (cardinal 32)))))
```

Total FD after recursive constituent unification:

```
((sem-cat action) (concept score) (tense past)
 (synt-cat clause) (cset (agent medium))
 (agent ((sem-cat individual) (concept c-player) (name Robinson)
        (SYNT-CAT PROPER-NAME)))
 (medium ((sem-cat set) (concept c-point) (cardinal 32)
        (SYNT-CAT NP))))
```

Fig. 1. An example of unification

The semantic input is a structured representation. It consists of a top-level predicate with embedded arguments. In the single unification shown in Fig. 1, however, only the top-level FD is enriched. The FDs embedded under **agent** and **medium** are not enriched. To properly refine the structured semantic input into a syntactic description we need to process these sub-FDs, by reaccessing the grammar at each level.

The way FUF proceeds at this point, is based on the notion of *constituent*: a constituent of a complex FD is a distinguished sub-FD. The special label **cset** (Constituent Set) identifies constituents. The value of **cset** is a list of attributes naming the constituents of the FD as shown in Fig. 1. Intuitively, constituents bring structure to functional descriptions.

To handle constituents, the complete unification procedure is:

1. Unify top-level input with grammar (single unification).
2. Identify constituents in result.
3. Recursively unify each constituent with the grammar.

Constituents therefore trigger recursion in FUGs. However, this description of the unification mechanism does not specify what control regime must be used to traverse the constituent structure. FUF implements the following regime: *top-down* and *breadth-first* traversal of the constituent structure. At each level of the structure, constituents are processed in the order they are declared in the **cset**. So in our example FD, the constituent structure is processed as follows: top-level first, then **agent**, then **medium**. The resulting FD at the end of the process is shown at the bottom of Fig. 1.

The two remaining FUF constructs we need to discuss in this section are the meta-variables **given** and **any**.

A well-known problem with top-down control regimes is their handling of left-recursive rules. For example, the grammar for NPs specifies that the determiner of an NP can be a possessive NP. In a phrase-structure formalism, this is encoded by a left-recursive rule such as $np/NP \rightarrow det/NP, nbar/NP$ (Shieber et al 1989, p.10). With a top-down regime, such a rule can lead to non-termination. In FUF, this problem is avoided by the use of the special construct **given**. The **given** construct checks that a given feature is instantiated in the input FD *before* unification starts. By adding a pair (**possessor given**) in the NP sub-grammar, we can ensure that a possessive NP gets added in determiner position only when a **possessor** constituent is given in the semantic input. Thus, recursion is only triggered when necessary and will always terminate.

Another meta-variable, **any**, implements a powerful delaying mechanism. A feature (**x any**) constrains **x** to be instantiated with *some* value at the *end* of the unification. The unifier enforces this constraint as follows: if **x** is already instantiated in the input FD, then **any** is satisfied; if it is not yet instantiated, the constraint is delayed and checked again at the end of the unification process. If at this point **x** is still not instantiated, the constraint fails and the unifier needs to backtrack. Therefore **any** is a meta-variable that triggers a delayed check.

In contrast to a procedural implementation of systemic grammars like NIGEL (Mann and Matthiessen 1983), where the control regime is driven by an *a priori*

grammatical structure, FUF's control regime is driven by the structure of the semantic input FD. It is therefore similar in spirit to the semantic-head-driven algorithm
presented by Shieber et al (1989). It also avoids the inefficiencies associated with a
bottom-up control regime, *e.g.*, the backtracking introduced by choosing the case of
an NP before knowing what syntactic role it will fill in a clause.

The control regime described thus far is the default regime followed by FUF. A
more flexible control regime can be implemented by explicitly controlling the value of
the cset feature in different parts of the grammar. In this paper, we do not attempt
to cover the many control issues related to lexical choice. Instead, we focus on the
special control devices we have implemented in FUF. A more complete description
of various control regimes for lexical choice implemented in FUF can be found in
(Elhadad 1992b) and (Robin 1992).

3 Bk-class and Floating Constraints

The task of the generator is to map from a semantic constituent structure to a
syntactic one. This task is difficult because, in general, these structures are not
isomorphic: *"a combination of semantic elements can be expressed by a single surface
element, or a single semantic element by a combination of surface elements* (Talmy,
1985, p. 57). For example, in the basketball domain, the clause pattern *"X edged Y"*
conveys two semantic elements: a semantic predicate - X won a game against Y -
and a manner qualification - the game was close.[3]

Moreover, the same semantic element can be realized by syntactic elements at
different linguistic ranks (*e.g.*, group, clause, sentence) For example, the low rating
of a team can be conveyed by a variety of syntactic constituents:

- Adjective (at the noun-group rank): *The hapless Denver Nuggets beat the Boston
  Celtics 101-99.*
- Verb (at the verb-group rank): *The Denver Nuggets stunned the Boston Celtics
  101-99.*
- Adverbial (at the clause rank): *The Denver Nuggets surprisingly beat the Boston
  Celtics 101-99.*

We call such semantic elements *floating constraints*. We distinguish them from
structural constraints such as semantic predications or references. Structural constraints require the presence of syntactic constituents at a given linguistic rank in
the output and thus guide the mapping process from the semantic structure to the
syntactic structure. For example, when an input event structure is mapped to a
clause, the semantic predicate c-win determines how the semantic roles are mapped
onto syntactic complements: winner to subject and loser to object.

The top-down regime implemented in FUF handles structural constraints efficiently because backtracking is circumscribed to the unification of the grammar
with a *single* input constituent. In contrast, the processing of floating constraints

---

[3] This non-isomorphism between syntactic and semantic structures is a pervasive phenomenon, as illustrated by Talmy's extensive cross-linguistic analysis of constructions
expressing motion and causation (Talmy 1976 and 1983).

can be very inefficient because it can trigger non-local backtracking, cutting across linguistic ranks and requiring the re-unification of the grammar with *several* input constituents. To illustrate this problem, consider a system reporting on the results of a basketball game and an input containing the following three constraints:

- Semantic Predication: convey that the Denver Nuggets defeated the Boston Celtics by a 101-99 score.
- Manner Qualification: convey that the game was tight.
- Argumentative Orientation: convey the low rating of the Denver Nuggets.

For example, the above input configuration of constraints is correctly satisfied by the following sentence: *"The hapless Denver Nuggets edged the Boston Celtics 101-99."*

But all these different linguistic devices cannot be freely combined, as illustrated by the following examples:

1. *? The Denver Nuggets narrowly stunned the Boston Celtics 101-99.*
2. *? The Denver Nuggets surprisingly nipped the Boston Celtics 101-99.*
3. *? Against all odds, the Denver Nuggets narrowly beat the Boston Celtics 101-99.*

In sentence (1), it is not clear which semantic aspect of the verb *"stunned"* is modified by *"narrowly"*: the expression of the game result or its unexpectedness. Similarly in (2), the modification of *"nipped"* by *"surprisingly"* is ambiguous. In (3), the scope of *"against all odds"* is ambiguous: it could be either *"narrowly"* - in which case the Nuggets are presented as highly rated - or *"beat"* - in which case the Nuggets are presented as lowly rated.

The input FD shown at the top of Fig. 2 encodes the three constraints we want to satisfy. The central part of Fig. 2 shows a fragment of a lexicon specifying the mapping between concepts and lexical items. The fragment shows how different verbs impose constraints on the features **AO** or **manner**, or no constraint for "neutral" verbs. The branch order in the **win-lex** alt enforces the stylistic preference for semantically rich verbs over neutral verbs with adverbials.[4] In addition, to avoid generating adverbials with ambiguous scope, the grammar enforces that (1) clauses contain a single adverb and (2) only neutral verbs are used in combination with adverbials.

Consider the realization of the semantic input at the top of Fig. 2 with the grammar at the bottom of this figure. FUF's top-down regime allows it to map the structural constraints to syntactic constituents right away: first the semantic predicate to a verb-group, and then the roles **winner**, **loser** and **score** to **subject**, **object** and **adjunct** respectively. In contrast, the mapping of the "floating" constraints **AO** and **manner** must be delayed.

Figure 2 illustrates this delaying mechanism by showing how the **manner** input constraint is handled by the grammar. The feature **manner-conveyed** is used to record the syntactic category of the constituent realizing the manner constraint. It

---

[4] FUF tries the branches of an **alt** construct in order. When no order is preferable, the construct **ralt** (standing for Random Alternation) whose branches are tried at random is used instead.

A semantic input expressing three constraints:

```
(;; Semantic predication
 (sem-cat action) (concept c-win) (token t-win-666) (tense past)
 (winner ((sem-cat individual) (concept c-team) (name Nuggets)))
 (loser ((sem-cat individual) (concept c-team) (name Celtics)))
 (score ((sem-cat quantity) (concept c-game-score)
         (winner-score 101) (loser-score 99)))
 ;; Manner constraint
 (manner ((sem-cat quality) (concept c-tight)))
 ;; Argumentative constraint
 (AO ((sem-cat scale) (concept c-rating)
      (carrier {winner}) (orientation -))))
```

Choice of verb in the lexico-grammar:

```
(...
 ((sem-cat action)
  (alt (index on concept)
    ;; Map the concept game-result to a verb
    (((concept win)
      (alt win-lex (:bk-class (AO manner))
        (;; The winner's rating is poor
         (({AO} ((concept c-rating) (carrier {winner})
                 (orientation -) (conveyed yes)))
          (lex ((alt ("stun" "surprise"))))
          ({adverb} none))

         ;; The victory is narrow
         (({manner} ((concept c-tight) (conveyed yes)))
          (lex ((alt ("edge" "nip"))))
          ({adverb} none))

         ;; Default neutral verbs
         ((lex ((alt ("beat" "defeat" "down"))))))))))
      ... ))))
```

Floating constraints mapping in the lexico-grammar:

```
( ...
 (verb ((alt ...))) ...
 (AO ((alt ...))) ...
 (manner ((alt manner-adverbial (:bk-class manner)
          (;; Can be realized by other means - delay
           ((manner-conveyed any))

           ;; Map manner to an adverbial adjunct
           ;; and mark that manner has been realized
           (({adverb} ((synt-cat adverb) (concept {^ ^ concept})))
            (manner-conveyed adverb)))))))
  ... )
```

Fig. 2. Handling floating constraints with bk-class

remains nil as long as the constraint is not conveyed. In the first branch of the manner-adverbial alt, we first check whether the manner constraint has already been handled by some other constituent. This check is implemented by the feature (manner-conveyed any). This first branch delays the decision to use an adverb with the any construct. This gives other devices a chance to express the manner constraint. However if no other linguistic device can be found that satisfies the manner constraint, the grammar resorts to using an adverbial adjunct, by choosing the second branch of the alt. The feature (manner-conveyed any) therefore prevents the generation of semantically incomplete sentences like *"The Denver Nuggets stunned the Boston Celtics 101-99."* The argumentative constraint is similarly handled with a feature ao-conveyed.

Let us now consider how the manner and argumentation constraints interact. In a top-down regime, the verb-group is first processed and the concept c-win is lexicalized. FUF is now traversing the lexicon fragment in the middle of Fig. 2 and first chooses the verb "stun" which satisfies both the semantic predication and the argumentative constraint. It then maps the semantic constituents to syntactic functions and proceeds to the argumentative constraint. This constraint is already satisfied by the verb, so no modifier needs to be introduced.

At this point FUF attempts to take into account the manner constraint. It first delays the use of an adverb with the any construct and completes the traversal of the constituents top-down. It eventually checks the any construct and finds that the manner constraint has not been satisfied. Backtracking is triggered. Consider at this point the state of the backtracking-point stack: the whole grammar has been traversed, all the subconstituents processed. Basically, all potential backtracking points are on the stack. If FUF blindly backtracks, search is maximized. Since we cannot know *a priori* where in the syntactic structure the floating manner constraint will fit, the decision whether to use an adverb must be delayed until the end of the traversal. There is therefore no way to detect failure before this point.

To avoid the cost of a blind backtracking, we introduce the bk-class construct. It implements a version of dependency-directed backtracking (de Kleer et al 1979) specialized to the case of FUF. The bk-class construct relies on the fact that in FUF, a failure always occurs because there is a conflict between two values for a certain attribute at a certain location in the total FD. In our example, we have to backtrack because an equation requires that the value of the feature {manner manner-conveyed} be instantiated, but the actual feature is not. The path {manner manner-conveyed} defines the *address of the failure*.[5]

The idea is that the location of a failure can be used to identify the only decision points in the backtracking stack that could have caused it. This identification requires additional knowledge that must be declared in the FUG. More precisely, we first allow the FUG writer to declare certain paths to be of a certain bk-class. We then require the explicit declaration in the FUG of the choice points that correspond to this bk-class.

For example, the statement: (define-bk-class manner {manner manner-conveyed})

---

[5] In an FD, each embedded feature can be viewed as an equation between the path leading to the feature in the total FD and the feature value.

specifies that the path {manner manner-conveyed} is of class manner. In addition, we tag in the FUG all alts that have an influence on the handling of the manner constraint with a declaration (:bk-class manner) as shown in Fig. 2.

When the unifier fails at a location of class manner, it *directly* backtracks to the last choice point of class manner, ignoring all intermediate decisions. In our example, when the any constraint fails, we directly backtrack to the manner choice point in the grammar (bottom of Fig. 2). If this last option fails again, we backtrack up to the choice of verb in the lexicon (middle of Fig. 2). We therefore use the knowledge that *only* the verb or the adverb can satisfy the manner constraint in a clause to drastically reduce the search space. But, this knowledge is *locally* expressed at each relevant choice point, retaining the possibility of independently expressing each constraint in the FUG.

In general, the determination of the address of failure is more complex and it is necessary to distinguish between *initial failures* and *derived failures*. An initial failure always occurs at a leaf of the total FD, when trying to unify two incompatible atoms. Failures however can also propagate up the structure of the total FD. For example, when unifying ((a ((b 1)))) with ((a ((b 2)))) the original address of failure is the path {a b}. When the unifier backtracks, it also triggers a failure at address {a}, which is not a leaf. This type of failure is called a derived failure. In the implementation of bk-class, FUF ignores derived failures and directly backtracks to the first choice point whose bk-class matches the last initial failure.

For the example of Fig. 2, we have measured the number of backtracking points required to generate different clauses conveying the same core content. Table 1 summarizes these measurements.[6]

Table 1. Measuring the effect of bk-class

		Backtracking points	
Input	Output	w/o bk-class	w/ bk-class
No floating constraints	*The DN beat the BC*	110	110
Manner in the verb	*The DN edged the BC*	110	110
Manner as adverbial	*The DN surprisingly beat the BC*	>10000	214
AO in the verb	*The DN stunned the BC*	112	112
AO as adjective	*The hapless DN beat the BC*	1,623	239
AO as adverbial	*The DN surprisingly beat the BC*	>100,000	277
AO & manner together	*The hapless DN edged the BC*	1,178	238

The number of backtracking points required to generate each example clause is listed with and without bk-class. The numbers for the first clause, which does not include any floating constraints, give an indication of the size of the grammar. It can be interpreted as the number of decisions the grammar makes to generate a basic clause for which practically no backtracking is required. It roughly corresponds to the number of unretracted decisions made by the grammar. It is the optimal number of

---

[6] In this table, *DN* abbreviates *Denver Nuggets* and *BC* abbreviates *Boston Celtics*.

backtracking points that a search control regime can obtain for the given input with this grammar. Without **bk-class**, the wide variation in number of backtracking points among the examples indicates the exponential nature of the blind search which floating constraints impose on the standard control regime. In contrast, with **bk-class**, the variation in number of backtracking points remains within a factor of three among all the examples.

The dependency-directed mechanism implemented in FUF with **bk-class** therefore complements a general top-down control regime to make the processing of floating constraints efficient. The performance penalty imposed by a floating constraint depends on the number of sites in the syntactic structure where it can be realized. For example, the AO constraint can be realized at three levels and it may require the unifier to re-traverse the grammar three times until it finds a site to convey the AO constraint. Each floating constraint can be characterized by its range of possible attachment nodes. In general, it would be desirable to delay the attachment until it is proven compatible with the other constraints. In FUF, an explicit annotation called **wait** implements such a delaying mechanism. It is similar to Naish's implementation for Prolog (Naish 1985). In FUF, a **wait** annotation freezes the choice of a branch in a disjunction until values for a given set of paths in the total FD are available.

While backtracking can be minimized by the use of **wait**, it cannot be avoided entirely. When FUF's input contains several mutually dependent floating constraints, they are all delayed in a deadlock situation. To break the deadlock, FUF selects one of the constraints arbitrarily. This non-deterministic choice can lead to backtracking. In this case, a combination of **bk-class** and **wait** is necessary to minimize backtracking. We are currently evaluating the efficiency gains of this combination of control tools over the use of **bk-class** alone.

The **bk-class** mechanism improves FUGs' efficiency while preserving their desirable properties - declarativeness and bidirectional constraint satisfaction. It can be declaratively read as a statement of dependency between a decision in the grammar and a class of constraints in the input. Using **bk-class**, however, is not always easy for the grammar writer since it requires thinking about the control strategy of the unifier - the same drawback as for Prolog's **cut** mechanism. But **bk-class** annotations are optional, and can be added only when needed to optimize a grammar.

4 External and Modularity

Content realization consists of mapping a semantic input structure onto a syntactic tree. In addition to the constraints present in the input, this process is constrained by a heterogeneous set of factors. Such factors are surveyed in (Matthiessen 1991) and (Robin 1990). They include:

- grammar rules
- a conceptual lexicon specifying the mapping between domain concepts and lexical items
- a grammatical dictionary providing the special grammatical properties of lexical items

- a collocation dictionary providing the restrictions on lexical co-occurrences
- a discourse model keeping track of the structure of the text as it is generated
- a domain knowledge base representing the encyclopedic context of generation
- a user-model representing the interpersonal context of generation

These sources vary along several dimensions:

- *Structure*: the grammar rules and the conceptual lexicon express *structural* constraints. They specify a transformation from one regular structure to another. Other sources like the collocation dictionary express inherently non-structural constraints (Halliday 1976, p. 73).
- *Portability*: the grammar rules, the grammatical dictionary (Cumming 1986) and to some extent the collocation dictionary (Smadja 1991a) are domain-independent. The other sources are highly domain-dependent.
- *Dynamism*: the discourse model is inherently dynamic, changing from one sentence to the next. In some applications (Dale 1988), this is also the case for the domain model and the user-model. The other sources are static.

How can these knowledge sources be combined?

One approach would be to integrate all these constraints into a single FUG. In addition to being non-modular and thus hindering portability, this approach is impractical for dynamic constraints: being a monotonic process, unification is inadequate to update dynamic models as generation unfolds.

A modular architecture is therefore preferable. The structural constraint sources - conceptual lexicon and grammar rules - can readily be implemented as a FUG as they are well handled by FUF's top-down regime. During unification, this backbone FUG needs to communicate with the other sources when necessary. What we need is a mechanism allowing constraints that lie outside of both the input FD and the FUG to be taken into account at any point during the unification process.

We introduce the **external** construct to address this need. When FUF encounters a feature of the form (a #(external F)) it performs the following operation:

1. Unification is suspended.
2. The external function F - a LISP function returning a sub-FD - is evaluated.
3. The value returned by F becomes the new value of the attribute a in the total FD.
4. Unification resumes where it was suspended with the updated total FD.

Therefore **External** allows the dynamic expansion of a FUG at unification-time.

To illustrate the use of the **external** construct in FUF, consider again the task of generating the sentence: *"The hapless Denver Nuggets edged the Celtics 101-99."* As explained in Sect. 3, the verb *"to edge"* in this sentence not only realizes the predicate element of the semantic input but also the manner constraint. This floating constraint provides a qualitative evaluation of the basketball game reported by the sentence. Such a qualitative evaluation does not depend only on the final score of the game[7] but on other quantitative factors as well, such as the number of lead

---

[7] In which case it would be redundant with the quantitative expression of the score in the sentence.

changes in the final minutes or the largest lead by either team at any point during the game. Several such quantitative facts about a game are abstracted and conflated with the semantic predicate by verbs like *"to edge"*, *"to hammer"*, *"to outlast"* or *"to rally past"*. Choosing among these verbs requires deciding which combination of quantitative facts is abstracted by the manner connotation of each verb.

In Sect. 3, we assumed that this decision was performed by the content planner building the FUG semantic input as illustrated by the presence of the (concept c-tight) feature in the input of Fig. 2. Performing such a mapping, however, requires knowledge of the existing lexical resources available in a given sublanguage (Kittredge and Lehrberger 1983). The fact that a given combination of quantitative data about a basketball game can be compactly expressed in English by describing the game as *"tight"* is *linguistic knowledge*. It should therefore be located in the lexicon portion of the FUG. Using **external** allows FUF to enforce this separation between linguistic and conceptual knowledge. In this case, the semantic input to the FUG no longer needs to provide a pre-linguistic specification of the manner. It needs only indicate that one of the sentence's communicative goals is to express the manner. Instead of the feature: (**manner** ((**sem-cat quality**) (**concept c-tight**))), the semantic input just contains the feature: (**manner any**). The lexico-grammar is now in charge of choosing a lexical item to appropriately qualify the game. To perform this choice, it must access the description of the game in the encyclopedic knowledge base. Figure 3 shows a fragment of a lexicon where the **external** construct implements an example of such query.

Unification of the semantic input with the **win-lex alt** of this lexicon fragment triggers calls to external functions. Each of these functions queries the knowledge base for quantitative data and returns an FD containing corresponding qualitative features. For example, the function **get-lead-changes** shown in Fig. 3 enriches the total FD with the feature **lead-changes**. These external functions connect the FUG with the knowledge base. Within the body an external function, one can access any feature in the total FD by specifying its path prefixed by @. In Fig. 3, note how this notation is used in the **get-lead-changes** function to retrieve information from the knowledge base about the particular token given in the semantic input.[8]

After the external functions return, the features added to the total FD are used for choosing a verb conveying the manner connotation appropriate to this particular game. For example, the verb *"to edge"* is preferred when a combination of features signals that (1) there was no overtime (2) no team built a big lead and (3) there were many lead changes. As we have identified about 100 different verbs in the basketball sublanguage to express the victory of a team, many features are required to discriminate between them. However, in a given situation, only a few features will actually be needed. Having the content planner systematically retrieve all the knowledge base information necessary to discriminate between all the words of the lexicon would thus be computationally wasteful.

In addition, the set of features required to discriminate between words depends on the part of speech. For example, there are many fewer adverbs available to convey the manner connotation than there are verbs. Fewer features are therefore required

---

[8] Recall that the semantic input is part of the total FD at any point during unification.

An external query function:

```
(defun get-lead-changes ()
  (let ((lead-change-num (get-role-value (get-token @{token})
                                          'lead-change-num)))
    (cond ((> lead-change-num 15) '((lead-changes numerous)))
          ((and (> lead-change-num 5) (> 15 lead-change-num))
           '((lead-changes average)))
          ((> 5 lead-change-num) '((lead-changes few)))))))
```

Backbone lexico-grammar with **external** *constructs:*

```
(...
 ((sem-cat action)
  (concept c-win)
  (alt win-lex (:bk-class (AO manner))
    ((({manner} any)

      ;; Knowledge base query for information discriminating
      ;; among manner-conveying verbs.
      ({manner} ((overtime #(external #'get-overtime))
                 (biggest-lead #(external #'get-biggest-lead))
                 (lead-changes #(external #'get-lead-changes))
                 ...))
      (alt win-and-manner-lex

        (;; The victory was obtained in overtime after many lead changes
         (({manner} ((overtime yes) (lead-changes numerous)))
          (lex "outlast"))

         ;; The victory was close and obtained in regulation
         (({manner} ((overtime no) (biggest-lead small)
                     (lead-changes numerous)))
          (alt (((lex "edge") (lex "nip")))))
         ...)))))))
```

Fig. 3. Accessing an external knowledge source from the lexicon

to select an adverb than to select a verb. Requiring the content planner to provide the features for all classes of lexical choice in advance would therefore impair modularity between linguistic and conceptual knowledge.

To summarize, the **external** construct enhances FUF in the following ways:

- It provides a co-routine control structure to interact with external processes.
- It enforces an information-hiding principle between different knowledge sources.
- It is a way to fetch constraints lying outside the FUG *on demand*, only when needed by FUF to choose between alternatives.

These different points correspond to needs that have been identified in many generation systems. TELEGRAM (Appelt 1985) implemented a mechanism where a FUG and a content planner cooperated to generate referring expressions. The **external** construct is a generalization of this mechanism. With PAULINE, Hovy (1988) advocated interleaving pervasively content realization with content planning. With **external**, FUF can implement such an interleaving while benefiting from the declarative nature of FUGs. While traversing a systemic linguistic network, PENMAN (Mann 1983) accesses its environment by calling functions called *inquiries*. FUF's **external** functions provides a similar facility in the context of FUGs. Finally, DIO-GENES, (Nirenburg and Nirenburg 1988) uses a blackboard to communicate with and control specialized modules working with their own separate knowledge sources. With **external**, a similar cooperation among specialized modules can be implemented in FUF with the total FD playing the role of the blackboard.

5 Conclusion

In this paper, we have addressed the issue of using FUGs to perform content realization as a whole, including lexical choice. When unifying a non-lexicalized semantic input with an integrated lexico-grammar, two new problems occur: (1) dealing with floating constraints and (2) accessing external knowledge sources. We have presented two control tools in FUGs to address these problems: **bk-class** and **external**.

To improve efficiency, **bk-class** implements a form of dependency-directed backtracking, taking advantage of the knowledge of what choice points in a grammar can influence the realization of a floating constraint. Naish (1985, p. 59) lists heuristics to improve efficiency in search, including "detect failure early" and "avoid failure." We have shown in Sect. 3 that there are good linguistic reasons why an early detection of failure for "floating" constraints is very difficult. In such cases, **bk-class** implements the heuristic of avoiding failure.

To achieve modularity in text generators, **external** implements a co-routine mechanism for communication between a FUG and other knowledge sources during unification. This mechanism generalizes approaches introduced in earlier work and addresses a criticism often expressed against FUGs.

Both **bk-class** and **external** augment the general semantic structure driven top-down regime of FUGs. They have been implemented and tested extensively in a wide variety of applications: COMET (McKeown et al 1990), a system that generates explanations in a multimedia setting, COOK (Smadja 1991b) a sentence-generation system that addresses the issue of collocations in stock market reports, ADVISOR (Elhadad 1991b, 1992a), a question-answering system that generates argumentative paragraphs and STREAK (Robin 1992) a system that generates information-packed report leads in the basketball domain.

Acknowledgments Many thanks to Kathy McKeown, David Kurlander, Becky Passoneau and Tony Weida. The research reported in this paper was partially supported by ONR grant N00014-89-J-1782, DARPA grant N00039-84-C-0165 and NSF grants IRT-84-51438 and IRI-90-24069.

References

D. Appelt. *Planning Natural Language Utterances.* Studies in Natural Language Processing. Cambridge University Press, 1985.

S. Cumming. The lexicon in text generation. In *Proceedings of the 1st Workshop on Automating the Lexicon*, Pisa, Italy, 1986.

R. Dale. *Generating referring expressions in a domain of objects and processes.* PhD thesis, University of Edinburgh, Scotland, 1988.

J. de Kleer, J. Doyle, G.L. Steele, and G.J. Sussman. Explicit control of reasoning. In Winston P.J. and R.H. Brown, editors, *Artificial Intelligence: an MIT Perspective*, pages 93–116. MIT Press, 1979.

M. Elhadad. Types in functional unification grammars. In *Proceedings of the 28th Annual Meeting of the Association for Computational Linguistics*, Detroit, MI, 1990. ACL.

M. Elhadad. FUF: The universal unifier - user manual, version 5.0. Technical Report CUCS-038-91, Columbia University, 1991.

M. Elhadad. Generating adjectives to express the speaker's argumentative intent. In *Proceedings of the 9th Annual Conference on Artificial Intelligence.* AAAI, 1991.

M. Elhadad. Generating coherent argumentative paragraphs. Submitted to COLING'92, 1992.

M. Elhadad. *Using argumentation to control lexical choice: A functional unification-based approach.* PhD thesis, Computer Science Department, Columbia University, 1992.

M.A.K. Halliday. *System and function in language.* Oxford University Press, Oxford, 1976.

E. Hovy. *Generating natural language under pragmatic constraints.* L. Erlbaum Associates, Hillsdale, N.J., 1988.

M. Kay. Functional grammar. In *Proceedings of the 5th Annual Meeting of the Berkeley Linguistic Society*, 1979.

R. Kittredge and J. Lehrberger. *Sublanguages: studies of language in restricted semantic domains.* Walter DeGruyter, New York, 1983.

W.C. Mann. An overview of the PENMAN text generation system. Technical Report ISI/RR-83-114, ISI, Marina del Rey, CA, 1983.

W.C. Mann and C.M. Matthiessen. *Nigel: a systemic grammar for text generation.* Technical Report ISI/RR-83-105, USC/ISI, 1983.

C.M. Matthiessen. Lexicogrammatical choice in text generation. In C. Paris, W. Swartout, and W.C. Mann, editors, *Natural Language Generation in Artificial Intelligence and Computational Linguistics.* Kluwer Academic Publishers, 1991.

K. R. McKeown. *Using Discourse Strategies and Focus Constraints to Generate Natural Language Text.* Studies in Natural Language Processing. Cambridge University Press, 1985.

K. R. McKeown, M. Elhadad, Y. Fukumoto, J.G. Lim, C. Lombardi, J. Robin, and F.A. Smadja. Text generation in comet. In R. Dale, C.S. Mellish, and M. Zock, editors, *Current Research in Natural Language Generation.* Academic Press, 1990.

Lee Naish. *Negation and Control in Prolog*, volume 238 of *Lectures Notes in Computer Science.* Springer Verlag, 1985.

S. Nirenburg and I. Nirenbrug. A framework for lexical selection natural language generation. In *Proceedings of the 11th International Conference on Computational Linguistics.* COLING, 1988.

C. L. Paris. *The use of explicit user models in text generation: tailoring to a user's level of expertise.* PhD thesis, Columbia University, 1987. Also available as technical report CUCS-309-87.

J. Robin. Lexical choice in natural language generation. Technical Report CUCS-040-90, Columbia University, 1990.

J. Robin. A revision-based architecture for reporting facts in their historical context. To appear in Horacek H. and M. Zock, editors, *Proceedings of the Third European Workshop on Language Generation*, 1992.

S. Shieber. *An introduction to Unification-Based Approaches to Grammar*, volume 4 of *CSLI Lecture Notes*. University of Chicago Press, Chicago, Il, 1986.

F. Smadja. Microcoding the lexicon with co-occurrence knowledge. In Uri Zernik, editor, *Lexical Acquisition: Using on-line resources to build a lexicon*. Lawrence Erlbaum, 1991.

F. Smadja. *Retrieving Collocational Knowledge from Textual Corpora. An Application: Language Generation*. PhD thesis, Computer Science Department, Columbia University, 1991.

S.M. Shieber, G. Van Noord, R.M. Moore, and Pereira F.C.P. A semantic head-driven generation algorithm for unification-based formalisms. In *Proceedings of the 27th ACL*, pages 7–17, Vancouver, British Columbia, Canada, 1989. ACL.

L. Talmy. Semantic causative types. in M. Shibatani, editor, *The grammar of causative constructions*, volume 6 of *Syntax and semantics*. Academic Press, 1976.

L. Talmy. How language structures space. In Pick, H.L. and L.P. Acredolo, editors, *Spatial orientation: theory, research and application*, Plenum Press, 1983.

L. Talmy. Lexicalization patterns: semantic structure in lexical form. In T. Shopen, editor, *Grammatical categories and the lexicon*, volume 3 of *Language typology and syntactic description*. Cambridge University Press, 1985.

Syntactic Selection in Linguistic Realization: A Comparative Study

Ishizaki Masato

Human Communication Research Centre, University of Edinburgh,
2 Buccleuch Place, Edinburgh EH8 9LW, Scotland, U.K.

Abstract

This paper clarifies the differences between structural and functional grammar theories from the viewpoint of syntactic selection in linguistic realization. Structural theories such as Context Free Grammar and Head-driven Phrase Structure Grammar are based on immediate dominance and linear precedence while functional theories such as Systemic Functional Grammar are based on functions and linear precedence. To bridge the gap between two theories, we need to develop a structural theory which permits any kinds of immediate dominance, or which can specify a particular node to construct a grammatical structure.

1 Introduction

This paper clarifies the differences between structural and functional grammar theories from the viewpoint of syntactic selection in linguistic realization. Context Free Grammar (CFG), Head-driven Phrase Structure Grammar (HPSG) [PS87] [PS91] and Systemic Functional Grammar (SFG) [Ha85] [HM81] will be examined in this paper. CFG is not a grammar for natural language, but a framework for describing the grammar. HPSG and SFG are grammars for natural language. In this paper, HPSG and SFG will be reconsidered as descriptive frameworks. This abstraction enables us to compare HPSG and SFG with CFG.

CFG is characterized by rules and rewriting operations over them. Naive CFG grammars are not used in current generation systems. Still, CFG offers a good starting point for reconsidering the role of grammar in generation. CFG rules simultaneously stipulate immediate dominance and linear precedence. Features are associated with the rules which many generation systems employ. HPSG is a member of the family of the Unification Based Grammars (UBGs), which includes Lexical Functional Grammar [Bj82], Categorial Unification Grammar [Us86] and Unification Categorial Grammar [ZK87]. In this paper HPSG is characterized by a few rules, constraints over feature value structures, and lexical items. This treatment is so general that it can be applied to other UBGs. SFG has always played a central role in generation, but the comparison with other theories seems to be difficult due to its totally different construction. SFG is composed of systemic features, systemic functions and realization rules over the functions. This paper focuses on systemic functions and realization rules which are directly connected to linguistic realization

McKeown and Paris examined Definite Clause Grammar (DCG) and Functional Unification Grammar (FUG) from the aspect of grammatical descriptions for syntactic selection [MP87]. They showed the representational inefficiency of DCG through their examples. Their comparison is understandable, but still insufficient in that they consider little about SFG. Mellish [Me88], Brew [Bc90], and Carpenter and Pollard [CP91] formalized SFG in terms of feature value structures. These studies are suggestive, but they are not appropriate for comparing grammars from the viewpoint of linguistic realization in that they do not consider the realization rules in SFG which play very important roles in linguistic realization. The SFG formalization in this paper is based on Patten's analysis [Pa88]. Still, the treatment of immediate dominance is revised to clarify the role of immediate dominance in SFG.

One of the reasons for difficulties in comparing linguistic realization algorithms lies in differences among input semantic expressions. Since the aim of this paper is to explore the relationship between syntactic selection in generation and syntactic information, we do not have to assume a specific semantic representation scheme. Still, we need to assume that an input semantic expression can be decomposable into smaller pieces of the expression in a certain way. One example of such expressions is a predicate-argument structure based on the first order predicate logic.

The relationships between syntactic and semantic rules must be specified in grammar based linguistic realization. Semantic rules in structural theories such as CFG and HPSG are assumed to be attached to syntactic rules one by one. This type of rule has desirable properties of compositionality and declarativeness. Semantic specification by logical forms appear to be irrelevant to SFG. However, SFG has chooser inquiry semantics which maps from logical forms to systemic features.[1]

Transformational Grammar has revealed much data on sentences with the same meaning [AH75]. Transformation refers to the positions of elements and the introduction of functional elements.[2] For example, *Dative Movement* and *Extraposition* refer to the position of elements. *Passive* and *There Insertion*, on the other hand, refer to both the position of elements and the introduction of functional elements.

Realization strategies such as top-down, bottom-up and semantic-head driven impose restrictions on semantic expressions. A top-down algorithm needs decomposable semantic expressions. Decomposability requires semantic rules to have inverse functions which produce decomposed semantic expressions from an original expression. A bottom-up algorithm uses a set of the decomposed semantic expression which corresponds to lexical information. The bottom-up algorithm needs a semantic decomposition algorithm to a lexical level which dispenses with syntactic information. A semantic-head driven algorithm assumes that semantic expressions have heads or pivot nodes which are the lowest node in the tree such that it and all higher nodes up to the tree have the same semantics [SN90].

---

[1] Inspection sources of inquiry semantics include not only logical forms, but also context and other various factors.

[2] Expressions are classified into substantial elements which contribute to the whole meaning, and functional elements which do not influence the whole meaning [Is90].

This paper examines grammar formalization, licensed structure definition and syntactic selection in CFG, HPSG and SFG.

2 Generation in the Framework of CFG

2.1 Formalization

(a) S → NP VP   (d) NP → they
(b) VP → V NP   (e) NP → poems
(c) VP → Aux V (f) V → composed
                        (g) Aux → were

Fig. 1. Rule Fragments of CFG

CFG is formalized as a quintuple shown in (1): a set of symbols V, a set of non-terminal symbols V_N, a set of terminal symbols V_T, a start symbol s_0 and a set of rules R which is defined over the symbols. Figure 1 shows rule fragments in the CFG framework which can handle active/passive sentences.

$$\langle V, V_N, V_T, s_0, R \rangle \tag{1}$$

Example rules can be encoded in the quintuple: the set of symbols V corresponds to {S, NP, VP, V, Aux, they, poems, composed, were}; the set of nonterminal symbols V_N is {S, NP, VP, PP, V, Aux, V, P}; the set of terminal symbols V_T is {they, poems, composed, were}; the start symbol s_0 is S; and the set of rules R consists of rules (a)–(i) shown in Figure 1.

2.2 Licensed Structures

A CFG licensed structure is defined as a quintuple as shown in (2). It consists of a set of nodes N, a set of labels L, the dominance relation D between mother and daughter nodes, the precedence relation P between sister nodes and the labeling function LaF from a node to a label. Figure 2 shows CFG licensed structure examples based on the rules in Figure 1.

$$\langle N, L, D, P, LaF \rangle \tag{2}$$

The tuple (2) can represent the example tree structure shown in Figure 2. The set of nodes N consists of nodes (1)–(8) shown in Figure 2. The set of labels L is {S, NP, VP, V, Aux}. The dominance relation D is {[(1),[(2),(3)]], [(2),(4)], [(3),[(5),(6)]], [(5),(7)], [(6),(8)]]}. The precedence relation P is {(2)<(3), (4)<(5)}. The labeling function LaF is {⟨(1),S⟩, ⟨(2),NP⟩, ⟨(3),VP⟩, ⟨(4),they⟩, ⟨(5),V⟩, ⟨(6),NP⟩, ⟨(7),composed⟩ ⟨(8),poems⟩}.

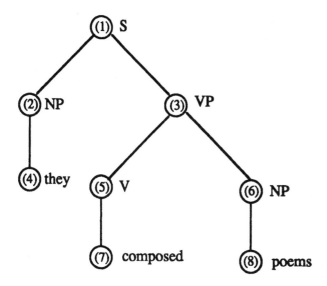

Fig. 2. A Licensed Structure Example in CFG-based Grammar

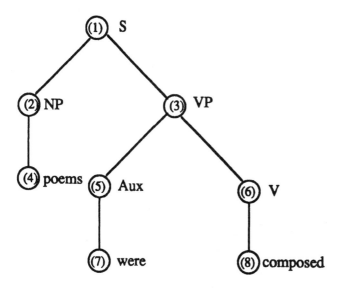

Fig. 3. A Passive Structure in CFG-based Grammar

2.3 Syntactic Selection

Linguistic realization with CFG grammars can be performed through top-down, bottom-up and semantic-head driven strategies. The top-down algorithm starts from the sentence symbol and rewrites it to a lexical level via the rules. In Figure 3, generation proceeds from node (1) to nodes (4), (7) and (8). As shown in the tuple (1), CFG-based rules stipulate both immediate dominance and linear precedence simultaneously. Thus, if functional elements constrain only one of them, some rule needs to be selected to allow generation to proceed at each choice point. This decision which depends on insufficient information might be incorrect. If it is found to be incorrect, backtracking and reselection of other rules is needed. In a passive construction as shown in Figure 3, even if the order between agent and patient is specified in a given semantic expression, the generation process suffers from two problems: one is that words to be dominated remain unknown until a verb is determined; and the other is that the order between agent and patient cannot be directly represented in CFG. Figure 4 shows some examples of how three elements are ordered in dominance structures. Since the dominance relations which CFG rules represent are local, the generation process cannot know correct structures in advance. We call this problem possible realizations of linear precedence. The top-down algorithm is efficient in that it does not produce other than sentences. However, it has the problem of left recursion which makes generation process infinite.[3]

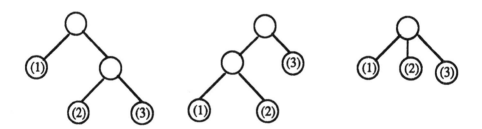

Fig. 4. Possible Realizations of Linear Precedence

The bottom-up algorithm starts from words derived from a semantic expression and organizes them into a sentence. In Figure 3, generation proceeds from nodes (4),(7) and (8) to node (1). In bottom-up generation, since semantically vacuous elements cannot be derived from a semantic expression, the algorithm must handle the problem of when the vacuous elements are introduced into the process. Since the dominance is local, the algorithm has the possible realizations of linear precedence even if all elements are ordered in a semantic expression. It can avoid the left

---

[3] In parsing, the left recursion problem can be avoided by using a book keeping mechanism like a Chart. In generation, on the other hand, it seems to be difficult to use a book keeping mechanism because the book keeping unit is not fixed.

recursion problem, but can produce other than sentences. Since the semantic-head driven generation is bottom-up by nature, it does not suffer from the left recursion problem. It also solves the semantically vacuous element and aimless production problems. Still, in realization, it suffers from the possible realizations of linear precedence.

3 Linguistic Realization based on HPSG

3.1 Formalization

Rules :
(a) M[SUBCAT $\langle\,\rangle$] $\rightarrow$ C, H[LEX $-$]
(b) M[SUBCAT $\langle[\,]\rangle$] $\rightarrow$ H[LEX $+$], C*
Constraints :
(c) M[HEAD [1]] $\Rightarrow$ H[HEAD [1]]
(d) M[SUBCAT [2]] $\Rightarrow$ H[SUBCAT $\langle$[1],[2]$\rangle$],C[SUBCAT [1]]
(e) [LEX $+$] $<$ [ ]
(f) complement $<<$ complement
(g) [PHON [1], PAST–PART [2], SUBCAT $\langle$[3],[4]$\rangle$] $\mapsto$
    [PHON fpsp([1],[2]), SUBCAT $\langle$(PP[BY [4]]),[3]$\rangle$]
Lexicon :
(h) [PHON burns; MAJ N; SUBCAT $\langle\,\rangle$; LEX $+$]
(i) [PHON poems; MAJ N; SUBCAT $\langle\,\rangle$; LEX $+$]
(j) [PHON composed; MAJ V; SUBCAT $\langle$NP,NP$\rangle$; LEX $+$]
(k) [PHON were; MAJ V; SUBCAT $\langle$VP[PAS]$\rangle$; LEX $+$]

Fig. 5. A Part of HPSG Specification

HPSG is stipulated as a tuple shown in (3). It consists of a set of features F, a set of values V, a set of feature value structures FVS, start feature value structures FVS_0, a set of rules R, and a set of constraints which consist of principles P , linear precedence LP and lexical rules LR, and a set of lexical items LI . The principles P specify the relations among feature value structures. The linear precedence LP constrains the order of constituents. The lexical rules are functions from feature value structures to feature value structures of lexical items. The lexicon contains lexical items which are represented by feature value structures.

Figure 5 shows an example of a HPSG specification.[4]

$$\langle F, V, FVS, FVS_0, R, P, LP, LR, LI\rangle \tag{3}$$

---

[4] Since the aim of this paper is not an introduction to HPSG, we provide an informal explanation to aid understanding of the examples of generation processes based on HPSG. *SUBCAT, LEX, HEAD, MAJ, PHON* and *PAST–PART* represent feature names: *SUBCAT* indicates subcategorization; *LEX* is lexicality; *HEAD* is a collection of features which include *MAJ, CASE* and so on; *MAJ* is a part of speech; *PHON* is a phonological form; and *PAST–PART* is a past particle form. Bracket notation embraces feature value structures, in which feature-value pairs are delimited by semicolon. Numbers in

The rules specify only immediate dominance. They say that a mother node can immediately dominate one head and one complement nodes, or one head and any number of complement nodes. Conditions on rule (a) are that a mother node has no subcategorization and a head node is not a lexical item. Conditions on rule (b) are that a mother node has one subcategorization and a head node is a lexical item. Principle (c) states that the head feature value structures of a mother node are equivalent to those of a head daughter node. Principle (d) says that the subcategorization list of a mother node is composed of that of a complement daughter and a head node. Linear precedence (e) requires lexical items to come before other items. Linear precedence (f) restricts complements to be ordered by their obliqueness which roughly corresponds to the place in the subcategorization list. Lexical rule (g) is the rule for passivization: phonological forms are determined by the function *fpsp* from a base form to a past particle form; subcategorization order is reversed and one element in subcategorization becomes an optional prepositional phrase with a preposition *by*. Lexical item (h) and (i) specify nouns whose phonological form *they* and *poems* respectively. Lexical item (j) and (k) say that verb *composed* and *were* have subcategorization lists $\langle NP,NP \rangle$ and $\langle VP[PAS] \rangle$ the latter of which has the passive feature.

An example specification is encoded in the tuple as follows. The set of features F is {PHON, MAJ, VFORM, SUBCAT, LEX, PAST–PART}. The set of values V is $\{V, N, +, -, \langle \rangle, \langle NP \rangle, \langle NP,NP \rangle, \langle VP[PAS] \rangle,$ they, poems, composed, were$\}$, and variables which can represent values and feature value structures. The set of feature value structures FVS is $\{\langle LEX,+ \rangle, \langle LEX,- \rangle, \langle LEX,x \rangle, \langle MAJ,V \rangle, \langle MAJ,N \rangle, \langle MAJ,x \rangle,$ $\langle SUBCAT,\langle NP \rangle \rangle, \langle SUBCAT,\langle NP,NP \rangle \rangle, \langle SUBCAT,\langle VP[PAS] \rangle \rangle, \langle SUBCAT,x \rangle, \cdots \}$, where x represents a distinct variable. The start feature value structures FVS_0 are $\{\langle MAJ,V \rangle, \langle SUBCAT,\langle \rangle \rangle \}$. The set of rules R is $\{M \rightarrow C,H, M \rightarrow H,C^* \}$. The set of principles P, linear precedence LP and lexical rules LR is as elements those constraints shown in Figure 5 as (c)–(g).

3.2 Licensed Structures

A HPSG licensed structure is defined as a tuple shown in (4). It consists of a set of nodes N, a set of feature value structures FVS, the dominance relation D between mother and daughter nodes, the precedence relation P between sister nodes and the labeling function LaF from a node to feature value structures. Figure 6 shows HPSG licensed structure examples based on the rules in Figure 5.

$$\langle N, F, V, D, P, LaF \rangle \tag{4}$$

brackets are used to indicate for equality of feature value structures. M, C and H before brackets represent mother, complement and head nodes, respectively. Brackets without node names in constraints mean that they can be applied irrespective of the kind of node. Angle brackets list subcategorization elements. Various arrows represent different kinds of relations: usual arrows shows immediate dominance; double arrows are relations among features value structures; and functional arrows are functions between feature value structures. A '<' represents linear precedence. A '<<' restricts linear precedence with obliqueness which roughly corresponds to the order of subcategorization list. For more detail about HPSG, please refer to [PS87] [PS91] .

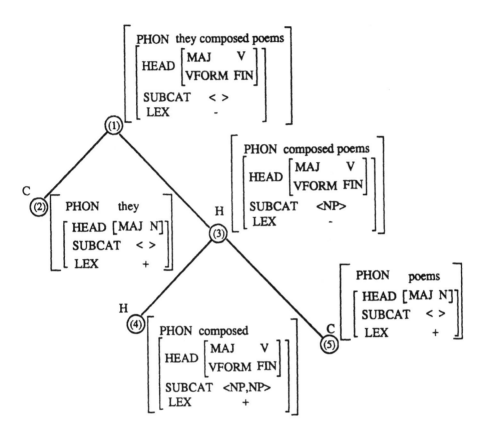

Fig. 6. A HPSG Licensed Structure Example

The tuple (4) represents an example tree structure shown in Figure 6. The set of nodes N consists of nodes (1)–(5) shown in Figure 6. The set of features F is {PHON, MAJ, VFORM, SUBCAT, LEX}. The set of values V is {V, N, +, −, ⟨ ⟩, ⟨NP⟩, ⟨NP,NP⟩, they, poems, composed}, The dominance relation D is {[(1),[(2),(3)]], [(3),[(5),(6)]]}. The precedence relation P is {(2)<(3), (4)<(5)}. The labeling function is {⟨(1),FVS1⟩, ⟨(2),FVS2⟩, ⋯}, where FVS1 is ⟨⟨PHON,*they composed poems*⟩, ⟨MAJ,V⟩, ⟨VFORM,FIN⟩, ⟨SUBCAT,⟨ ⟩⟩, ⟨LEX,−⟩⟩ and FVS2 is ⟨⟨PHON,*they*⟩, ⟨MAJ,N⟩, ⟨SUBCAT,⟨ ⟩⟩, ⟨LEX,+⟩⟩.

3.3 Generation with HPSG

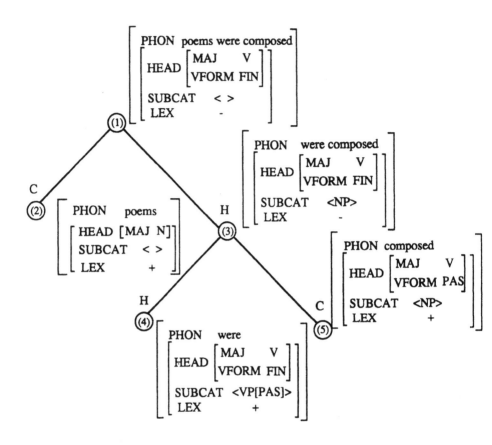

Fig. 7. A Passive Structure in HPSG

Since top-down, bottom-up and semantic-head driven strategies are closely related to the characteristics of semantic expressions, linguistic realization with HPSG can distinguish three strategies depending on whether semantic expressions have properties of decomposability, total decomposability to a lexical level and headness. Top-down HPSG generation is stipulated as the process of going from feature value structures which represent a sentence to ones which represent words. Bottom-up generation is stipulated as reverse processes to the top-down. As shown in (3), HPSG rules stipulate immediate dominance and linear precedence separately. Hence, even if functional elements constrain only one of them, generation can proceed without making any assumptions about dominance and precedence at each choice point. However, since the dominance relation is local, the possible realization problem still exists.

Since every feature is not orthogonal to each other, the relation between features must be restricted to avoid feature overspecification which causes the contradiction between feature value structures. Overspecification is handled by *feature Co-occurrence restrictions* in Generalized Phrase Structure Grammar (GPSG) [GK85], the antecedent of HPSG. HPSG exploits lattice structures to cope with overspecification which has the same effects as the *feature co-occurrence restrictions*. Some features, on the other hand, are not fully specified, which is called underspecification. Underspecification is handled by *feature specification defaults* in GPSG. The problem of handling defaults in the generation process is that if some features depend on the feature whose value is specified by default, backtracking and resetting of the default value to a correct one are necessary when default values are found to be incorrect during generation.

4 Linguistic Realization based on SFG

4.1 Formalization

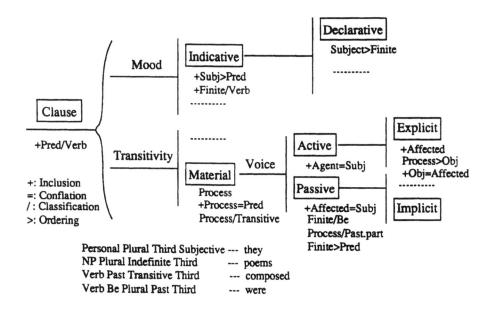

Fig. 8. A Part of SFG Network

SFG contains systems composed of systemic features, systemic functions and realization rules over the systemic functions. Realization rules make statements about *inclusion* which introduces functions, *conflation* which unifies one function with another function, *classification* which assigns grammatical features to functions, *ordering* which stipulates the order of functions and *agreement* which states that two distinct functions must agree. SFG is formalized as a tuple shown in 5. It consists of a set of systemic features Fe, a set of systemic functions Fu, realization rules RR which are defined over systemic functions, a set of relations RS among systemic features, a set of functions Frf from systemic features to realization rules, and a set of lexical items LI,

$$\langle Fe, Fu, RR, RS, Frf, LI \rangle \qquad (5)$$

Figure 8 represents a part of SFG network partly extracted from [Wi83].[5] The systemic feature *Clause* has systemic function *Pred* which is classified as the function Verb. *Clause* consists of *Mood* and *Transitivity* systems. The systems *Mood* and *Transitivity* consist of the systemic features *Indicative* and *Material*, respectively. The example network of SFG is encoded into the tuple (5). The set of systemic features Fe is {Clause, Mood, Indicative, Transitivity, Material, Declarative, Active, Passive, Explicit}. The set of functions Fu is {Pred, Subj, Obj, Finite, Process, Agent, Affected, ···}. The set of realization rules RR is {+Pred/Verb, +Subj>Pred, +Finite/Verb, ···}.[6] The set of relations RS among systemic features is {(Clause≡(Mood∧Transitivity), ···}. The set of functions Frf from realization rules to a systemic function is {⟨Clause,[+Pred/Verb]⟩, ···}. The set of lexical items LI is {they, poems, composed, were}.

4.2 Licensed Structures

A SFG licensed structure is defined as a quintuple as shown in (6). It consists of a set of nodes N, a set of systemic functions SF, the precedence relation P between sister nodes, the labeling function LaF from a node to systemic functions, and the lexical mapping function LL from a node to a phrase which is mapped using another systems, or to a lexical item. The dominance relation of SFG is a little different from that of CFG or HPSG. SFG exploits *minimal bracketing* which forces tree structures to be shallow not to contradict functional specification. The lexical mapping function plays a role in making functional analysis consistent. In Figure 9, realization rules operates functions on one level, which is *Group* level. Figure 9 shows a SFG licensed structure example based on the rules in Figure 8.

$$\langle N, SF, P, LaF, LL \rangle \qquad (6)$$

---

[5] The boxes show systemic features. The expressions under the boxes are realization rules. The curly bracket notation indicates a conjunction of systemic features. The vertical bar notation represents a disjunction of systemic features. For more detail about SFG, please refer to [Ha85] [HM81] [Pa88][Wi83].

[6] One caveat about SFG notation is that a '>' in SFG is meant to be converse precedence to one in HPSG.

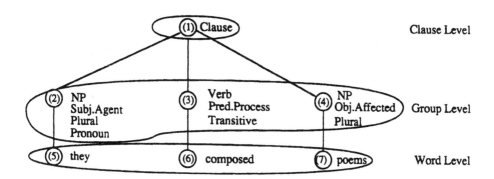

Fig. 9. A SFG Licensed Structure Example

The tuple (6) represents the example tree structure shown in Figure 9. The set of nodes N consists of nodes (1)–(7) shown in Figure 9. The set of systemic functions SF is {Subj.Agent, NP, Plural, Pronoun, Pred.Process, Verb, Transitive, Finite, $\cdots$}. The precedence relation P is {(2)>(3), (3)>(4)}. The labeling function LaF is {⟨(1),Clause⟩, ⟨(2),[Subj.Agent,Plural,Pronoun]⟩, $\cdots$}. The lexical mapping function LL is {⟨*they*,[Personal,Plural,Third,Subjective]⟩, $\cdots$}.

SFG generation is performed through the execution of realization operations along systemic features. In Figure 10, generation proceeds from (a) to (k) along the systems shown in Figure 8. For example, when the systemic feature *Clause* is selected, the function *Pred* is introduced and is restricted to the function *Verb*. Then, when the systemic feature *Indicative* is selected, the function *Subj* is introduced and is ordered before the function *Pred*, and the function *Finite* is introduced and is restricted to the function *Verb*.

Since SFG treatment of semantic expressions and licensed structures are very different from others, top-down, bottom-up and semantic-head driven strategies are hard to distinguish. Bottom-up generation is similar to SFG generation in that they distinguish word selection from sentence construction. However, they differ because SFG word selection systematically embraces semantically vacuous elements. While structural theories such as CFG and HPSG need to consider immediate dominance and linear precedence, functional theories such as SFG need not to consider immediate dominance as shown in (6). Hence, SFG does not suffer from the insufficient information problem and the possible realization problem.

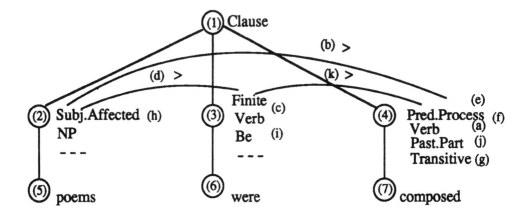

Fig. 10. A Passive Structure in SFG

5 Conclusion

The differences between structural and functional grammar theories are mainly caused by immediate dominance. CFG rules specify immediate dominance and linear precedence simultaneously. HPSG rules represent them separately. SFG, on the other hand, uses functions and linear precedence to stipulate grammatical sentences.

Bateman and Momma [BM91] implemented SFG in Typed Feature System espoused by Emele and Zajac [EZ90]. As discussed in section 2, 3 and 4, SFG is less restricted in the sense that it mainly uses linear precedence. Hence, if semantic treatment problems are sorted out, it is easy to predict that the conversion of SFG is possible. However, incorporating structural theories into SFG is certain to be difficult because immediate dominance hinders functional specification of SFG. To bridge the gap between two theories, we need to develop a structural theory which permits any kinds of immediate dominance, or which can specify a node to construct a grammatical structure:

Acknowledgments

The author wishes to extend his sincere gratitude to Dr. Akira Ishikawa, Dr. Robert Dale of the Centre for Cognitive Science and Dr. Chris Mellish of the Department of Artificial Intelligence at the University of Edinburgh for their helpful suggestions on the draft of this paper. He thanks anonymous referees for their useful comments to improve his paper. He also thanks the members of the Human Communication Research Centre and the Centre for Cognitive Science at the University of Edinburgh for their encouragement.

References

[AH75] Adrian Akmajian and Frank Heny.: *An Introduction to the Principles of Transformational Syntax*. Cambridge:The MIT Press. (1975)

[BM91] John A. Bateman and Stefan Momma.: The nondirectional representation of Systemic Functional Grammars and Semantics as Typed Feature Structures. ms. (1991)

[Bj82] Joan Bresnan (Ed.).: *The Mental Representation of Grammatical Relations*. Cambridge: MIT Press (1982)

[Bc90] Chris Brew.: Partial Descriptions and Systemic Grammar. In *Proceedings of the 13th International Conference on Computational Linguistics* (1990) 36–41

[CP91] Bob Carpenter and Carl Pollard.: Inclusion, Disjointness and Choice: The Logic of Linguistic Classification. In *Proceeding of the 29th Annual Meeting of the Association for Computational Linguistics* (1991) 9-16

[EZ90] Martin Emele and Remi Zajac.: Typed Unification Grammar. In *Proceedings of the 13th International Conference on Computational Linguistics* (1990) 293–298

[GK85] G.Gazdar, E.Klein, G.Pullum and I.Sag.: *Generalized Phrase Structure Grammar*. Cambridge:Harvard University Press (1985)

[Ha85] M.A.K.Halliday.: *An Introduction to Functional Grammar*. London:Edward Arnold (1985)

[HM81] M.A.K.Halliday and J.R.Martin. (Eds.).: *Readings in Systemic Linguistics*. London:Batsford Academic and Educational Ltd. (1981)

[Is90] Masato Ishizaki.: A Bottom-up Generation for Principle-based Grammars Using Constraint Propagation. In *Proceedings of the 13th International Conference on Computational Linguistics* (1990) 188–193

[MP87] Katheleen R. McKeown and Cecile L. Paris.: Functional Unification Revisited. In *Proceedings of the 25th Annual Meeting of the Association for Computational Linguistics* (1987) 97–103

[Me88] Chris S. Mellish.: Implementing Systemic Classification By Unification. In *Computational Linguistics* 14(1) (1988) 40–51. (1991) 11–17

[Pa88] Terry Patten.: *Systemic Text Generation as Problem Solving*. Cambridge: Cambridge University Press (1988)

[PS87] Carl Pollard and Ivan A. Sag.: *Information-Based Syntax and Semantics Volume 1*. Number 13 of CSLI Lecture Notes (1987)

[PS91] Carl Pollard and Ivan A. Sag.: *Information-Based Syntax and Semantics Volume 2*. ms. (1991)

[SN90] Stuart Shieber, Gertjan van Noord, Fernando C.N. Pereira and Robert C. Moore. Semantic-Head-Driven Generation. In *Computational Linguistics* 16(1) (1990) 30–42

[Us86] H. Uszkoreit. Categorial Unification Grammar. In *Proceedings of the 11th International Conference on Computational Linguistics* (1986) 187–194

[ZK87] H.Zeevat, E.Klein and J.Calder.: Unification Categorial Grammar. In Haddock, Klein and Morrill (Eds.).: *Categorial Grammar, Unification Grammar and Parsing*. (1987) 195-222

[Wi83] Terry Winograd. *Language as A Cognitive Process*. London:Addison-Wesley Publishing Company (1983)

A Constraint Logic Programming Treatment of Syntactic Choice in Natural Language Generation

Patrick Saint-Dizier

IRIT Université Paul Sabatier
118 route de Narbonne
31062 Toulouse (Cedex)
France
email: STDIZIER@IRIT.IRIT.FR

Abstract

In this document, we show how a constrained-based approach to lexical choice can overcome the problem of choosing lexical structures a priori and having to revise these judgements when more information is available. We focus on the treatment of linear precedence and on the determination of syntactic rules using a constraint logic programming approach.

1 Introduction

Syntactic choice is a crucial problem in natural language processing and in particular in natural language generation, where it has rarely been addressed in depth. By syntactic choice we mean being at a certain point in the generation procedure and choosing a syntactic rule in a grammar that could contribute to producing a certain well-formed surface form from the input internal representation of an utterance. Independently of the generation strategy (bottom-up or top-down), a certain syntactic choice can be confirmed or rejected at subsequent stages depending on the new information available. This new information has mainly three origins: the input internal representation which has been further analyzed and processed, the data associated to the words used in the generated surface sentence and constraints from the grammar. Real natural language processing systems usually involve quite large syntactic systems which exhibit a high degree of non-determinism. As a result, syntactic choice is a complex task, which entails a lot of revisions, and thus a lot of backtracking.

Furthermore, usual syntactic choice systems offer little flexibility: it is indeed difficult to incorporate into such systems external parameters coming from, for example, the discursive level which could impose a certain construction, and the user level which could impose structural preferences.

The problem of syntactic choice can be more or less fully solved by different approaches. The first one is to rewrite the grammar so as to make it as deterministic as possible. This approach has however severe limitations. First the degree of generality of most current syntactic systems (e.g. X-bar, GPSGs (Gazdar et al 1986), HPSGs (Pollard and Sag 1987) makes such a transformation extremely complex and entails the introduction of a large number of linguistically unmotivated symbols. Second, the presence of new grammar symbols increases the complexity of the natural language generation system and makes it more difficult to maintain. Finally, flexibility of the system is seriously altered.

A second type of approach, much more promising, is to modify or adapt the generation strategy. Both top-down and bottom-up approaches have proven to be of much interest. They should be preserved in their main, general principles. It is more appropriate to improve deeper aspects of the strategy. Intelligent backtracking, where backtracking points can be specified in the grammar, permits to avoid computing several times the same structure and exploring choices which would necessarily lead to a failure. This approach is very recent and has not yet been explored at all, as far as we know, for language processing. Another possibility is the use of lazy evaluation techniques. This technique is clearly of much interest to us, it needs however to be embedded into a larger formal and practical framework which would appropriately handle it. Constraint Logic Programming (hereafter noted as CLP) seems to us to be such an appropriate framework.

This document shows that CLP techniques are very well adapted to handling the problem of syntactic choice. Our approach can also be used to solve other problems involving multiple choices such as lexicalization or text planning. The next section presents the basic foundations of CLP and its main motivations for natural language processing in general. Section 3 addresses the problem of constituent precedence in natural language generation, treated as a CLP constraint, which constitutes the first step of syntactic choice. Section 4 presents a constraint propagation and resolution technique which manages syntactic rules. Instead of using the classical generate and test schema, this technique proceeds by reducing the search space of syntactic choices a priori. The final choices are made only when all necessary information is available.

2 An introduction to Constraint Logic Programming

Constraint Logic Programming is a new area of Logic Programming. Its main aim is to replace some of the Prolog general procedures on some domains by more specialized and refined treatments. This is the case for example for the treatment of rational numbers and booleans, which are treated in CLP as in ordinary languages, allowing e.g. the expression of partially instantiated equations. Basically, CLP consists in identifying a domain (rationals, a finite domain of semantic values, etc.), in defining an operator (e.g. precedence, logical operators) and its porperties and from these properties in defining a resolution method that will properly handle the constraints expressed by the operator on that domain.

We first introduce the abstract CLP machine (derived from Prolog III (Colmerauer 1990)). This abstract machine can be defined at a certain level i of the resolving process:

(1) { W, t0 t1 t2 ... tn, S }

where:

- W is a list of variables occuring in the original query (each variable is typed),

- t0 t1 t2 ... tn is a list of terms (current goal), and

- S is the current set of (satisfiable) constraints.

Then, a CLP rule is selected in the current programme, according to a certain selection procedure:

(2) s0 :- s1, s2, ..., sm, {R}.

The result is the following new resolvant (if we apply Prolog's computation rule):

(3) { W, s1 s2 ... sm t1 t2 ... tn, $S \cup R \cup (s0 = t0)$ }

if $S \cup R \cup (s0 = t0)$ is satisfiable, notice that simplifications may also occur on this set of constraints. Notice that the notion of most general unifier is replaced by a more general operation: equality (s0 = t0), which can be defined in different ways, depending in particular on the domain of the variables (e.g. equality on boolean structures).

The CLP approach has several advantages over more 'standard' approaches (like using Prolog), it indeed permits to:

- improve efficiency of the current system, whereas Prolog uses constraints (encoded by terms) according to the "generate and test" schema, CLP systems use them to reduce the search space *a priori*, i.e. before generation of any values.
- improve expressivity since active constraints have a different, more general semantics. CLP introduces new computation domains (i.e. boolean domain, arithmetic domain, finite domains ...) besides of the usual Herbrand one. We thus can directly describe more naturally the objects and their properties in the discourse domain. We do not have to encode them as Prolog terms or predicates. Resolution encodes the properties of the domain with respect to the operator considered and some other basic operations, like simplifications.
- improve genericity and reusability of the tools developed for language processing so that they can be used for different subareas and purposes.
  The major aspects of active constraints of the constraint logic programming framework (Jaffar and Lassez 1987, Dincbas et al 1988, Colmerauer 1990, Van Hentenrick 1989, Macworth 1987) are the following:
- their coherence is checked at each step of the proof construction,
- they are maintained active throughout the whole proof construction process until they can be adequately resolved,
- they introduce a greater modularity since each constraint system is dealt with independently,
- the result of a query is a set of constraints on variables from which it is straightforward to define domains of values for variables, furthermore, constraints cannot only be viewed as coming down to defining domains for variables, they also express complex relations between variables.
- they are fully declarative,
- and thus, they are a priori fully independent of the way they are used (e.g. for parsing or generating sentences, with a bottom-up or a top-down strategy).

3 Generating sentences with an active precedence constraint

The linear precedence constraint has extensively been studied in the computational linguistics literature. The degree of generality and of linguistic adequacy it confers to syntactic systems has proven to be very useful. From our point of view, linear precedence is specified at two levels:

- at the syntactic level, to account for general syntactic organization principles,
- at the lexical level, to capture, at subcategorization level, the distributional properties of each lexical item.

A well-formed sentence has to meet the requirements of these two levels.

The CLP approach to linear precedence offers two major advantages. First, it avoids making precedence choices which could reveal later to be incorrect, and would then provoque backtracking. Useless computations can then be avoided. Second, it can handle several mutually exclusive precedence choices in parallel, without having the practical limitations of a breadth-first search strategy. Each precedence choice is characterized by a set of precedence constraints. Thus the CLP system handles a set of sets of precedence constraints, each set corresponding to a well-formed sentence with respect to the grammar and to the internal representation from which the sentence is generated. If a set of precedence constraints does not define a complete order, then several sentences may be produced. This set of sets is managed dynamically, i.e., at each step of the generation process, incoherent sets are discarded. This process is fully monotonic and independent of the generation strategy (bottom-up or top-down).

The linear precedence constraint is uniformly represented by a predicate of the form:

p(A,B)

where A and B denote terminal or non-terminal symbols of the syntactic system. Its associated resolution mechanism being quite technical, it is included in this document as an appendix. We will mainly show here its general behaviour and illustrate it.

Let us now examine the main features of the precedence constraint resolution mechanism. Each time a new step in the sentence processing is performed, constraints are added to the current set of active constraints and their consistency is checked. At the beginning σ_0 of the generation process, the set of active constraints is empty. The general process can then be summarized as follows:

step σ_i: satisfiable set (or sets) of active precedence constraints { S }

selection of a rule describing a phrase structure of the form: T :- R

    where R is a set (possibly empty) of active precedence constraints.

step σ_{i+1}: set of active precedence constraints = combination of S, R and R'. This combination operation is detailed in the appendix.

We now define R' more in detail. One of the major motivations of R' is that the generation of sentences will be done on the basis of precedence constraints on terminal elements. This is the reason why each time a phrase structure construction A $\rightarrow$ B, C is used, the constraints on A must also be applied to B and C by transitivity, whenever appropriate, or the reverse if the system proceeds bottom-up. To derive these new constraints, we now introduce the notion of left and right corner of a derivation and then give a formal specification of the new precedence constraints which apply to these two corners. This fully defines R'.

When a phrase structure construction rule does not have a complete order on its right-hand side symbols, then left and right corners are not unique. R' is then a disjunction of sets of constraints, each element of the disjunction correreponding to a choice of left and right corner. When such a element is not coherent with $S \cup R$, then it is eliminated.

To illustrate this constraint resolution mechanism, let us consider a simple natural language grammar, slightly modified for the sake of clarity and conciseness, precedence constraints are specified by the predicate defined above:

s → np(subj), vp. (no precedence constraint)

np(C) → det(C), n(C) , { p(det,n) }.

vp → v, np(obj).

suppose now we want to generate a sentence from a certain internal representation, starting from the symbol s. Here are summarized the different steps of the generation process:

1. rule: s → np(subj), vp. precedence: 2 sets corresponding to the 2 possible cases: [[p(np(subj),vp)], [p(vp,np(subj))]]]

2. rule: np(subj) → det(subj), n(subj). associated sets of constraints: [[p(det(subj),n(subj)),p(n(subj),vp),p(np(subj),vp)],

[p(det(subj),n(subj)),p(vp,det(subj)),p(vp,np(subj))]]]

This new set reflects the adjunction of the constraint p(det,n) and the treatment of the transitivity of the det and the n with respect to the vp which either precedes of follows the subject np.

3. rule: vp → v, np(obj). New associated sets of constraints:

New sets of constraints:

[[p(v,np(obj)),p(n(subj),v),p(np(subj),v),p(det(subj),n(obj)),p(n(subj),vp),

p(np(subj),vp)],

[p(v,np(obj)),p(np(obj),det(subj)),p(np(obj),np(subj)), p(det(subj),n(subj)),

p(vp,det(subj)),p(vp,np(subj))],

[p(np(obj),v),p(n(subj),np(obj)),p(np(subj),np(obj)), p(det(subj),n(obj)),

p(n(subj),vp),p(np(subj),vp)],

[p(np(obj),v),p(v,det(subj)),p(v,np(subj)),p(det(subj), n(subj)),

p(vp,det(subj),p(vp,np(subj))]]]

etc.

On these sets of constraints lexical precedence coherence controls are applied as soon as lexical items having precedence constraints are reached. Suppose that for example a certain verb imposes its object np to follow it, then all the sets with: p(np(obj), v) become incoherent and are discarded. When all constraints have been taken into account, then the surface sentence(s) can be directly generated from the sets of precedence constraints.

The risk of combinatory explosion with this approach for languages exhibiting a high degree of free phrase order can be limited by considering that in most laguages free order is limited within a certain domain, for example within bounding nodes. As a consequence, the resulting sets of precedence constraints remain relatively small. On the other hand, this approach offers a great flexibility in producing all the possible word orderings, in a way which is more efficient than if they had been computed via backtracking.

4 A dynamic treatment of syntactic rules

The dynamic treatment of syntactic rules we propose here has some similitudes in its principles with the treatment of precedence. The basic idea is that when starting generating a sentence (either in a top-down or a bottom-up fashion), we only have partial information, in terms of e.g. morphological and subcategorization information about the words that will appear in the generated surface sentence. Then, when processing each sub-component of the input internal representation, the information becomes more and more precise, thus the surface structure of parts of the sentence become more precise. At the end of the process, the structure of the surface sentence is fully determined. It may then originate several possible surface realizations.

This process is very general. We think it has a certain psychological reality. It can be applied to many different approaches including the generation from RST structures and DRT representations, etcI It is not restricted to the treatment of isolated sentences and can be as well applied at both lexicalization level (a micro-level) (MacDonald, 1991), (Viegas 1992) and discourse level (a macro-level) (e.g. Paris et al. 1991). In this section, we first introduce the notion of hierarchy of syntactic and semantic types, then we present the input semantic representation and how it is treated. Finally, we present the constraint propagation mechanism which handles multiple choices.

4.1 Introducing syntactic and semantic types

Let us first consider our typology of syntactic types. There are several ways to define it, in particular, it can be more or less ad'hoc and more or less closely related to the form of the internal representation. We think, in order to guarantee generality of the process, ease of maintainance and re-usability, that it must have a quite high degree of generality. We have defined hierarchies of types for each class of syntactic object: s, np, vp, pp, preposition, etc.

From almost any type of grammar, it is possible to define abstract types representing syntactic and semantic information at various levels of generality. Each type represents, for example in terms of trees, the set of subtrees of depth one which root is identical. For example, consider the following simple grammar G:

$$1: s \rightarrow np, vp.$$
$$2: s \rightarrow inf, vp.$$
$$3: s \rightarrow comp, vp.$$
$$4: vp \rightarrow v.$$
$$5: vp \rightarrow v, np.$$
$$6: vp \rightarrow v, np, pp.$$
$$7: vp \rightarrow v, pp.$$
$$8: vp \rightarrow v, inf.$$
$$9: np \rightarrow det, n.$$
$$10: np \rightarrow poss, n.$$

The type s has in its denotation the rules 1, 2 and 3:

$$[| \, s \, |]_G = \{(s \rightarrow np, vp), (s \rightarrow inf, vp), (s \rightarrow comp, vp)\}.$$

The elements in the right-hand part of these rules are themselves types (np, vp, inf and comp). The type vp is characterized by its denotation, namely rules 4 to 8. Each of these types can be represented by a minimal type structure representing here subcategorization information (or consistuency information). For the type s, we have the following type structure (written Login (Aït-Kaçi and Nasr 1986)):

s = {xp(cat ⇒ [s],
        const1 ⇒ xp(cat ⇒ [np, inf, comp]),
        const2 ⇒ xp(cat ⇒ [vp])) }.

Under const1, we have a type of level xp (phrasal level) which can be either an np, an inf or a comp.

In case of incompatible right-hand sides, the type is represented by a set of type constructors. For example, for the type np, we have the following set of type constructors:

np = { xp(cat ⇒ [np], const1 ⇒ x0(cat ⇒ [det, poss]),
              const2 ⇒ x0(cat ⇒ [n])),
       xp(cat ⇒ [np], const1 ⇒ x0(cat ⇒ [n], type ⇒ proper_noun)) }.

x0 denotes a terminal type (see Saint-Dizier 1991a). To be more comprehensive, here is the type hierarchy for the French verb phrases:

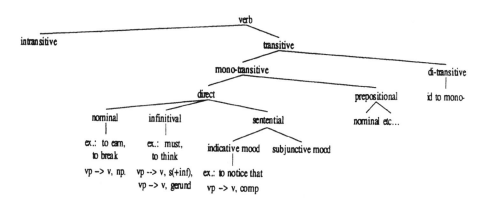

Fig. 1.

Each node in this tree is a type, to leaves are associated sets of syntactic rules defining the denotation of these types. The type vp is polymorphic since it has several incompatible subcategorization frames.

Similarly, semantic types for prepositions can be defined. Combined with the noun phrase they subcategorize for, they contribute to the determination of the most appropriate preposition(s) for prepositional phrases when they are combined with the semantic features of the np they introduce. Here is a part of the tree of semantic types for prepositions:

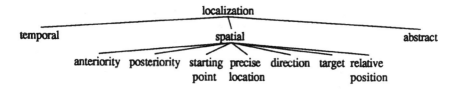

Fig. 2.

To each leaf of that tree corresponds one or more preposition(s). For example, to the leaf 'direction' corresponds in French the following prepositions: 'vers, en direction de, à '. Notice that we find almost the same subtree under the temporal and abstract types than under the spatial type.

The set of types we have defined forms a finite domain of types. This domain is structured by the subtype hierarchy. Types may be restricted by additional feature-value pairs. The operator on this domain we consider is the subtype operator. The constraint propagation mechanism handles the management of subtypes, as explained in section 4.3, using the operation of greater lower bound (GLB) at various levels for performing simplifications.

4.2 Form of the input semantic representation

We consider a very neutral input internal representation form, which could be find for example in HPSG and LFG - based systems. The following sentence:

The car has four wheels.

is represented by the following semantic form:

Each of the predefined labels (e.g. SUBJ) refers to a substructure in a sentence. Labels themselves have sub-parts representing, for example, for a noun phrase its quantification, its nature (pronominal or overt), etc. To each of these labels it is possible to attach a set of syntactic types corresponding to all their possible surface realizations. The structure of the semantic form does not a priori follow any sentence surface structure, but it is clear however that a label used inside another label refers to a substructure of the structure associated to the outermost label (e.g. QUANT is inside SUBJ). When generating a sentence from this representation, the different subtypes attached to each label are combined by the constraint resolution mechanism in charge of the syntactic type management.

4.3 Propagation of syntactic and semantic constraints

Let us now examine how the generation process works and how syntactic types are selected and restricted. For the sake of readability, we illustrate the constraint propagation process on a simple example, and give in the same time the general principles which are used at each level.

$$\begin{bmatrix} \text{Focus} : \quad \text{SUBJ} \\[2em] \text{SUBJ} : \begin{bmatrix} \text{QUANT} : \text{the} \\ \text{PRED} : \text{car} \end{bmatrix} \\[2em] \text{PRED} : \text{have(SUBJ, OBJ1)} \\[2em] \text{OBJ1} : \begin{bmatrix} \text{QUANT} : \text{four} \\ \text{PRED} : \text{wheels} \end{bmatrix} \\[2em] \text{Tense} : \quad \text{past} \end{bmatrix}$$

Fig. 3.

To each abstract label that may occur in the input internal representation (e.g. OBJ, Focus, SUBJ, etc.) is associated a set of types defined in the above type hierarchies that covers all the possible syntactic realizations of that label. Terminal elements of the internal representation are predicates or constants (like preterit for the label Tense, or the predicate associated to a verb). To these terminal elements are associated either lexical entries (for example for verbs and nouns) or syntactic features which have to be assigned to the types dominating these terminal elements, such as the feature Tense with value past for the verb. The information under the Focus label will produce a feature for the type s saying for example that the sentence will be in the active voice (if the focus is the subject) or in the passive voice (if the focus is the object). For example, we have the following attached types:

to labels:

SUBJ : [np, inf, comp]

OBJ1 : [np, pp]

COMP : [sentential , infinitive]

PRED : [verb, adj, n]

QUANT : [det, poss]

Tense : [s(tense $\Rightarrow$ T : tense)]

> (a feature tense is incorporated into the type s, its value is not yet known and it is thus represented as a variable T of type tense).

to terminal elements:

past : [s(tense $\Rightarrow$ past)] (the feature tense of type s has value past)

have(subj, obj1) : [verb(string $\Rightarrow$ W , pred $\Rightarrow$ have(X, Y))]

The above form can be paraphrased as follows: the predicate have with two arguments refers to a feature 'string' which represents the surface realization of that predicate. To string is associated a value W. The denotation of W of type string is the set of values associated to the feature string of those lexical entries which unify with the type specification:

$[|\ W\ |]_{Lexicon} = \{W\ |\ \forall\ T\epsilon Lexicon,\ \text{subsumes}(\text{verb}(\ \text{string} \Rightarrow W\ ,$

$\text{pred} \Rightarrow \text{have}(X, Y)\ )\ ),\ T)\ \}.$

Other features associated to the selected verb can also be included in the type which is percolated in the grammar. Notice that all these specifications are fully declarative.

The basic principle of the generator can be summarized as follows. At the beginning of the generation process, the system only knows that it is going to generate from the input semantic representation for example a sentence, represented by the general type s. Then, suppose, the system processes the subject subpart of the internal representation. The subject (node SUBJ) can a priori be an np, an s or a comp (in French), which are themselves denoted by types. When the structure of the subject is known, then the type s is restricted to only include subjects of a certain type. The process goes on with the verb phrase, the general type associated to it is vp. Then, when examining its complements this type is further restricted, e.g. to transitive verb. This procedure of reducing the search space of possible applicable syntactic rules to generate a sentence is monotonic. At the end of the process, the denotations of the remaining types for each substructure describe the different possible well-formed phrase and sentence constructions with respect to the input form and to the grammar.

Let us now illustrate this process on a simple but comprehensive example, using the semantic representation given in 4.2. Starting from the outermost part of the semantic representation, we start with the construction of an s. As given in 4.1, we have the following starting structure:

xp(cat ⇒ s,

   const1 ⇒ xp(cat ⇒ [np, inf, comp]),

   const2 ⇒ xp(cat ⇒ [vp])).

Let us now follow the Prolog standard computation rule (from left to right) and let us process the SUBJ node. This node confirms the choice [np, inf, comp] for const1. Then, the first constituent of SUBJ is QUANT, which has two possible types [det, poss]. Det and poss are constituents that only appear as constituents of the type np. As a consequence (1) a type np is generated and (2) the disjunction of types [det, poss] is assigned to the first constituent (morphological features and other features are ommited for the sake of readability):

xp(cat ⇒ [np],

   const1 ⇒ x0(cat ⇒ [det,poss]),

   const2 ⇒ x0(cat ⇒ [n])).

Now, when the string 'the' is processed, it is, from lexical insertion, associated to a det type. This is consistent with the specification in the type, and poss is withdrawn, giving:

xp(cat ⇒ [np],

   const1 ⇒ x0(cat ⇒ [det], string ⇒ [the]),

   const2 ⇒ x0(cat ⇒ [n], string ⇒ [car])).

Next, the n is processed and entails no changes in the structure. The const1 substructure has been fully treated and it is incorporated in the s type:

xp(cat ⇒ s,
    const1 ⇒ xp(cat ⇒ [np],
                const1 ⇒ x0(cat ⇒ [det], string ⇒ [the]),
                const2 ⇒ x0(cat ⇒ [n], string ⇒ [car])),
    const2 ⇒ xp(cat ⇒ [vp])).

The const2 substructure is now considered. The system first considers the PRED node. To the PRED node is associated the list of types [verb, n, adj]. The type is then identified via lexical insertion from the predicate itself to be mono-transitive (it has 2 arguments) which is a subtype of verb (see 4.1) ; it corresponds to the structure:

xp(cat ⇒ [mono-transitive],
    const1 ⇒ x0(cat ⇒ [v], string ⇒ [has]),
    const2 ⇒ xp(cat ⇒ [np, pp, inf])).

Next, the node OBJ1 is considered. It has the following associated set of types [np, pp]. Similarly to the SUBJ node, the following subtype is produced for the OBJ1 level, of type np:

xp(cat ⇒ [np],
    const1 ⇒ x0(cat ⇒ [det], string ⇒ [four]),
    const2 ⇒ x0(cat ⇒ [n], string ⇒ [wheels])).

At this stage, the system does not know where to include the OBJ1 structure. It can either be attached direcly at s level or at vp level. In our example, since the outermost level does not have any const3 level, the np type must be included within the const2 level of the vp type which is waiting for an np under const2. The resulting representation then becomes :

xp(cat ⇒ s,
    const1 ⇒ xp(cat ⇒ [np],
                const1 ⇒ x0(cat ⇒ [det], string ⇒ [the]),
                const2 ⇒ x0(cat ⇒ [n], string ⇒ [car])),
    const2 ⇒ xp(cat ⇒ [mono-transitive],
                const1 ⇒ x0(cat ⇒ [v], string ⇒ [has]),
                const2 ⇒ xp(cat ⇒ [np],
                        const1 ⇒ x0(cat ⇒ [det], string ⇒ [four]),
                        const2 ⇒ x0(cat ⇒ [n], string ⇒ [wheels])))).

where the different string feature labels permit the construction of the expected sentence. If there are several possible places where a subtype can be included (for example the verb has several vp and sentence arguments), then the inclusion is postponed untill more information is available about the other elements such as nps, inf and comp. If there are still several possibilities, then a disjunction of subtypes is created. Notice that the result may not necessarily be a single, fully instanciated type, but it may be polymorphic, reflecting the different possible sentences that may be constructed from the input semantic representation.

Taking into account focus and tense permits the system to determine whether the sentence is in the active or passive form and what will be the tense of the verb. These two labels are treated in a similar way. If they are treated before the verb, their associated value is left pending (with a type representation that matches the verb's type description) and they are propagated till more information is available to incorporate them into a structure, here the vp type.

In the case where the denotation of a type is a disjunction of type constructors, as in:

np = { xp(cat ⇒ [np], const1 ⇒ x0(cat ⇒ [det, poss]),
                       const2 ⇒ x0(cat ⇒ [n])),
       xp(cat ⇒ [np], const1 ⇒ x0(cat ⇒ [n], type ⇒ proper_noun)) }.

and when new information N has to be merged within the denotation, then the system tries all the merge operations it can on each type constructor. The type constructor which cannot merge with the new information N are discarded from the denotation : they are no longer coherent with the specifications of the sentence being generated. For example, if we want to merge the type constructors of np with N = x0(cat ⇒ [det]), then only the first constructor will remain coherent and will be kept. The second one has no greater lower bound with N (except the empty type which is the contradiction).

The constraint resolution mechanism constructs partial types and propagates type information, it is very simple and general. It can be summarized by the following processes (which are not ordered a priori) :

(0) initialization at s level: type s.

(1) restriction of a set S1 of types, with respect to another set S2 (S2 often being a subset of S1, where types may possibly be restricted by features), the resulting set S is the greater lower bound of S1 and S2.

(2) specialisation of a type under a consti label: the present type is T1 and a type T2 must be merged, the result is also the greater lower bound of the two types T1 and T2 at the consti level, as in:

T1 = xp(cat ⇒ s, const2 ⇒ xp(cat ⇒ [np, pp])),
T2 = xp(cat ⇒ [np],
          const1 ⇒ x0(cat ⇒ [det], string ⇒ [four]),
          const2 ⇒ x0(cat ⇒ [n], string ⇒ [wheels])),
gives T = xp(cat ⇒ s, const2 ⇒ xp(cat ⇒ [np],
                        const1 ⇒ x0(cat ⇒ [det], string ⇒ [four]),
                        const2 ⇒ x0(cat ⇒ [n], string ⇒ [wheels]))).

(3) propagation of a partial type, to be included later under a certain $const_i$.

(4) creation of a disjunction of types when several attachments are possible. For example, if we have:

main type:
xp(cat ⇒ [vp], const1 ⇒ x0(cat ⇒ [v]),
            const2 ⇒ xp(cat ⇒ [np,pp]), const3 ⇒ xp(cat ⇒ [np, inf]))
type to be merged as explained in (2) above:
xp(cat ⇒ [np]).

The result is a disjunction of type constructors associated to the main type level (here vp):

{xp(cat ⇒ [vp], const1 ⇒ x0(cat ⇒ [v]),
            const2 ⇒ xp(cat ⇒ [np]), const3 ⇒ xp(cat ⇒ [np, inf])),
  xp(cat ⇒ [vp], const1 ⇒ x0(cat ⇒ [v]),
            const2 ⇒ xp(cat ⇒ [np,pp]), const3 ⇒ xp(cat ⇒ [np])) }.

Notice that this set may be further restricted by future additional information determined from the semantic representation.

5 Comparison with Related Works

The works in natural language generation which are the closest to ours is the MUM-BLE system (MacDonald 1984, Huettner et al. 1987). This system has realization specifications which represent the relations between the semantic form and the surface sentence. These specifications are managed by a planner which plays the role of a supervisor (or a meta-interpretor) and which interleaves planning and surface realization. The realization is top-down and proceeds from the outermost specifications to the innermost ones.

Our system has major differences with this system. First in our system, we do not have the notion of planning: the semantic form is traversed and constraints on the nature of syntactic realizations are propagated, realizations can be done at any time after all the necessary information is available for a given structure. The planning system of Mumble is here replaced by the more general propagation technique of CLP. Next, semantic information is processed in the order it is found. Semantic descriptions originate syntactic information which is stored in the type descriptions as shown in 4.3. They permit the production of surface forms only when all the necessary information is present.

Within CLP, the result of a goal is the set of constraints that correspond to the execution of the goal. As a consequence, our approach permits the production of constraints corresponding to all the possible surface realization of a semantic form. Choices can then be made on the basis of external criteria such as user preferences of pragmatic factors (focus). Also, all the other constraints that may appear in the grammar (e.g. precedence, finite domains, etc.) play a role in the realization of the surface form in a uniform and homogenous way.

Finally, the generation method we have presented here can be used with many types of semantic forms and syntactic systems. We have presented in 4.1 the means to define types from most rule-based syntactic systems.

6 Conclusion

The constraint resolution mechanisms we have presented here, namely precedence and syntactic rules selection, have been fully implemented by means of a CLP meta-interpreter. This implementation proves feasability. However to have a better idea of the gain in efficiency, a more direct interpretation is necessary. We are now integrating this system into our main generation system, presented in (Saint-Dizier 1991a, 1991b).

Our approach is not limited to syntactic choice. It can indeed be used in a quite similar way for any kind of choice problem, such as the treatment of RSTs, the problem of lexical choice or lexicalization (word-sense are represented as types) and the generation of texts where the planning aspect also originates complex choices which can be revised. We are currently working on the integration of the lexical coercion rules of (Pustejovsky 1991) using exactly this system. Work in progress show that a general procedure like 'coerce-α' 'coerce any structure α' (to make a parallelism with the GB's move-α) can be applied to lexical entries in case of a need of coercion and that additional information will restrict this principle during the generation process. There is then no coercion applied a priori, which would risk to be revised later. Simply the possible space of coercion is restricted further and further when generating a sentence.

Finally, our approach, besides the innovative aspect of using CLP and constraint propagation techniques, also claims for a certain psychological reality in the sense that when uttering a sentence, we have in mind all the parameters associated to the contents of the sentence.

7 APPENDIX

We present here more in detail the resolution algorithm of the precedence constraint given in section 3.

Defining Left and right corners

Let a phrase structure type be of the form (we use the rule notation to facilitate understanding, but this is equivalent to the type notation previously introduced):

A → B, P.

where B is a set of symbols and P is a set of precedence constraints. The set of possible left corners CG for B given P is defined as follows:

$CG = B - \{E \epsilon B \mid \exists X \epsilon B, p(X, E) \epsilon P\}$.

E is thus a symbol which must be preceded by another symbol in B, it cannot therefore be a left corner. Similarly, we define the set of possible right corners CD for B given P:

$CG = B - \{E \epsilon B \mid \exists Y \epsilon B, p(E, Y) \epsilon P\}$.

In this case a symbol E which must precede another symbol cannot be a right corner.

From the CG and CD, we can define the set CGCD of all possible pairs of left and right corners for B given P; it is the cartesian product of the two set without pairs with identical elements since a symbol cannot be at the same time a left and a right corner:

$CGCD = CGXCD - \{(X, Y) \mid X = Y\}$.

At this stage, we must say a few words about the case where B has only a single element. Then, since this rule cannot have any precedence constraints, the single element is both a left and a right corner. To end up this section, let us consider a simple example. Consider the rule:

a → b, c, d, e, f, p(b,c), p(d,e).

We then have:

CG = { b, d, f },

CD = { c, e, f },

CGCD = { (b,c), (b,e), (b,f), (d,c), (d,e), (d,f), (f,c), (f,e) }.

Precedence constraints associated to each pair in CGCD

Besides precedence constraints coming from the rule itself (i.e. R), there are additional constraints (R') which have to be added to the set of of active constraints (cf. 3.1). Let us consider again the general rule format given in 6.2 above, we then have the following constraints in R':

(1) The first constraint follows from the choice of a give pair in CGCD. If p(W,Z) is selected, then we have the precedence constraints p(W,Z). From this choice will follow additional constraints. Each pair in CGCD originates a different set of precedence constraints. As a result, we will have a disjunction of sets of precedence constraints.

(2) From a pair in CGCD, we deduce that all symbol preceding the left-hand side symbol A of the rule also precedes the left corners of the rule and that all symbols preceded by A is also preceded by all its right corners. More formall, for each left corner cg in CG we have the following additional constraints:

$\{p(X, cg) \mid \exists p(X, A) \epsilon S\}$ (S is the current set of actice constraints).

Similarly, we have for each right corner cd in CD:

$\{p(cd, Y) \mid \exists Y, p(A, Y) \epsilon S\}$.

To summarize, from the set of pairs (cg,cd) in CGCD, we get a set R' of constraints of the form:

R' = $\{ R'_1, R'_2, \ldots, R'_n \}$

where:

n = card(CGCD),

R'_i, to which corresponds the pair $(cg_i, cd_i) \epsilon$ CGCD such that:

$R'_i = p(cg_i, cd_i) \cup \{p(X, cg_i) \mid \exists p(X, A) \epsilon S\} \cup \{p(cd_i, Y) \mid \exists Y, p(A, Y) \epsilon S\}$.

Finally, $S \cup R$ is merged with R', the R'$_i$ which are inconsistent are withdrawn. Possible simplification, to avoid redundancy, are also performed at this level. The result is a disjunction of sets of constraints. If the disjunction is empty, then there are no solutions to the sentence being processed (i.e. it is ill-formed or it cannot be generated). As an illustration, if we consider the above example and have:

S = { p(f,a), p(g,a) },

we then have, for the pair in CGCD (b,c) the following set R'$_j$:

R'_j = { p(f,b), p(c,g) }

and for the pair (d,c), we get:

R'_k = { p(f,d), p(c,g) }

suppose (for short) that we only have the two above pairs in CGCD, we then get the following new set S of active constraints composed of a disjunction of two sets:

S = { { p(f,a), p(a,g), p(b,c), p(d,e), p(f,b), p(c,g) },
      { p(f,a), p(a,g), p(b,c), p(d,e), p(d,c), p(f,d), p(d,c) } }.

in the first set an occurence of p(b,c) has been eliminated to avoid redundancy.

References

Aït-Kaçi, H., Nasr, R.. LOGIN: A Logic Programming Language with Built-in Inheritance, journal of Logic Programming, vol. 3, pp 185-215, 1986.

Colmerauer, A., An Introduction to Prolog III, CACM 33-7, 1990.

Dincbas M., Van Hentenryck P., Simonis H., Aggoun A., Graf T. eand Berthier F. (1988) "The Constraint Logic Programming Language CHIP", Proceedings of the International Conference on Fifth Generation Computer Systems, pp 693-702, ICOT, Tokyo.

Emele, M., Zajac, R., Typed Unification Grammars, in proc. COLINGU90, Helsinki, 1990.

Freuder E. C. (1978) "Synthetising Constraint Expressions" Communications of the ACM, 21:958-966.

Gazdar, G., Klein, E., Pullum, G.K., Sag, I., Generalized Phrase Structure Grammar, Harvard University Press, 1985.

Huettner, A., Vaugham, M., MacDonald, D., Constraints on the Generation of Adjunct Clauses, in proc. 25th meeting of the ACL, Stanford university, 1987.

Jaffar, J., Lassez, J.L., Constraint Logic Programming, Proc. 14th ACM Symposium on Principles of Programming Languages, 1987.

MacDonald, D., Description Directed Control : its Implications for Natural Language Generation, in Computational Linguistics, N. Cercone (Edt), Plenum Press, 1984.

MacDonald, D., On the Place of Words in the Generation Process, in Natural Language Generation in Artificial Intelligence and Computational Linguistics, C. Paris et al. Edts, Kluwer Academic, 1991.

Mackworth A. K. (1987) Constraint Satisfaction, in Shapiro (ed.), Encyclopedia of Artificial Intelligence, Wiley-Interscience Publication, New-York.

Paris et al. (Edts), Natural Language Generation in Artificial Intelligence and Computational Linguistics, Kluwer Academic, 1991.

Pollard, C., Sag, I., Information-based Syntax and Semantics, vol. 1, CSLI lecture notes no.13, 1987.

Pustejovsky, J., The Generative Lexicon, Computational Linguistics, 1991.

Saint-Dizier, P., Constrained Logic Programming for Natural Language Processing, proc. E. ACL-89, Manchester, 1989.

Saint-Dizier, P., Processing Language with Types and Active Constraints, in proc. E. ACL 91, Berlin, 1991.

Saint-Dizier, P., Generating sentences with Active Constraints, in proc. 3rd European workshop on language generation, Austria, 1991.

Sheiber, S., An Introduction to Unification-Based Approaches to Grammar, CSLI lecture notes no 4, Chicago University Press, 1986.

Van Hentenrick P. Constraint Satisfaction in Logic Programming, MIT Press, Cambridge, 1989.

Viegas, E., The Semantics-Pragmatics of Lexicalization, in proc. 2nd Computational Lexical Semantics seminar, Toulouse, 1992.

Generating Utterances in Dialogue Systems

Nick J. Youd[1] and Scott McGlashan[2]

[1] Logica Cambridge Ltd, Betjeman House, 104 Hills Road, Cambridge, U.K.
[2] Social and Computer Sciences Research Group, Department of Sociology, University of Surrey, Guildford, U.K.

Abstract

This paper describes the language output component of the Sundial spoken dialogue system. Following a dialogue planning decision to produce an utterance, an utterance planning component derives a semantic description drawing on a model of speakers' knowledge of the domain. This semantic description is linguistically realised by a generation component which draws on a bi-directional lexicon-grammar. The algorithm recycles structure from a contextual history of previous utterances, where this is possible.

1 Introduction

The language generation work described in this paper forms part of the Sundial project[3], which is concerned with building real-time integrated computer systems capable of maintaining co-operative dialogues with users of information services, over standard telephone lines, within limited task domains which include flight reservations and train enquiries. In this paper, we describe and illustrate the Sundial approach to the generation of system utterances[4].

One requirement on generation in dialogue systems is that system utterances are coherent with the current state of the dialogue. This constrains the communicative purpose of utterances. For example, unlike text-based dialogue systems, generation in speech-based systems must be sensitive to problems of poor recognition arising

---

[3] Sundial (Speech UNerstanding in DIALogue) is partly funded by the Commission of the European Communities under the ESPRIT II programme as project P2218, and involves partners from France (CNET, CAP GEMINI INNOVATION and IRISA – University of Rennes), Germany (Daimler Benz, Siemens and the University of Erlangen), Italy (CSELT, Saritel and Politechnico di Torino), Sweden (Infovox) and the UK (Logica and the University of Surrey).

[4] In addition to the authors, design and implementation of the dialogue manager and message generation modules has been carried out by Eric Bilange, Wieland Eckert, Norman Fraser, Nigel Gilbert, Marc Guyomard, Paul Heisterkamp, Jill House, Mouloud Kharoune, Jean-Yves Magadur, Jacques Siroux and Robin Wooffitt. The views expressed in this paper are those of the authors and do not necessarily reflect those of our collaborators.

from continuous speech from untrained users (Young and Proctor 1989). Accordingly, the system may have to confirm, implicitly or explicitly, its interpretation of the user's utterance. The conceptual content and linguistic form of utterances are also constrained by the current dialogue state. Utterances must express the concepts necessary for the user to build an extension to their conceptual model of the dialogue. For example, in response to the user's request *what time does flight ba123 arrive?*, the system's response needs to include a 'confirming' context, as with *flight ba123 arrives at 17 15*, if the flight has not been previously referenced in the dialogue or if there are doubts as to the interpretation of the request. At the linguistic level, not only must concepts be lexically realizable, but concepts already referenced in the dialogue may 're-use' previous linguistic realizations, thereby simplifying the realization process and maximizing conceptual and linguistic correspondence between system and user utterances (Garrod and Anderson 1987).

Figure 1 presents an overview of the Sundial architecture. Utterance generation comes about firstly on the basis of decisions by the *dialogue planner*, which is concerned with coherence at a conversational level (Bilange 1991). In generating a system utterance, the dialogue planner determines on the basis of the dialogue model its communicative purpose and schematic conceptual content. Generation makes use of two contextual knowledge bases: the *belief model* or discourse model – a repository of semantic knowledge, and the *linguistic history*, a record of analysis trees of spoken user and system utterances. The utterance planning module builds a detailed semantic description on the basis of the current state of the belief model. This description, together with a portion of the linguistic history, is passed to the message generation module which constructs a linguistic representation using a head-driven UCG algorithm extended to re-use, where appropriate, representations in the linguistic history.

2 Planning System Utterances

At the end of each user turn in the dialogue, the dialogue planner constructs a set of *moves* for the system: i.e. a set of continuations given the current state of the dialogue model. This model is hierarchically structured into exchanges, interventions and dialogue acts. The communicative purpose of each move is indicated by a *dialogue act* label. The conceptual content of a move is indicated by a reference to information in the belief model. In the examples shown, this is done in terms of parameters of the current task entity. For example, if the system requires the departure date of a flight, the dialogue planner constructs a system move with the dialogue act label OPEN_REQUEST, an index *dbflight1* referencing the current task, and a parameter label with unspecified value: [*id : dbflight1, date : _*].

The utterance planning module maps the set of moves into a linguistically-oriented representation which consists of *Utterance Field Objects* (UFOs). These may be complex or atomic. Complex UFOs are used to represent system turns which consists of more than one utterance as in (1):

(1) You want to travel from London to Paris. What date do you want to travel on?

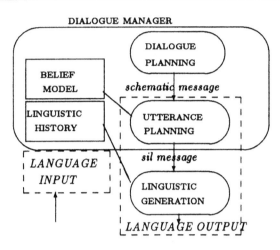

Fig. 1. Schematic architecture showing relation of dialogue manager to language output component

Atomic UFOs, used to represent the individual utterances, are sign-based representations which have been extended to characterize dialogue information (see Sect. 3.1 for a description of other sign attributes). For example, (1) is initially characterized as the complex UFO in (2):

(2)

$$
\begin{bmatrix}
id : ufo4 \\
card : 2 \\
ufo\_1 : \begin{bmatrix}
id : ufo5 \\
dialogue : \begin{bmatrix} dact : confirm \end{bmatrix} \\
semantics : \begin{bmatrix} id : dbflight1 \\ goalcity : paris \\ sourcecity : london \end{bmatrix}
\end{bmatrix} \\
ufo\_2 : \begin{bmatrix}
id : ufo6 \\
dialogue : \begin{bmatrix} dact : open\_request \end{bmatrix} \\
semantics : \begin{bmatrix} id : dbflight1 \\ date : \_ \end{bmatrix}
\end{bmatrix}
\end{bmatrix}
$$

where *ufo4* is a complex UFO composed of two atomic UFOs (indicated by the value of the *card* attribute). Both of these specify values for dialogue and semantics attributes; in *ufo5*, for example, the value of the dialogue attribute indicates that the communicative purpose is a confirmation (*dact:confirm*) and the value of the semantic attribute indicate the parameters to be confirmed – the departure and arrival cities of a flight referenced by the index *dbflight1*.

Simple planning rules are then used to determine whether a full semantic description is required to replace the semantic index and, if so, the type of description appropriate for the dialogue act. For some dialogue acts, semantic descriptions are unnecessary since they are realized as 'stock phrases' such as *hello* or *good bye*. With the majority, however, the planning rules specify the type of semantic description to be built by the belief module. For example, ufo_2 in (2) triggers a rule which specifies that the discourse object is to be described using describe_in_context (see below).

Building semantic descriptions involves the extraction of discourse objects in the belief model which are sufficient to enable the hearer to build appropriate structure in their own belief model. Discourse objects are represented using the SIL knowledge representation language (Youd and McGlashan to appear). The language specifies a number of object types ordered in terms of a subsumption hierarchy. Each type is associated with one or more roles; for example, objects of the type ARRIVE have *thetheme*, *thetime* and *theplace* roles where the value of each role is itself a typed object (the lexical entry for *arrive* is shown in (6)). Discourse objects in the belief model are instantiated SIL objects: they have been assigned an index by which they may be externally identified.

Using the semantic index, the belief module identifies a root object in the current belief space and a SIL representation describing its contents is produced by recursively descending through its roles. Both the search for a root object as well as the number of subdescriptions that are required starting at a given root, are constrained through *lexical tagging*: i.e. tagging SIL types and roles which are explicitly referenced in the lexicon. In this way, only descriptions capable of mapping onto SIL expressions within the generation lexicon are built.

Each of the following description types introduce variants on this basic description building process:

describe is the default type, which describes the minimum possible. If there is only one object to describe, it uses the basic description routine. If there are several objects which do not contain a common root, it uses describe_with_context.

describe_with_context is typically used where a number of objects $O_1 \ldots O_n$ need to be described. In the simplest case, these objects have a common (spanning) root object O_r; the result is then the SIL representation which describes O_r and contains sub-descriptions for all of $O_1 \ldots O_n$. A variant is *tandem-description*, for which more than one root is proposed. In order to constrain search it is necessary that the two descriptions are in some sense parallel, as for example:

(3) Flight BA 123 *leaves London at 17.15* and *arrives in Paris at 18.39*.

where the first conjunct corresponds to the root object DEPART and the second ARRIVE and both share the value of *thetheme* role here realized as the subject of *leave*.

describe_in_context is typically used for describing queries, such as *what time do you want to leave?*, or for attributive descriptions, such as *the time of departure*. An object O_q is not described in terms of its value (which may not be known), but in terms of some description whose root O_r is known, and which references it. Although it uses the same root-proposal mechanism as describe_with_context, once O_r is found, only sufficient material is added to the description to provide an external description of O_q. The description for *ufo6* in (2) is given in (4):

(4)

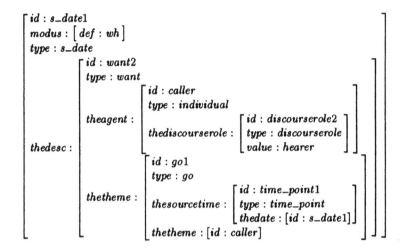

where the value of the role *thedate* in <thedesc thetheme thesourcetime> references *s_date1*.

describe_and_context combines describe_in_context, with basic description. It is used when an *assignment* description is required, as in

(5) The price of the ticket is three hundred pounds.

Two parts are returned: the external description *the price of the ticket* (obtained using describe_in_context) and the internal description corresponding to *three hundred pounds*.

3 Linguistic Realization

Using the UFOs built in the dialogue manager module, the message generation module generates a linguistic representation suitable for speech synthesis. Here we describe the grammar-lexicon, the basic generation algorithm as well as refinements emerging from 're-use' of linguistic representations.

3.1 UCG Grammar Lexicon

The grammar is modelled closely on UCG (Calder et al. 1988). An example lexical entry is given in (6).

(6)

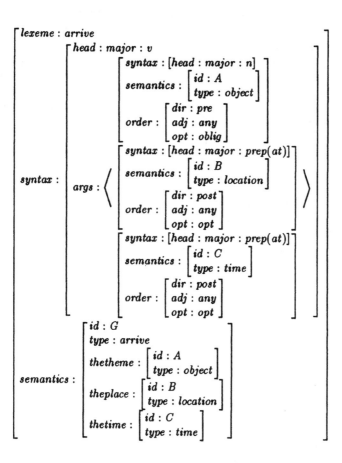

It will be seen that the subcategorisation frame is defined in a list at the <syntax args> position. In addition to the basic *phonology, syntax, semantics*, the sign has fields for *slash* and *order*. The former is used in the gap-threaded treatment of movement (see Sect. 5 below). The latter is instantiated in argument categories, to indicate their surface position with respect to the functor (head).

The grammar used here specialises standard UCG in two respects. Firstly, domain-specific semantics are incorporated in the lexicon to a much greater extent. The <semantic type> feature can take any value from the subsumption hierarchy defined in SIL. The type ARRIVE in (6) is subsumption-compatible with EVENT; therefore the entry can be inserted into an environment which requires a sign of this semantic type. The subcategorisation frame can thus be simultaneously syntactically and semantically constraining. Secondly, the rules of functional application:

$A/B \ B \rightarrow A$

$B \ A\backslash B \rightarrow A$

(where '/' and '\' indicate order of application) have been elaborated to permit underspecified order, adjacency and optionality. In (6), *theplace* argument is optional and can occur in any position after the functor.

The lexicon is defined using the DATR language (Evans and Gazdar 1989). Starting with a set of *definitional sentences* in which redundancy and reduplication is kept to a minimum, the principles of inheritance with defaults are applied to derive a lexicon with rich structure-sharing both within and among entries. The lexicon is compiled out of the DATR sentences offline (Andry et al. to appear).

The lexical entries for generation and parsing incorporate the same knowledge, being derived from the same source. However the generation lexicon differs from the parsing lexicon in its compiled form, because:

1. a *morphological lexicon* is compiled out separately from the lexicon of base forms. The entries in this are ordered according to specificity, lexical exceptions being first; each entry serves to map an uninflected form onto a surface form, given a certain specification of syntactic features;
2. the generation lexicon is indexed principally by the *semantics* field. Entries are indexed firstly by semantic type, and secondly ordered according to the amount of semantic detail they are capable of absorbing from the input description.

Additionally a reverse index, from lexical base forms to the nodes in the semantic hierarchy at which their entries are indexed, is provided, for use in constraint-relaxation search by the re-use algorithm (see Sect. 5.3).

4 Basic Algorithm

The *head-driven bottom-up generation* algorithm (vanNoord 1990) is particularly suitable for lexicon-based grammars such as ours. It also has the advantages of being goal-directed (hence of greater efficiency), and of not being limited by the recursion problem present in top-down algorithms.

The Sundial generation algorithm, in simplified form, can be described as the process of finding a lexical candidate for the input sign whose semantics unifies with that of the input, then recursively generating its arguments. However, a so-called *lexical pivot*, chosen on the basis of its semantics, does not guarantee syntactic coherence. For example, given the SIL description in (7):

(7)

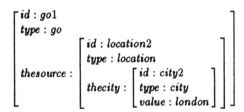

the algorithm generates:[5]

(8)

$$travellondon : \mathbf{v} : \text{GO} \rightarrow$$
$$travel : \mathbf{v} : \text{GO}$$
$$london : \mathbf{n} : \text{LOCATION} \rightarrow$$

where *london* is syntactically an np, but is required by the subcategorisation frame of *travel* to be a prepositional phrase. To deal with this, we introduce *specifiers*, which simply act as category raisers, and *modifiers*, which may add material to the semantics while maintaining the correspondence between goal semantics and pivot semantics. Either of these will be referred to as *raisers*. In the analysis tree shown in (8), the raiser given in (9) is required above *london*.

(9)
$$\left[syntax : \begin{bmatrix} head : [major : prep(from)] \\ args : \left\langle \begin{bmatrix} syntax : \begin{bmatrix} head : [major : n] \\ args : [\,] \end{bmatrix} \\ semantics : C \end{bmatrix} \right\rangle \end{bmatrix} \\ semantics : C \right]$$

This is a semantically transparent functor, whose only effect is to raise the syntactic type n to $prep(from)$.

The function *GENERATE* specified in (10) takes as input a *sign* of which only the semantics need be specified and produces an analysis tree *signout*. The algorithm requires that the arguments in the subcategorisation frame of *lexcand* are recursively generated first; after this an attempt is made to find a chain of raisers which will raise the semantics and the syntax of the result of applying *lexcand* to *Args*, to meet the input constraints.

(10)

---

[5] The analysis trees shown here and elsewhere represent a condensed form of the feature structures actually generated. The semantics (shown in small capitals) in particular show only the semantic type of the constituent. Order with respect to the head is shown by arrows; the lexical head of every node is shown immediately below the sign for the node, and does not have an order marking.

$$
\begin{array}{|l}
\underline{\;GENERATE\;}\\
sign, signout, lexcand, arg, arg', unraised : SIGN\\
args\_to\_gen, argsout : \mathbb{F}\;SIGN\\
lexcand : LEX\\
raiser : RAISER\\
raisers : \mathbb{F}\;RAISER\\
\hline
raisers = POSSIBLE\_CHAINS[sign.syntax])\\
can\_raise[raisers, raiser, sign, lexcand]\\
\theta = UNIFY[lexcand.semantics, sign.semantics]\\
args\_to\_gen = \{arg \circ \theta \mid arg \in lexcand.args \wedge arg \circ \theta \neq arg\}\\
argsout =\\
\quad\{argout \mid arg' \in args\_to\_gen \wedge\\
\qquad argout = GENERATE[arg']\}\\
unraised.args = argsout\\
signout = RAISE[raiser, unraised]\\
\end{array}
$$

The algorithm is described here using a variant of the 'Z' language, a notation which uses set-theoretic constructs and predicate calculus in a structured way, to build formal specifications. The notation '$\mathbb{F}\;T$' refers to objects which are finite sets of elements of type T. The definition for $GENERATE$ is structured in terms of a set of declarations, followed by sentences which must become true during the process of generation. In order to specify clearly that $UNIFY$ exports its bindings to the environment, the bindings θ are shown returned as the result of $UNIFY$, and applied using the operator '$\circ$'.

The types used in the specification are as follows:

> $SIGN$ the set of all well-formed signs, as defined above
> LEX the subset of $SIGN$ corresponding to lexical entries
> $RAISER$ the set of raising categories

The operation $RAISE$ matches the sign *raiser* against the chain of lexical raisers which make it up, recursively raising *lexcand* as it goes. Morphological instantiation is delayed until this point, to avoid the possibility of backtracking that might arise from instantiating a feature structure when other constraints are not all present.

With raising, instead of (8) the correct form given in (11) is generated:

(11)

> $travelfromlondon : \mathbf{v} : \mathrm{GO} \rightarrow$
> $travel : \mathbf{v} : \mathrm{GO}$
> $fromlondon : \mathbf{prep} : \mathrm{LOCATION} \rightarrow$
> $from : \mathbf{prep} : \mathrm{LOCATION}$
> $london : \mathbf{n} : \mathrm{LOCATION} \rightarrow$

5 Refinements

5.1 Moved Constituents

The basic algorithm assumes that while the input *sign* may be partially specified for syntactic features, it has no specified arguments. This is not always the case. For example, in the case of an equi verb such as *want*, the input sign for the recursive call to *GENERATE* which will produce the embedded verb-phrase, already has its subject argument instantiated. It is therefore necessary to match such arguments against those of the candidate lexical entry*lexcand*, but ignore them in testing for instantiation and in recursively generating. For example, with *do you want to travel to Paris from London*, the subject of *travel*, which is specified in its *args* list, is not generated for this reason.

Moved constituents may be handled by a threaded argument to *GENERATE* constraining the nature of any expected gap. Gaps are introduced by *wh* constituents, or by non-lexical rules such as topicalisation (Gazdar et al. 1985). A gap is threaded through the generation tree, on the basis that most lexical constituents, and hence most phrasal constituents, simply pass the gap on. So-called 'island constraints' on movement may be enforced by specifying in the lexicon that certain phrasal categories cannot pass gaps. A gap is eliminated, leaving instead of an expected constituent a placeholder or *trace*, when the constraints of that constituent match the constraints of the gap.

The following example shows an analysis tree for the second utterance in (1) where the gap has been proposed by the entry for *what* and eliminated by the argument of the *pp(on)*:

(12)

       whatdatedoyouwanttotravelon : **v** : S_DATE
          what : **v** : S_DATE
          date : **n** : S_DATE →
              date : **n** : S_DATE
          doyouwanttotravelon : **v** : WANT →
              do : **v** : WANT
              you : **n** : INDIVIDUAL →
              wanttotravelon : **v** : WANT →
                 want : **v** : WANT
                 to : **v** : UNSPEC →
                 travelon : **v** : GO →
                   travel : **v** : GO
                   on : **prep** : S_DATE →
                      on : **prep** : S_DATE

5.2 Morphological instantiation and string building

Instantiation of a lexical entry is delayed at least until all that can be known about its environment is known (Calder et al. 1989). This requires (i) that its *args*, if any, have been generated, and (ii) that the category-raising chain corresponding to *raiser* has been instantiated. The first requirement will allow agreement and control dependencies to be satisfied: for example, a verb is not morphologically instantiated until its subject has been generated, because in general it will inflect according to agreement features of the subject. The second requirement is so that constraints outside the current constitituent may take effect. For example, the base form of *want* in *you want to travel to Paris from London* depends on the category-raising chain consisting of the infinitival complementiser *to* having been determined.

The surface string for a sign is built by applying the rules of categorial combination to its head and arguments. In order for a constituent's string to be generated, and hence be capable of being spoken, all subconstituent strings must be complete. Where order is underspecified, the string is produced using the default order of the lexical entry. However constituents from which material has been extracted, and constituents containing prosodic emphasis (Youd and House 1991) are moved rightwards if possible.

5.3 Recycling Previous Utterances

There are two constraints on generating from a previous entry in the linguistic history: firstly, an appropriate entry which is sufficiently recent must be chosen; secondly, generation should take place in such a way as to maximise use of the previous structure. A number of patterns have been defined, according to which a newly generated sign draws on a previous analysis tree:

1. An *echo* corresponds exactly to all or part of the previous structure;
2. A *substitution* corresponds closely, but not exactly, to all or part of the previous structure;
3. An *embedded echo* has part(s) of it identical to all or part(s) of the previous structure;
4. An *embedded substitution* is like an embedded echo, except that the embedded substructure is not identical to, but may be derived via some simple substitution, from its antecedent.

Figure 2 illustrates the four possibilities. The echoes are a special case of substitutions (where there are no differences); the embedded cases may be handled by beginning the attempt to reuse previous material at some recursive stage within generation. We therefore shall concentrate on describing the substitution algorithm.

Firstly, a suitable candidate from the linguistic history must be found. Two criteria seem to be needed. Firstly, it must form part, or all, of a recent entry. Non-recent candidates would appear to be ruled out by psycholinguistic results, that memory for surface structure is short-lived, and because if they were to be allowed, the amount of search required to find them would undo any benefit to be gained from re-using a previous structure. Secondly, its semantics must match that of the target in a non-trivial way. This would be the case, for example, if the candidate entry and the target shared the same semantic type, or if their types were closely related in the type hierarchy, and they shared a number of attributes. Thus, for the

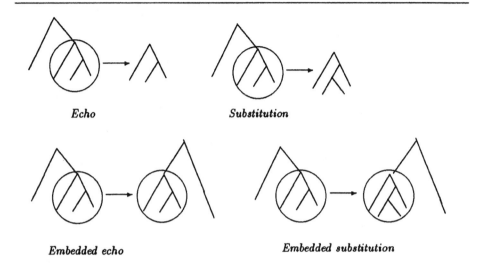

Fig. 2. Echoes, substitutions, and their embedded versions

candidate antecedent *nine fifty six* and the target utterance *five fifty six*, both are of type s_TIME and so are compatible; furthermore, since the structure of an object of type s_TIME is schematically the same for both instances:

$$
\begin{bmatrix}
type : s\_time \\
thehour : \begin{bmatrix} type : hour \end{bmatrix} \\
theminutes : \begin{bmatrix} type : minutes \end{bmatrix}
\end{bmatrix}
$$

they may correspond in their arguments.

The recycling algorithm, which combines lexical search with comparison of the source and target structures, is given in (13):

(13)

```
┌─ GENERATE_FROM_ENTRY ──────────────────────────────
│ S_src, S_trg : Analysis_tree
│ L_cand : LEX
│ Aligned_args : IF Analysis_tree × Analysis_tree
├────────────────────────────────────────────────────
│ (S_src.semantics ≡ S_trg.semantics ⇒ UNIFY[S_src, S_trg]
│ ∨
│ (∃ L_cand • LEXICALLY_NEAR[L_cand, S_src.lexeme] ⇒
│       UNIFY[S_src.semantics, L_cand.semantics] ∧
│       Aligned_args = ALIGN_ARGS[L_cand, S_src] ∧
│       ∀ < Arg_{src_i}, Arg_{trg_i} > ∈ Aligned_args •
│             GENERATE_FROM_ENTRY[Arg_{src_i}, Arg_{trg_i}]
│ ∨
│ GENERATE[S]
└────────────────────────────────────────────────────
```

This algorithm is as follows: if the antecedent and the target have identical semantics, then use all the antecedent. This is the echo, or embedded echo, case; otherwise, attempt to find a lexical head for the target, searching in the proximity of its semantic type in the class hierarchy; having found this, align its arguments, where possible, with arguments of the antecedent, and call the procedure recursively for each of these. If neither identity nor lexical closeness are possible, default to the normal generation algorithm which ignores previous structures.

The algorithm in (13) may be illustrated by considering the generation of the phrase: *I drive to Paris*, when an analysis tree for *I fly to Paris* is in the linguistic history. First, this entry is chosen, because its semantics:

$$
\begin{bmatrix}
id : \mathit{flight}41 \\
type : flight \\
thetheme : \begin{bmatrix} id : speaker \\ type : individual \end{bmatrix} \\
thegoal : \begin{bmatrix} id : paris \\ type : city \end{bmatrix}
\end{bmatrix}
$$

is sufficiently similar to the target semantics

$$
\begin{bmatrix}
id : drive23 \\
type : drive \\
thetheme : \begin{bmatrix} id : speaker \\ type : individual \end{bmatrix} \\
thegoal : \begin{bmatrix} id : paris \\ type : city \end{bmatrix}
\end{bmatrix}
$$

However, the lexical head of the former analysis tree, *fly*, is incompatible with the target semantics, and there is no other suitable candidate at the node indexed by *FLIGHT*. So the search continues in the proximity, first at the node *TRAVEL*, which is successful but not specific enough, then (successfully) at its daughter node

DRIVE. Next, the syntactic *args* of the instantiated lexical head *drive*:

$$\left\langle \begin{bmatrix} syntax : head : n \\ semantics : \begin{bmatrix} id : speaker \\ type : individual \end{bmatrix} \end{bmatrix} \begin{bmatrix} syntax : head : prep \\ semantics : \begin{bmatrix} id : paris \\ type : city \end{bmatrix} \end{bmatrix} \right\rangle$$

are matched off against corresponding subtrees in the former analysis tree, on the basis of their semantics. Since an exact match is possible, these subtrees are copied over onto the target analysis tree in their entirety.

6 Updating the Dialogue Manager

Generation of system utterances results in the extension of dialogue, belief and linguistic history models in the dialogue manager (in Fig. 1 the dialogue model is within the dialogue planning component). The dialogue model is updated when a set of moves for the system utterance is constructed by the dialogue planner. This process may close existing exchanges or open new ones; for example, the move underlying *you want to travel from London to Paris* in (1) opens a confirmation exchange. The belief model is updated when the description of objects referenced in the move is built for the utterance planner. When the belief model is updated, existing objects may be modified or new ones created; with the above example, the *owner* attribute of the GO object changes from *user* to *shared* reflecting its status as shared knowledge. Finally, the linguistic history is updated after linguistic generation: the complete semantic and syntactic analyses are passed back to the dialogue manager and recorded in the linguistic history. The recycling algorithm can re-use these analyses in subsequent generation cycles.

7 Implementation

The work described here has been implemented in Quintus Prolog. The planning and description routines form part of the Sundial dialogue manager, which has been designed to be maximally application- and language-independent. Linguistic generation is driven as a subroutine by the planning component. The lexicon, and the generation algorithm, currently employ DAG-coding. Tools exist for conversion between DAG-encoded and term-encoded data-structures; it is intended in the future to use term-coding to improve efficiency. Currently the linguistic generator has been developed and tested with English lexica covering two domains: financial transactions and flight enquiries; work is currently underway to customise it for a French UCG lexicon.

8 Conclusion and Future Research

We have shown how felicitous language generation can come about by referencing contexts about which the interlocutor knows. Because utterance planning depends on a conceptual model, different contexts will give rise to different descriptions. For a planner built along these lines, the 'logical equivalence problem' does not arise. Linguistic generation may also owe something to context, especially when there is a noticeable degree of redundancy in interlocutors' contributions – often the case in spoken dialogue systems.

The context-intensive approach to generation described here is also of importance for that other aspect of spoken language output, prosody (Youd and House 1991). Work is planned to evaluate the communicative effectiveness of spoken system output, from both prosodic and textual points of view.

References

Andry, F., Fraser, N., McGlashan, S., Thornton, S., Youd, N. J.: Making DATR work for speech: Lexicon compilation in Sundial. Computational Linguistics (to appear)

Bilange, E.: A task independent oral dialogue model. In proceedings of EACL, Berlin (1990)

Calder, J., Klein, E., Zeevat, H.: Unification categorial grammar: a concise extendable grammar for natural language processing. In proceedings of COLING (1988) 83–86

Calder, J., Reape, M., Zeevat, H.: An algorithm for generation in unification categorial grammar. In proceedings of EACL (1989) 233–240

Evans, R., Gazdar, G.: Inference in DATR. In Proceedings of EACL (1989) 66–71

Garrod, S., Anderson, A.: Saying what you mean in dialogue: A study in conceptual and semantic co-ordination. Cognition 27 (1987) 181–218

Gazdar, G., Klein, E., Pullum, G., Sag, I.: Generalised Phrase Structure Grammar. London: Basil Blackwell (1985)

Noord, G.: An overview of head-driven bottom-up generation. In Dale, R., Mellish, C., Zock, M.: Current Research in Natural Language Generation. London: Academic Press (1990) 141–165

Youd, N. J., House, J.: Generating intonation in a voice dialogue system. In proceedings of EUROSPEECH (1991) 1287–1290

Youd, N. J., McGlashan, S.: Semantic interpretation in dialogue. Submitted to COLING 1992

Young, S. J., Proctor, C. E.: The design and implementation of dialogue control in voice operated database inquiry systems. Computer Speech and Language 3 (1989) 329–353

MONOLOGUE AS A TURN IN DIALOGUE: towards an integration of exchange structure and rhetorical structure theory*

Robin P. Fawcett and Bethan L. Davies

The Computational Linguistics Unit
Human Communication Research Centre
University of Wales
College of Cardiff
University of Edinburgh
e-mail: fawcett@cf.ac.uk
e-mail: bethan@cogsci.ed.ac.uk

Abstract

This paper identifies a major problem in planning discourse, and then points to a solution. The problem is that of the relationship between models for monologue and dialogue. Rhetorical structure theory (RST) is selected as the current best prospect for modelling monologue. A model for exchange structure is then outlined - the systemic flowchart model - and we conclude by showing how the two can be related to each other in an integrated overall model.

1 Locating the problem

[2]We suggest the value of recognizing **two broad types** of structure — and so two types of 'grammar' — at the discourse level of planning. These are related to each other by **rank** (rather than **realization**), i.e. one type of structure is nested inside the other. For the first we shall use the term **genre** [Halliday and Hasan 1985; Ventola 1987], and for the second **exchange structure** [Sinclair and Coulthard 1975; Fawcett, van der Mije and van Wissen 1988]. Here we shall assume that a

---

* The work reported here has been supported by grants from The Speech Research Unit at DRA Malvern under contract no. ER1/9/4/2181/23, by the University Research Council of International Computers Ltd, and by Longman. We would like to thank the unknown referees of this paper and our immediate colleagues Calum Gordon, Yuen Lin and Ruvan Weerasinghe for their comments on an earlier version of this paper, and the last three and Gordon Tucker for many fruitful discussions of our developing ideas in this and related areas.

[2] Owing to publication constraints, this version of the paper omits large sections of the original. A full–length revised version of that is now published as Fawcett and Davies 1992. The latter contains additional sections on: (1) the problems of modularization in this area of NLP; (2) an overview of relevant work in NLG and NLU (where we point out that there are some surprising differences between what are, effectively if illogically, two different research paradigms); (3) a summary and justification of RST; and (4) more details of our implementation. We strongly urge that anyone considering implementing the SFM should take account of Fawcett et al [1988], Fawcett and Davies [1992], and, if appropriate, Fawcett and Taylor [1989].

single grammar of exchange structure serves all of the many types of genre, even when they have the form of monologue. While the relations of rhetorical structure theory (RST) may well also be relevant to larger, genre-sized units of discourse, it is exchange structure that is the locus for our proposal.

Much valuable work has been done in natural language understanding (NLU) research in modelling dialogue [e.g. Litman and Allen 1987; Carberry 1990], with particular attention given to the interpretation of goals and plans. Interestingly, NLU researchers have made little use of the 'discourse grammars' of text-descriptive linguistics such as Sinclair and Coulthard [1975]. In contrast, natural language generation (NLG) researchers in discourse planning have drawn on 'grammars of discourse' produced by text–descriptive linguists, but they have worked almost entirely on written monologue. Our basic assumption is that these two research paradigms need to be brought closer together, and on two dimensions: our models of discourse generation and discourse understanding should inform each other, as should our models of monologue and of **dialogue**. In other words, we suggest that all discourse can be insightfully approached as, essentially, dialogue (which can be extended to 'multilogue'). In this approach paragraphs, or indeed **monologues** of any size or structure, are regarded as **extended turns in dialogue**. The optimal model of discourse will therefore comprehend both NLG and NLU, and both dialogue and monologue. (However, we must also provide for the ways in which the expectations about the internal structure of different genres vary; see Sections 3.2 and 3.4 below.)

2 A model of monologue: rhetorical structure theory

McKeown and Swartout [1988] provide an excellent overview of work on NLG prior to 1988. Since then interest in **rhetorical structure theory** (RST) has grown considerably [e.g. Mann and Thompson 1987, Hovy 1988, 1990a, 1991], so that is now widely seen in the NLG community as a more promising long-term framework for paragraph planning than are **schemas** of the sort proposed by McKeown [1985].[3] RST is more open–ended — but also more problematical. It is our goal to integrate the best available work in this framework with that in our own framework (to be described shortly). We agree with the position taken by Hovy [1990a], namely that it is a theoretical framework within which there remain many issues — many more, indeed, than were observable when the theory was younger, even in its classic exposition by Mann and Thompson [1987]. Here we shall assume familiarity with the basic concepts of RST, e.g. as in (a) in Figure 1.

For reasons that will become clear in Section 4, we wish to suggest an alternative notation. Let us represent the nucleus and the satellite as being in a 'constituency'

---

[3] While the whole theoretical thrust of RST research is in monologue, Moore [1989] uses an approach that incorporates RST in a model of 'interactive explanation'. The overall framework is essentially that of a monologue, like most other generation systems, but it is one in which it is possible to ask follow-up questions of various sorts. However, this in no way affects the basic point, which is that RST has been developed essentially as a model of monologue. The model presented in Fawcett et al. [1988] and summarized in Section 3 provides for such 'break' exchanges.

relationship to each other, i.e. as sister elements of the structure of a higher unit, as in (b) in Figure 1. We shall use as labels for the **elements** in that higher unit the RST symbols 'N' and 'S' (for 'nucleus' and 'satellite'). The S to N relationship is one of **dependence**; it therefore captures the dependence expressed in (a) by the arrow (as does the familiar 'modifier' to 'head' relationship in syntax). If we then (1) express the nature of the **relation** as the label for the **class** of the **unit** (i.e. the span of text) that 'fills' the satellite, and (2) introduce an equivalent term ('basis') for the unit that fills the nucleus, then the relationships identified in RST have been captured in a notation that is fully consistent with the notation to be introduced in Section 3.4 for exchange structure. It also allows us to represent in a natural way the recursion in RST, whether of embedding or the sister units of 'sequence', etc.

One focus of interest in recent RST work has been the compilation of a 'maximum list' of possible relations and the search for the optimal way to subcategorize them; see especially Hovy [1990b] and Maier and Hovy [to appear]. The bases for such a taxonomic organization that have been discussed include: (1) a distinction between relations motivated by subject matter and by presentational criteria (in Mann and Thompson [1987], reminiscent of Halliday and Hasan's [1976] 'external' vs. 'internal' relations); (2) the various conjunction relations recognized in Halliday and Hasan's [1976] approach to 'cohesion' (in Hovy [1990b]); and (3) Halliday's proposal that each clause realizes simultaneously three (sometimes four) 'meta-functional' types of meaning: ideational (experiential and logical), interpersonal and textual [e.g. Halliday 1985] (in Maier and Hovy [to appear]). Our proposal is that there is no single overall network. In the proposal to be put in Section 4, the RST relations would be grouped according to their potential place in structure. And if it turned out that a large number were all possible at some point in structure, then the network should show just that. While experience suggests that systems normally have between two and six features, there is no virtue in building in features that are not well motivated (e.g. by reflecting some aspect of a higher level of planning). We therefore offer to those working in the RST tradition of paragraph planning the idea that it is the organization of **the discourse grammar itself** that breaks down the list into smaller groupings. Some (or all) of the distinctions mentioned above could still be relevant within these networks.

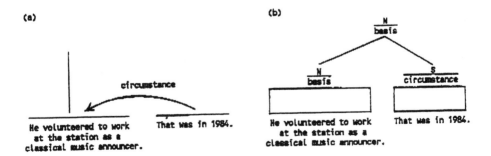

Fig. 1. Two alternative RST notations

3 A model of dialogue: The systemic flowchart model

3.1 The setting of the model

We shall now outline the main concepts involved in the approach to discourse being taken in the COMMUNAL Project[4] Figure 2 summarises the project's overall
structure, showing how the discourse grammars fits into the larger design. While
the model to be proposed here has been implemented in this framework, there is no
reason why it should not also be borrowed for use in other frameworks.

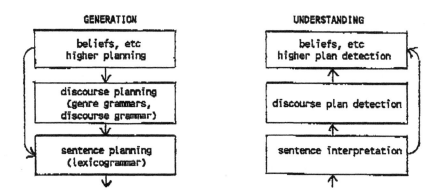

Fig. 2. The major levels of planning in COMMUNAL

The original **systemic flowchart model** (SFM) was developed by Fawcett, van
der Mije and van Wissen [1988] and was there termed the 'local discourse grammar'
(in contrast with the 'global discourse grammar' of the genres). What follows here
is a much shortened account of that 28-page description, and any NLG researcher
considering exploring this model further is urged to consult that paper and Fawcett
and Taylor [1989].

The SFM was originally developed as a tool for use in analyzing the discourse
of spoken interactive texts, including the language of children aged 6–12 and adult
coffee–conversation, but it has since been tested and thereby developed on a variety
of types of interactive text. It draws on a wide range of earlier work, including speech

---

[4] COMMUNAL is a major research project that applies and develops Systemic Functional
Linguistics in a very large, fully working computer system. The acronym COMMUNAL
stands for COnvivial Man–Machine Understanding through NAtural Language. The principles underlying the project are set out in Fawcett [1988]. The project has been planned
for an initial five-year period ending in 1993, and normally has 4–6 researchers in the
team. Some descriptions of COMMUNAL available in the public domain include Tucker
[1989], Fawcett [1990], Fawcett and Tucker [1990], Fawcett, Tucker and Lin [in press] and
Fawcett [to appear]. For a 'generationist's' view of computational linguistics see Fawcett
1992a, and for the reversibility of the grammar see Fawcett 1992b and O'Donoghue 1991.

act theory and discourse analysis, and in particular the work of the 'Birmingham School' (e.g. Sinclair and Coulthard's [1975] seminal study of classroom discourse, and the further developments in the school (e.g. Coulthard and Montgomery [1981]; see especially those of Berry and Burton). The SFM's three main claims to be an advance over earlier work are (1) that it is an explicit and so predictive model; (2) that substantial parts of it have been implemented in a computer model of discourse planning; and (3) that it generates a very wide range of discourse structures. There is a continuing process of revision and expansion.

3.2 Four axioms for modelling discourse

In developing the model four basic assumptions about the nature of discourse grammars were made.

The first is that, while there are different **grammars** (c.p. scripts) for higher units of structure (i.e. for casual conversation, classroom discourse etc.), they will all make use of the same grammar for the unit of **exchange** and its parts (in our case, the SFM). However, choices made in different genre grammars will set **different probabilities** (including zero) within the SFM, so that appropriate choices are made for different situation types. In some genres, such as service encounters or quiz shows, a high proportion of the choices are pre-selected, whereas in others such as casual conversation many more options would be left unprescribed.

Second, we assume that a grammar of discourse is an attempt to model (partially, as always) **psychological reality**.

Third, the model should not be merely **descriptive**, as are most other discourse models, but **predictive**. Earlier models were intended to be used in the analysis of discourse, not for discourse production. Fawcett et al.'s aim was to make their model **predictive**.

Fourth, we should expect the grammar of discourse to be reasonably complex. After all, sentence grammar is highly complex.

3.3 Five important characteristics of the model

Before introducing the grammar itself, we will outline the main areas in which it differs from earlier 'grammars of discourse' (**some** of which of course have some of the same characteristics).

First, the grammar provides for a much wider set of non-canonical but **discoursally grammatical** moves and acts in discourse. These include:

a. **Challenges**, e.g. *Don't say that about your sister!*

b. **Seek clarifications**, e.g. *But why can't I stay in bed this morning?*

c. **Oblique moves**, which operate on an ostensible and an ulterior level, e.g. *And you say I make a mess in the kitchen!*

d. **Unreal encounters**, where an utterance is not a communicative act in the normal sense, e.g. (to self, having just avoided being button–holed by someone who is not liked): *That was close!*

e. **Act-internal breaks**, which include self-repairs, interruptions that continue another interactant's act, and other communicative difficulties which are resolved (or otherwise) within an act. A SFM for these phenomena is given in Fawcett and Taylor [1990].

Second, the grammar models discourse as an ongoing **process**, rather than a **product**. When a user interacts with a computer, the structure of the **discourse** builds up gradually throughout the interaction. Therefore it is vital that a grammar of exchange structure destined for this type of environment (and, we suggest, any discourse grammar) should be **dynamic** rather than **synoptic** (c.f. Martin [1985]). What formalism can capture this? Not a phrase structure grammar, and not a systemic grammar — at least, not without supplementation.

The third characteristic is thus the formalism that gives the model its name. By supplementing the concept of the **system network** with that of the **flowchart**, we have a happy combination of formalisms that give us what we require. The flowchart relationships link up many relatively small system networks, where the networks are an expanded version of what is typically represented in flowcharts as a diamond-shaped decision boxes. Both decision boxes and networks provide **choices**, thus expressing **paradigmatic** relations. However, the choices provided by a system network are more complex those encountered in a conventional decision box. The dominant **syntagmatic** relationship is **sequence** between speakers' moves; this is the 'flowchart' element of the model (represented in Figure 3 by a line with an arrow). There is also the part-whole relationship of **componence**, which we shall meet later.

The fourth main characteristic of the model is that it is not merely cognitive, but **socio-cognitive**. A discourse is a joint production, being built in the minds of all the interactants (whether they are directly participating or not).

Finally, it should also be emphasized that the interactants are not only jointly producing a structured discourse, they are also creating a 'new' or 'modified' **reality** in their belief systems.

3.4 A simplified grammar of exchange structure: moves only

Figure 3 (taken from Fawcett et al. [1988:125]) presents a simplified version of the SFM. We shall explore the way it is used to generate exchanges through working an example. Each interactant is of course using his or her own version of the grammar as they build co-operatively the exchange, so the turn is passed (or taken) from one to another.

In terms of the network that we shall encounter in Figure 5, the discourse is both 'real' (addressed to a human (or other 'agent')) and 'straight' (has no ulterior purpose).

The choices among the number and types of act that may occur within each move (which we shall come to in Figure 5) have been limited to a single typical class of act per move. Thus the full SFM provides for many more choices than are shown in Figure 3.

We will assume that there are two interactants, A and B, who will jointly work through the system until an END is selected for the top–level exchange.

A selects [initiate exchange] and so enters the first system. (The names of features are enclosed in square brackets in running text.) A thus activates a realization rule

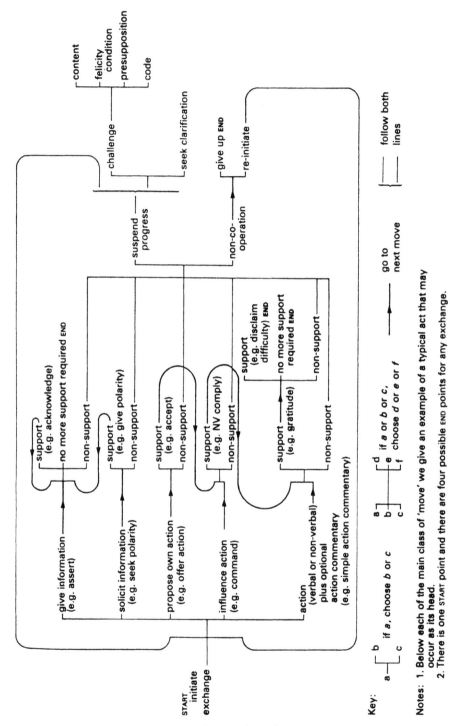

Fig. 3. A systemic flowchart model of moves in exchanges

to generate the **unit** of **exchange**, whose leftmost daughter element is an **Initiate** (represented as 'I'). See the left-most part of (b) in Figure 4 [adapted from Fawcett et al. 1988:126], which illustrates the structure we are generating. A must now choose between five types of move. In this example we choose [solicit information], and in this mini–grammar the head of the move is filled by the act [seek polarity] (i.e. seeking Yes or No as an answer). Notice that the five possible types of move fall roughly into two groups: the top two are both concerned with 'information', and the lower three are concerned with 'action'. The S–shaped lines in the section of the network concerned with 'support' neatly illustrate the dependencies within these two sets of move.

The line with an arrow following the choice of move signifies a **change of turn**. The addition of this extra element, necessary for the operation of the SFM, has raised some interesting issues in the grammar's implementation (see Section 3.5).

The change of turn leads into another system. Whichever class of move was chosen to initiate the exchange, B now has to choose between [support], [no more support required] or [non–support].

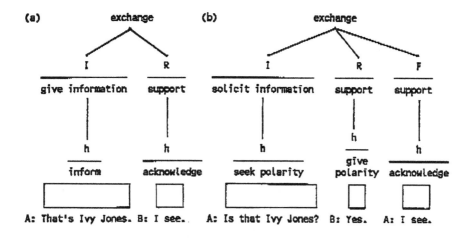

Fig. 4. Examples illustrating the common structure of two types of 'information' exchange

The term 'support' needs some comment. It is not a matter of 'psychological support' for the goals of the other interactant; the issue is whether the discoursal predictions set up by the preceding move(s) will be supported. In our case, the choice of [support] reflects B's decision to supply the information requested by A. A **Respond** element (represented by 'R') is generated; it is filled by a **move** of the 'support' class, and its head is in turn filled by an appropriate act such as [give polarity] (typically mediated by Yes or No).

What comes after B's choice of [support]? You will notice that the traversal loops back in the network to a point which can also be reached through selecting [give information] on the initial move. This illustrates the similarity in structure of the two types of exchange from this stage onwards, and also achieves economy in the grammar. (As you will see, even greater economy is achieved in the lower thee classes of move.)

At this point, the interactant can choose either [support] (which will result in the generation of a **Follow–up**), or [non–support] (the result of which will be discussed shortly), or [no more support required], which simply ends the exchange. In the full grammar there would be probabilities that show the likelihood of each of these. For brevity, we will assume that the latter is selected, so that our demonstration traversal is completed (in Figure @(b) [support] was chosen.).

So far we have only considered [support] moves. What if [non–support] is chosen? The interactant would then have to decide between [suspend progress] or [non–cooperation]. If [suspend progress] were selected, a further choice of [challenge] (various types) or [seek clarification] would be encountered. Both of these choices would cause a **Break** element to be generated, which would be filled by an **embedded bound exchange**. The selection of [non–cooperation] can either mean abandoning the exchange (i.e. ending it abruptly) or re–initiating. If B were to choose to re–initiate, the 'R' element would be added to the structure at the present layer of embedding — an embedded structure would not be generated. This is because choosing [non–cooperation] implies that the existing exchange will not be returned to, while, if a [suspend progress] is selected, the original exchange may, subject to memory limitations, be taken up again.

3.5 A fragment of a fuller network

The network that is actually being implemented in the COMMUNAL Project is very much fuller than the one shown in Figure 3. A large fragment of it is shown in Figure 5 (reproduced from Fawcett et al. 1988). As often happens, the computer implementation of the network model has led to useful modifications to the model; it has also provided the occasion to make certain improvements that were known to be needed in any case, such as the probabilities (to prevent it over-generating).[5]

The main points to notice are (1) the use of curly brackets to lead on to more than one simultaneous (i.e. parallel) systems — not all of which are in fact parallel, as we shall see; and (2) the proliferation of systems offering choices between classes of acts. These come from three main sources: the literature of linguistic studies of discourse (so that there is an overlap with some of the relations in RST): speech act theory, especially for the primary subcategories of [give information]; and new labels prompted by the needs of the analysis of which the SFM was first developed, and subsequent corpora upon which it has been tested.

We shall now describe an important extension to the model which both tightens up its predictive power and allows us to express **probabilities**. Suppose the type of question asked had been a [seek now content] (a 'Wh–question' such as Where's

---

[5] The discourse grammars consist of a PROLOG program and a set of grammar files; the files contain a representation of the system networks and realization rules in the form of PROLOG facts, which are then interpreted by the DEFREL program (so called because it DEFines RELations). The whole system operates in the POPLOG environment on a SUN 4 SPARCstation.

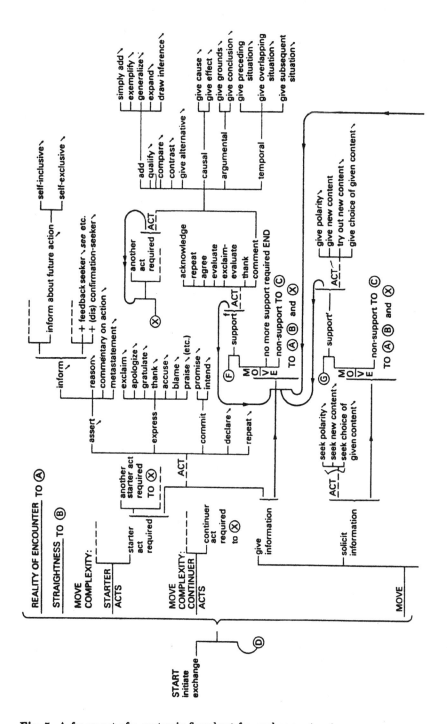

Fig. 5. A fragment of a systemic flowchart for exchange structure

Utah?) A support move would probably be a [give new content], like In the US, but it might be a [try out new content], like In the US? We represent the difference in probabilities by ensuring that, whenever [seek new content] and [support] are chosen, there is a **change in the probabilities in the subsequent ACT system** (which is bottom right in Figure 5). In our case [give new content] gets 99%, [try out new content] 1%, and the others (such as [give polarity], etc.) get 0%. If [seek polarity] is chosen the new probabilities reflect the very different predictions. In any particular case, of course, interactants' higher goals and plans guide their choices, but we see a value (especially in discourse interpretation but also in generation) in modelling the interactants' knowledge of their discourse grammar. The **preferences** mechanism for implementing this is taken over from the sentence grammar in GENESYS; see Fawcett et al [1992] and Fawcett [to appear]. The great advantage of using probabilities in this way for discourse is that one can represent the interactants' knowledge of the **relative** likelihood of a particular choice being made in a particular environment — something that can simply not be done with the 'all–or–nothing' type of grammatical rule. (Before leaving probabilities, we should point out that they additionally provide a mechanism through which choices in the genre grammar can pre–select options in the grammar of exchanges.)

However, there is a **notational ambiguity** in the representation used in Figure 5 that needs to be cleared up. We have noted that a change of turn is represented by a line marked with a single arrow; it emerges from a curly bracket which also leads, via a broken line, to the specification of the class that fills the head of the move being generated. In the systemic notation such curly brackets normally mean that the systems to its right are to be traversed in parallel, it being immaterial which of the systems is traversed first. But this is not so in the present discourse grammar. Here, clearly, the head act of the current move - and indeed any continuer acts that it contains — must be generated before the turn is passed to another interactant. This has been handled in the implementation through the following two procedures (one for each type of line). The more basic of the two is that the 'flowchart' relationship (shown in Figures 7 and 9 as lines with single arrows) is implemented by a turn-passing algorithm (for which see Davies 1991:94f.). But **before this applies** we must first implement the second type of 'syntagmatic' relationship in Figure 5 (represented by the broken line). This is the step down the rank scale from move to the various small systems specifying the choice of act, and it is implemented as a re–entry rule (rather as in the lexicogrammar).

Another change made in the computer implementation was to move the systems relating to starter and continuer acts so that they appear in an appropriate syntagmatic relation to the head acts. In so doing, the somewhat crude recursive mechanism for starter and continuer acts (the line with a double arrow) has been replaced (For further details see Fawcett and Davies [1992]).

In other words, the generation process for exchange structures such as those in Figure 4 is a series of relatively short passes through small, independent networks.[6]

---

[6] For a fuller account of the changes made to Fawcett et al., together with a 'walk through' of the stages of generation of a discourse in which the tree structure is built up stage by stage, see Davies [1991].

4 Towards a merger of the two models

RST and the SFM already have a considerable amount common.[7] The desirability
of a merger of the two comes from the **complementarity** of their strengths. While
RST has been developed for monologue, the SFM focuses on dialogue. Each can
claim with some legitimacy that it is the most highly developed model of its kind
in its field, and each is based in the analysis of large bodies of text. Neither claims
to have reached a 'final' stage of development, but each is fairly confident about the
value of its central assumptions. The key questions are:

(1) Are the two models indeed compatible?

(2) Where would the connection be made?

The proposal that we wish to make may by now have become self–evident. As
we saw when looking at the acts in Figure 5, there is a strong similarity between the
relations in RST and the continuer acts in the SFM. Moreover, we noted that the
SFM is acknowledged to need further development in this vital area. Our proposal
is that RST, as currently represented, is (or includes, see below) what is in SFM
terms effectively a **description of moves of the 'give information' class and
their constituents**. This is because the model was developed with written texts
of this type — though it is likely that many RST categories will also be relevant to
other types of move. As we saw in Section 2, the difference in the way in which the
structures are represented in RST and in the SFM is less great than it might at first
appear; Figure 1(b) and Figure 4 are capture the same relationships (though the
labels are, of course, different). There already exists in the COMMUNAL Project a
discourse grammar for generating exchanges of the sort shown in Figure 4, so that
it is clear that it could, with appropriate adjustments, have RST relations built into
it.

One of the current problems about RST as a grammar is that it fails to make
strong predictions as to what configurations of structures are discoursally grammatical and what are not. The work of Moore and Paris [1988] suggests one way of
constraining the apparent lack of control in the framework presented by Mann and
Thompson. We suggest the value of exploring the incorporation of insights such as
theirs in an expanded SFM, by foregrounding 'favourite' patternings through the
use of probabilities. The method for handling continuer acts introduced in Fawcett
and Davies [1992] and described in full in Davies [1991] may also have a role to play.

Clearly, the next step is for those working in the two traditions to explore this
exciting possibility. We might attempt to relate the categories recognized in RST to
the generative apparatus available in the SFM for the internal structure of moves —
initially for 'give information' moves and then for the other classes. If the current
RST predictions are right, there would be no more than one starter or continuer act
in most cases, but a considerable amount of embedding.

There is one apparent problem for the SFM in the RST approach. This is what
might be termed the 'rank scale issue'. The SFM currently makes use of a rank

---

[7] Both have evolved as complements to large systemic functional sentence generators
(NIGEL in Penman [Matthiessen and Bateman 1991] and GENESYS in COMMUNAL
[Fawcett and Tucker 1990]). In fact, the influence of SFG on each has been different (see
Maier and Hovy [to appear] for RST and Fawcett et al. [1988] for the SFM).

scale relationship between the units of exchange, move and act. But in RST there is no limitation on how many layers of structure appear in a text — each choosing from the same set of choices of relation. There is thus the potential for infinitely recursive embedding. This may be less of a problem than might at first appear, in that (1) the SFM already allows for recursive embedding (though so far only for whole exchanges), and (2) we who are working on the development of the SFM have no a priori commitment to an exhaustive application of Halliday's original rank scale concept [Halliday 1961] (as the Birmingham model appears to). If the evidence is that the relations recognized in RST are equally relevant at all layers of the structure of a complex move, then we will be happy to adapt the model to accommodate this.

In conclusion, Figure 6 illustrates how an RST structure may be located within a SFM structure. The text is taken from Mann and Thompson [1987], except that we have added the Initiate move and the following Well, and slightly adapted the text to make it a little more plausible as a spoken text. The analysis in the Respond move follows that in Mann and Thompson [1987], expressed in the SFM formalism. However, in a spirit of give and take, we have replaced (1) our term 'head' by the RST term nucleus (N), and (2) our terms 'starter' and 'continuer' by the RST term 'satellite' (S). The somewhat uninformative term 'basis', introduced in Section 2, is replaced by a specification of the class of act ('inform') wherever it is a 'free clause'.

Finally, we should point out that there is also a need to consider the relevance of the relations recognized in RST to the structure of discourse above the exchange, i.e. in the relevant types of genre grammar.

5 Conclusions

There are clearly already many issues to explore that arise in considering a merging of the two models. Inevitably, others will arise as the work proceeds. And we should note that any such experiment should also bear in mind some at least of the many unresolved issues pointed out by Hovy [1990a]. It will be interesting to see if fresh light is cast upon these through the implementation of the ideas suggested here.

We do not expect a 'seamless join' between the two models to occur effortlessly; there are bound to be difficulties of many kinds as we explore possible ways of bringing the two models together. But, given the richness and flexibility of the descriptive and implementational tools available to us, it is an enterprise on which we can enter with an expectation of some measure of success. In particular, we emphasize the increasing role that we expect the concept of probabilities on choices in systems to play in generation — at the level of discourse planning as at the level of sentence planning.

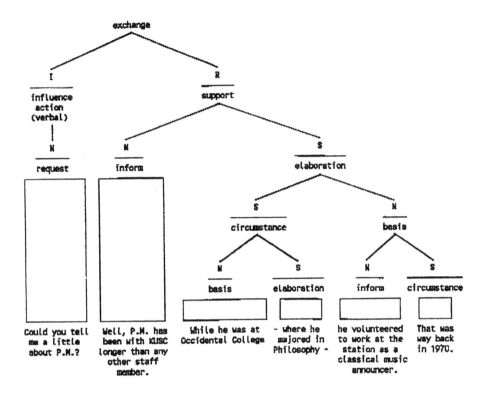

Fig. 6. Towards an integration of RST and the SFM

References

Carberry, S. (1990): *Plan Recognition in Natural Language Dialogue.* Cambridge. Mass. The MIT Press.

Coulthard, M.; Montgomery, M. (Eds) (1981): *Studies in Discourse Analysis.* London. Routledge and Kegan Paul.

Davies, B. L. (1991): *A Discourse on Discourse: Aspects of Implementing a Systemic Flowchart Model of Discourse Generation.* Msc Dissertation. Cardiff. University of Wales College of Cardiff. Dept. of Computing Mathematics.

Fawcett, R. P. (1988): *Language generation as choice in social interaction.* In Zock and Sabah (Eds) 1988b. Pages 27–49.

Fawcett, R. P. (1990): *The computer generation of speech with semantically and discoursally motivatedintonation.* In Procs of 5th International Workshop on Natural Language Generation. Pittsburgh.

Fawcett, R. P. (1992a): *The State of the Craft in Computational Linguistics: a Generationist's Viewpoint.* COMMUNAL Working Papers No. 2. Cardiff. Computational Linguistics Unit. University of Wales. CF1 3EU.

Fawcett, R. P. (1992b): *A Generationist Approach to Grammar Reversibility in Natural Language Processing.* COMMUNAL Working Papers No. 4. Cardiff. Computational Linguistics Unit. University of Wales. CF1 3EU.

Fawcett, R. P. (to appear): *A systemic functional approach to selectional restrictions, roles and semantic preferences.* Accepted for Machine Translation.

Fawcett, R. P.; Davies, B. L. (1992): *Some Issues in Discourse Planning: Towards a Marriage of Rhetorical Structure Theory and the Systemic Flowchart Model of Exchanges.* COMMUNAL Working Papers No. 3. Cardiff. Computational Linguistics Unit. University of Wales. CF1 3EU.

Fawcett, R. P.; van der Mije, A.; van Wissen, C. (1988): *Towards a systemic flowchart model for localdiscourse structure.* In Fawcett, R. P.; Young, D. J. (Eds) 1988. New Developments in Systemic Linguistics. Vol 2. Theory and Application. London. Pinter. Pages 116–143.

Fawcett, R. P.; Taylor, M. M. (1989): *A discourse grammar that allows flexibility.* In Taylor M. M.; Neel, F.; Boushuis, D. G. (Eds) 1989. The Structure of Multi–modal Dialogue. Amsterdam. North Holland. Pages 173–182.

Fawcett, R. P.; Tucker, G. H. (1990): *Demonstration of GENESYS: a very large, semantically basedsystemic functional grammar.* In Procs of COLING 90. Vol 1. Pages 47–49.

Fawcett, R. P.; Tucker, G. H.; Lin, Y. Q. (1992): *The Role of Realization in Realization: How a Systemic Functional Grammar Works.* COMMUNAL Working Papers No. 1. Cardiff. Computational Linguistics Unit. University of Wales. CF1 3EU. Also in Horacek and Zock (to appear).

Halliday, M. A. K. (1961): *Categories of the theory of grammar.* In Word 17. Pages 241–292.

Halliday, M. A. K. (1985): *An Introduction to Functional Grammar.* London. Arnold.

Halliday, M. A. K.; Hasan, R. (1976): *Cohesion in English.* London. Longman.

Horacek, H.; Zock, M. (Eds) (to appear): *Planning and Realization in Natural Language Generation.* London. Pinter.

Hovy, E. H. (1988): *Planning coherent multi–sentential text.* In Procs of 26th Ann. Meet. of ACL.

Hovy, E. H. (1990a): *Unresolved issues in paragraph planning.* In Dale, R.; Mellish, C.; Zock, M. (Eds) 1990a. Current Research in Natural Language Generation. London. Academic Press. Pages 17–45.

Hovy, E. H. (1990b): *Parsimonious and profligate approaches to the question of discourse structure relations.* In Procs of 5th International Workshop on Natural Language Generation. Pittsburgh.

Hovy, E. H. (1991): *Approaches to the planning of coherent text.* In Paris, C. L.; Swartout, W. R.; Mann, W. C. (Eds) 1991. Natural Language Generation in Artificial Intelligence and Computational Linguistics. Dordrecht. Kluwer.

Litman, D.; Allen, J. (1987): *A plan recognition model for sub–dialogues in conversation.* In Cognitive Science 11. Pages 163–200.

McKeown, K. R. (1985): *Text Generation: Using Discourse Strategies and Focus Constraints to Generate Natural Language Text.* Cambridge. Cambridge University Press.

McKeown, K.; Swartout, W. R. (1988): *Language generation and explanation.* In Zock and Sabah (Eds) 1988a. Advances in Natural Language Generation Vol 1. London. Pinter. Pages 1–51.

Maier, E.; Hovy, E. H. (to appear): *Organizing discourse structure relations using metafunctions.* In Horacek and Zock (to appear).

Mann, W. C.; Thompson, S. A. (1987): *Rhetorical structure theory: a theory of text organization.* In Polyani, L. 1987. Discourse Structure. Norwood, NJ. Ablex.

Martin, J. R. (1985): *Process and text: two aspects of human semiosis*. In Benson, J. D.; Greaves, W. S. (Eds) 1985. Systemic Perspectives on Discourse. Vol 1. Selected Theoretical Papers from the Ninth International Systemic Workshop. Norwood, N.J.. Ablex. New York. Academic. Pages 248–274.

Matthiessen, C. M. I. M.; Bateman, J. (1991): *Text Generation and Systemic-Functional Linguistics*. London. Pinter.

Moore, J. D. (1989): *A Reactive Approach to Explanation in Expert and Advice-Giving Systems*. PhD thesis. University of California. Los Angeles.

Moore, J. D.; Paris, C. L. (1988): *Constructing coherent text using rhetorical relations*. In Procs. 10th Cog. Sci. Conf. Pages 199–204. Montreal.

O'Donoghue, T. F. (1991): *A semantic interpreter for systemic grammars*. In Proceedings of the ACL Workshop on Reversible Grammars (Berkeley, California). 1991. Morristown NJ. Bell Communications Research.

Sinclair, J. McH.; Coulthard, R. M. (1975): *Towards an Analysis of Discourse*. London. Oxford University Press.

Ventola, E. (1987): *The Structure of Social Interaction: a Systemic Approach to the Semiotics of Service Encounters*. London. Pinter.

Zock, M.; Sabah, G. (Eds) (1988a): *Advances in Natural Language Generation*. Vol 1. London. Pinter.

Zock, M.; Sabah, G. (Eds) (1988b): *Advances in Natural Language Generation*. Vol 2. London. Pinter.

Abducing Temporal Discourse*

Alex Lascarides and Jon Oberlander

Centre for Cognitive Science *and* Human Communication Research Centre
University of Edinburgh
2, Buccleuch Place, Edinburgh EH8 9LW
Scotland, UK

Abstract

We focus on the following question: given the causal and temporal relations
between events in a knowledge base, what are the ways they can be described
in extended text? We argue that we want to be able to generate *laconic* text,
where certain temporal information remains implicit but pragmatically inferrable.
An algorithm for generating laconic text is proposed, interleaving abduction and
nonmonotonic deduction over a formal model of pragmatic implicature. We demonstrate that the nonmonotonicity ensures that the generation of laconic text is influenced by the preceding linguistic and extra-linguistic context.

1 Introduction

Given the causal and temporal relations between events in a knowledge base (KB),
what are the ways they can be described in extended text?

Elsewhere, we have argued that amongst the various ways, we will prefer those
which allow the reader-hearer H to retrieve all and only the causal and temporal
relations which the author-speaker S intended to convey. Such utterances we call
temporally adequate, a notion we define precisely below. Among those temporally
adequate utterances will be some which, although not marking the correct relations
explicitly, allow H to infer them successfully. Utterances which are both temporally
adequate and leave information S intends to convey implicit we call *laconic*.

We'll argue below that in some cases, laconic text is the most natural and so
its generation shouldn't be precluded. But generating laconic discourse can be a
risky business, since it requires S to assess which implicatures H will draw from it.
Having S reason about implicature may be an attractive idea, but without a logical
theory to underpin it, it is hard to assess its utility. Lascarides and Asher (1991a)
developed a particular formal model of temporal implicature. They extended the
formal interpretative framework of discourse representation theory (Kamp 1981) by

---

* The support of the Science and Engineering Research Council through project number
GR/G22077 is gratefully acknowledged. HCRC is supported by the Economic and Social
Research Council. We thank Robert Dale, Masato Ishizaki and two anonymous reviewers
for their helpful comments.

incorporating discourse (or rhetorical) relations. By representing knowledge of the world and of linguistic pragmatics by defeasible conditionals in a nonmonotonic logic, they showed formally how the knowledge could be used to augment the relatively neutral semantic representations with their richer pragmatic implicatures, including discourse relations and temporal relations.

Here, we consider how to recruit this framework in the service of generation. The current goal is to retain the same defeasible rules, and assess the extent to which the model can inform the generation process. In Oberlander and Lascarides (1991), we investigated one possible strategy, based Joshi *et al*'s (1986) Interactive Defaults. We concluded that it left the calculation of discourse implicatures in a peripheral position, and that a deeper model was required. We have therefore turned to a model which views generation as abduction, as proposed in Hobbs *et al* (1990). We offer a possible abductive generation algorithm. We conclude that the abductive generation of laconic discourse in the defeasible framework requires the interleaving of abduction and deduction; and that the nonmonotonicity of the logic permits context-sensitive generation, which is currently difficult in Hobbs *et al*'s system of weighted abduction.

In the next section, we motivate the need for generating laconic discourse. We then state the temporal constraints that define temporal adequacy, introduce the theory of discourse structure and nonmonotonic inference, and outline the shift from interpretation to generation. We then show in detail how the generation algorithm proposed treats some simple, specific examples. Finally, we contrast our approach with weighted abduction.

2 Laconic Discourse

It is generally agreed that it is not always possible, or even desirable, to syntactically mark all the temporal information that the speaker S wishes to convey to the hearer H (Hobbs 1979, Joshi *et al* 1986, Oberlander and Lascarides 1991). In particular, it is not always appropriate to mark temporal progression with cue phrases such as *after that* or *and then*. Sometimes, simplest is best: (1) is at least as coherent as text (2) if not more so, and one would not want to preclude (1)'s generation.

(1)   Max entered the office. John greeted him with a smile. He showed Max to the seat in front of his desk and offered him a cup of coffee.

(2)   Max entered the office. Then, John greeted him with a smile. After that, he showed Max to the seat in front of his desk. He then offered Max a cup of coffee.

But leaving temporal progression unmarked has ramifications. Although in some cases it produces the most natural text, in others it can mislead H. Consider the case where Jon switches off the heating, and then Judy comes in and says the room is hot. Unlike text (1), the fact that this temporal progression is left unmarked in text (3) is potentially misleading for H, for the second event described could mistakenly be interpreted by H as the *cause* of the first event: text (4) would be better in this case.

(3)   Jon switched off the heating. Judy came in and said the room was too hot.

(4)   Jon switched off the heating. Then, Judy came in and said the room was too
      hot.

If temporal information is to be left implicit, then S must ensure that not only
does the semantics of the linguistic structures she uses produce suitable entailments,
but that the pragmatic implicatures H infers from the linguistic structures must be
appropriate too. A discourse is *laconic* if it keeps some temporal information implicit
while retaining the right implicatures. We wish to generate laconic texts like (1) but
preclude the generation of misleading texts like (3).

3 Temporal Constraints and Implicature

To build a process that can generate laconic discourse we certainly need a character-
isation of what it actually means for a text to be pragmatically appropriate. Equally
obviously, we require a formal model of discourse implicature that can inform NL
generation. We now address these issues.

3.1 Temporal Constraints

We concentrate on those properties required of the generated utterance that are
central to temporal import. As in Lascarides and Oberlander (1992), necessary (but
insufficient) properties of an adequate utterance are *temporal coherence* and *temporal
reliability*. Following Bach (1986), we take 'eventualities' to cover both events and
states. Temporal coherence and temporal reliability are defined in terms of a set C of
relations between eventualities. This set intuitively describes when two eventualities
are connected. The relations in C are: causation, the part/whole relation,[2] temporal
overlap, and the immediately precedes relation (where 'e_1 immediately precedes e_2'
means that e_1 and e_2 stand in a causal or part/whole relation that is compatible
with e_1 temporally preceding e_2).[3] The definitions are:

- **Temporal Coherence**
  A text is *temporally coherent* if H can infer that at least one of the relations C
  holds between the eventualities described in the sentences.
- **Temporal Reliability**
  A text is *temporally reliable* if one of the relations in C which H infers to hold
  does in fact hold between the eventualities described in the sentences.

A text is temporally *incoherent* if the natural interpretation of the text is such that
there are no inferrable relations between the events. A text is temporally *unreliable*
if the natural interpretation of the text is such that the inferred relations between
the events differ from their actual relations in the world. It follows from these definitions that a text can be coherent but unreliable. On the other hand, there may be

---

[2] We think of 'e_1 is part of e_2' in terms of Moens and Steedman's (1988) event terminology.

[3] We assume that an event e_1 precedes an event e_2 if e_1's *culmination* occurs before e_2's. So
there are part/whole relations between e_1 and e_2 that are compatible with e_1 temporally
preceding e_2.

no question of reliability simply because we cannot establish a temporal or causal relation between the two eventualities. An utterance is temporally *adequate* only if it is both coherent and reliable. Laconic text is adequate, and also leaves some intended temporal information implicit. Ensuring that such a candidate is adequate thus requires a model of implicature. Of course, the set of laconic discourses describing a given temporal-causal structure need not be a singleton: there may be a further choice, or there may be no laconic description. We do not consider how to choose between rival laconic utterances; however, the approach as currently envisaged will proceed from inadequate laconic text to an adequate non-laconic one.

3.2 Discourse Structure and Implicature

The basic model of implicature which we wish to embed in the generation process starts with traditional discourse representation structures (cf. Kamp 1981), but goes on to assume that candidate discourses possess hierarchical structure, with units linked by discourse relations modelled after those proposed by Hobbs (1979, 1985) (cf. also Mann and Thompson 1987, Reichman 1984, Scha and Polanyi 1988). Lascarides and Asher (1991a) use *Narration, Explanation, Background, Result* and *Elaboration*. These are the discourse relations central to establishing the temporal structures, and they are therefore the only ones we consider here.

Lascarides and Asher provide a logical theory for determining the discourse relations between sentences in a text, and the temporal relations between the events they describe. The logic used is the nonmonotonic logic CE proposed by Asher and Morreau (1991). Implicatures are calculated via default rules. For example, they motivate the rules below as manifestations of Gricean-style pragmatic maxims and world knowledge, where the clauses α and β appear in that order in the text, and "α and β are discourse-related" means that one of the five discourse relations holds between α and β. Informally:

- **Narration**
  If clauses α and β are discourse-related, then normally $Narration(\alpha, \beta)$ holds.
- **Axiom on Narration**
  If $Narration(\alpha, \beta)$ holds, and α and β describe events e_1 and e_2 respectively, then e_1 occurs before e_2.
- **Explanation**
  If clauses α and β are discourse-related, and the event described in β caused that described in α, then normally $Explanation(\alpha, \beta)$ holds.
- **Axiom on Explanation**
  If $Explanation(\alpha, \beta)$ holds, then event e_1 described in α does not occur before event e_2 described in β.
- **Push Causal Law**
  If clauses α and β are discourse-related, and α describes the event e_1 of x falling and β the event e_2 of y pushing x, then normally e_2 causes e_1.
- **Causes Precede Effects**
  If event e_2 causes e_1, then e_1 doesn't occur before e_2.

The rules for Narration and Explanation constitute defeasible linguistic knowledge, and the axioms on them indefeasible linguistic knowledge. In particular, Narration and its axiom convey information about the pragmatic effects of the descriptive order of events; unless there is information to the contrary, it is assumed that the descriptive order of events matches their temporal order in interpretation. The Push Causal Law is a mixture linguistic knowledge and world knowledge; given that the clauses are discourse-related somehow, the events they describe must be connected as defined in $\mathcal{C}$; here, given the events in question, they must normally stand in a causal relation. That Causes Precede their Effects is indefeasible world knowledge.

A more formal notation makes clear both the logical structure of these rules, and the problems involved in calculating implicature. Let $\langle \alpha, \beta \rangle$ be a function: the clause β is to be attached to the clause α, where α is part of the discourse structure already. Let $fall(max, e_\alpha)$ mean that the main eventuality described by the clause α is a Max falling event. Let $e_1 \prec e_2$ mean the eventuality e_1 wholly precedes e_2, and $cause(e_1, e_2)$ mean e_1 causes e_2. Finally, we represent the defeasible connective as in Asher and Morreau (1991) as a conditional $>$: so $\phi > \psi$ means 'if ϕ, then normally ψ'. The rules for modelling implicature are then represented as schemas:[4]

- **Narration**
  $\langle \alpha, \beta \rangle > Narration(\alpha, \beta)$
- **Axiom on Narration**
  $Narration(\alpha, \beta) \rightarrow e_\alpha \prec e_\beta$
- **Explanation**
  $\langle \alpha, \beta \rangle \wedge cause(e_\beta, e_\alpha) > Explanation(\alpha, \beta)$
- **Axiom on Explanation**
  $Explanation(\alpha, \beta) \rightarrow \neg e_\alpha \prec e_\beta$
- **Push Causal Law**
  $\langle \alpha, \beta \rangle \wedge fall(max, e_\alpha) \wedge push(john, max, e_\beta) > cause(e_\beta, e_\alpha)$
- **Causes Precede Effects**
  $cause(e_2, e_1) \rightarrow \neg e_1 \prec e_2$

It should be stressed that the formal theory of implicature contains many other rules, including rules concerning information conveyed by aspectual classification, the different tenses featured and temporal adverbials. We highlight the current rules because they are relevant to the simple illustrative examples we consider below. We won't tackle here examples where an eventuality should be described as a state rather than an event, or by a clause modified by the pluperfect tense rather than the simple past. But because the generation process we supply is informed by the *whole* model of implicature, it is powerful enough to tackle such choices.

---

[4] Discourse structure is given a model theoretical interpretation in Asher (1991); e_α abbreviates $me(\alpha)$, which is formally defined in Lascarides and Asher (1991b) in an intuitively correct way. For simplicity, we have here ignored the modal nature of the indefeasible knowledge; in fact, an indefeasible rule is embedded within the necessity operator $\square$.

4 Interpretation by Deduction

Let us now briefly review how CE and the defeasible rules are used deductively, during interpretation, to infer the discourse structures of candidate texts. CE represents monotonic validity as $\models$, and non-monotonic validity as $\approx$. Two patterns of nonmonotonic inference are particularly relevant:

  - **Defeasible Modus Ponens**
    $$\phi > \psi, \phi \mathrel{\vrule height 1.6ex width 0pt}{\approx} \psi$$
e.g. Birds normally fly, Tweety is a bird; so Tweety flies
  - **The Penguin Principle**
    $$\phi \rightarrow \psi, \psi > \chi, \phi > \neg\chi, \phi \mathrel{\vrule height 1.6ex width 0pt}{\approx} \neg\chi$$
e.g. Penguins are birds, birds normally fly, penguins normally don't fly, Tweety is a penguin; so Tweety doesn't fly.

For example, in interpreting text (5) we assume the text is coherent and so attempt to attach the second clause to the first with a discourse relation (so $\langle \alpha, \beta \rangle$ is true).

(5)   Max stood up. John greeted him.

In the absence of further information, the only rule whose antecedent is satisfied in interpreting text (5) is Narration. Other things being equal, we infer via Defeasible Modus Ponens that the *Narration* relation holds between (5)'s clauses. This then yields, assuming logical omniscience, an interpretation where the standing up precedes the greeting. Defeasible Modus Ponens and logical omniscience entail that in (6), the greeting preceded the standing up.

(6)   John greeted Max. Max stood up.

Texts (5) and (6) show why it's essential that the temporal information conveyed by textual order should be represented. But it's also essential that this information should be represented as a default, for descriptive order doesn't *always* match temporal order, even if there are no syntactic markers to indicate this:

(7)   Max fell. John pushed him.

Text (7) verifies the antecedents to *two* of our defeasible laws: Narration and the Push Causal Law. The consequents of these default laws cannot both hold in a consistent KB. By the Penguin Principle, the law with the more specific antecedent wins: the Causal Law, because its antecedent logically entails that of Narration. Hence (7) is interpreted as a case where the pushing caused the falling. In turn, this entails that the antecedent to Explanation is verified; and whilst conflicting with Narration, it's more specific, and hence its consequent—*Explanation*—follows by the Penguin Principle. Compare this with (5): similar logical forms are assigned to the clauses because of the similar syntax, but different discourse structures, and different temporal structures are derived.[5]

---

[5] The formal details of how the logic CE models the Penguin Principle, and these interpretations, are given in Lascarides and Asher (1991a, 1991b). Note that although the double application of the Penguin Principle, as in (7), is not valid in general, they show that for the particular case considered here, CE validates the double application.

The discourse relations constrain the topic of a discourse segment, as defined in Asher (1991). Since we consider only the temporal domain here, we can replace topics with the simpler notion of *key events*, as used in Maybury (1991). Constraints between discourse structure and key events are used below to explain incoherence.

Intuitively, in describing an event structure, some events are more important in the story than others. Following Obermeier (1985), we assume that keyness is a two place relation on eventualities. The formula $key(e_1, e_2)$ means that e_1 is a key event relative to e_2; intuitively, the text segment containing a description of e_2 is *about* e_1. We assume that deciding a text's key events depends on the text's purpose and S's and H's points of view. Formally stating rules that represent relationships between purpose, point of view and key events are beyond the scope of this paper; this problem is tackled in Maybury (1991).

We provide event- and discourse-constraints on keyness: $key(e_1, e_2)$ entails that e_1 and e_2 stand in one of the relations in $\mathcal{C}$. Furthermore, the law below states that $Narration(\alpha, \beta)$ holds only if the eventualities described by α and β have a distinct common key event (cf. Asher's (1991) topic constraints on *Narration*):

- **Distinct Common Key Event for Narration**
  $Narration(\alpha, \beta) \rightarrow (\exists e)(key(e, e_\alpha) \land key(e, e_\beta) \land \neg key(e_\alpha, e_\beta) \land \neg key(e_\beta, e_\alpha))$

This rule is used to explain the incoherence of (8): as long as WK about cars breaking down and dying hair is represented as intuitions would dictate, one cannot find a common distinct key event, and so *Narration* between the clauses can't be inferred.

(8)   ?Max's car broke down. Mary died her hair black.

But no other relation can be inferred given the above defeasible laws. And hence no discourse structure for (8) is constructed.

The relations of *Elaboration* and *Explanation* also constrain the value of key: the following rule states that the event that's explained is key relative to the events that explain it.

- **Key Event of Explanation**
  $Explanation(\alpha, \beta) \rightarrow key(e_\alpha, e_\beta)$

Support for this rule comes again from explaining incoherence, this time of a text first cited in Caenepeel (1991):

(9)   ?Everyone laughed. Fred told a joke.

In (9), there is likely to be a causal law much like the one for pushes: if laughing and telling a joke are connected, then normally the latter caused the former. Accordingly, H will infer this causal relation, so Explanation's antecedent is verified. But in this minimal context, it is hard to see how laughing (on its own) could be a key for joke telling (on its own). This new constraint therefore blocks *Explanation* from being inferred; in essence laughing in (9) simply doesn't warrant explanation. But *Narration* cannot be deduced either, since this is blocked by the causal relation already inferred. Hence no discourse structure for (9) is constructed.[6] By a parallel argument, *Elaboration* constrains keyness in a similar way.

---

[6] Replacing *Everyone laughed* with *Everyone laughed until their sides split* improves coherence, even though the causal relation is the same. One can envisage a purpose for the

5 Generation by Abduction

Declarative grammars are regarded as appealing partly because they can be used bidirectionally. So how can our theory of implicature for text interpretation inform text generation? One answer is: through abduction.[7] Abduction is inference that is classically logically invalid, but is nonetheless plausible: it is 'inference to the best explanation'. Essentially, abduction permits us, from $p \rightarrow q$ and q, to assume p. p is then an explanation of why q is true. Abduction can be compared to the creation of plans via theorem-proving; generation by abduction thus bears some general similarities to generation by planning.

Making the antecedent of an indefeasible law true yields the consequent, *whatever* other premises are in the KB. But with defeasible laws, we must check that the context, as characterised by H's KB, actually permits the conclusion. If other facts are available, or if other rules are logically stronger, then the conclusion may not follow. Because of this, the algorithm for generation described below interleaves abduction and deduction. A nonmonotonic deductive check (NMDC) guides the abduction process so that a defeasible rule δ is used in abduction only if it is reliable to do so.

Abduction can be viewed as a process of support-location, as in Selman and Levesque (1990). We have a knowledge structure we want to support, and abduction helps us find ways of doing so. So, for example, $Narration(\alpha, \beta)$ supports e_α before e_β (via the Axiom on Narration). Some types of support are more desirable than others; in generation, we will prefer abduction to find supports for event structures that are directly linguistically realisable. That is, we will not rest until we have shown how to prove all the knowledge structure from a set of assumptions A which are actually justified by the text, without any defeasible inferential links between A and the text. Let's call such assumptions *concrete*. Assumptions concerning discourse relations and event-relations are not concrete; those concerning textual order or the presence of temporal connectives are concrete.

The process of abducing a description of a temporal structure will terminate when all the assumptions are directly realisable; that is: abductive generation is a search for concrete support, and it is not complete until all other supports have been shown to be grounded by concrete ones.

The generation process unfolds as follows. The initial knowledge sources for S consists of three sets: Δ, EC and ET. Δ contains the purpose of the text (we here assume it to be to inform) and also the KB H uses to interpret language—in other words, all the defeasible and indefeasible laws introduced earlier, and the facts H already knows about the eventualities to be described. EC is a pair of sets; the first contains the names of the eventualities, and the second contains all causal and part/whole relations between them. These relations induce a hierarchical structure on the eventualities: the part/whole relation is a subordinating one, and the

---

text that makes the latter event key relative to joke telling, making it worth explaining.
[7] Konolige (1991) proves certain equivalence results between defeasible reasoning and abduction. But these results hold only for those systems of defeasible reasoning that do not validate the Penguin Principle, and hence don't directly apply to CE.

cause/effect relation a coordinating one (cf. Nakhimovsky 1987). ET is the set of temporal relations between the eventualities.

The first process S undertakes in generation is to use the purpose of the text and S's and H's points of view to determine which eventualities in EC are the key ones. This produces an additional hierarchical structure EK, which describes which eventualities are key relative to others in the database. As we've mentioned, abduction to EK from the S's initial knowledge sources is beyond the scope of this paper, but see Maybury (1991).

Given the knowledge sources Δ, EC, ET and EK, the generation algorithm proceeds as described below. But first, some comments about discourse structure will help elucidate the algorithm. A discourse structure D is hierarchical on the clauses: *Explanation* and *Elaboration* are subordinating relations, and *Narration*, *Result* and *Background* are coordinating ones. D also fixes the textual order of the clauses via the semantics of discourse structure in Lascarides and Asher (1991a): textual order corresponds to the depth-first left-to-right path through D. Hence D will entail concrete assumptions about textual order, such as $\langle \alpha, \beta \rangle$, which essentially means "utter α before β". The construction of D described below will also fix what eventuality each clause describes; so, for example, D will entail concrete assumptions such as $fall(max, e_\alpha)$.

1. Start at the topmost leftmost eventuality in EC, and proceed in a depth-first, left-to-right manner on EC, abducing discourse assumptions pairwise (via Δ, EC, ET and EK) that will prove the relations in EC, ET and EK between the current pair of eventualities. Do this until all events have been covered. This produces a set D, which is the discourse structure.

2. We now proceed in a depth-first, left-to-right manner on D. We name the set of discourse relations between the current pair of clauses CDR; CER names the event relations between the eventualities that these clauses describe.

   (a) We add to the set $Conc$ the set of concrete assumptions arising from D that concern just the current pair of clauses.

   (b) We do an NMDC on Δ and $Conc$. This produces a set of inferences Inf.

      i. If Inf includes the relations in CER and CDR, then either (i$'$) abduce extra concrete assumptions about the current pair of clauses via Δ, and then go on to (i$''$); or else directly (i$''$) go on to next pair in D and start at (a); if there is no further pair in D, send $Conc$ to the surface grammar.

      ii. If Inf does not include the relations in CER and CDR, then abduce on any rule in Δ with a relation from CER or CDR in the consequent, which will add a *further* concrete assumption to the set of existing concrete assumptions in $Conc$. Add these further assumptions to $Conc$, and go back to (b).

Proceeding depth first left to right on EC ensures that each abduction is on a pair of events that are in temporal proximity. The output of each abduction is a discourse relation between the clauses. Given the constraints on which clauses in a text can be related by a discourse relation—the so-called openness constraints—the clauses must appear in textual proximity. Hence temporal proximity induces textual proximity.

Sibun (1992) argues in favour of a related 'localist' approach for generating coherent spatial descriptions.[8]

The KB used in the NMDC does not contain all of D, nor any of EC, EK or ET. This is because what the NMDC is trying to prove are the discourse relation for the clause currently being generated, and assertions about its event structure. The fact that these are provable from a KB containing them as premises would be trivial. We would fail to expose the contextual side effects of using default rules.

Notice that the NMDC is nonmonotonic, and the inferences drawn are sensitive to *all* the premises in the relevant KB, including in particular the concrete assumptions for clauses in D that have already been through the abduction process. Abduction for the clause currently being processed is therefore contextually bound, a fact discussed in more detail in the final section.

6 Worked Examples

We now consider two very simple examples in formal detail. These illustrate some general properties of the process we propose, and also expose some of its limitations. We are primarily concerned with the specification of the clausal semantics, textual ordering, and connectives, including cue phrases. So, while basically glossing over the selection of key events, let us consider in detail what is abduced after that.

6.1 The Push and the Fall

Suppose that the event structure to be described consists of two events—John pushing Max and Max falling—and a relation that the push caused the fall (and so preceded it). Thus EC is $\{\{fall(max, e_1), push(john, max, e_2)\}, \{cause(e_2, e_1)\}\}$, and ET is $\{e_2 \prec e_1\}$. The first task is abduce EK, in accordance with the purposes of the discourse.

Suppose that resulting EK is $\{key(e_1, e_2)\}$, so falling is the key. Let α be the clause that is to describe Max falling, and β the clause describing John's pushing him. Then abduction on Δ, EC, ET and EK will yield the discourse structure $Explanation(\alpha, \beta)$, where $fall(max, e_\alpha)$ and $push(john, max, e_\beta)$ must be true of whatever linguistic realisation we eventually choose for α and β. The rules abduced on are Key Event of Explanation and Axiom on Explanation; in this case, no other choice of rules in Δ will do. $Explanation(\alpha, \beta)$ fixes the textual order; α is to be uttered before β.

Now we construct $Conc$: it is $\{\langle \alpha, \beta \rangle, fall(max, e_\alpha), push(john, max, e_\beta)\}$. The NMDC on Δ and $Conc$ yields the inferences Inf, which are $Explanation(\alpha, \beta)$ and $cause(e_\beta, e_\alpha)$. Thus Inf includes CER and CDR. So the NMDC in this case has shown that no additional assumptions need to be made about α and β, although of course they may be made if S wishes: either step (i') or step (i'') could be now taken.

---

[8] However, unlike Sibun, we concur with Hovy (1988), and assume that calculating discourse structure is an essential part of text generation: there are constraints on which clauses can be related in a coherent discourse; generation should be informed by these constraints; and discourse structure encodes them (cf. also Polanyi 1985, Webber 1991).

Suppose we take the latter. Then $Conc$ is sent to the surface grammar for realisation, resulting in the reliable text (7).[9]

(7)   Max fell. John pushed him.

Alternatively, suppose we take step (i').[10] Then abduction on *any* law, defeasible or indefeasible, with elements in CER or CDR in the consequent is permitted. There may be a number of rules in H's KB that could be used. For example, Non-evidential Because, which is glossed as 'if α and β are discourse related and β features the connective *because*, then $cause(e_\beta, e_\alpha)$ normally holds'.

- **Non-evidential Because**
  $\langle \alpha, \beta \rangle \wedge because(\beta) > cause(e_\beta, e_\alpha)$

Abducing on Non-evidential Because will entail that $because(\beta)$ must be made true; this is added to $Conc$. So the text generated would be (10) instead of (7).

(10)   Max fell because John pushed him.

We don't address here the problem of choosing between (7) and (10); but we have fulfilled a task that's necessary to making such choices. We have spelt out in detail exactly what temporal information can remain implicit without misleading H.

6.2 Exception to the Causal Law

The NMDC that preceded abduction on the discourse structure in the previous example may seem superfluous. It didn't constrain the rules in H's KB that could be used for further abduction. In general, however, the NMDC is required, because of the context sensitivity of inference involving defeasible laws. We now consider a simple example that demonstrates the need for the NMDC.

Suppose that the event structure to be described involves the two events of Max falling and John pushing him once more, but this time the temporal relationship between them is different: the falling *immediately precedes* the pushing. This is represented by EC_1 and ET_1, respectively $\{\{fall(max, e_1), push(john, max, e_2)\}, \{\}\}$ and $\{e_1 \prec e_2\}$. Suppose furthermore that the discourse structure arising from abduction on Δ, EC and ET is $Narration(\alpha, \beta)$, where α describes the fall and β the pushing. Now assume for the sake of argument that there is no NMDC on Δ and $Conc$, which is $\{\langle \alpha, \beta \rangle, fall(max, e_\alpha), push(john, max, e_\beta)\}$. Then nothing will block S from using abduction on Narration. Suppose S uses abduction on Narration, *and nothing more*. Then the text generated will be (7).

(7)   Max fell. John pushed him.

---

[9] In Oberlander and Lascarides (1991), we discuss how this model of generation indicates why the occurrence of such 'unmarked' temporal reversals is rare in naturally occurring data. It should be stressed that we do not claim (7) is always optimal, although in certain contexts it may be (as urged in Caenepeel 1991).

[10] Whether (i') is used is a question of textual optimality; an issue we don't address here.

But given that the Push Causal Law and Explanation also form part of H's KB, H won't interpret (7) in the way S would hope. In this case, although the antecedent to Narration is verified by uttering (7), the consequent of this defeasible law won't be inferred by H because of the other premises in the KB. Of course, it would be possible for S to generate (7), test how H would interpret it, and then debug it if necessary. But it would be more efficient if the abduction process were guided so that S didn't generate (7) in the first place. The NMDC is there to play this role.

Consider now how the NMDC will block abduction on Narration in this example. The NMDC yields the nonmonotonic inferences from Δ and $Conc$, which as before are $cause(e_\beta, e_\alpha)$ and $Explanation(\alpha, \beta)$. These don't include CER or CDR; they are contrary to what S requires. So according to the above algorithm, abduction on rules that provide *additional* (rather than different) assumptions about the linguistic structure of the clauses must be made, in order to ensure that H will infer $Narration(\alpha, \beta)$. But abduction on Narration would not involve the assumption of additional linguistic structure, since its antecedent is already in $Conc$. So the NMDC precludes abduction on Narration in this case.

S must find another rule whose consequent is $Narration(\alpha, \beta)$, and whose antecedent must be proved by making additional assumptions about linguistic structure. Cue And Then is just such a law:

- **Cue And Then**
  $\langle \alpha, \beta \rangle \wedge andthen(\beta) \rightarrow Narration(\alpha, \beta)$

Abducing on this rule will involve the additional assumption that the clause β features the phrase *and then*. Hence, this path would ultimately yield the following, reliable text, the NMDC having ensured that (7) was never generated, in this context:

(11)   Max fell and then John pushed him.

This example may have an air of artificiality: under what circumstances would we want to describe EC_1 and ET_1? The example (13) below provides such a circumstance and also demonstrates the degree of context sensitivity featured in the generation process, arising from the NMDC.

7 Related Work

There is considerable interest in recruiting abduction for natural language interpretation. Advantages and disadvantages of various approaches are investigated in work by Hobbs *et al* (1988, 1990), Charniak and Goldman (1988, 1989), Norvig and Wilensky (1990), Appelt and Pollack (1991). Abduction in generation is considered by Hobbs *et al* (1990:26–28) and by Ishizaki and Ishikawa (1991). We here consider briefly two points of comparison with Norvig and Wilensky and Hobbs *et al*.

7.1 Commensurability and Optimality

Norvig and Wilensky (1990) contrast several abductive interpretation methods. They concede the attraction of measure- (or probability-) based approaches, noting that these enable information from various components of the grammar to be handled in a uniform framework. They go on to point out, however, that a single dimension of measure is not enough to represent cost, goodness of explanation and heuristic search control altogether. In this respect, we should observe that we do not have any measure at all available for representing these factors. We have here been concerned only with the generation of *adequate*, rather than *optimal* texts. To extend our account to deal with optimality, a mechanism—such as weighted abduction—taking into account more complex preferences could be exploited. On the other hand, even without a measure, we do capture part of the appeal of commensurable models: all the information manipulated, from event structures to textual assumptions, is represented in a uniform context-sensitive logical framework.

7.2 Weighted Abduction and Context Sensitivity

Hobbs *et al* (1990) have discussed the use of *weighted abduction*, which allows algorithmic choice between competing sets of assumptions. Weighting guides abduction via assertions about the relative cost of assuming each predicate featured in the antecedent. Costs are assigned to antecedents in a global fashion and are represented by superscripts. For example in (12), the cost of assuming p_1 and p_2 in order to prove q is $\omega_1 c + \omega_2 c$, where c is the cost of assuming q.

(12) $p_1 \omega_1 \wedge p_2 \omega_2 \rightarrow q$

We prefer to assume antecedents that prove the result and that have the lowest cost. Such a framework could thus provide a mechanism for preferring one adequate utterance over another.

On the other hand, weighted abduction has problems with the context-sensitive nature of language processing; in this respect, our approach has certain advantages. Consider again the NMDC with the event structure defined by EC_1 and ET_1. It might seem that weighted abduction would obviate the need for a deductive check. Perhaps we could weight the antedecent of the rule for Cue And Then (which is of the form $p_1 \wedge p_2$) so that its assumption cost is lower than that for Narration (of the form p_1). With such a scheme, (11) would certainly be the preferred description of EC_1 and ET_1. However, even if we could arrange this, we wouldn't want to. Under the suggested algorithm, Narration's antecedent could never be assumed at zero cost. The context-free nature of the weighting then means that Narration, as the higher cost rule, would *never* be preferred. And this would mean that the relatively natural text (1) would never be generated.

In fact, an NMDC is ineliminable in a system which permits abduction over a set of rules which incorporate default information. Hobbs *et al* (1990:47–48) observe that incorporating 'et cetera' predicates into their scheme means that certain literals can only be assumed once it has been established that no contradiction results. They further observe that the difficulty of handling the side-effects of assumptions 'may be fundamental, resulting from the fact that the abduction scheme attempts to make global judgments on the basis of strictly local information' [p48].

In this connection, we wish to note two points. First, the use of a nonmonotonic logical framework allows for a relatively graceful treatment of contextual side-effects.

Secondly, we can indicate the means by which we incorporate discourse-contextual factors by turning once more to example (7) with event structure defined by EC_1 and ET_1. Generating descriptions of event pairs *in vacuo* may seem a little strange; but generating them in context seems more natural.

The NMDC exploits the context-sensitivity of nonmonotonic inference, permitting a logical explanation of how linguistic and extra-linguistic context influence what can remain reliably implicit in a clause being generated, and hence when that text can be laconic. This property is, of course, most significant in extended text. By adding rules in H's KB concerning how the preceding discourse structure affects interpretation, we can supply an explanation of why (7) is unreliable in the 'null' context we considered in the previous section, but reliable below:

(13)   John and Max were at the edge of a cliff. Max felt a sharp blow to the back of his neck. He fell. John pushed him. Max rolled over the edge of the cliff.

Briefly, the following element of H's KB distinguishes the 'null' context case from (13). We assume H's KB contains a rule of LK that one doesn't describe events in the order: cause, effect, further cause:

- **Maintain Causal Trajectory**
  $R(\gamma, \alpha) \wedge cause(e_\gamma, e_\alpha) \wedge \langle \alpha, \beta \rangle > \neg cause(e_\beta, e_\alpha)$

For (13), consider γ to be the clause describing Max feeling the sharp blow, and α and β to be the clauses describing the falling and pushing, as before.

The logically unrelated antecedents of Maintain Causal Trajectory and the Push Causal Law are both satisfied in the NMDC; their consequents conflict. Under these circumstances, akin to the standard Nixon Diamond in default logic, CE produces no conclusion. Now, there is arguably a principle of *inertia* in the interpretation of text: if all else fails, assume that the discourse relation for the current sentence is the same as those used already in the discourse. A version of the principle is formally represented in Lascarides, Asher and Oberlander (1992); informally, its says that if you derive a Nixon Diamond of irresolvable conflict when attempting discourse attachment, you should assume the discourse relation is that which was used previously. If the principle is available in processing (13), the preceding discourse relation—in this case *Narration*—will be inferred between α and β. In contrast with the previous example, the NMDC will confirm that the discourse structure is compatible with what S wishes to prove. With the same temporal structure EC_1 and ET_1, the textual pair in (7) is reliable in the context of (13), but not in the 'null' context.

8 Conclusion

A formal model of the temporal implicatures underlying discourse can be incorporated into an NL generation process. By exploiting a nonmonotonic logic, we can extend DRT with a theory of discourse relations, and by employing abduction within this framework, we can show how to generate laconic discourse. A certain amount of nonmonotonic deduction must be interleaved with this abduction. We would argue that this is a price worth paying, if we want to generate texts like (1), where the descriptive order of the events guides the implicatures drawn.[11] Furthermore, although there is a cost, there is also a gain: abduction becomes context sensitive, and so we are able to explain why, in describing the same event structure, generation will yield different linguistic structures in different discourse contexts. The model's most significant current limitation is that it only provides adequate discourses, rather than optimal ones; this is therefore our current area of investigation.

References

Appelt, D. E. and Pollack, M. E.: Weighted Abduction for Plan Ascription. User Modeling and User-Adapted Interaction 1 (4) (1991)

Asher, N. and Morreau, M.: Common Sense Entailment: A Modal Theory of Nonmonotonic Reasoning. Proceedings of the 12th International Joint Conference on Artificial Intelligence. Sydney Australia, August (1991)

Asher, N.: Reference to Abstract Objects in English: A Philosophical Semantics for Natural Language Metaphysics. Book manuscript submitted to Kluwer Academic Publishers (1991)

Bach, E.: The algebra of events. Linguistics and Philosophy 9 (1986) 5-16

Caenepeel, M.: Event Structure versus Discourse Coherence. Proceedings of the Workshop on Discourse Coherence. University of Edinburgh, April (1991)

Charniak, E. and Goldman, R: A Logic for Semantic Interpretation. Proceedings of the 26th Annual Meeting of the Association for Computational Linguistics, State University of New York at Buffalo N.Y., 7-10 June (1988) 87-94

Charniak, E. and Golman, R.: Plan Recognition in Stories and in Life. Proceedings of the Uncertainty Workshop, International Joint Conference in Artificial Intelligence, Detroit USA (1989)

Grice, H. P.: Logic and Conversation. In Cole, P. and Morgan, J. L. (eds.) *Syntax and Semantics*, Volume 3: *Speech Acts* 41-58. New York: Academic Press (1975)

Hobbs, J. R.: Coherence and Coreference. Cognitive Science 3 (1979) 67-90.

Hobbs, J. R.: On the Coherence and Structure of Discourse. Report No. CSLI-85-37, Center for the Study of Language and Information, October (1985)

Hobbs, J. R., Stickel, M., Martin, P. and Edwards, D.: Interpretation as Abduction. Proceedings of the 26th Annual Meeting of the Association for Computational Linguistics, State University of New York at Buffalo, N.Y., 7-10 June (1988) 95-103

Hobbs, J. R., Stickel, M., Appelt, D. and Martin, P.: Interpretation as Abduction. Technical Note No. 499, Artificial Intelligence Center, SRI International, Menlo Park, December (1990)

Hovy, E. H.: Planning coherent multisentential text. Proceedings of the 26th Annual Meeting of the Association for Computational Linguistics. State University of New York at Buffalo, N.Y., 7-10 June (1988) 163-169

Ishizaki, M. and Ishikawa, A.: Taking 'Generation As Abduction' Seriously. Submitted to *COLING92*.

Joshi, A. K., Webber, B. L. and Weischedel, R. M.: Some Aspects of Default Reasoning in Interactive Discourse. LINC LAB 24 No. MS-CIS-86-27, School of Engineering and Applied Science, University of Pennsylvania, Philadelphia, April (1986)

---

[11] Note that changing the descriptive order in text (1) would yield a distinct temporal order of events in interpretation.

Kamp, H.: A theory of truth and semantic representation. In Groenendijk, J. A. G., Janssen, T. M. V. and Stokhof, M. B. J. (eds.) *Formal Methods in the Study of Language* **136** (1981) 277-322. Amsterdam: Mathematical Centre Tracts.

Konolige, K.: Abduction vs. Closure in Causal Theories. Technical Note No. 505, Artificial Intelligence Center, SRI International, Menlo Park (1991)

Lascarides, A. and Asher, N.: Discourse Relations and Defeasible Knowledge. Proceedings of the 29th Annual Meeting of Association for Computational Linguistics, Berkeley, Ca, June (1991a) 55–63

Lascarides, A. and Asher, N.: Discourse Relations and Common Sense Entailment. Research Report HCRC/RP-16, HCRC, University of Edinburgh, January (1991b)

Lascarides, A., Asher, N. and Oberlander, J.: Inferring Discourse Relations in Context. Technical note (1992)

Lascarides, A. and Oberlander, J.: Temporal Coherence and Defeasible Knowledge. Theoretical Linguistics **18** (1992)

Mann, W. and Thompson, S.: Rhetorical Structure Theory: A theory of text organisation. Technical Report ISI/RS-87-190, USC/ISI, June (1987)

Maybury, M.: Planning Multisentential English Text using Communicative Acts. PhD thesis, University of Cambridge (1991)

Moens, M. and Steedman, M. J.: Temporal ontology and temporal reference. Computational Linguistics **14** (1988) 15-28

Nakhimovsky, A.: Temporal Reasoning in Natural Language Understanding: the Temporal Structure of Narrative. Proceedings of the 3rd European Meeting of the Association for Computational Linguistics, Copenhagen (1987) 262-269

Norvig, P. and Wilensky, R.: A Critical Evaluation of Commensurable Abduction Models for Semantic Interpretation. In Karlgren, H. (ed.) *Proceedings of COLING90* (1990) 225-230

Oberlander, J. and Lascarides, A.: Discourse Generation, Temporal Constraints, and Defeasible Reasoning. Paper presented at the AAAI Fall Symposium on Discourse Structure in Natural Language Understanding and Generation, Asilomar, Ca, November (1991)

Obermeier, K.: Temporal Inferences in Medical Texts. Proceedings of the 23rd Annual Meeting of the Association for Computational Linguistics, University of Chicago, Chicago, Illinois, 8-12 July (1985) 9-17

Polanyi, L.: A Theory of Discourse Structure and Discourse Coherence. In Eilfort, W. H., Kroeber, P. D. and Peterson, K. L. (eds.) *Papers from the General Session at the 21st Regional Meeting of the Chicago Linguistics Society*, Chicago, April (1985) 25-27

Reichman-Adar, R.: Extended Person-Machine Interface. Artificial Intelligence **22** (1984) 157-218

Scha, R. and Polanyi, L.: An augmented context free grammar. Proceedings of the 12th International Conference on Computational Linguistics and the 24th Annual Meeting of the Association for Computational Linguistics, Budapest Hungary, 22-27 August (1988) 573-577

Selman, B. and Levesque, H. J.: Abductive and Default Reasoning: A Computational Core. Proceedings of the 8th National Conference on Artificial Intelligence, Boston (1990) 343-348

Sibun, P.: Generating Text without Trees. Computational Intelligence: Special Issue on Natural Language Generation **8** (1992)

Webber, B. L.: Structure and Ostension in the Interpretation of Discourse Deixis. Language and Cognitive Processes **6** (1991) 107-135

Using System Networks to Build Rhetorical Structures[*]

Keith Vander Linden, Susanna Cumming and James Martin

University of Colorado, Boulder CO 80309-0430, USA

Abstract

We are currently engaged in a project to study the generation of instructional texts for common consumer devices. Our initial efforts have focused on an exhaustive corpus-based analysis of instruction booklets for cordless telephones. In this paper, we present our analysis of the way the various processes used in this domain are expressed. Our emphasis here is on the relationship between the surface grammatical coding of these processes and the underlying rhetorical structure of the text. This analysis has been formalized using a systemic-functional framework, with the resulting system networks forming the basis for the IMAGENE text generation system.

1 Introduction

We are engaged in a project to study the generation of a kind of text we call *instructional text*. By instructional text we have in mind the kind of booklet you find when you purchase a common household appliance such as a telephone, alarm clock or VCR. Our initial efforts have centered around a detailed corpus-based analysis. This analysis is leading to a characterization of the overall structure of these kinds of texts, and characterizations of several interesting linguistic phenomena as they occur within this domain.

This paper will focus on the relationship between rhetorical structure and grammatical coding. In particular, it will present our analysis of the surface grammatical coding of a variety of local rhetorical relations in this domain. To make this discussion more concrete, consider the following alternatives for expressing a volume adjustment in the telephone domain.

(1) Adjust the volume to your preferred level *with the VOL LO/HI switch.*

(2) *Use the VOL LO/HI switch* to adjust volume to your preferred level. (code) [2]

---

[*] This work was supported in part by NSF Grant IRI-9109859.

[2] Our convention will be to add a reference to the end of all examples that have come from the corpus, indicating which manual they came from. (code) and (exc) will stand for examples from the Code-a-Phone and Excursion manuals respectively (Code-a-phone, 1989; Excursion, 1989). All other examples are contrived.

Given that a process such as volume adjustment can be represented as an action frame with an instrument slot, it would seem that (1) would be the most congruent alternative to choose. However, our analysis of the corpus indicates that instrument clauses such as the one used in (2) are the preferred form. The alternation hinges on whether the switch itself is the local topic, in which case the clause form is used. The clause form naturally appears most often since these texts are typically organized around the buttons and switches that control the device. The alternative form appears most often in initial installation instructions before the controls have been fully explained.

We have encountered many of these sorts of alternation during our exploration of this domain. Following a brief motivation of the theoretical tools we have used, this paper will describe our methodology for finding, analyzing and formalizing these distinctions and then will present the results of the analysis and how they were implemented in the IMAGENE (Instruction MAnual GENErator) text generation system.

1.1 Systemic-Functional Grammar

We have used the Penman implementation of the system network from systemic-functional grammar (Mann, 1985) to formalize the results of our study. Both theoretical and practical considerations have converged in dictating this choice for the current project. From a theoretical point of view, we are attracted to the system as an implementation of a functional approach to language. The basic research problem in text generation is identical to that of functional and cognitive linguistics: to discover the principles which allow speakers/writers to navigate the lexicogrammatical resources of their language and produce utterances/texts which satisfy simultaneous goals at a variety of levels, both cognitive and social in nature. As an implementation of the functional approach to language, Halliday's systemic theory is particularly useful, because the systemic formalism provides a convenient and consistent architecture for the description and implementation of the links between communicative goals and linguistic forms.

1.2 Rhetorical Structure Theory

We have used Rhetorical Structure Theory (or RST) (Mann and Thompson, 1988) as a descriptive tool in our corpus analysis and as a constructive tool in IMAGENE (Mann and Thompson, 1987c). It was developed at USC/ISI as a means of representing text structure — viewed in terms of the semantic and pragmatic relations that hold between text units at all levels — in a computational context. It was developed jointly by linguists and computer scientists, and is valuable in that it provides a means of incorporating well-established approaches from linguistics into a uniform notation.

While its suitability for representing interactive discourse is questionable, it has been successfully applied to a variety of written genres (Hovy, 1989; Hovy and McCoy, 1989; Moore and Paris, 1988). Generally a new domain has dictated modifications to the inventory of relations, but this very adaptability is one of its most useful features.

Earlier work on RST has focused on the higher levels of text structure: while a few researchers mentioned the desirability of extending rhetorical analysis below the clause level, this possibility has not yet been exploited. In our corpus, however, we found that most of the rhetorical complexity was located at the clausal and subclausal levels. This required the extension of RST into the clause in order to provide a uniform treatment for clauses and subclausal relations such as prepositional phrases. Consider the following examples of purpose relations, some at the clause level and some at the phrase level:

(3a) *To end a previous call*, hold down FLASH [6] for about two seconds, then release it. (code)

(3b) Follow the steps in the illustration below, *for desk installation*. (code)

(3c) The OFF position is primarily used *for charging the batteries*. (code)

Such examples, which are very prevalent in our data, challenge the widely held assumption that the principles governing inter-clausal relations are very different in kind from those governing intra-clausal relations. According to this view, the former can be characterized as simple (a single type of structural relation and a small finite set of relation types), highly productive, universal, and uniform (a single type of representation is appropriate for all levels from text to paragraph to sentence). Conversely, the latter is characterized as complex (requiring a large number of rules), highly constrained, language-specific (and thus learned), and diverse (different principles are involved in the organization of the noun phrase than the sentence; and within the noun phrase, different kinds of relations obtain between the head noun and e.g. its determiners and its adjectives). While this contrast does indeed hold at the level of form, at the levels of meaning and of discourse function we must recognize some degree of interpenetration between these two types of organization – specifically, phrasal constituents (such as the "for" phrases in the above examples) can have semantic content like that of the typical clause (they refer to actions or states) and relations with other constituents similar to interclausal relations, such as "purpose" (Cumming, 1991). Consequences of these observations for our implementation will be discussed below.

2 Corpus Analysis: Using a Database Tool

In order to design a generator for instructional text, it was necessary to first do an analysis of the rhetorical and lexicogrammatical characteristics of "natural" instructional text. The basic problem we face is to identify systematic covariation between forms and functional environments; for this study, we focus on the grammatical realization (clause or phrase type) of sets of actions and states bearing various rhetorical relations to each other. Various aspects of this problem have of course been addressed in the functional syntax literature, which mention a variety of relevant factors (among more recent work, see e.g. Cumming, 1984; Haiman and Thompson, 1989; Ford, 1988; the papers by Noonan, Thompson and Longacre in Shopen (Shopen, 1985); and various analyses in the RST framework, including Ford,

1986; Mann and Thompson, 1987a; Mann and Thompson, 1987b; Matthiessen and Thompson, 1987; Sanders et al., 1990). These works have proved fruitful as sources of hypotheses; however, they have all focussed on conversation, narrative, or expository prose, and we could not assume that the results would transfer to a new genre: in fact, clause combining strategies vary notoriously across genres (see e.g. Chafe, 1982; Beaman, 1984; Biber, 1988).

In conducting our analysis, we adopted a methodology of doing a comprehensive analysis of each of a small number of texts. Currently, the corpus is made up of the procedural text from two cordless telephone manuals, comprising around 1700 words of text. This approach is motivated by the need in functional analysis for the identification of multiple instances of both target linguistic forms and functional environments across a single text so that recurring correlations can be identified. A full grammatical and rhetorical analysis of the entire text is necessary, since it is not possible to determine beforehand what aspects of the context may be relevant.

The analysis was carried out by hand, since any automatic parser inevitably embodies assumptions about the answers to some of the very questions we were trying to address. We proceeded by creating a database containing three tables relating to different levels of structure: prepositional and noun phrases, clauses, and nodes in the rhetorical structure[3]. Hierarchical relationships in the text, both syntactic and rhetorical, were indicated via pointers between these files. Clause and phrase records contain, in addition to the text of the unit, fields for coding information such as determiner, number, and modification (for NPs) or linker, verb form, and argument structure (for clauses). The rhetorical structure file contains fields for indicating the nucleus and type of relation for each satellite, and the parent for each nucleus; all nodes contain pointers to the associated clause or phrase. In this way information about the core relations between rhetorical functions and morphosyntactic forms could easily be obtained, and it was a simple matter to test hypotheses against the entire corpus as they emerged.

3 Results of the Analysis: The System Networks

To formalize the results of this study, we have built system networks for the most important local rhetorical relations we found in our corpus: procedural sequences, purposes, preconditions, and results. These relations make up about 55% of the relations we identified in the corpus. Of the other types of rhetorical relations, joint and functional lists, which we address in the architecture but have not studied, make up about 20%, elaboration and title relations, tending to be at higher levels, another 20%, and seven other less common relations, 5%.

Our findings indicate that, not surprisingly, sequences of actions are expressed as sequences of imperative sentences. Purposes and preconditions are expressed as phrases fronting the actions they describe and results as separate declarative sentences following the actions they describe. There are, however, numerous conditions

---

[3] The actual RST and grammatical analyses of the text were carried out by one of the authors and the examples crucial to the formalization of the results were reviewed by all the authors.

that can alter this basic pattern. Actions, under certain circumstances, may be expressed as phrases attached to the end of the immediately following action. We call this process *rhetorical demotion* because the action, for rhetorical reasons, is not being stated as a separate imperative clause. Similarly, circumstances may dictate that relations normally expressed as subordinate clauses may be expressed as separate sentences. We call this *rhetorical promotion*. Here are some examples of these processes:

(4) Lift the handset and set the OFF/STBY/TALK [8] switch to TALK. Return the OFF/STBY/TALK switch to STBY *after your call.* (code)

(5) *1. Make sure the IN USE/CHARGE Light [10] is OFF.* 2. Tap the PAGE [11] button. (code)

In (4), the "after your call" is coding the action of calling someone, but the writer considered this to be obvious, and thus rhetorically demoted it. In (5), the writer considered having a particular light off important enough to rhetorically promote it. Occasionally, problems in understanding an instructional text arise from the inappropriate use of these promotions and demotions.

We have chosen the terms "promotion" and "demotion" because they employ a metaphor which implies a change from a more "basic" status. It is an undisputed universal of human languages that main, finite clauses function primarily to code new, independent actions and events, while noun phrases function to code time-stable entities. Non-finite clauses and nominalizations code actions and events which are either not new or dependent in some way (such as time, participants, or causality) on another event. These are the "prototypical" (in the sense of Hopper and Thompson, 1984) or "congruent" (in the sense of Halliday, 1985) functions of the various coding types. This claim has been justified both by means of cross-linguistic studies of the functions of similar forms in various languages (as in e.g. Hopper and Thompson, 1984) and by means of frequency counts in a single language (as in e.g. Thompson, 1987): the "congruent" mapping occurs more often. In our data, for instance, only 5% of the 65 reader actions were coded as demoted phrases, the rest were coded as imperative clauses. Similarly, only 9% of the 54 precondition expressions were coded as separate sentences.

Space limitations prevent us from detailing the entire set of system networks, so we will focus on the purpose network. We will discuss the functional distinctions the systems in this network make and how they use text-based realization statements to construct a rhetorical structure. The details of the other networks are similar in coverage and form to those presented here.

3.1 Purpose Relations in Instructional Text

Instructional text is action oriented and very often includes some statement of purpose for the actions it prescribes. Our study of these purpose clauses has resulted in the network shown in Fig. 1. Here are some representative examples of the purpose clauses/phrases we found in the corpus:

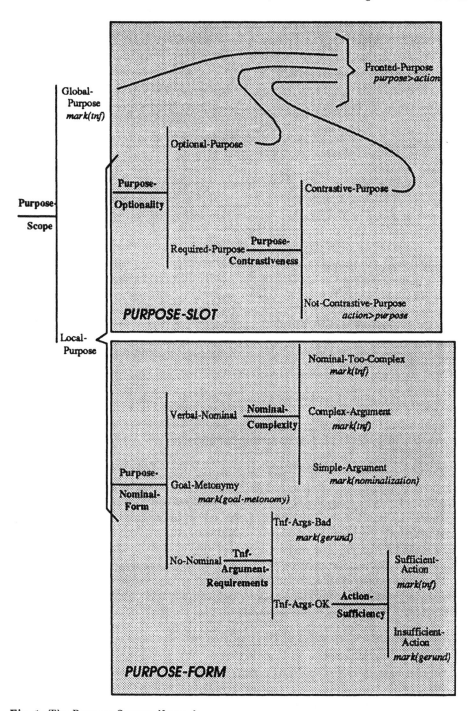

Fig. 1. The Purpose System Network

(6a) *To end a previous call,* hold down FLASH [6] for about two seconds, then release it. (code)

(6b) Follow the steps in the illustration below, *for desk installation.* (code)

(6c) The OFF position is primarily used *for charging the batteries.* (code)

(6d) *For frequently busy numbers,* you'll want to use REDIAL [7], and the pause will have to be in Redial memory. (code)

We can see two issues of choice at the rhetorical level in these examples. First, the purpose clauses/phrases can occur either before or after the actions which they motivate. Second, there are four grammatical forms to choose from. In (6a) we see a "to" infinitive form, in (6b) a "for" prepositional phrase with a nominalization ("installation") as the complement, in (6c) a "for" preposition with a gerund phrase as a complement, and in (6d) a "for" preposition with a noun phrase as a complement that is the goal of the corresponding action.

We'll now give a brief discussion of how the systems in the **purpose-slot** and **purpose-form** sub-networks address these two issues. The **purpose-slot** sub-network formalizes Thompson's notion of the "vastly different functions" for initial and final purpose clauses (Thompson, 1985). In keeping with her analysis, **purpose-form** represents the factors determining the form of the purpose expression separately from those determing the slot. Taken together, they can generate a greater range of purpose expressions than is typical in generation systems (see e.g. Hovy, 1988) and identify the functional reasons for choosing one form over the other. The purpose system as a whole handles 96% of the 29 purpose expressions in the corpus.

Purpose Slot. The **purpose-slot** sub-network places the purpose clause/phrase in the final position in most cases. The exceptions to this are when the scope of the purpose is multiple, the purpose is considered optional, or the purpose is considered contrastive.

The first exception, handled by the **purpose-scope** system, concerns the number of actions the purpose pertains to. We could not, for instance, restate (6a) as "?? Hold down FLASH [6] for about two seconds, then release it *to end a previous call.*" As Thompson points out (Thompson, 1985), the purpose clause is often used, as it is here, to state a context in which the prescribed actions are to be interpreted, and thus should be fronted. The restatement also implies, incorrectly, that the purpose applies to the last action alone rather than to the sequence of actions.

The remaining exceptions occur when the purpose is considered optional or contrastive and are handled by the **purpose-optionality** and **purpose-contrastiveness** systems respectively. Here are examples of them from the corpus:

(7) *For more information and wall installation instructions,* see the Installation Notes on page 3. (code)

(8) If your battery is not holding a charge and you believe it has developed a "MEMORY" condition, drain it and recharge according to the outlined instructions. *In order to prevent "MEMORY" from occurring,* keep your handset out of the base for at least 2 hours a day. (exc)

In (7), the purpose is optional, that is, the reader may or may not want more information at this point in the text. The purpose is, therefore, stated first to set the appropriate context for the prescribed action. In (8), the purpose of preventing "MEMORY" is stated in contrast to the state of affairs in the previous sentence. It is thus fronted to set the appropriate context for the prescribed action.

Purpose Form. The **purpose-form** sub-network, which determines the grammatical form of purpose expressions, is more complicated. As illustrated in the diagram, the form and slot sub-networks share the **purpose-scope** system. For a purpose whose scope includes more than one action, the "to" infinitive form is used. Example (6a) illustrated this. These sorts of context-setting purposes are not demoted to phrase status.

The remainder of the **purpose-form** sub-network is based on the observation that instructional text is oriented toward reader actions. Because purpose clauses/phrases are not reader actions, they tend to be demoted to phrase status whenever possible. Thus, the **purpose-nominal-form** system will realize a prepositional phrase with a nominalization as the complement whenever possible[4] This use of phrases with nominalizations in rhetorical relations is common in instructional text and elsewhere (Cumming, 1991).

Even if a nominalization exists, however, it still may not be used depending upon the determination of the **nominal-complexity** system. This system, based on the examples in our corpus, restricts nominalizations to a single, non-complex argument. Consider the following examples, each of which corresponds to one of the possible features of this system:

(9a) Use the VOL LO/HI [2] switch *to adjust volume to your preferred listing level.* (code)

(9b) ?? Use the VOL LO/HI [2] switch *for volume adjustment to your preferred listening level.*

(10a) FLASH uses proper timing *to avoid an accidental hangup.* (code)

(10b) ?? FLASH uses proper timing *for accidental hangup avoidance.*

In cases (9a) and (10a), taken from the corpus, there was a nominalization available, "adjustment" and "avoidance", but neither was used. The "adjustment" nominalization in (9b) was not used because it required more than one argument. The "avoidance" nominalization in (10b) was rejected because the argument "accidental hangup" was itself a nominalization and thus too complex. In both cases, the "to" infinitive form was preferred.

Goal Metonymy occurs in purposes when the goal of the purpose clause is more important than its action. This occurs in:

(11) *For frequently busy numbers,* you'll want to use REDIAL [7], and the pause will have to be in Redial memory. (code)

---

[4] The **purpose-form** sub-network currently represents three discrete points along the continuum from fully nominal to fully verbal forms expressing the same action (Quirk et al., 1985), namely the nominalization, the gerund, and "to" infinitive.

Here we have an ellipsis where the full purpose would be something like "to deal with frequently busy numbers" or "for dealing with frequently busy numbers". The object of the verb, in this case, is considered more important than the verb itself, allowing the metonymy.

If no nominalization is available, the **tnf-argument-requirements** and **action-sufficiency** systems will typically produce the "to" infinitive except when the infinitive form requires unwanted arguments or the action in the main clause is not sufficient to achieve the purpose. Here are examples of these cases:

(12a) The BATT LOW Light [9] comes ON when the battery is weak. The handset must be returned to the base *for recharging.* (code)

(12b) ?? The BATT LOW Light [9] comes ON when the battery is weak. The handset must be returned to the base *to recharge (the battery).*

(13a) OFF is used primarily *for recharging the battery.* (code)

(13b) ?? OFF is used primarily *to recharge the battery.*

Examples (12a) and (13a) were found in the corpus, while the alternate "to" infinitive expressions, (12b) and (13b) seem suspect; (12b), because we would be required to restate "the battery" which is unacceptable in this context, (13b), because the "to" infinitive clause implies that putting the handset in OFF position is all that is required for recharging the battery (which is not the case with this telephone).

3.2 Realization Statements for Text

The system networks we have developed, such as the purpose network, employ realization statements for text. These statements are similar to Nigel's realization statements except that they operate on rhetorical structures. We have used four basic types: **insert**, **order**, **mark**, and **remove**.

Insert adds a particular text function to the rhetorical structure tree. This statement is similar to Nigel's **insert** except that it is iterative and the functions it inserts are subscripted. By iterative, we mean that it adds an arbitrary number of whatever function is indicated. We can use it to add an arbitrarily long list of procedural actions as children of a text node, or to add a list of preconditions to a particular action. By subscripted functions, we mean that it is capable of adding any number of nodes of action type, and subscripts them. This way we can indicate, for example, which purpose nodes go with which action nodes.

Order is very similar to Nigel's **order** realization statement. It allows us to textually order two functions in the rhetorical structure. The **purpose-slot** system, for example, uses the **order** realization statement (denoted by < and > in Fig. 1) to specify the slot of the purpose clause/phrase.

Mark adds an annotation to a node in the tree. These annotations are used to determine which Nigel inquiries should be preset before the call to Nigel for a particular clause/phrase. The **purpose-form** system, for example, marks purposes as "to" infinitives (tnf), gerunds, etc.

Remove allows us to remove a particular node or link from the rhetorical structure. In a rhetorical demotion, for example, we **remove** the rhetorical link signifying that a node is an action, and **insert** the link for the same node indicating that it is a precondition satellite of another action.

3.3 Information Sources for Inquiries

Responding to the inquiries for the purpose system network, as with all the other networks we have developed, requires consulting four different sources of information:

1. The Process Representation — This source represents the process that the writer wants to talk about. It can be used, for example, to respond to the **purpose-scope** system in the purpose network which inquires about the number of actions the purpose in question pertains to.
2. The User Model — This source represents the information the user is expected to know and is used to respond to the inquiries concerning the level of detail of the instructions.
3. The Lexicogrammar — This source represents the lexical and grammatical tools available to the system for expression. It can be used, for example, to respond to the **purpose-nominal-form** system in the purpose network which inquires about the availability of a nominalization for a particular action. This approach uses the lexicogrammar as a resource, as Bateman has proposed in (Bateman, 1991).
4. The Style Parameters — This set of parameters represents the writing and formatting style of a particular technical writing shop. The result network, for example, consults this set to determine whether result relations be explicitly bulleted or not. The identification of such parameters for instructional text should aid in the ongoing effort to model register variation (Paris and Bateman, 1990).

Currently, we are defining the inquiry interface and have not built the tools to run them in what Nigel refers to as *implemented* mode (Nigel, 1988). We feel that building this interface is an important first step in determining what a text generator needs from these sources; from this information we can go on to design the required knowledgebases in the appropriate way as discussed in (Paris and Maier, 1991).

4 Implementation of the Results: IMAGENE

The results of the analysis just described, are being implemented in IMAGENE. The overriding goal of this project is to produce an instructional text generation system that is capable of taking the output of a planner and producing the appropriate instructional text. Thus, our goals overlap with those of other recent projects concerning instructions (Mellish and Evans, 1989; McKeown et al., 1990; Dale, 1990). We, however, have concentrated on the construction of realistic rhetorical structures and the generation of the appropriate syntactic structures corresponding to them. IMAGENE's architecture is designed to present an inquiry interface in generating texts, much like Nigel does when generating sentences and is depicted in Fig. 2.

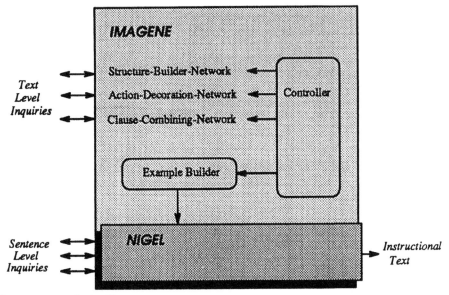

Fig. 2. IMAGENE's Architecture

IMAGENE's controller executes the three system networks depicted to produce a rhetorical structure. The resulting rhetorical structure is represented using an implementation of RST in LOOM (MacGregor, 1989) which includes those aspects of RST necessary for instructional text including purpose, precondition, and result relations and facilities for recursive depth of procedural and functional lists. This structure is then walked and Nigel is called for each expressible sentence. IMAGENE presets all of the attributes for each sentence that it identifies as relevant to the text structure, and Nigel, in turn, inquires about the remaining attributes that are relevant for the sentences. The inquiries that IMAGENE makes pursuant to building the text structure are presented in the same format as those that Nigel makes pursuant to building the individual sentences.

This architecture provides the flexibility to build a rhetorical structure and then pass back over it as many times as necessary making modifications. It also has the flexibility to use system networks or any other form of control structure on each pass depending upon the requirements of the task. Currently, only system networks are used, but it would be possible, for example, to include a spreading activation account of clause combining should that prove to be a more useful paradigm.

The remainder of this section outlines a sample run of the program, detailing the construction of the rhetorical structure, the attachment of local rhetorical relations to each of the actions in that structure (called *action decoration*), and the invocation of Nigel for each collection of nodes constituting a sentence. The example text includes two actions, moving a switch and extending the antenna, and both a precondition and a result.

4.1 The Structure Builder

The structure-building tool starts with a rhetorical structure of one root node and determines what type of children that node will have and then iteratively adds those children to the structure using the **insert** realization statement. It then recursively calls itself for each of the children using Nigel's **preselect** statement. This process results in a partial RST tree of arbitrary depth containing no nodes for preconditions, purposes, or results.

4.2 Action Decoration

IMAGENE then walks the partial RST tree, calling the action-decoration network for each action at the leaf level. This network attaches various local rhetorical relations to the actions and performs some restructuring. Figure 3 shows the root of the action-decoration network.

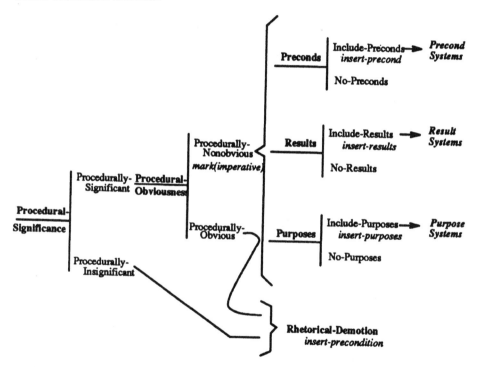

Fig. 3. The Action Decorator

The systems **procedural-significance** and **procedural-obviousness** specify that actions become imperative commands unless they are deemed procedurally insignificant or procedurally obvious, in which case they are rhetorically demoted and attached to the following action by the **rhetorical-demotion** gate. For actions that are significant and non-obvious, this network calls decoration sub-networks, such as the purpose network discussed above, to realize any desired preconditions, results, and purposes. Currently, the **Preconds**, **Results**, and **Purposes** systems simply inquire whether or not to include their respective relations.

The result of this pass is a decorated rhetorical structure. This is the partial rhetorical structure built by the structure-builder, extended with preconditions, results, and purposes and modified by any rhetorical promotions and demotions. The structure for our example is depicted in Fig. 4. It includes a root node called `text-root1` which has two procedural children, `action1` and `action2`. `Action1` has both a precondition and a result. In this example the environment/user has mapped the functions `action1` and `action2` to the abstract actions of moving a switch and extending the antenna respectively, `precondition1` to having the battery charged and `result1` to having the phone ready. This structure with these mappings is reflected in the resulting text shown in the next section.

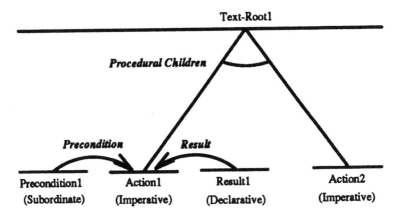

Fig. 4. A Sample IMAGENE Rhetorical Structure

4.3 Calling Nigel

When the decorated rhetorical structure has been produced, IMAGENE traverses the tree again, calling Nigel for each set of leaf nodes that constitute a sentence. All of the information about the sentence that is known at this time is preset in an example record, which keeps Nigel from making the same inquiries again. This includes information such as the mood and tense of the sentences and whether or not there are subordinate clauses. Nigel will inquire about any other information that it needs to produce the sentence, including the particular verb and whether or not there is a direct object. The resulting output of our example is:

When the battery has charged for 8 hours, move the OFF/STBY/TALK switch to STBY. The phone is now ready to use. Extend the base antenna.

This includes the two actions "move" and "extend", the precondition that the battery has charged, and the result the phone is ready to use. We did not specify any functional information that would dictate any rhetorical promotions or demotions, although we could, for example, have promoted the precondition which would produce "Make sure that the battery has charged for 8 hours. Move the OFF/STBY/TALK switch to STBY. ...".

5 Conclusion

We have discussed IMAGENE, a text generator that uses system networks to translate process structures into grammatically annotated rhetorical structures. We have shown how these system networks are capable of capturing the functional distinctions we found in our analysis of a corpus of instructional texts and have noted the requirements imposed by this analysis on the knowledgebases supporting text generation. Our plans for this work include: the inclusion of other forms of instructions in the corpus; the development of a process representation and user model which include the information we have identified as important; an investigation of the high level organization of instructional text; an analysis of lexical selection in instructional text including the use of non-literal language and referring expressions; and a study of when and why instructional texts include the local rhetorical relations we have been working with.

References

Bateman, J. A.: Decision making in text generation: Towards a negative definition. In Meteer, M. and Zukerman, I., editors, Proceedings of the IJCAI-91 Workshop on Decision Making Throughout the Generation Process, August 24–25, Darling Harbor, Sydney, Australia (1991)

Beaman, K.: Coordination and subordination revisited: syntactic complexity in spoken and written narrative discourse. In Tannen, D., editor, Coherence in Spoken and Written Discourse pages 45–80. Ablex Norwood, NJ (1984)

Biber, D.: Variation Across Speech and Writing. Cambridge University Press Cambridge (1988)

Chafe, W. L.: Integration and involvement in speaking, writing and oral literature. In Tannen, D., editor, Spoken and Written Language pages 35–53. Ablex Norwood, NJ (1982)

Code-a-phone Code-A-Phone Owner's Guide. Code-A-Phone Corporation P.O. Box 5678, Portland, OR 97228 (1989)

Cumming, S.: Local cohesion in Chinese and English: an approach to clause combining. In Proceedings of the Tenth Annual Meeting of the Berkeley Linguistics Society pages 465–471 (1984)

Cumming, S.: Nominalization in English and the organization of grammars. In Proceedings of the IJCAI-91 Workshop on Decision Making Throughout the Generation Process, August 24–25, Darling Harbor, Sydney, Australia (1991)

Dale, R.: Generating recipes: An overview of Epicure. In Dale, R., Mellish, C., and Zock, M., editors, Current Research in Natural Language Generation chapter 9. Academic

Press (1990) Selected readings from the 2nd European NLG Workshop, April, 1989, Edinburgh

Excursion Excursion 3100. Northwestern Bell Phones, A USWest Company (1989)

Ford, C.: Overlapping relations in text structure. In Proceedings of the Second Annual Meeting of the Pacific Linguistics Society (1986)

Ford, C.: Grammar in ordinary interaction: the pragmatics of adverbial clauses in conversational English. PhD thesis UCLA (1988)

Haiman, J. and Thompson, S., editors Clause combining in grammar and discourse. Benjamins Amsterdam (1989)

Halliday, M. A. K.: An Introduction to Functional Grammar. Edward Arnold London (1985)

Hopper, P. J. and Thompson, S. A.: The discourse basis for lexical categories in universal grammar. Language 60(4) (1984) 703–752

Hovy, E. H.: Planning coherent multisentential text. In Proceedings of the Twenty-Sixth Annual Meeting of the Association for Computational Linguistics (1988) State University of New York, Buffalo, NY, USA, June 7-10

Hovy, E. H.: Approaches to the planning of coherent text. Technical Report ISI/RR-89-245 USC Information Sciences Institute from the 4th International Workshop on Text Generation, Catalina Island, CA, July, 1988, edited and to appear in Natural Language In Artificial Intelligence and Computational Linguistics, 1990. (1989)

Hovy, E. H. and McCoy, K. F.: Focusing your RST: A step toward generating coherent multisentential text. In Program of the Eleventh Annual Conference of the Cognitive Science Society, August 16–17, Ann Arbor, MI pages 667–674. Lawrence Erlbaum Association, Publishers (1989)

MacGregor, R.: The LOOM Users Manual. USC Information Sciences Institute Draft (1989)

Mann, W. C.: An introduction to the Nigel text generation grammar. In Benson, J. D., Freedle, R. O., and Greaves, W. S., editors, Systemic Perspectives on Discourse: Selected Theoretical Papers from the 9th International Systemic Workshop volume 1. Ablex (1985)

Mann, W. C. and Thompson, S. A.: Antithesis: a study in clause combining and discourse structure. In Steele, R. and Threadgold, T., editors, Language Topics: Essays in honor of Michael Halliday volume 2. Benjamins Amsterdam (1987a) Also published as USC tech report ISI/RS-87-177

Mann, W. C. and Thompson, S. A.: Rhetorical structure theory: a framework for the analysis of texts. IPRA Papers in Pragmatics 1 (1987b) Also published as USC tech report ISI/RS-87-185

Mann, W. C. and Thompson, S. A.: Rhetorical structure theory: Description and construction of text structures. In Kempen, G., editor, Natural Language Generation: New Results in Artificial Intelligence, Psychology, and Linguistics. NATO Scientific Affairs Division Martinus Nijhoff (1987c) Proceedings of the NATO Advanced Research Workshop on Natural Language Generation, Nijmegen, The Netherlands, August 19-23, 1986

Mann, W. C. and Thompson, S. A.: Rhetorical structure theory: A theory of text organization. In Polanyi, L., editor, The Structure of Discourse. Ablex (1988) Also available as ISI tech. report ISI/RS-87-190

Matthiessen, C. M. I. M. and Thompson, S. A.: The structure of discourse and "subordination". In Haiman, J. and Thompson, S., editors, Clause Combining in Discourse and Grammar. Benjamins Amsterdam (1987) Also available as ISI tech. report ISI/RS-87-183

McKeown, K. R., Elhadad, M., Fukumoto, Y., Lim, J., Lombardi, C., Robin, J., and Smadja, F.: Natural language generation in COMET. In Dale, R., Mellish, C., and Zock, M., editors, Current Research in Natural Language Generation chapter 5. Academic Press (1990)

Mellish, C. and Evans, R.: Natural language generation from plans. Computational Linguistics 15(4) (1989) 233–249

Moore, J. D. and Paris, C. L.: Constructing coherent text using rhetorical relations Submitted to the Tenth Annual Conference of the Cognitive Science Society, August 17–19, Montreal, Quebec (1988)

Nigel The Nigel Manual. USC Information Sciences Institute, Penman Natural Language Group Draft (1988)

Paris, C. L. and Bateman, J. A.: User modeling and register theory: A congruence of concerns Draft – Submitted to Journal of User Modeling (1990)

Paris, C. L. and Maier, E.: Knowledge resources or decisions. In Proceedings of the IJCAI-91 Workshop on Decision Making Throughout the Generation Process, August 24–25, Darling Harbor, Sydney, Australia (1991)

Quirk, R., Greenbaum, S., Leech, G., and Svartvik, J.: A Comprehensive Grammar of the English Language. Longman (1985)

Sanders, T. J. M., Spooren, W. P. M. S., and Noordman, L. G. M.: Towards a taxonomy of coherence relations. Technical report Discourse Studies Group, Department of Language and Literature, Tilburg University, The Netherlands (1990)

Shopen, T., editor Language Typology and Syntactic Description. Cambridge University Press Cambridge, England (1985)

Thompson, S. A.: Grammar and written discourse: Initial and final purpose clauses in English. Text 5(1–2) (1985) 55–84

Thompson, S. A.: "Subordination" and narrative event structure. In Tomlin, R. S., editor, Coherence and Grounding in Discourse pages 435–454. John Benjamins Publishing Co. (1987) Outcome of a Symposium, Eugene, Oregon, June, 1984, and published as vol. 11 of the series Typological Studies in Language

Customizing RST
for the Automatic Production
of Technical Manuals

Dietmar Rösner[1] *and Manfred Stede*[2]

[1] FAW
  P.O.Box 2060
  D - 7900 Ulm
  Germany
  ROESNER@DULFAW1A.bitnet

[2] Dept. of Computer Science***
  University of Toronto
  Toronto M5S 1A4
  Canada
  MSTEDE@CS.TORONTO.EDU

Abstract

Rhetorical Structure Theory (RST) has emerged as a promising candidate for text representation in NLG. We investigated the applicability of RST in the automatic production of multilingual technical manuals. Starting from a domain knowledge base, we construct an RST-tree for a particular manual section, which is then converted to a set of sentence plans. These plans serve as input to sentence generators that produce the final text. In this paper, we report first on a number of open questions regarding general aspects of RST. Arguing that the original set of RST relations is not specific enough for practical *generation* purposes, we suggest a number of new relations that we found useful in our domain. After briefly examining the stage of RST tree construction, we then outline a procedure for converting RST trees to a sequence of sentence plans.

1 Introduction

The availability of technical documents in multiple languages is a problem of increasing significance. Not only do consumers demand adequate documentation in their mother tongue; there are also legal requirements, e.g. with respect to the upcoming European common market: the product reliability act forces merchants to offer technical documentation in the consumer's native language. The need to provide such a massive amount of multilingual material is likely to exceed both the capacities of human translators as well as those of currently available machine translation technology. We feel that this situation calls for the investigation of a potential alternative: to exploit available natural language generation technology in order to help overcome the documentation problem.

*** Part of the work reported in this paper was carried out during an internship at FAW Ulm funded from the ICSI exchange program. The work has also been supported by a University of Toronto Open Doctoral Fellowship.

This paper reports on the role of RST in subsequent phases of our ongoing work in the TECHDOC project, which aims at the automatic production of automobile maintenance manuals. Our initial step was the analytical production of RST trees for a corpus of manual texts in several languages, which lead to a few general observations regarding basic assumptions made by RST. These are discussed in section 2, and section 3 lists some additional rhetorical relations we found helpful in this particular genre. We developed a knowledge base that captures aspects of the automobile engine in order to be able to automatically reproduce instructional text. From this KB we build an RST tree, as sketched in section 4, and then convert it into sentence plans, which are finally handed to generator modules. At current these are PENMAN (1989) for English and SEMTEX (Rösner 1988) for German. This conversion step is the topic of section 5. For a more detailled description of the overall system architecture see Rösner and Stede (1992).

2 General Experiences with RST Analyses

We carried out our analyses as a prerequisite for the subsequent attempts to reconstruct the texts from a knowledge base. This perspective poses additional questions since an RST tree with (unformalized) segments from a text as leaves is an intermediate step only.

2.1 What is a minimal unit in RST analysis?

We have been looking at texts that present the same information (about maintaining a technical product) in different languages and tried to find out if identical RST analyses can be set up for corresponding text segments. In many cases this was obvious and straightforward (cf. Figure 1) but there are problems that are due to weaknesses and vagueness in basic definitions of RST.

For minimal units Mann and Thompson (1987) (henceforth M&T) demand that they "should have independent functional integrity"; in their analyses, units are essentially clauses. We found it difficult to rely on surface cues only, especially when we compared English and German text segments in parallel. Some Examples:

> "Check the coolant level in the reserve tank <u>when the engine is at normal operating temperature</u>."
> "'Den Kühlmittelstand im Reservetank <u>bei normaler Betriebstemperatur</u> des Motors kontrollieren."
>
> "... add a 50/50 solution of anti-freeze and water <u>to bring it up to MAX</u>."
> "...eine Lösung von Antifrost und Wasser im Verhältnis von 50 : 50 <u>bis zur 'MAX'-Linie</u> nachfüllen."

When we carried out our analyses, we employed two tests for the separation of the example texts into minimal units: The "paraphrase test" and the "gloss test".

The *"paraphrase test"* may help when a sentence is not immediately separable into "basic units" for RST, e.g., when the status of a prepositional adjunct is debatable. Is there a reformulation for the same content that uses a subordinate clause

...

4. Nachdem die Zündkerze am Zylinderkopf aufsitzt,   (7a)

   mit einem Zündkerzenschlüssel um 1/2 Umdrehung anziehen,   (7b)

   um den Dichtungsring zusammenzupressen.   (7c)

...

4. After the plug seats against the cylinder head,   (7a)

   tighten 1/2 turn with a spark plug wrench   (7b)

   to compress the washer.   (7c)

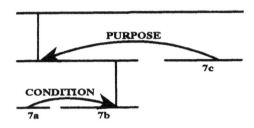

Fig. 1. RST analysis of parallel text segments

or separate sentences? If so, there is strong evidence to treat the adjunct as the realisation of a proposition in its own right.

The *"gloss test"* is a kind of multilingual version of the "paraphrase test". When we analyzed English, German and – recently – French versions of manual paragraphs in parallel, we asked whether in cases of differing surface constructions "glosses" of the other language's version would be possible as alternatives as well. If so, we were more convinced that the common RST analysis was well-founded.

2.2 Simultaneous analyses revisited

As M&T already stated (p. 28): "Sometimes there is a pair of spans in a text for which the analyst recognizes that more than one relation definition holds, i.e., the analyst affirms the defining conditions of more than one relation".

We found such examples as well:

> *"Never use spark plugs with an improper heat range; they will adversely affect engine performance and durability."*
> *"Replace plugs one at a time, so you don't get the wires mixed up."*
> *"Thread the new spark plug in by hand to prevent crossthreading."*

These recommendations can be analyzed as MOTIVATION relations if we allow the nucleus to present an action that should *not* be performed (example 1) or that should be performed *in a certain manner* (examples 2, 3). On the other hand the examples could as well be read as instances of OTHERWISE.

A way to reconcile such differing analyses could be – as in the systemic tradition – to distinguish different metafunctions:

The OTHERWISE relation is appropriate for the *ideational* level, the concern of which is, what the factual consequences of disobeying the advice will be; MOTIVA-TION is chosen on the *interpersonal* level: Why is the writer telling this; what effect is to be achieved on the reader (e.g., warn him or her)?

2.3 How to handle complex dependencies?

The RST analysis of the following text segment is given in Figure 2:

"[The spark plugs must be securely tightened]$_{8a}$, but [not over-tightened]$_{8b}$. [A plug that's too loose]$_{9a}$ [can get very hot]$_{9b}$ and [possibly damage the engine]$_{9b'}$; [one that's too tight]$_{10a}$ [could damage the threads in the cylinder head]$_{10b}$."

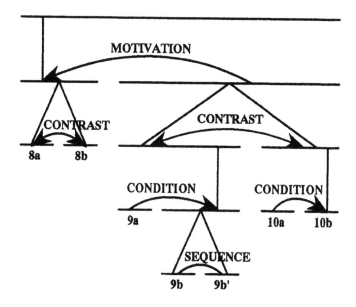

Fig. 2. Example from "Spark Plugs"

The problem with this segment is that the adjacency restrictions of M&T lead to an unsatisfactory analysis. 8a and 8b are in a CONTRAST relation that reappears – comparable to a 'respectively' construction – in the CONTRAST relation between sentences 9 and 10. On the other hand the pairs of non-adjacent segments 8a, 9 and 8b, 10 resp. are related also via MOTIVATION links but these links are not expressible in the RST tree. They could of course be made explicit in an arrangement like:

"[The spark plugs must be securely tightened]$_{8a}$, because [a plug that's too loose]$_{9a}$ [can get very hot]$_{9b}$ and [possibly damage the engine]$_{9b'}$. [On the other hand it should not be over-tightened]$_{8b}$, because [a plug that's too tight]$_{10a}$ [could damage the threads in the cylinder head]$_{10b}$."

In such an arrangement the MOTIVATION relations are explicit but the CONTRAST between the minimum and maximum value of the tightening has been stretched over a long distance, probably a too long one.

The general issue here is that on the message level we actually have not a simple tree but a net of related propositions and some of these relations are no longer represented in the RST tree.

2.4 What is in a text segment?

According to "classical RST", not only single propositions, but whole text segments function as nuclei and satellites of relations. We feel that there are still open questions with respect to the status of parts of a text segment when the whole segment in turn functions as part of an RST relation on a "higher level" in the tree. The CD player example (cf. Section 5.1) may serve as a case in point. Our analysis of the example text is shown in Figure 6.

The alternative propositions 1 and 2 serve as satellite of a NON-VOLITIONAL CAUSE relation with proposition 3 (the possibility that moisture may condense on the lens inside the player). Through the link *"should this occur"* (see discussion in Section 5.1), proposition 3 is related to proposition 4 (the player will not operate). RST forces us to take the whole text segment 1 to 3 as satellite, although the propositions 1 and 2 are no longer relevant (there may be other reasons for moisture condensing on the lens) for the relation between 3 and 4. As a first hypothesis, one might argue that only the nucleus of a text segment may be "accessible" on the next higher level. But: The isolated proposition 4 alone (the player will not operate) cannot sensibly be related to the recommended procedure in propositions 5 to 7, since only in the case of moisture causing the non-operability this procedure will have the desired effect. (Another way to rephrase this: In *"should this occur"* the demonstrative *"this"* has a narrow reading referring only back to proposition 3, whereas in *"in this case"* we have a wide scope reading, i.e., reference to the combination of 3 and 4).

We are faced with some evidence against the RST principle of (strict) connectedness, according to which a schema application spans the subordinate nuclei and satellites *in their entirety*, and all their parts have the same status. The example has shown that certain parts of a text segment can be much more prominent in the superordinate relation than others, and that the RST operation of always "drawing the line" over the complete spans does not take such differences into account.

3 RST in the Production of Technical Manuals

3.1 Local vs. global structuring

In the domain of maintenance information in manuals, RST relations are most relevant on a local level whereas the global structuring is much better accounted for by schematizing maintenance information as a plan with the following ingredients: Preconditions, a sequence of plan steps, post-conditions. The texts found in our analysis more or less followed this general layout. There are enhancements of this skeleton of the schema: Each step in the plan can have annotations that are warnings of various degrees of emphasis, or hints about potential errors or failures (cf. figures 3 and 4, and further discussion in section 4).

Changing Oil
1. Warm up the engine.
2. Remove the engine oil filler cap and drain bolt, and drain the oil.

    CAUTION: A warmed-up engine and the oil in it are hot; be careful not to burn yourself.

3. Reinstall the drain bolt with a new washer and refill the engine with the recommended oil to the upper mark on the dipstick.

    ENGINE OIL CHANGE CAPACITY: 3.5 ℓ (3.1 Imp qt, 3.7 US qt): Incl. oil in filter

4. Start the engine and make sure oil is not leaking from the drain bolt.

    ① Engine Oil Filler Cap   ② Engine Oil Drain Bolt

Ölwechsel
1. Motor warmlaufen lassen.
2. Motoröleinfülldeckel und Ablaßschraube entfernen und Öl ablassen.

    VORSICHT: Bei heißem Motor ist auch das Öl heiß; geben Sie acht, damit Sie sich nicht verbrennen.

3. Die Ablaßschraube mit einer neuen Dichtungsscheibe anbringen, den Motor mit dem empfohlenen Öl auffüllen, bis der Stand die obere Marke am Tauchmeßstab erreicht.

    MOTORÖLWECHSELMENGE: 3,5 Liter (Einschließlich Öl im Filter)

4. Den Motor anlassen und sichergehen, daß kein Öl an der Ablaßschraube ausläuft.

    ① Motoröleinfülldeckel   ② Motorölablaßschraube

Fig. 3. Excerpt from a manual page (Honda Civic)

3.2 RST (re)definitions needed

M&T based their definitions of RST relations on the material they had investigated. They did not assume to have defined a closed list: "We see it as an open set, susceptible to extension and modification for the purposes of particular genres and cultural styles" (p. 48). In the manual domain we frequently encountered structures that could not adequately be described using "classical RST". Some examples:

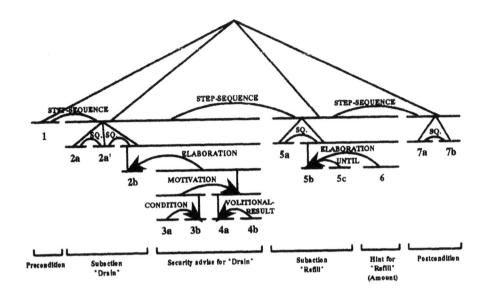

Fig. 4. RST-Analysis for excerpt from Fig. 3

PRECONDITION The CIRCUMSTANCE definition in M&T must be interpreted generously in order to cover cases like the following with the precondition as satellite:

> "Check the coolant level in the reserve tank when the engine is at normal operating temperature."
>
> "Fill the reserve tank up to the MAX mark with the engine cold."

CONDITION will not be adequate either. A reformulation as *"IF engine at normal operating temperature THEN check the coolant ..."* would actually be misleading.

The examples are best analyzed using a new relation named PRECONDITION (or something similar) with the following definition in the style of M&T:

---

relation name:	PRECONDITION
constraints on N:	presents an action
constraints on S:	presents an unrealized situation
constraints on the N + S combination:	S must be realized in order to make it possible or sensible to carry out N
the effect:	R recognizes that situation S must be realized in order to successfully carry out action N
locus of the effect:	N and S

UNTIL We frequently found examples like:

> "... turn the radiator cap counterclockwise until it stops."
> "Fill the radiator with new coolant up to the filler opening."
> "Flush the cooling system by pooring clean water into the radiator until it drains out clear."

If we want to see these examples as made up from two minimal units at all (cf. 2.1) we should have a relation – named UNTIL or similarly – where the nucleus presents an action and the satellite presents a "stopping" condition for the nucleus action, which often is at the same time the result of it.

relation name:	UNTIL
constraints on N:	presents an action
constraints on S:	presents an unrealized situation
constraints on the N + S combination:	N is carried out as long as S is not yet true; S may result from N
the effect:	R recognizes that N has to be carried out only as long as S is unrealized
locus of the effect:	N and S

In order to be helpful as a piece of advice, a "stopping condition" in an UNTIL-relation must be easily observable. This is not the case in the following example:

> "... leave the player for about an hour until the moisture evaporates"

One should not be mislead by the proposition "until" as surface cue; the example is better analyzed as VOLITIONAL RESULT relation (with the until-phrase as satellite), the "stopping condition" is here given as temporal information ("for an hour").

ALTERNATIVE Sometimes propositions are alternatives, but CONTRAST is not really applicable, as in the following example:

> "If the player is brought directly from a cold location to a warm location or is placed in a very damp room, ... "

Such arrangements may be analyzed using a multinuclear relation named ALTER-NATIVE[1] or similarly.

relation name:	ALTERNATIVE
constraints on N:	multi-nuclear
constraints on the combination of nuclei:	The situations or actions presented in the nuclei are alternatives
the effect:	R recognizes the nuclei as alternatives
locus of the effect:	multiple nuclei

---

[1] Scott and Souza (1990) refer to a relation with this name, but do not give a definition.

STEP-SEQUENCE In the manual domain, a typical text structure is an enumerated list of instruction steps. These steps correspond to the decomposition of the overall activity (which is encoded in the knowledge base, cf. Chapter 4). Therefore, the numbered sequence of instructions is of a different status than other SEQUENCE-relations, as for example within one instruction step: *"Remove the dipstick and check the oil level."* We suggest to represent the higher-level sequence, as prescribed in the KB, by a distinct relation named STEP-SEQUENCE and use the ordinary SEQUENCE relation for all other cases.

Other relation variants Beside providing new relation definitions, another obvious and practical way to achieve a more fine-grained text representation is the factorization of existing RST relations into more specific variants. For example, a CONDITION can be of temporal or causal nature, and its expression in natural languages may depend on that (in English, it does: 'when' vs. 'if'; in German it does not necessarily: 'wenn' covers both cases). As another example, the family of ELABORATION relations that M&T specify (set:member, abstract:instance, etc.) is to be linked to possible realizations in language.

4 The Production of RST Trees

In the last few years, the automatic construction of RST trees has been pursued by other researchers who formalized the conditions and effects of some relations, and suggested top-down planning mechanisms (Hovy 1988, Hovy 1990 and McCoy 1989, Moore and Paris 1989). In th system, however, tree construction is performed in a different manner, which we describe here only briefly (but see Rösner and Stede 1992). Due to our domain of choice, automobile maintenance instructions, the *macrostructure* of the text to be produced is highly regular and can be encoded in a similar way as the schemata used by McKeown (1985). We implemented the schemata in the same knowledge base that holds the underlying domain knowledge (in the KL-ONE dialect LOOM), thus providing for easy linkages between text structure schemata and domain knowledge concepts, which fill the slots of the schemata. This close relationship facilitates the construction of the RST tree, which represents the *microstructure* of the text, i.e., the local relations between text spans.

The schema that we extracted from the instructional texts we investigated has the following structure: First the location of the object(s) in question is described. Then, if appropriate, suitable as well as improper replacement parts or substances are listed. The actual steps of the repair or maintenance activities (which fall into three categories: checking, adding, replacing) constitute a plan in the traditional AI sense, where steps may have pre- or post-conditions, and may be refined by a complete sub-plan. Besides, additional advice can be given for a step or an entire plan.

The schemata consist of LOOM objects, and the RST tree is built up by methods that are attached to them. For example, the method defined for the object 'plan' checks whether this particular plan instance has a defined precondition, and if so contributes its propositional content to the RST tree via a CONDITION relation.

The steps of the plan are being realized as the nuclei of a STEP-SEQUENCE relation, and since every step itself can be a complex object, the 'plan' method calls the 'plan-step' method for each of them and integrates the results. Moreover, if a step consists of a refinement plan, the original 'plan' method is called recursively, and the result is combined with the RST representation for this step by a PURPOSE relation. This short characterization should suffice to illustrate the general idea of tree construction that we employed.

5 From RST Trees to Sentence Plans

In contrast to tree construction, the process of transforming it into language has received little attention in the literature so far. However, the development of principles for producing text from RST trees is an important step for judging their suitability as text representation vehicle on the whole. Only when non-ad-hoc mechanisms for converting trees to sentences exist do we have a testbed that allows to assess the true quality (and specifically the language-independence) of the intermediate RST representation. For the pursuit of this goal we intend to provide a start. Assuming at this point that the existing tree ensures the reasonable ordering of the represented information, i.e., the text will be *coherent*, the task of the rules we are after now is to produce a good, *cohesive* text from this tree.

5.1 Two examples

Let us illustrate the tree-to-text translation task with two examples. The translation is a one-to-many mapping, because the tree of course can be realized in a wide variety of ways. Some of the possible realizations are more acceptable than others. The aim in automating this translation step is to identify principles that ensure the production of texts that lean towards the 'positive' end of the scale. Consider the following excerpt from an automobile manual:

> "[Open the radiator cap]₁ and [drain valve]₂ to [drain the coolant]₃. Then [flush the cooling system]₄ by [pouring clean water into the radiator]₅ until [it drains out clear]₆."

Given this as an RST-tree (cf. Fig. 5), we can translate it into texts like the following:

1. *Open the radiator cap. Open the drain valve. This will drain the coolant. Pour water into the radiator. Stop when the water drains out clear. This will flush the cooling system.*
2. *In order to drain the coolant, open the radiator cap, then open the drain valve. Then, in order to flush the cooling system, pour water into the radiator until it drains out clear.*
3. *After draining the coolant by opening the radiator cap and the drain valve, pour water into the radiator until it drains out clear, which will flush the cooling system.*

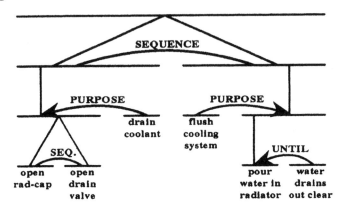

Fig. 5. RST analysis of "radiator cap"

These three variants should suffice to demonstrate that the texts resulting from a simple RST tree can be of very different nature and quality. What we are looking for, then, are general mechanisms that avoid mistakes like the too simplistic structure in (1), monotonous repetition of cue phrases in (2) or overloaded structure in (3).

The next excerpt, taken from a CD player manual, shows that the choice of relation signals depends crucially on the size of the involved text portions.

> If [the player is brought directly from a cold location to a warm location]₁, or [is placed in a very damp room]₂, [moisture may condense on the lens inside the player]₃. Should this occur, [the player will not operate]₄. In this case, [remove the disc]₅ and [leave the player in a warm place for about an hour]₆ until [the moisture evaporates]₇.

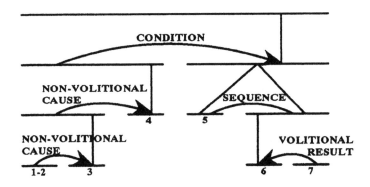

Fig. 6. RST analysis of "CD player"

The relation NON-VOLITIONAL CAUSE between (1,2) and 3 is quite similar to CONDITION and is expressed using 'if... (then) ...', because both nucleus and satellite behave like single propositions. This does not hold for the NON-VOLITIONAL CAUSE in (1-3,4): The satellite is complex, and therefore the expression *"should this occur"* is used to attach it to the nucleus. The combination of both is then in turn a satellite of a CONDITION, and this time, the expression *"in this case"* is chosen, which has the same function as *"should this occur"* (and therefore, one could replace the other).

5.2 The translation steps

Mann (1988) enumerates the following problems that are to be solved after building RST structure (p. 65): theme control, sentence scope, conjunction uses, lexical choice, formulaic text, grammatical realization. In our model, the last step is left to a sentence generator (PENMAN), for which we want to construct the input, i.e., sentence plans. We concentrate here on the first three items of the above list, and we treat theme control only as the question of ordering nucleus and satellite of relations. A task for future work is the integration of theme or focus development, which also influences the choice of sentence structure (see e.g. Derr and McKeown 1984).

An important factor for the enterprise at hand is the content of a leaf node. As mentioned earlier, RST does not make any commitments as to the kind of information that can constitute a 'minimal unit'. For generation to be possible, however, some commitment must be made, and our working assumption is that a leaf contains a single proposition that can in principle be expressed by a single sentence (but in practice is often part of a more complex sentence).

Linear order of nucleus and satellite For a subset of the RST relations, M&T list a 'canonical order' of nucleus and satellite (p. 17), which we can by and large confirm after carrying out our manual analyses. There are a few relations where the order is almost fixed; among them are ELABORATION, BACKGROUND, CONDITION, and UNTIL. Slightly more flexible, but still with a strong preference for one order, are ENABLEMENT, SOLUTIONHOOD, and others. Finally, at the opposite end of the spectrum, are relations where the order can vary freely (reflected by the connective chosen, including none), for example PURPOSE (contrary to M&T's suggestion), CONTRAST, MOTIVATION, or PRECONDITION.

Sentence boundaries As long as the question of producing simple or complex sentences, to be handled on the basis of theme/focus development, is left out, the decision on sentence boundaries can be made solely in accordance with the connective choice. In most cases a relation involving leaf nodes or a subtree of depth 1 gives rise to a single sentence. An exception is a SEQUENCE with more than two nuclei.

Connectives The question of generating connectives needs to be approached from two angles: First, given a rhetorical relation, should it be signalled by a suitable connective? Second, how does this choice relate to other decisions involving sentence structure or lexical selection? Given the scarcity of complicated syntax in the genre of repair instructions, we did so far not focus on the latter question. We only employ the coarse-grained distinction between simple (single propositions or trees of depth 1) and complex (trees of depth > 1) nuclei and satellites, the relevance of which was illustrated in the last subsection.

The other point is the decision whether to explicitly signal the presence of a rhetorical relation. This can be done by syntactic means (which we have not investigated in detail) or by using a proper connective. Some relations go typically unsignalled, like BACKGROUND or certain cases of ELABORATION and CIRCUMSTANCE; the propositional content suffices to communicate the intended link to the reader. Also, a relation like CONTRAST can be established on the basis of word semantics, for example by using terms that express the opposite ends of some scale. Therefore, the heuristic to "always generate accurate and unambiguous textual markers of the rhetorical relations", as proposed by Scott and Souza (1990), certainly requires some refinement: Apart from the fact that unsignalled relations are often felicitous, the notion of unambiguous markers is not clear, because often several relations can be signalled by the same connective (like the various CAUSE and RESULT relations, or MOTIVATION and PURPOSE).

The stated heuristic can be employed (somewhat pragmatically) for the purpose of generation, though: Using a connective usually doesn't hurt, so, as a general rule, use one. The next issue is the choice from a set of alternative connectives, where the guideline is to avoid repeating the same word. (This is, again, a genre-dependent matter; for certain purposes like advertising, the ostensive repetition of cue words may achieve some stylistic effect.) In our system, we elected to avoid repeating the same connective as long as there are others available. More fine-grained choices, as discussed by Elhadad and McKeown (1990), are currently not made, but their approach seems to be in principle compatible with our pattern- and constraint-based procedure (see below), since they also define connectives as a set of constraints holding between the involved propositions.

5.3 The translation algorithm

The decisive constraint for transforming an RST-tree into language is the set of options available for expressing the rhetorical relations. We encode these options as a set of patterns that express how nucleus and satellite can take part in one or more sentences. The patterns' applicability is subject to constraints on both nucleus and satellite, which in the first place check for atomicity or complexity of the subtrees. Moreover, patterns are occasionally matched not only against the RST tree, but also against the linearization generated so far, in order to check for existing sentence boundaries (see example below). All the factors discussed in the previous subsection are encoded in the patterns: N/S order, presence or absence of connectives, sentence structure (to a small extent), and sentence boundaries.

One additional pattern element encodes preferences for expressing relations. For instance, we prefer a CONDITION with an atomic satellite to start a new sentence; when the context doesn't allow this, however, we choose a different pattern. Hence, the patterns corresponding to a relation are partially ordered with respect to a numeric preference value. The two CONDITION patterns alluded to as well as a few exemplary others are shown in table 1.

In general, a pattern for relations with one nucleus and one satellite has the following form (curly brackets denote optionality):

< (PREF. VALUE) (CONSTRAINTS ON N/S) {TEXT} (N|S) {TEXT} (N|S) {TEXT} >

In particular, 'TEXT' can include a full stop, indicating a sentence boundary.

Table 1. Realization patterns for some relations (smp = simple, cpx = complex)

Relation	Patterns
PURPOSE	< 0 (N smp, S smp) ". To" <S> "," <N> "." >
	< 0 (N smp, S smp) <N> "in order to" <S> "." >
	< 0 (N cpx, S smp) <N> ". As a result," <S> "." >
CONDITION	< 1 (S smp) ". If" <S> "," <N> "." >
	< 0 (S smp) "if" <S> "," <N> "." >
NON-VOL	< 0 (N smp, S cpx) <S> ". In this case, " <N> "." >
CAUSE	< 0 (S smp) "if" <S> "," <N> "." >
VOL-RESULT	< 0 (N smp, S smp) <N> "such that" <S> "." >
	< 0 (N cpx, S cpx) <N> ". The result is: " <S> "." >
SEQUENCE	< 1 (N1 smp, N2 smp) <N1> "and" <N2> "." >
with 2 Ns	< 0 () <N1> "." <N2> "." >

The overall translation procedure comprises the following steps:

1. Apply aggregation rules that combine adjacent propositions, as it has been suggested in other work (e.g., by Hovy 1990) For example, when the same activity is performed with different objects, the rule converts "Remove the engine oil filler cap. Remove the drain bolt." to "Remove the engine oil filler cap and the drain bolt." These changes are made directly to the RST tree.

2. Tree traversal: The RST tree is linearized by traversing it in depth-first, left-to-right manner. At each node, the constraints in the patterns for the relation at hand determine which patterns are applicable. The first one is chosen, the others may be accessed later via backtracking. If the traversal succeeds without problems, i.e. every node can be mapped onto a pattern, the first possible linearization is generated. Then backtracking starts in order to explore all variations and to choose the one with the highest preference ranking. When some pattern successfully applies, the algorithm checks whether the same pattern has been used in the preceding three clauses of this linearization; in this case the preference value is decreased by one. Whenever a dead end occurs during tree traversal, i.e., there is no (more) suitable pattern for a node, the search backs up to the last choice point. This exhaustive search produces the set of admissible linearizations, and the winning one is chosen according to the preference values.

3. Now it needs to be decided how referring NPs are to be realized (in/definite full NPs or pronouns). This step depends on focus development as well as on the particular language and has not yet been fully worked out in our current

procedure.
4. The propositions and the connectives are converted into the input format of the sentence generator (in our case, PENMAN).

5.4 A short example

Based on the pattern table given above, here is the successive expansion of the CD-player RST-tree from Fig. 6 given in the form: (RELATION NUCLEUS SATELLITE) or (RELATION $NUCL_1 \ldots NUCL_n$). We list only the choice of those patterns that ultimately win:

Initial Tree:
(CONDITION (SEQUENCE (5) (VOL-RESULT (6) (7)))
                (NON-VOL-CAUSE (4) (NON-VOL-CAUSE (3) (1-2))))

Pattern: CONDITION < "." <S> ". In this case," <N> "." >
Result: ((NON-VOL-CAUSE (4) (NON-VOL-CAUSE (3) (1-2))). In this case, (SEQUENCE ...).)
Pattern: NON-VOL-CAUSE < <S> ". Should this occur," <N> "." >
Result: ((NON-VOL-CAUSE (3) (1-2)). Should this occur, (4). In this case, (SEQUENCE ...).)
Pattern: NON-VOL-CAUSE < "If" <S> "," <N> "." >
Result: (If (1-2), (3). Should this occur, (4). In this case, (SEQUENCE ...).)
Pattern: SEQUENCE < <N> "and" <N> "." >
Result: (If (1-2), (3). Should this occur, (4). In this case, (5) and (VOL-RESULT (6) (7)).)
Pattern: VOL-RESULT < <N> "such that" <S> "." >
Result: (If (1-2), (3). Should this occur, (4). In this case, (5) and (6) such that (7).)

6 Summary and Outlook

RST is a useful basis for a language-independent text representation in NLG. However, we identified several problematic areas of the theory that require further investigation: First, the definition of 'minimal units'; second, the nature of simultaneous analyses; third, certain difficult cases of linearization and of the scope of relations, where the adjacency constraint is questionable.

For using RST in a practical system, we supplemented the original framework with a set of more specific relations. A pool of possible linguistic realizations for the relations has been identified and encoded as patterns, which are successively applied when the RST tree is traversed. This algorithm is currently being implemented and will replace a more provisional procedure that is part of our prototypical system for the multilingual generation of instructional text from a knowledge base.

An important task for future work on generation from RST trees, including our own, is an investigation of the relationship between linguistic realizations of rhetorical relations and the actual propositional content in a tree leaf. The type of this content determines to a considerable extent what connectives can be used and what sentence structures are possible. The relevant features for describing this type need to be established, while, at least for our purposes, the tree should be kept free from information pertaining to a specific language.

However, what an RST tree cannot be kept free of are implicit dependencies on the genre that is being dealt with. Our assumption of the correspondence between leaf nodes and single propositions is, for example, motivated by what we find in instructional texts. Also, the translation algorithm outlined in section 5 is in several respects geared towards the phenomena encountered in this particular kind of text. In the absence of truly *universal* mechanisms regarding RST tree construction and processing, we think that this is a reasonable approach; the parameters that distinguish various genres are for the time being far from well understood.

References

Marcia A. Derr, Kathleen R. McKeown. *Using Focus to Generate Complex and Simple Sentences.* Proceedings of COLING-84, pp. 319-326, 1984.

Michael Elhadad, Kathleen R. McKeown. *Generating Connectives.* Proceedings of COLING-90, pp. 97-101, 1990.

Eduard H. Hovy. *Planning Coherent Multisentential Text.* In: Proceedings of the 28th Annual Meeting of the Association for Compuational Linguistics, pages 163-169. Buffalo, NY. 1988.

Eduard H. Hovy, Kathleen F. McCoy. *Focusing Your RST: A Step Toward Generating Coherent Multisentential Text.* In: Proceedings of the 11th Annual Conference of the Cognitive Science Society. Ann Arbor, MI. 1989.

Eduard H. Hovy. *Unresolved Issues in Paragraph Planning.* In: Robert Dale, Chris Mellish, Michael Zock (Eds.): Current Research in Natural Language Generation. Academic Press. 1990.

William C. Mann. *Text Generation: The Problem of Text Structure.* In: D. McDonald, L. Bolc (Eds.): Natural Language Generation Systems. Springer. New York. 1988.

William C. Mann, Sandra A. Thompson. *Rhetorical Structure Theory: A Theory of Text Organization.* In: L.Polanyi (Ed.) : The Structure of Discourse. Norwood, N.J.: Ablex, 1987. Also available as USC/Information Sciences Institute Research Report RS-87-190.

Kathleen F. McKeown. *Text Generation: Using Discourse Strategies and Focus Constraints to Generate Natural Language Text.* Cambridge University Press. 1985.

Johanna D. Moore, Cecile L. Paris. *Planning Text for Advisory Dialogues.* In: Proceedings of the 27th Annual Meeting of the Association for Computational Linguistics, pages 203-211. 1989.

The Penman Documentation. Unpublished documentation for the Penman language generation system. USC/Information Sciences Institute, 1989.

Dietmar Rösner. *The Generation System of the SEMSYN Project: Towards a Task-Independent Generator for German.* In: M. Zock, G. Sabah (Eds.): Advances in Natural Language Generation: An Interdisciplinary Perspective. Pinter Publishers. London. 1988.

Dietmar Rösner, Manfred Stede. *TECHDOC: A System for the Automatic Production of Multilingual Technical Manuals.* Submitted. 1992.

Donia R. Scott, Clarisse Sieckenius de Souza. *Getting the Message Across in RST-based Text Generation.* In: Robert Dale, Chris Mellish, Michael Zock (Eds.): Current Research in Natural Language Generation. Academic Press. 1990.

Text Revision: A Model and Its Implementation

Kentaro Inui, Takenobu Tokunaga and Hozumi Tanaka

Department of Computer Science
Tokyo Institute of Technology
2-12-1 Ôokayama Meguro Tokyo 152 Japan
{inui,take,tanaka}@cs.titech.ac.jp

Abstract

To generate good text, many kinds of decisions should be made. Many researchers have spent much time searching for the architecture that would determine a proper order for these decisions. However, even if such an architecture is found, there are still certain kinds of problems that are difficult to consider during the generation process. Those problems can be more easily detected and solved by introducing a revision process after generation. In this paper, we argue the importance of text revision with respect to natural language generation, and propose a computational model of text revision. We also discuss its implementation issues and describe an experimental Japanese text generation system, WEIVER.

1 Introduction

During the course of text generation, many kinds of decisions should be made. These decisions are generally classified into two categories: *decisions on what-to-say*, that is, topic selection and topic organization, and *decisions on how-to-say*, that is, decisions on grammatical choices and lexical choices. Many of the text generation systems proposed thus far make these decisions in a fixed sequential order. The order usually begins with decisions on what-to-say and ends with decisions on how-to-say.

These decisions, however, are interdependent, and a more versatile architecture is required to handle these interactions [4, 8, 16]. For example, the number of propositions contained in a sentence is constrained by 2 sets of decisions, the rhetorical relations among the propositions (what-to-say) and the complexity of the sentence (how-to-say). These decisions are interdependent. Furthermore, within each of the sets, there are other interactions among decisions. To account for this, some researchers have developed devices that allow interactions among decision modules [1, 8, 16, 17]. For example, Hovy proposed an architecture that can dynamically decide the order of decisions during the generation process [8].

One limitation to these approaches is that the system needs to foresee how a generation decision constrains subsequent decisions. There are, however, certain kinds of problems that are difficult to detect before the text is actually generated. Structural ambiguities, for example, are difficult to detect before lexical choice, word order, and punctuation decisions are all made. We call these kinds of problems *surface problems*.

Whatever decision order we adopt, there is the possibility that surface problems will still remain (see Sect. 3).

This leads us to the idea of revising text once generated. We introduce a text revision process that solves surface problems. In this paper, we argue the importance of text revision with respect to natural language generation, and propose a computational model of text revision. We also describe an experimental Japanese text generation system, WEIVER, which incorporates a revision module.

Since our target language is Japanese, we provide a brief introduction to Japanese in the next section. In Sect. 3 we give examples illustrating why the revision process is necessary. In Sect. 4 we provide a summary of our approach to solve the problems presented in Sect. 3. The implementation issues are discussed in Sect. 5.

2 Brief Introduction to Japanese

A simple Japanese sentence consists of a sequence of postpositional phrases (PPs) followed by a predicate (a verb or an adjective). A PP consists of a noun phrase (NP) followed by a postposition, which indicates the case role of the NP. We say "each PP modifies the predicate" and call PPs the *modifiers* and the predicate the *modifiee*. For example, both "*John-ga*"[1] and "*Tokyo-ni*" modify "*sundeiru*" in sentence (1).

(1) *John-ga   Tokyo-ni sundeiru.*
    John-NOM   in Tokyo lives.

The order of PPs is not strictly fixed, so it is possible to scramble PPs without changing the meaning of the sentence[2]. For example, the sentence "*Tokyo-ni John-ga sundeiru.*" has the same meaning as that of sentence (1). As with prepositional phrase attachments in English, one of the important constraints in Japanese is that no two modification relations cross each other[3].

When a sentence has only one modifiee, the modification relation can be uniquely determined. However, this is not always the case. Sentence (2) is an example in which the noun "*Mary*" is modified by the verb "*satteiku*." In this example, "*Poochie-to*" can modify either "*satteiku*" or "*miteita*."

(2) *John-ga   Poochie-to   satteiku   Mary-wo   miteita.*
    John-NOM   with Poochie   departing   Mary-ACC   look at-PAST

Depending on which verb "*Poochie-to*" modifies, this sentence gives two interpretations[4]:

- John looked at [Mary departing with Poochie].
  (the case "*Poochie-to*" modifies "*satteiku*")

---

[1] We denote PP in "NP-postposition" form for convenience of explanation.

[2] Of course, scrambling may change nuances and the naturalness of the sentence.

[3] There are some exceptions but this is generally considered a reasonable constraint.

[4] It is interesting that the translation in English is also ambiguous. We make the difference clear by using brackets and inversion.

   – With Poochie, John looked at Mary departing.
     (the case "*Poochie-to*" modifies "*miteita*")

Given no contextual information, both interpretations are equally acceptable. Determining the correct modification relation is one of the major problems of natural language understanding. In natural language generation, it is important to avoid generating such an ambiguous sentence.

3 Why Revision?

In this section, we argue that to solve surface problems, text generation should exploit the revision process.

Consider sentence (2) again. Assume that we want to generate a sentence representing the second meaning, "With Poochie, John looked at Mary departing." If the system made a decision on the word order as that in sentence (3), then "*Poochie-to*" could only modify "*miteita*," and we would obtain a desirable sentence. This is because modifiers can only modify succeeding elements in Japanese.

(3) *John-ga   satteiku   Mary-wo   Poochie-to   miteita.*
    John-NOM departing Mary-ACC with Poochie look at-PAST
    (With Poochie, John looked at Mary departing.)

The ambiguity of sentence (2) could also be resolved by inserting a comma (sentence (4)). This is because a modifier preceding a comma will not modify the element immediately following the comma.

(4) *John-ga   Poochie-to,   satteiku   Mary-wo   miteita.*
    John-NOM with Poochie departing Mary-ACC look at-PAST
    (With Poochie, John looked at Mary departing.)

In the same way, we can avoid structural ambiguities through proper decisions on word order and punctuation. This seems to imply that you have only to make these decisions at the end of the process. This strategy, however, does not work for the following reasons:

   – It is not always possible to find a proper word order that does not cause any ambiguities.
   – Word order should not be decided only with respect to avoiding structural ambiguities. There are many factors that decide word order, such as old/new information, focus, etc.

The following example demonstrates this difficulty[5].

(5) *John-wa,*   [[*Tom-ga*   *Φ*   *Φ*   *yôkyûsita*   *node*]
    John-TOP Tom-NOM (John-DAT) (position of   request-PAST because
                                    president-ACC)

---

[5] We enclose subordinate clauses with brackets. *Φ* denotes an ellipsis.

kare-ni	syatyô-wo	yuzuru-to]	kôhyôsita.
him-DAT	position of	transfer-COMP	announce-PAST
(Tom)	president-ACC		

Due to the structural ambiguity, sentence (5) also has two possible interpretations:

- John made an announcement that in response to Tom's request, John would transfer the position of president to Tom.
  (the case "*Tom-ga yôkyûsita node*" modifies "*yuzuru*")
- John made an announcement, in response to Tom's request, that John would transfer the position of president to Tom.
  (the case "*Tom-ga yôkyûsita node*" modifies "*kôhyôsita*")

Assume the first interpretation is the intended meaning. To avoid the ambiguity, try an alternative word order, as in sentence (6), taking the same tactic as in sentence (3). Note that "*kare-ni*" has been moved in front of "*Tom-ga*," and compare with sentence (5).

(6) *John-wa,*   [*kare-ni*   [*Tom-ga*   Φ   *yôkyûsita*   *node*]
     John-TOP   him-DAT   Tom-NOM   (position of   request-PAST   because
                (??)   president-ACC)

     syatyô-wo   *yuzuru-to*]   *kôhyôsita.*
     position of   transfer-COMP   announce-PAST
     president-ACC

This word order, however, causes another problem. Although "*kare*" should refer to "*Tom*" as in sentence (5), "*kare*" in sentence (6) instead refers to "*John.*" This problem arises because all of the lexical choices had already been decided before deciding on the word order.

In this example, the intended meaning can be attained, however, by adopting another syntactic structure, like that in sentence (7). The subordinate clause in sentence (5) is realized as a coordinate clause.

(7) *John-wa,*   [*Tom-ga*   Φ   *yôkyûsita*   *node*]
     John-TOP   Tom-NOM   (position of   request-PAST   because
                                 president-ACC)

     syatyô-wo   *yuzurukoto-wo*   *kim*   *e,*   *sore-wo*   *kôhyôsita.*
     position of   transferring-ACC   decide   and   it-ACC   announce-PAST
     president-ACC

From this we can see that, for certain sentences, some syntactic structures inherently have structural ambiguities. This suggests that at the decision point on the syntactic structure you have to foresee whether, or not, your decision will cause any structural ambiguities. This task, however, is very difficult unless the text is actually generated. In this sense, it is a surface problem.

The complexity of a sentence, e.g. length, depth of embedding, etc., is also a kind of surface problem. For example, consider the case when a proposition "My car is new." is embedded into the other proposition "My car is French." You can produce *"My new car is French."* as well as *"My car, which is new, is French."* [19]. There is no syntactic embedding in the first sentence. Therefore, the depth of (syntactic) embedding can be measured only after lexical and grammatical choices are made.

Even if the system has the ability to decide the order of decisions dynamically, it does not alleviate this problem. By introducing the revision process, we can easily find and solve such kinds of problems. This is one of the most important motivations of our research.

4 Our Approach

Text generation consists of two processes: *initial generation process*, followed by *revision process*. The revision process solves the surface problems, which are difficult to consider during the initial generation, as we discussed in Sect. 3.

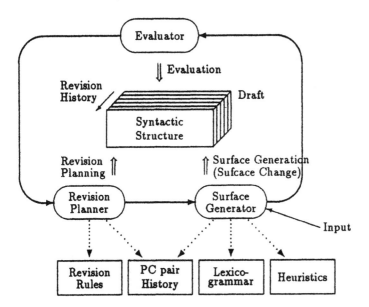

Fig. 1. Model of text generation

Figure 1 illustrates our model of text generation. At the moment we focus on how-to-say decisions, so we assume that the input to the system is a rhetorical structure, that represents what-to-say information. The system has three modules: *surface generator, evaluator* and *revision planner*.

In the initial generation, the surface generator makes decisions on grammatical and lexical choices to generate a text from the input by referring to the two kinds of resources: the *lexico-grammar* and the *heuristics*. The lexico-grammar provides the grammatical and lexical constraints [14]. The heuristics provide the pragmatic and textual preferences, such as referring expressions and topicalization. The heuristics are used at each decision point where the surface generator has more than one choice that satisfies the grammatical and lexical constraints. The output of the surface generator is called the *draft*, because it may not be the final (optimal) version of the text, as a result of surface problems.

The revision process consists of repetitions of the *revision cycle*. Each revision cycle consists of *evaluation, revision planning*, and *surface change*. In a revision cycle, first the evaluator evaluates the current draft to detect surface problems. Then, the revision planner selects one of them, and suggests a change that will solve the problem. The surface generator actually changes the draft. A revision cycle ends when the surface change is successfully accomplished. By repeating revision cycles, the draft can be gradually improved into the final version of the text.

4.1 Evaluation

Here we focus on the following two surface problems.

- structural ambiguity
- sentence complexity
    - the length of sentences, clauses and phrases
    - the depth of embedding and modification relations
    - the depth of center embedding

The evaluator evaluates the draft, which is an actual text rather than some intermediate representation. The draft is represented as its syntactic structure, which provides helpful information for the evaluation.

Even with the state-of-the-art techniques of natural language understanding, it is difficult to find structural ambiguities. The evaluator has to detect the structural ambiguities that even humans cannot disambiguate. For example, the examples shown in Sect. 2 and 3 may not be ambiguous if proper contexts are given. At the moment, our system requires human assistance to detect structural ambiguities.

The complexity of the sentence mainly affects the readability. Several criteria for measuring the complexity of the Japanese sentence have been proposed in research on machine translation systems and text revision support systems. We focus on the criteria itemized above regarding sentence complexity. In the current system, we establish upper and lower bounds for each criteria. An example of the values is shown in Table 1.

Table 1. An example of the criteria regarding sentence complexity

Criteria	Upper bound	Lower bound
Length of sentence (words)	40	5
Depth of clause embedding	3	0
Depth of modification relation in NP	3	0
Depth of center embedding	1	0

4.2 Revision Planning

The revision planner selects one of the problems detected by the evaluator, and suggests a change to solve it using heuristics. We call these heuristics the *revision rules*. The rules are assigned static preference. The revision planner chooses the most preferable rule from the rules of which preconditions are satisfied. Then the revision planner sends the surface generator a *message* that describes the change in the chosen revision rule. When the change cannot be realized because of a reason such as grammatical constraints, the surface generator requests an alternative message from the revision planner. If the revision planner cannot suggest any alternative change for the problem, it tries another problem. The revision planner manages the history of the drafts and the changes (*revision history*). By monitoring the history, the revision planner keeps the revision process from falling into an infinite loop.

Our model repeats the revision cycle until we produce an acceptable text. Therefore, even if a surface change introduces new problems, these can be detected and solved in the subsequent cycles. This means that the revision planner need not seriously consider the side effects of the changes. At this point, our model is significantly different from previous one-pass generation models, in which the system has to foresee the effects of each decision on the subsequent processes.

4.3 Surface Change

In addition to the initial generation, the surface change is also handled by the surface generator. The examples in Sect. 3 show that solving the surface problems involves various kinds of surface changes, such as changes of word order, punctuation, lexical choice, syntactic structure, and so on. Moreover, each surface change should produce an alternative draft that both satisfies the grammatical and lexical constraints, and is supported by the pragmatic and textual preferences as well as the initial draft. Otherwise, the draft may becomes worse due to the changes.

5 Implementation

The generation model described in the previous section has been partially implemented as WEIVER. In this section, we discuss implementation issues of WEIVER. In particular, we focus on the surface change.

5.1 Lexico-grammar

The generation process can be considered as a set of decisions, each of which is made at a choice point in a decision tree. From this point of view, we can regard a surface change as a change of decisions. The system is required to change various kinds of decisions on grammatical and lexical choices to solve the surface problems. It is thus desirable that both grammatical and lexical knowledge are described in a uniform representation.

We therefore adopt a *phrasal lexicon*, which integrates the grammar and the lexicon into a unified representation [14]. In addition, the phrasal lexicon contributes to the generation of fluent text [11]. Basically, we follow Jacobs' representation, which represents the phrasal lexicon as a collection of PC pairs (Pattern-Concept pairs) [10]. In Jacobs' framework, each PC pair defines a mapping from a part of the semantic structure to the syntactic/lexical fragments, and the generator constructs surface sentences from these fragments. Decisions on how-to-say can be considered as choices among PC pairs. From the viewpoint of revision, a surface change can be attained by replacing PC pairs with alternatives.

```
CONTEXT: [ ],
MAP-FROM: [ [$1, con:@action,
                  required-slots:[agt:$2, obj:$3], optional-slots:[ ],
                  constr:[type:sentence] ],
           [$2, con:@animate],
           [$3, con:@concrete-object],
MAP-TO: [ [$1, con:@action,
               slots:[agt:$2, obj:$3],
               constr:[type:sentence, voice:passive, pos:VP, connect:period] ],
          [$2, con:@animate],
          [$3, con:@concrete-object,
               constr:[type:TOP, pos:NP, connect:V],
EFFECTS: [current-focus($3), . . . ]
```

Fig. 2. An example of extended PC pair

To realize the revision process, we made some extensions on PC pairs. Each PC pair defines a tree-to-tree mapping. By applying PC pairs, the surface generator incrementally transforms the input rhetorical structure into a syntactic structure (see Fig. 3). We call the structures that are partially transferred the *intermediate structures*. Figure 2 shows an example of our PC pair [6]. A PC pair consists of four parts: CONTEXT, MAP-FROM, MAP-TO and EFFECTS. A PC pair can be applied only if both its CONTEXT and MAP-FROM unify with a subtree of the rhetorical/intermediate structure. If more than one PC pair is applicable at a decision point, the surface generator refers to the heuristics to choose one of them. After choosing a PC pair, the surface generator replaces the subtree of the rhetorical/intermediate structure, specified by MAP-FROM, with the MAP-TO subtree. EFFECTS defines the effects that will be achieved when the PC pair is applied. The PC pair in Fig. 2 is applied to realize a proposition as a passive sentence when an object of an action (node $3) is the current local focus.

The extensions to Jacobs' are as follows. First, our PC pair maps from tree structures to tree structures, while Jacobs' maps conceptual structures to linear strings. Because the result of applying our PC pairs is always a uniform representation, the generator can treat the various kinds of decisions, such as lexical, grammatical and, even textual ones, in a uniform manner. Jacobs' PC pair is only for single sentence

---

[6] "$N" and "@X" are typed variables to unify with an identifier of a node and a concept, respectively.

generation. Furthermore, the tree structures provide more information for evaluation than strings do. Secondly, in selecting PC pairs, the newly introduced EFFECTS part enables the system to take into account not just semantic constraints but also pragmatic preferences. The EFFECT part is also used by the revision planner to suggest the decisions to be changed (see Sect. 5.4).

5.2 An Example

In this section, we show another brief example. In the following sections we discuss several features of WEIVER using this example.

The Initial Generation. The rhetorical structure shown in Fig. 3 (a) is the input[7]. It has four propositions. At the first step of the initial generation, the surface generator divides the input propositions into some sentences. This is realized by applying PC pairs to the subtree near the root node of the input rhetorical structure. If there is more than one applicable PC pair, the generator chooses one of them by referring to the heuristics. Scott and Souza [20] proposed the heuristics of organizing propositions. Their heuristics guide the linguistic realization of the rhetorical structure including embedding and coordination. Our heuristics follow them.

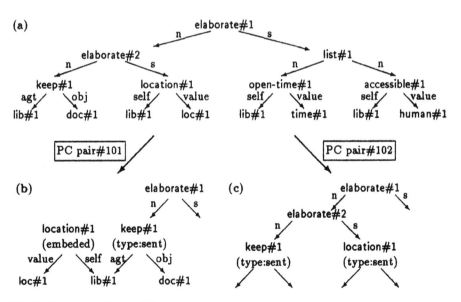

Fig. 3. Transformation of Structure

At the decision point (a) in Fig.3, there are two applicable PC pairs, PC pair#101 and PC pair#102. Assume PC pair#101 is chosen by referring to the heuristics. As

---

[7] Actually, the input includes the other information, such as focus.

a result, proposition location#1 is embedded to proposition keep#1 (Fig. 3 (b)), and these two propositions will be realized as one sentence, as in the first sentence in draft (8).

(8) *siryô-wa,*   [*tonari-no tatemono-no 4kai-no itiban'oku-ni aru*]
     document-TOP   in the most inner part of the next building on the 4th floor

    siryôsitu-ni   *hokansareteimasu.*   *siryôsitu-wa*   *9zi-kara 5zi-made*
    library-LOC   keep-PASS   Library-TOP   from 9 to 5

    aitei   *te*   *darede-mo*   *tukaemasu.*
    open   and   everybody   accessible.

(The document is kept in the library in the most inner part of the next building on the 4th floor. The library is open from 9 to 5 and is open to the public.)

The Revision Cycle. After the initial generation, WEIVER enters the first revision cycle. First, the evaluator evaluates draft (8) and detects a surface problem; the modification of the noun phrase "*siryôsitu*," that is "*tonari-no ... aru*," is too deep according to the criterion shown in Table 1[8]. Next, the revision planner suggests that PC pair#101 should be replaced in order to solve the problem. Following this suggestion, the surface generator actually replaces it with PC pair#102 at the decision point (a) in Fig. 3. As a result, the proposition location#1, which was embedded in draft (8), will be realized as a separate sentence. The new draft is shown in draft (9).

(9) *siryô-wa*   *siryôsitu-ni*   *hokansareteimasu.*   *siryôsitu-wa*
     document-TOP   library-LOC   keep-PASS   library-TOP

    tonari-no tatemono-no 4kai-no itiban'oku-ni arimasu.
    in the most inner part of the next building on the 4th floor

    Φ   *9zi-kara 5zi-made*   *aitei*   *te*   *darede-mo*   *tukaemasu.*
    (siryôsitu-TOP)   from 9 to 5   open   and   everybody   accessible

This is the end of one revision cycle. In the following process, WEIVER repeats revision cycles as well. In the following sections, we explain the following points using the above example:

- how to find the PC pair to be replaced,
- how to change the draft with its intended meaning preserved,
- how to change the draft without degrading the quality of the draft.

---

[8] This problem is difficult to avoid in the initial generation, because it is difficult to foresee that the referring expression of loc#1 in Fig. RS (a) will be such a long NP when one decides the embedding.

5.3 PC Pair History

First, we introduce the *PC pair history* as a resource for the revision planning and the surface change.

In the initial generation, the surface generator keeps track of the process as a PC pair history. It is represented as a data structure similar to the dependency network used in the truth maintenance system (TMS) [5]. From the viewpoint of TMS, we can roughly regard the input (rhetorical structure) as a set of facts, each decision (PC pair) as an assumption, and the resultant subtree as a conclusion.

Figure 4 (a) shows a fragment of a sample PC pair history. It shows that PC pair#72 (see Fig. 2) was applied under the precondition represented as the nodes above and, as a result, produced the several features represented as the nodes below. "n_i" denotes the identifier of the node in the rhetorical/intermediate structure. The surface generator records the PC pair history by gathering subnetworks, like those shown in Fig. 4 (a). In general, the resultant network is a directed acyclic graph (see Fig. 4 (b)). We also call this the *dependency network*. In the dependency network, each node has a state, either *in* or *out*. The states propagate along the links as they do in TMS. This mechanism enables us to reconstruct the intermediate structure, which is the result of removing a PC pair (see Sect. 5.6).

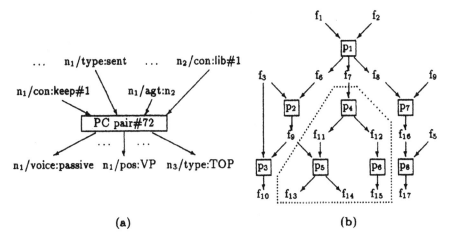

(a)   (b)

Fig. 4. Dependency network

The dependencies among the PC pairs exist not only because of their preconditions but also because of the heuristics. The PC pair history holds both kinds of dependencies. A number of heuristics on how-to-say have been proposed in the previous research on text generation, although at the moment we have implemented only a few of them in WEIVER. The heuristics are used to generate anaphora [3], ellipsis [9], exophora [2, 19], connectives [6], etc. They are also used to make the pragmatic decisions (formality, etc.) [8].

Most heuristics are context sensitive. Consider the focusing heuristics as an example. Generating an anaphora is partially dependent on the current focus state described as in the rule below [15].

> If a noun phrase denotes the "given" information and
>   it was the previous current discourse focus,
> then pronominalize it.

Thus, most heuristics can be represented as production rules. In the PC pair history, the preconditions of the applied heuristics are also recorded to represent these heuristics dependencies.

5.4 Suggesting a PC pair to Change

The revision planner suggests an appropriate change and sends the message to the surface generator. In the above example, the following revision rule will be applied.

> If an adjective phrase M, which modifies a noun phrase, is too deep, and
>   there exists a node in M whose semantic node has a feature "*embedded*,"
> then remove the feature.

Generally, the revision rules suggest which feature should be removed from the current draft. Sometimes they even suggest which feature should be added in place of the removed feature. After choosing an applicable revision rule, the revision planner searches the PC pair history for the PC pair that introduced the features in question. That is easy because the PC pair history holds the dependencies among the PC pairs and the features. In this example, the feature "*embedded*" of location#1 is in question. Fig. 3 shows "*embedded*" is introduced by PC pair#101. Therefore, the message "*Remove PC pair#101*." is sent to the surface generator. The revision planner further refers to the EFFECTS part in the PC pairs if pragmatic constraints are involved in addition to grammatical features.

5.5 Internal/external Dependencies

Next, the surface generator actually changes the draft with respect to the message. In this example, the surface generator replaces PC pair#101 with PC pair#102 at the choice point shown in Fig. 3 (a). As a result, the feature "*embedded*" in location#1 will be removed, and the first sentence in draft (8) will be divided into two separate sentences.

Because of this change, some of the PC pairs that were applied after the decision point (a) to generate draft (8) may now become inapplicable. For example, the PC pair that realized location#1 as an adjective phrase is not applicable any longer. Thus, there are dependencies among the PC pairs that are applied together to generate a draft. Such dependencies can be found by referring to the PC pair history. Here, we define two types of dependencies: *internal* and *external dependencies*.

Internal Dependency. Assume PC pair p_4 is replaced with PC pair p_4' in Fig.4 (b). Since the features f_{11} and f_{12} may not be produced by p_4', both p_5 and p_6 may not be applicable anymore. In other words, p_5 and p_6 are dependent on p_4. We call these *internal dependencies*. The internal dependencies can be found by traversing the dependency network.

External Dependency. Note that the topicalized subject *"siryôsitu-wa"* was omitted in draft (9). Such ellipses are introduced not because of the grammatical constraints, but because of the textual preferences. The heuristic applied in this example is "The topic in the current sentence should be omitted when it is the same as one in the latest sentence." Thus, some PC pairs are dependent on the replaced PC pair not because of the preconditions of the PC pairs, but because of the heuristics. We call these *external dependencies*. The external dependencies can be found by referring to the preconditions of the heuristics. In general, A PC pair p_i depends externally on the replaced PC pair p_j only when p_i does not depend internally on p_j, and when p_j is included in the preconditions of the heuristics applied to choose p_i.

5.6 Generating Alternatives

In this section, we show how the surface generator realizes the surface changes with respect to the internal and external dependencies. The procedure is as follows:

1. receive the message from the revision planner,
2. make the state of the PC pair in question *out*, spread the state over the dependency network, and construct the intermediate structure (S) from the features whose current states are *in*,
3. invoke the ordinary generation process (apply the PC pairs to S until all the required decisions are made),
4. make the collection of the PC pairs (C) which depend externally on the changed parts,
5. if C is empty, terminate the process, otherwise, choose and remove a PC pair from C that corresponds to the left most part in the draft,
6. if the PC pair chosen in 5 still satisfies the heuristics, go to 5, otherwise go to 2.

For example, assume the PC pair to be replaced is p_4 in Fig. 4 (b). The PC pairs and the features enclosed by the dotted line are set to *out*, and the intermediate structure is constructed of the features with *in* states. Then the surface generator applies the alternative PC pairs to generate an alternative draft. Our procedure ensures that the new draft does not degrade, by also considering the external dependencies as described in steps 4 through 6.

Although this procedure often works successfully, it still has drawbacks. Assume PC pair p_5 was introduced in the previous revision cycle, that is, at that time WEIVER replaced a PC pair with PC pair p_5 to solve a surface problem. If WEIVER now removes p_4, p_5 may also be removed and the previous surface problem may be introduced again. To avoid this problem, step 3 in the above procedure should be extended as follows:

3'. if the PC pairs depending internally on the PC pair to be replaced include a PC pair (p_i) that was introduced in the previous revision cycle, upgrade the priority of p_i and invoke the generation process, otherwise, invoke the ordinary generation process.

In our method, because the surface generator generates an alternative draft from the same rhetorical structure, it is ensured that the new draft keeps the intended meaning intact. Moreover, because the surface generator also considers the external dependencies, the new draft satisfies not only the grammatical and lexical constraints, but also the pragmatic and textual preferences. Thus, it is guaranteed that the surface change will not worsen the quality of the draft.

5.7 From the Viewpoint of Backtracking

Our method is very similar to a dependency-directed backtracking (DDB) in a justification-based TMS (JTMS). Actually, we believe that the text revision can be realized naturally in this line. As mentioned in Sect. 5.3, each decision can be regarded as an assumption that is justified by its preconditions. That is, replacing a PC pair can be seen as retracting an assumption and adding an alternative one. Thus, with respect to efficiency, our method has the advantage over a naive depth-first backtracking, as discussed in Doyle's paper [5].

However, there needs to be some extensions to JTMS for text revision. Because the heuristics make it difficult to specify the dependencies (see Sect. 5.3), one cannot utilize the JTMS algorithm for the dependency propagation. In our method, the surface generator starts the generation process from an intermediate structure, and then sees if the heuristics are still satisfied. Furthermore, the surface generator prefers the previous surface changes, as discussed in Sect. 5.6.

6 Related Work

We have discussed text revision as a means of solving surface problems. The importance of text revision has also been argued from other points of view. Those arguments are summarized by Wong as follows [21]:

- Revision has psychological reality [22].
- Revision enables feedback from how-to-say to what-to-say. This is important because some factors are detectable only after realization [18].
- With revision, the giant step of the whole generation task can be divided into smaller tasks [22].

Our model also inherits these advantages.

Mann and Moore's KDS [13] and Gabriel's *Yh* [7] are examples of systems that have implemented the revision component. They are different from WEIVER in two ways. First, they never change the decisions, and second, instead of the surface text they evaluate the intermediate representation. Because of these differences, they have difficulties in detecting and solving the surface problems.

Several models have been proposed that evaluate the surface text in revision. Mann's Penman [12] and Wong's blackboard model [21] evaluate the draft, referring to information such as the syntactic structure. Meteer [18] and Yazdani [22] propose models that parse the draft. Our model is very similar to these four models. However, the implementation issues of these models have not yet been fully discussed.

7 Concluding Remarks

In this paper we argued the importance of text revision with respect to natural language generation, and proposed a model that incorporated a revision module. Although we focused on the revision in terms of solving the surface problems, we believe that the revision plays important roles in the other aspects of improving text, as discussed by Meteer [18]. We also discussed the implementation issues of our model. We adopted the JTMS-like approach to keep several constraints consistent in changing the draft.

At present, there is little documented research on text revision. This is due, in particular, to the difficulty of text evaluation. There is no consensus on criteria for evaluation and improvement. Observing the human writing process may provide valuable insight into this problem, as Meteer has indicated [17]. We have also conducted a psychological experiment to extract criteria for the evaluation and improvement. The collected data is now under analysis. We will feed the result back into the system. At the same time, we will extend the current system, and evaluate its performance with more examples.

Acknowledgments

The authors would like to thank Dr. Christian Matthiessen for his fruitful discussions on realization of lexico-grammar, and the reviewers for their helpful comments on the early version of this paper. The authors owe a great debt to Craig Hunter and Megan Withycombe, who patiently read the draft and contributed to improving the how-to-say of this paper.

References

1. D. E. Appelt. TELEGRAM: A grammar formalism for language planning. In *the Proceedings of the International Joint Conference on Artificial Intelligence*, pages 595–599, 1983.
2. D. E. Appelt. Planning natural-language referring expressions. In D. D. McDonald and L. Bolc, editors, *Natural Language Generation Systems*, chapter 3, pages 69–97. Springer-Verlag, 1988.
3. R. Dale. The generation of subsequent referring expressions in structured discourse. In M. Zock and G. Sabah, editors, *Advances in Natural Language Generation*, chapter vol. 2, 4, pages 58–75. Ablex Publishing Corporation, 1988.
4. L. Danlos. Conceptual and linguistic decisions in generation. In *the Proceedings of the International Conference on Computational Linguistics*, pages 501–504, 1984.
5. J. Doyle. A truth maintenance system. *Artificial Intelligence*, pages 231–272, 1979.
6. M. Elhadad and K. R. McKeown. Generating connectives. In *the Proceedings of the International Conference on Computational Linguistics*, pages 3:97–101, 1990.
7. R. P. Gabriel. Deliberate writing. In D. D. McDonald and L. Bolc, editors, *Natural Language Generation Systems*, chapter 1, pages 1–46. Springer-Verlag, 1988.
8. E. H. Hovy. *Generating Natural Language under Pragmatic Constraints*. Lawrence Erlbaum Associates, 1988.

9. S. Ishizaki. Generation Japanese text from conceptual representation. In D. D. Mc-Donald and L. Bolc, editors, *Natural Language Generation Systems*, chapter 7, pages 256–279. Springer-Verlag, 1988.

10. P. S. Jacobs. PHRED: A generator for natural language interfaces. In D. D. McDonald and L. Bolc, editors, *Natural Language Generation Systems*, chapter 7, pages 256–279. Springer-Verlag, 1988.

11. K. Kukich. Fluency in natural language reports. In D. D. McDonald and Leonard Bolc, editors, *Natural Language Generation Systems*, chapter 8, pages 280–311. Springer-Verlag, 1988.

12. W. C. Mann. An overview of the Penman text generation system. In *the Proceedings of the National Conference on Artificial Intelligence*, pages 261–265, 1983.

13. W. C. Mann and J. A. Moore. Computer generation of multiparagraph English text. *American Journal of Computational Linguistics*, 7(1):17–29, 1981.

14. C. Matthiessen. Lexico(Grammatical) choice in text generation. In *Natural Language Generation in Artificial Intelligence and Computational Linguistics*, chapter 10, pages 249–292. Kluwer Academic Publishers, 1991.

15. M. Maybury. Using discourse focus, temporal focus, and spatial focus to generate multisententiai text. In *the Proceedings of the Fifth International Workshop on Natural Language Generation*, pages 70–78, 1990.

16. K. R. McKeown and M. Elhadad. A contrastive evaluation of functional unification grammar for surface language generation: A case study in choice of connectives. In C. L. Paris, W. R. Swartout, and W. C. Mann, editors, *Natural Language Generation in Artificial Intelligence and Computational Linguistics*, chapter 14, pages 351–396. Kluwer Academic Publishers, 1991.

17. M. W. Meteer. *The Generation Gap: The Problem of Expressibility in Text Planning*. PhD thesis, University of Massachusetts, 1990.

18. M. M. Meteer (Vaughan) and D. D. McDonald. A model of revision in natural language generation. In *the Proceedings of the Annual Meeting of the Association for Computational Linguistics*, pages 90–96, 1986.

19. E. Reiter. Generating descriptions that exploit a user's domain knowledge. In R. Dale, C. Mellish, and M Zock, editors, *Current Research in Natural Language Generation*, chapter 10, pages 257–286. Academic Press, 1990.

20. D. R. Scott and C. S. Souza. Getting the message across in RST-based text genertion. In R. Dale, C. Mellish, and M Zock, editors, *Current Research in Natural Language Generation*, chapter 3, pages 47–74. Academic Press, 1990.

21. W. C. Wong and R. F. Simmons. A blackboard model of text production with revision. In *the Proceedings of the AAAI Workshop on Text Planning and Realization*, pages 99–106, 1988.

22. M. Yazdani. Reviewing as a component of the text generation process. In G. Kempen, editor, *Natural Language Generation*, chapter 13, pages 183–190. Martinus Nijhoff, 1987.

Transparently–Motivated Metaphor Generation[*]

Mark A. Jones and Kathleen F. McCoy

University of Delaware, Newark DE 19716, USA

Abstract

This paper introduces the phenomena of transparently-motivated metaphor. It makes a case for its prevalence, and reports analysis of some of the textual goals that such metaphor can achieve. General principles that can explain many of the uses of metaphor are discussed. Our analysis of metaphors and the resulting principles have led to preliminary developments of a methodology for generating transparently-motivated metaphors that can account for metaphor generation from general principles. This methodology allows for novel metaphor generation, an account of the conceptual structures behind such expressions, as well as an account of the effects of the metaphors.

1 Introduction

Our understanding of the world influences the way we express ourselves, and so much of what we naturally say is metaphorical. These metaphorical expressions often reflect conceptual models which are the basis for how we understand the world. Mark Johnson (1987) has made some interesting observations about the building blocks of thought, most notably that the building blocks of thought are based closely to our bodily experience. Among the building blocks he has described are attraction, blockage, and containment. Consider, for example, when describing the purchase of shares of stock, one may say "I took $2500 out of my money market account and put it into Exxon common stock." The speaker did not literally put money into the stock, but rather bought stock with the money. This metaphor is based in the simplifying concepts that represent investments as containers which can hold money. When we write and talk we automatically use non-literal expressions that reflect our common conceptual groundings. These lead to very natural and easily understood expressions because we (speaker and hearer) share these common conceptual groundings.

Upon analyzing both spoken and written discourse, we find that the use of metaphor (of the kind we speak) is extremely prevalent to the point that many

---

[*] This work is supported by Grant #H133E80015 from the National Institute on Disability and Rehabilitation Research. Support has also been provided by The Nemours Foundation.

such expressions go unnoticed. Further analysis reveals that metaphor is frequently used as a textual device to help achieve the goals of the speaker. These goals range from focus management and perspective, to creating more understandable descriptions that depend on common conceptual groundings.

Typically, however, a natural language generation system only has available to it the literal information that it is to convey. It does not have the conceptual groundings (that we will argue underlie many metaphorical statements) that people do. As a result, the generator does not have available to it a very common tool that is useful for achieving certain kinds of discourse goals. Because of this, we argue that metaphor is not an added unnecessary feature of a natural language generation system, but is a necessary element. What we would like to do is supply a generator with necessary conceptual groundings so it can identify additional non-literal ways of expressing what it could only express before literally. This would yield additional options for the system to express itself.

In this paper we first isolate the phenomena that we call transparently-motivated metaphor and make the case of its prevalence. After this we analyze some of the textual goals that such metaphor can achieve and discuss some (conceptually grounded) principles that can explain many of the uses of metaphor found in our text analysis. Our analysis of metaphors and the resulting principles have led to initial developments of a methodology for generating transparently-motivated metaphors. This general methodology will be discussed.

2 Prevalence of Metaphor

When the topic of metaphor is first mentioned, many readers think primarily in terms of rather blatant metaphors. For example, Cornell Way (1991, p. 28) cites a case where a fever is described as "A stubborn and unconquerable flame Creeps in his veins and drinks the streams of life." Although we do not contest that such examples are in fact metaphors, we are interested in the more transparent metaphors. Such metaphors not only occur in friendly and artistic communication, but also in hard, factual domains. The pervasiveness of such metaphors in even rather mundane text is evidenced by not only our analysis of texts, but also the analysis of others such as Carbonell (1982) who found very frequent use of metaphors in the financial pages of the New York Times.

Consider just a few more expressions that often pass without notice. "Savings and Loan bail out" and "Chrysler bail out," although salient at different points in recent history, appear to come from the same conceptual roots. In literal terms, an entity is in trouble, and is getting outside (government) help. The term bail-out that is used to describe this situation is hardly literal, and maps to something more concrete (and thus closer to our conceptual roots (Johnson 1987)). This particular concrete situation is that of helping to bail out another's boat before it sinks into the water.

The actions of politicians are often described in terms of "political moves." Here, the import of the action is rarely linked to any physical motion per-se. Rather, the word *move* appears to suggest that the background model of such actions contains the notion of "politics as a game."

3 Non-Literal Expressions

One could object that in the previous examples with words such as *move*, there is no metaphor. Rather, there are multiple individual word senses. Admittedly, there appears to be a continuum between polysemy and metaphor (Anderson 1990). It is an open question whether certain uses of words reflect what should be treated as extra, individual word-meanings or metaphorical meanings which are expansions from some core (Norvig and Lakoff 1987). For example, should we treat the word *big* as having an individual abstract sense meaning significant (e.g., "we have a big problem") or should we treat the word as only physical and treat the less literal meaning as an extension via a metaphorical mapping? We will err on the side of general mechanisms of metaphoric extension and away from the more idiosyncratic solution of recognizing extra, explicit word senses. For instance, if we use a general metaphoric mechanism for representing less central meanings of the word *big*, we can also explain less central meanings of similar words like *huge*. In both cases, a metaphoric mapping can carry the physical meaning (i.e., large in size) into the abstract realm (i.e., significant). We can speak of a big problem or a huge problem. Although the magnitude of the significance may be different, they have the same relation to each other as they do in the more literal, physical domain. Martin (1990) describes this behavior in terms of words being "core-related." The more general approach described in this work can lead to a more parsimonious representation in the lexicon by capturing the deeper generalizations.

Metaphors can be divided into three basic categories: dead, conventional, and novel. Dead metaphors are basically frozen phrases. They may have once been novel metaphors, but the tracing of their meaning has been lost. Conventional metaphors have been connoted with the more transparent metaphors. They generally follow common patterns and associations (e.g., more is up, less is down) (Lakoff and Johnson 1980, Lakoff 1987). Finally, new metaphors that are not easily related to specific patterns are considered fresh, novel, or creative metaphors.

A metaphor is an expression that applies one domain to another. In the previous example of "putting money into a stock" the physical object domain is being used to describe something in the financial domain. The terminology we will use is consistent with that of Richards (1936). More technically, the physical object domain plays the role of the *vehicle* domain (the vehicle is what "carries" the metaphor). Likewise, the financial domain plays the role of the *tenor* domain.

The class of metaphors that we wish to investigate primarily falls under conventional metaphors, but by some judgments, may also enter the fresh domain. We wish to limit the scope of this work to what we shall call transparently-motivated metaphors. These are metaphors that are motivated by general principles and convey a meaning that is primarily not that of the mapping itself. These involve discussing things in more concrete terms or in terms that are conceptually grounded in common structures of thought. In addition, we restrict ourselves to "verb phrase" metaphors. In other words, we are not interested in metaphorical expressions to be used as noun phrase reference. Rather, we are interested in how a metaphorical use of a verb can be explained in a computational fashion.

The prevalence of such metaphor may not be at first apparent. The transparently-motivated metaphors are such a natural form of expression, built of very familiar concepts, that they often do not have the alerting quality that the most flowery metaphors do. Often, it requires several readings of the same page of text before these metaphors can be recognized. The test used to recognize these metaphors is to question the literalness of the expression (although the distinction of literalness is tenuous (Gibbs 1989), computationally, this is often accomplished with semantic restrictions).

It is important to distinguish metaphor from analogy and similes. A prototypical analogy is: "The sun is to the solar system as a nucleus is to an atom" (Gentner 1983). For the purpose of this work, the main distinction between metaphor and analogy is what is being expressed. An analogy makes the basic mapping between the tenor domain and the vehicle domain explicit (Carbonell 1982, p. 421). The mapping must be consciously recognized by the reader if it is to be understood. This is because the mapping is directly linked to the meaning of the expression. In metaphor the mapping may facilitate the expression of an additional meaning. Similarly, Cornell Way (1991, p. 160) shares this distinction, stating that analogy avoids the real question of what facilitates the isomorphism, instead, it just states it.

Furthermore, analogies typically do not employ motivation from common, ubiquitous conceptual groundings. Instead, they often employ novel background mappings. This is why analogies explicitly mark their background mappings. We are not interested in creating whole new background mappings. We are interested in generating new and familiar expressions based in common, familiar conceptual mappings.

It should be clear that similes do not qualify as transparently motivated, for the same reasons. Their mappings are novel and the meaning is closely tied to the mapping itself. There are expressions which are typically called metaphors that, according to these distinctions, may perhaps be better categorized as analogies or similes, such as "Men are wolves" (Black 1962). Under close inspection, we see that the mapping here is definitely not transparent. Although not stated in the prototypical form (using the form "is like") the statement has the effect of a simile. Black's example can be rephrased as "men are like wolves", and the meaning is preserved, perhaps even made more accessible. It appears that Tourangeau and Sternberg would agree to this analysis, in that they do not define simile in terms of the particular words "is like", rather they state "When an *overt* nonliteral *comparison* is made, it is usually called a simile" (1982, p. 204, emphasis ours).

In summary, transparently-motivated metaphors:

1. Are based on universal groundings that are often linked to bodily experience.

2. Convey a message that is something more than the mapping between vehicle and tenor. The mapping is used to convey this other message.

3. Are subtle in the way that they do not draw attention to themselves as blatant metaphors. In fact, at first glance, these metaphors are often not recognized as non-literal.

4 The Uses of Metaphor

We claim that it is not just the case that metaphor is a nice added attraction to text whose sole purpose is to make the text more enjoyable by adding a flowery flavor. Rather, metaphor can be harnessed in order to achieve certain textual goals that are difficult to achieve with strictly literal statements. Some of these goals are discussed here.

4.1 Focus of Attention

An important issue regarding metaphor generation is how it is used to direct a reader's focus of attention. Proper focus cues contribute to more coherent text. Different elements of a sentence can be raised in focus to achieve purposes of text planners at a higher level. The most simple example of manipulating focus of attention in a sentence is the passive construction. In the sentence "John hit the ball", John is naturally in focus because he is the actor and the subject of the sentence. But in "The ball was hit by John" the prominence of the ball has been raised. This is an example of an agreed upon method for raising the focus of some element of the sentence by using syntactic means to place that object into a prominent position (e.g., the first position) in a sentence.

The traditional view of focus of attention is that it is something that is accomplished by syntactic means, such as by making the desired focus the subject of the sentence (as was done in the sentence above with the passive construction). However, further inspection reveals that there is a relationship between semantic types and level of focus. There exist languages that do not allow the passivation of a sentence when the deep subject is more animate than the deep object. For example, in Navajo the expression equivalent to "The rock was carried by the man" would not be acceptable (Keenan 1985, p. 272). The reason for this is based in the semantic types of the objects. Presumably placing an inanimate rock before an animate object (man) in focus is so unacceptable that it has become a part of their grammar.

Not only is the animate feature important to focusing, but concreteness also appears to be. Concreteness has been found to positively correlate with several phenomena (Paivio et al. 1968), including free recall (Dukes and Bastian 1966), (Stoke 1929), (Paivio 1967), recognition memory (Gorman 1961) and short-term memory (Borkowski 1968). These studies have found that more concrete things tend to be remembered better than less concrete things. Although memory tests do not directly equate to focus at the time of reading, such techniques are as appropriate for the question as we can expect, due to the inappropriateness of on-line measures (e.g., eye fixation and reading time measurements) to this issue (see (Singer 1990, p. 21)). Thus the above studies show that more concrete items are given higher focus then non-concrete concepts.

Given this evidence, it is both reasonable and intuitive to conclude that the semantic types of words/concepts affect the perceived level of focus attributed to those words/concepts. We have chosen to model the effects of semantic types on perceived focus levels using a focus hierarchy. Items at the top of the hierarchy, by nature of their semantic features, are more likely to be focused than those at the bottom. Generally, concepts which are considered very concrete and volitional are toward the top while more amorphous and abstract things are toward the bottom.

Given the hierarchy which explains inherent focus level according to the semantic type of an object, it is interesting to note that one effect of metaphorical statements can be to alter the perceived semantic type of an object (and therefore potentially raise the perceived focus level). Consider the metaphorical statement "AI *is no stranger* to object-oriented paradigms" (Elliot 1991). Notice that the phrase "is no stranger" has the effect of conceptually personifying the objects involved (i.e., AI and object-oriented paradigms) since it is a phrase that, literally, can only be used with humans (or perhaps other animate objects). Compare the perceived focus level with that in a more literal rendition of the sentence such as: "AI and object-oriented paradigms have previously been incorporated together."

Thus one effect of metaphor can be seen in the area of focus of attention as manipulated by the semantic types of objects in a sentence. In the traditional view of focus of attention, a word is treated as having a static semantics. However the use of metaphor can make the semantic type of objects more fluid. By using them with a verb that only applies to humans, for example, the objects are pushed up the focus hierarchy towards the position that humans occupy.

Thus one principle we recognize is:

Semantic Focusing Principle. One way to raise the perceived focus of attention of an item is to use a metaphorical verb whose literal sense requires objects higher in the focus hierarchy. The effect is to raise the perceived semantic type of the object toward that position in the focus hierarchy.

Other examples of this principle at work include: "Lisp *has adopted* various object-oriented approaches" which personifies Lisp, and "The parties *have reached* a tentative agreement" where the agreement has been raised to the level of concrete physical object.

There are two ways that metaphor can raise the focus of an element. One way is the semantic shift of the element to a more concrete or animate level. The second way is that when the semantic shift is finally expressed in a sentence, the object may be placed in subject position. We claim that both together (the semantic shift and the positioning) should tend to have a more pronounced focusing effect than either in isolation.

4.2 Conceptual Fit

In the above section we saw how metaphor could be used to alter the perceived semantic type of a concept and thus alter its perceived level of focus. This same type of altering may make it possible to reach a better conceptual fit. There are really two aspects to the conceptual fit of a concept. To motivate these, consider the following two metaphorical expressions found in a conversation about financial planning.

- "...when did you put the money in?"
- "well how 'bout if you move it to a money market fund?"

The first element of conceptual fit can been seen in the way that money is being described in the above examples. Money is being viewed as a tangible object that can be physically moved. Please note that when money is transferred from one security to another, it typically is done without any tangible tender actually being manipulated. Yet, conceptually, it is often viewed, or spoken of, in this light. It should be pointed out that examples like this are not novel, it is quite natural for people to talk about abstract concepts in a more concrete sense; this grounding (informally) appears to make the concepts more understandable. Notice that making an abstract item concrete is often achieved by metaphor.[2]

This notion is captured in a principle that we call The Concreteness Principle.

The Concreteness Principle. People naturally tend to describe things in a more concrete manner, even when the issue at hand is rather abstract; such behavior generally yields more natural and understandable text.

While the concreteness principle might explain some of what is going on in the above two examples, it is not enough to explain the similarity of those metaphors with others such as:

- "I just put $84.79 *into* groceries."
- "Consider an object class *in* the object-oriented approach."
- "Anything can be *crammed into* an object oriented framework – including AI."

These metaphors have something in common. In each case, a concept is being viewed as a container, with (abstract) objects viewed (along more concrete lines) as being put into or taken out of the container. This is consistent with Johnson's (1987) work which emphasized that the building blocks of thought are based on bodily experience. In particular, he described "schemas" for these building blocks including one for containment.

Thus another common basis for metaphors is to view things in line with one of these pre-identified schemas that are commonly held by a population. This leads us to another principle:

Conceptual Roots Principle. It is natural to talk about things in the light of "basic building blocks" of thought that are commonly shared by a community.

4.3 Perspective

While a notion of perspective on an item or event is related to the notion of focus discussed above, they are distinct. Rather than concentrating on which object is focused on, perspective has to do with *how* an object is viewed. A given perspective on an item or event causes certain aspects of that item or event to be highlighted (and not others) (McCoy 1989).

---

[2] This reason for metaphor, on the face of it, looks similar to the kind of metaphors discussed above for focus reasons. Indeed, making an abstract object more concrete also raises the focus level. The point we are making here is that it can *also* make the concept easier to understand, or **grasp**.

Consider the meaning conveyed by a couple with young children attending a social event with all of their children's paraphernalia in tow. One may say to the other "It is time to pull up stakes". Here, the literal meaning of what is being communicated is that it is time to leave. However, the leaving was metaphorically taken from the camping domain, where leaving is a rather involved process. This use of metaphor has highlighted or put a particular perspective on the leaving that emphasizes the work involved in carrying out the task ahead. Another example of perspective casts enthusiasts of traditional AI Programming and the Object-Oriented programming approach in an antagonistic light, highlighting their differences: "Rather than suffering from two warring factions, we should aim to combine the best of both camps and overcome the weaknesses of each approach" (Elliot 1991). This metaphorical method for highlighting particular aspects of an item can often be found in text designed to persuade the reader.

4.4 Brevity and Filling Lexical Holes

Paivio (1979) lists three hypotheses explaining the usefulness of metaphor. One is that, through vivid imagery, metaphor makes its expression more memorable. This relates to focus, and less directly to perspective. The other two hypotheses listed are compactness, and inexpressibility. The compactness hypothesis recognizes that a metaphor allows large chunks of information to be transferred from vehicle to tenor. In this way metaphor can achieve the goal of brevity. It is natural and briefer to say that something is "...considered an object class *in* the object-oriented approach." (Ell91), than to say that it is "considered an object class *with respect to* the object oriented approach." Thirdly, the inexpressibility hypothesis states that a metaphor enables us to describe experiences for which appropriate words are not available. Lexical holes, however, differ from the goals listed. Lexical holes are not so much a goal that may yield additional texture to the text, rather they demand that a metaphor be generated.

5 Metaphor Understanding Research

Several researchers have made progress with the problems of metaphor recognition and understanding (c.f., Carbonell (1982), Fass (1991), Gentner (1983), Martin (1990), Tourangeau and Sternberg (1982) and Weiner (1985)). There is a great deal of background that the study of metaphor generation can borrow from existing metaphor understanding work.

The usefulness of an is-a hierarchy of concepts that can yield more general instances and siblings has been recognized in metaphor understanding work. Martin's work in understanding new metaphors has given us the concept of "core-relatedness" which we have previously described as helping to motivate this work. Metaphor understanding research has made progress in answering the question of what is carried from one domain to another by a metaphor. Carbonell's (1982) hierarchy of invariance grades ten conceptual relations in terms of whether they are maintained across domains. So, for example, the hierarchy specifies that goals are maintained somewhat more than causal structures which are maintained more than descriptive properties.

Although there is much background that we can borrow from metaphor understanding research, there are fundamental differences between the problems of metaphor understanding and metaphor generation. Metaphor understanding research can assume that the input that is given to it is natural. When working in generation, we must be careful to insure that the output is expressed naturally. We must choose when it is best to use metaphor rather than a more literal expression. Therefore the goals must be carefully examined and exploited.

In metaphor understanding, knowledge structures are used for the purpose of recognizing and interpreting the metaphorical input. These are not the problems of metaphor generation; we are fortunate to know what we want to express, and if we choose to, that we are employing the tool of metaphor. Instead, the knowledge that we use must be suited for choosing the most apt metaphor to generate expressions in the most effective manner. With a limitless number of possible metaphorical domains to choose from, we must be especially sensitive to the issues of size and tractability.

6 Previous Non-Literal Generation Research

Early work on non-literal generation concentrated on stylized sub-languages (Kukich 1983), (Kittredge et al. 1986). Although this work generated non-literal expressions, it did not capture the conceptual motivation behind the metaphors generated by general principle. Instead, non-literal expressions were not fundamentally distinguished from more literal expressions.

In his work on the KING generator, Jacobs (1985) developed a system to represent knowledge for generation. The purpose of Jacobs's work was parsimony of representation, not a general approach to metaphor generation. The representation scheme that KING used included VIEWs which could be used to represent alternative routes of expression. The information in these VIEWs could be motivated by metaphor. However, any metaphor that could be generated by the system would first essentially have to be individually encoded. To the system's credit, the specification was not necessarily at a particular sentence form, but at a somewhat conceptual level. For example, it was encoded that the action *punch* could be expressed as a transfer using *give* with *punch* being the object of the giving.

To our knowledge, there does not exist a computational theory that can account for metaphor generation from general principles. Such an approach should allow for novel metaphor generation, and account for the conceptual structures behind such expressions, as well as account for the effects of such manipulation.

7 Approach to a Solution

Instead of prescribing acceptable metaphors, we wish to prescribe general structures that motivate familiar metaphors as well as less familiar ones. We believe that transparently-motivated metaphors are a promising sub-class of metaphors in which to work, because they carry special requirements that restrict the possible search space from which they can be generated. We have begun preliminary work on specifying the basic structures and methodologies that together can generate good metaphors.

It is hardly a trivial matter to develop a computational approach to generating an appropriate metaphorical expression for a given meaning that we wish to convey. This is even more difficult when we consider that specific goals will also need to be met (e.g., be brief, raise the focus level of the subject, emphasize the difficulty of the action of the verb, etc.). Generating metaphors is not like finding square roots; there is no single path of reasoning that can be expected to yield a suitable metaphor. Our approach can be considered opportunistic because more than one vehicle domain may be isolated and tried. Failure will result when no suitable domain and mapping can be found. We appeal to two related, but distinct approaches which we describe below. The first handles metaphors between two similar domains (where similar means two domains sharing the role being metaphorically described). The second handles the more general metaphors that can occur between two very different domains.

7.1 General Role Filling

The idea behind the general role filling approach is to identify sibling domains to the tenor domain that are appropriate as vehicle domains. Both the tenor and vehicle domains share some roles. In particular we require that they share the role that is the focus of the metaphor (that aspect of an action which is being referred to metaphorically). We can identify a superordinate of the tenor domain from which the tenor domain inherits the role in question. The vehicle domain will also share this superordinate.

In addition to sharing the common superordinate, a reasonable metaphorical domain must have the following qualities:

1. *Be universal, or considered very familiar (with respect to the user model).* This restriction is rather self-evident; if the audience that is supposed to understand the metaphor is ignorant of the vehicle domain, there is little hope of the expression's success.
2. *Be concrete.* In particular, the selected vehicle domain must always motivate a description that is at least as concrete as the tenor domain. This restriction follows from the concreteness principle described earlier.
3. *Have the potential to achieve any special constraints due to the goal of the metaphor.* Recall earlier that a metaphor may be used for focus, brevity, etc. The metaphorical domain must be one which is able to achieve these goals.
4. *Have specialized lexical expressions in the vehicle domain for the role being described.* This restriction is particularly special to the transparently-motivated metaphors. It is necessary because the lexical expression used to describe the role is the only information that carries the mapping. Notice that this restriction would not be necessary in the case of other non-literal expressions which explicitly state the relevant mappings. It is this specialized expression that carries the vehicle domain to the full utterance. Without the specialized lexical expression, a transparently-motivated metaphor cannot be generated.

These specifications constrain what potential metaphorical domains will be considered. Not only are such specifications required[3] but by limiting what domains are appropriate to be considered metaphorical domains, the space and search time requirements, which may be very large in a complete system, will be held down.

To illustrate how this works here is a sketch of how the goal of perspective can be attained. Consider trying to generate the metaphorical expression conveying "leave the party", while at the same time emphasizing the effort that it takes to leave (as was the case for the couple described earlier with their children and paraphernalia). A party can be described via is-a links of the abstraction hierarchy as a human process. A process can have a termination. In the case of attending a party, leaving and saying goodbye to everyone can be considered part of the termination of this process.

After ascending the is-a hierarchy a level of abstraction, we can search for a candidate vehicle domain that shares this same parent. There are, of course, a number of possible vehicle domains that meet the first two criteria given above (i.e., are known to the user and are at least as concrete as partying). To narrow this choice further, a number of considerations come into play.

One of these considerations has to do with whether or not the possible vehicle domains have specialized expressions available for the termination (the role that the metaphor involves). Two possible vehicle domains (among many) that meet this criteria are camping, with "pulling up stakes", and electrical equipment, with "pull the plug".

Both domains are thus far potential candidates, however, now the constraints imposed by the goal of the metaphor must be considered: emphasize the complexity of the termination. Will an allusion to camping rhetorically make leaving the party appear more involved? Here we must appeal to more detailed knowledge about the termination of the camping experience. In this case we find that the termination of a camping experience is not trivial, it requires a moderate amount of work (as compared to the partying domain). Therefore, it appears that the quality of difficulty is transmitted via the metaphor to the expression.

On the other hand the electric equipment domain has a relatively simple termination. The process would not select this domain because the desired emphasis would be lost. However, notice that if a simple/fast termination was desired, this domain would have been suitable.[4]

There is a lot of challenging work yet to be done with regard to determining what qualities are appropriate for selecting a metaphorical domain. Generally speaking, an apt metaphor would map salient aspects (e.g., termination) between domains. In this specific example, the aptness of "pull up stakes" may in part be due to the special qualities of this particular leaving of a party, which is more complex than a prototypical leaving because of the children and their stuff. The qualities

---

[3] An exception to this, is perhaps for the quality *be concrete*, which is not technically necessary for every possible goal, but is compatible with all goals.

[4] A final process should be completed before any such metaphors are generated. We should have a test to insure that the metaphor is not misunderstood. In particular, we should be sure that the expression can not reasonably be interpreted as literal.

that lead to the deviation from prototypicality may be quite salient. Therefore, a good metaphorical domain should have an analog for them. Camping has such an analog, the equipment associated with camping. In section 7.2 we will discuss a more computationally tractable solution to this problem.

We noted earlier that if the goal of expressing the perspective of simplicity that "pull the plug" would be appropriate. Consider if the typical experience of this couple was that leaving was a complex process, but for once their children were not along, "pull the plug" would be reasonable for the way it emphasizes simplicity. This is because the lack of complicating factors would be salient, and would match better with this simple electrical experience which also is without extensive paraphernalia. In sum, an especially non-prototypical aspect in the tenor domain may be useful in selecting a metaphorical domain, if that aspect is to be emphasized.

7.2 Specific Role Filling via Conceptual Mappings

The previous approach works well for some transparent metaphors, but notice there is a severe restriction on the relationship between the tenor and vehicle domains – they must have the role involved in the expression in common. In this section we discuss a method for generating metaphors potentially concerning two very different domains. Its reasoning is dominated by top-down rules and associated mappings that are often triggered by the tenor domain.

Recall that earlier we discussed conceptual fit as a common reason for metaphor generation. From this reason, two principles for deriving metaphors were specified: the concreteness and the conceptual roots principle. The method introduced here is intended to help implement this second principle. If a system is to generate metaphors which follow from conceptual roots, those roots must be represented in the system. We will need *metaphorical domain selection rules* and related mapping information which will capture the conceptual roots by mirroring such common metaphorical behaviors as those pointed to in Lakoff and Johnson's work (1980), (Lakoff 1987). There should be selection rules related to such familiar patterns as "try to describe arguments in terms of war, and argument structure in terms of buildings", "describe progress in terms of a vehicle moving toward a goal" and "describe securities in terms of containers for money." These rules, and the mapping structures associated with them, are a major part of the attempt at the formal embodiment of human conceptual groundings.

Consider describing the progress with a publication or career, with the intention of being as intuitive as possible–requesting a relevant conceptual fit. A rule encoding the notion "describe progress in terms of a vehicle moving toward a goal" would be triggered. Closely attached to this rule should be the information about how the mapping from tenor domain to vehicle domain should relate. Such information would include mappings such as the following:

Notice that these expressions for progress in the vehicle domain of physical motion are natural and probably more frequent than the "literal" forms. This may be (similar to Mark Johnson's (1987) reasoning) because people *understand* progress in terms of motion. It is in this way that metaphor generation can yield a more conceptually appropriate expression, which may actually be easier to understand than

Table 1. A mapping for describing progress in terms of a moving vehicle

Tenor Domain		Vehicle Domain
progress	....	forward
negative progress	....	backward
no progress	....	still
unsatisfactory progress	....	slow

its literal counterpart.

This is specific information analogous to that provided by the is-a hierarchy and role information in the "pull up stakes" example. However, this process is more specific than that of using role filling terms from different domains. Here, some of the cognitive grounding of viewing progress in terms of motion is encoded.

Generating from More General Principles We are excited about the potential for abstracting beyond the level of information presented in section 7.2. Please recall the "career as moving object" example. Note that the moving object has some starting point, some goal and some points on its path. With time involved, it also has some speed. It appears that with a sophisticated model of this behavior in the vehicle domain and rules linking it to appropriate types of tenor domains, that the above four mappings could be derived. Interestingly, a more general structure matched with reasoning could yield other derived expressions. With the knowledge that energy is required to move objects, and given that a prototypical moving object is a car that runs on gas, we could hope to generate "My career is running out of gas." As the level of the information that motivates the metaphors reaches a higher level of abstraction, a greater degree of "creativity" is anticipated.

Not all selection rules lie at the same level of abstraction. The selection rules, and their associated mapping knowledge may need to be encoded in a hierarchical fashion. For example, the concept of possessions as containers of their purchase price may be a more specific version of the general concept that things are containers of what goes into their existence (e.g, "I put a lot of (time, energy, love, money) into this relationship!").

A more general level can be motivated by abstracting from existing rules and mappings, but some very general rules may be recognized in tact. Two examples of such general rules relate the notions "High (on a scale) is good" and "Large magnitude is significant". Consider the system employing such principles as these when needing to describe a lawyer's reputation as impressive, the generator might say, for example, "She has a very high reputation," or "She has a very big reputation."

This is an example of rather imprecise expression. Yet, it is the same type of imprecise expression that people naturally use every day, from which the appropriate meaning is understood. Some specific metaphors which follow from these general principles may be novel. Yet, they will always be motivated by universal principles based on familiar conceptual groundings. So even in the worst case, (barring the failure of being mistaken for literal) only the aptness may suffer, not the conveyed meaning itself.

7.3 Achieving the Goals

We have shown how a perspective goal can be accomplished through the general role filling approach, and how a conceptual fit goal can be accomplished with the specific role filling approach. Any goal that can take advantage of the general role filling approach can also benefit from the specific role filling approach. Although the specific role filling approach is well suited for goal of conceptual fit, we do not claim that only one of the approaches is right for accomplishing a particular goal. The only possible exception is the conceptual fit goal is somewhat limited to the rule-driven approach. Yet, there still might be hope for the conceptual fit goal without a suitable selection rule being discovered. We can imagine a more elaborate approach that would require that certain metaphorical domains be recognized for their special relationship with conceptual roots. For example, those metaphorical domains that are fairly general, and directly related to bodily experience (e.g., containment and motion) would be prime candidates for an extensive attempt at a match.

The goal of brevity need not add any more complexity to the model. When the candidate metaphorical domains are being considered, and we know what specific role need be filled, we can compare the length of the specialized lexical expressions once they are identified. Although the scope of our work does not cross into the final phase of sentence generation, we could merely pass several candidates as output, and the final sentence generator could temporarily generate them so they can be compared for brevity.

The goal of raising the focus level of a particular element of an expression would take advantage of the work described in section 4.1. In particular, candidate metaphorical domains must fill focusing criteria. The element to be raised must be shifted to a semantic type by the metaphorical domain(s) which is higher in the focus hierarchy than is the case in the more literal form. If many candidates are promising, we would then want to choose one which could allow the possibility of the element whose focus is to be raised to be located in subject position.

8 Application to Augmentative Communication

Some of the ideas in this work can be applied to the problem of Augmentative Communication, the field of developing tools to facilitate the expression of disabled people. A large population of non-speaking, motor-impaired individuals must rely on computer-based communication aids. These aids, in essence, present the user with a list of letters, words, or phrases that may be selected to compose the desired utterance. The resulting utterance may then be passed to a document preparation system. While many of these individuals desire to communicate in complete well-formed sentences, the expenditure in effort and time is often prohibitive. The sentence compansion (compression expansion) project's goal is to increase the communication rate of such individuals by decreasing the number of words that must be selected to form a sentence (McCoy et al. 1990), (Jones 1991). Input to the system is a list of uninflected content words (e.g., "apple eat john"), and the output is the desired sentence (e.g.,"The apple was eaten by John.") In order to do this, techniques from both NLU and NLG must be employed.

The success of the sentence compansion system is marred by one major shortcoming. It has carried the caveat that it was intended to handle only literal expressions. However, as this work reflects, not only are transparently-motivated expressions prevalent, they are often difficult to distinguish as non-literal. Therefore they are especially undesirable to exclude. We hope that the work here will help increase the coverage of the sentence compansion system.

9 Conclusion

A great deal of work is yet to be done. Before an implementation can be encoded, we must develop a more concrete theory of the knowledge structures and procedures based upon the groundwork here.

198zWe have introduced transparently-motivated metaphor and have made a case of its prevalence. We have analyzed some of the textual goals that such metaphor can achieve and discussed principles which can explain many of the uses of metaphor found in our text analysis. Our analysis of metaphors and the resulting principles have led to preliminary developments of a methodology for generating transparently-motivated metaphors that can account for metaphor generation from general principles. This allows for novel metaphor generation, and accounts for the conceptual structures behind such expressions, and accounts for the effects of such manipulation.

References

Anderson, R. C.: Inferences about word meanings. In Graesser, A. C. and Bower, G. H., editors, *Inferences and Text Comprehension* (1990)

Black, M.: *Models and Metaphors.* Cornell University Press, Ithica, NY (1962)

Black, M.: More about metaphor. In Ortony, A., editor, *Metaphor and Thought.* Cambridge University Press, Cambridge (1979) 19–43

Borkowski, J. G. and Eisner, H. C.: Meaningfulness and abstractness in short-term memory. *Journal of Experimental Psychology* 76 (1968) 57–61

Carbonell, J. G.: Metaphor: An inescapable phenomenon in natural language comprehension. In Lenhart, W. and Ringle, U., editors, *Strategies for Natural Language Processing,* Lawrence Erlbaum Associates, Hillsdale, NJ (1982) 415–434

Cornell Way, E.: *Knowledge Representation and Metaphor.* Kluwer Academic Publishers, Boston (1991)

Dukes, W. F. and Bastian, J.: Recall of abstract and concrete words equated on meaningfulness. *Journal of Verbal Learning and Verbal Behavior* 5 (1966) 455–458

Elliot, L. B.: The bandwagon blues *AI Expert* 6:5 May (1991) 11–13

Fass, D.: met*: A method for discriminating metonymy and metaphor by computer *Computational Linguistics Journal* 17:1 March (1991) 49–90

Fass, D. and Wilks, Y.: Preference semantics, ill-formedness and metaphor. *American Journal of Computational Linguistics* 9:3-4 July-Dec (1983) 178–187

Gentner, D.: Structure-mapping: A theoretical framework for analogy. *Cognitive Science* **7:2** (1983) 155–170

Gibbs, Jr., T. W.: Understanding and literal meaning. *Cognitive Science* **13** (1989) 243–251

Gorman, A. M.: Recognition memory for nouns as a function of abstractness and frequency. *Journal of Experimental Psychology* **61** (1961) 23–29

Jacobs, P. S.: *A Knowledge-Based Approach to Language Production.* PhD thesis, University of California at Berkeley Computer Science Division Report (1985)

Johnson, M.: *The Body in the Mind: The Bodily Basis of Reason and Imagination.* University of Chicago press, Chicago (1987)

Jones, M., Demasco, P., McCoy, K., and Pennington, C.: Knowledge representation considerations for a domain independent semantic parser. In *Proceedings of the 14th Annual Conference* RESNA, Kansas City, MO (1991) 109–111

Keenan, E. L.: In Shopen, T., editor, *Language Typology and Syntactic Description*, volume 1: Clause Structure. Cambridge University Press, Cambridge (1985)

Kittredge, R., Polguere, A., and Goldberg, E.: Synthesizing weather forecasts from formatted data. In *Proceedings of Coling86* (1986) 563–565

Kukich, K.: Design of a knowledge-based report generator. In *Proceedings of the 21st Annual Meeting of the ACL* Cambridge, MA June (1983) 145–150,

Lakoff, G.: *Women, Fire and Dangerous Things What Categories Reveal About the Mind.* University of Chicago Press, Chicago (1987)

Lakoff, G. and Johnson, M.: *Metaphors we live by.* University of Chicago Press, Chicago (1980)

Martin, J. H.: *A Computational Model of Metaphor Interpretation.* Academic Press (1990)

McCoy, K., Demasco, P., Jones, M., and Pennington, C.: Applying natural language processing techniques to augmentative communication systems. In *Proceedings of the 13th International Conference on Computational Linguistics*, Helsinki, Finland (1990)

McCoy, K. F.: Generating context sensitive responses to object-related misconceptions. *Artificial Intelligence* **41** (1989) 157–195

Norvig, P. and Lakoff, G.: Taking: A study in lexical network theory. In *Proceedings of the 13th Annual Meeting* Berkeley Linguistics Society (1987) 195–206

Paivio, A.: Paired-associate learning and free recall of nouns as a function of concreteness, specificity, imagery, and meaningfulness. *Psychological Reports* **20** (1967) 239–245

Paivio, A.: Psychological processes in comprehension. In Ortony, A., editor, *Metaphor and Thought* Cambridge University Press, Cambridge (1979) 150–171

Paivio, A., Yuille, J. C., and Madigan, S.: Concreteness, imagery, and meaningfulness values for 925 nouns. *Journal of Experimental Psychology* **76:1** (1968) Monograph Supplement part 2

Richards, I. A.: *The Philosophy of Rhetoric.* Oxford University Press (1936)

Singer, M.: *Psychology of Language.* Lawrence Erlbaum Associates, Hillsdale, NJ (1990)

Stoke, S. M.: Memory for onomatopes. *Journal of Genetic Psychology* **36** (1929) 594–596

Tourangeau, R. and Sternberg, R. J.: Understanding and appreciating metaphors. *Cognition* **11** (1982) 203–244

Weiner, E. J.: Solving the containment problem for figurative language. *International Journal of Man-Machine Studies* **23** (1985) 527–537

Generating Referring Expressions in a Multimodal Environment*

Wim Claassen

NICI, University of Nijmegen
Montessorilaan 3
Postbus 9104
6500 HE Nijmegen
The Netherlands
email: CLAASSEN@NICI.KUN.NL

Abstract

EDWARD is a system which is being developed to study multimodal human-computer interaction. It incorporates a graph-editor called Gr2 and a Dutch natural language dialogue system called DoNaLD. EDWARD is capable of realizing referring actions in three ways: it can utter unimodal referring expressions, it can generate pointing gestures and it can produce multimodal referring expressions which combine referring expressions with a pointing gesture. The system uses its knowledge base and a context model to decide the type and the conceptual content of its referring expressions. The context model used is based on Alshawi's notions of context factors and salience. Presently seven types of context factors are used. The decision tree and a set of rules used by EDWARD to guide the generation process are described.

1 Introduction

This paper deals with the automatic generation of referring expressions in a multimodal research prototype called EDWARD. The primary aim of our project is the development and assessment of an interaction module which combines the positive features of the conversation and the manipulation mode of interaction (Claassen, Bos and Huls, 1990). EDWARD combines a graph-editor called Gr2 (Bos, in press) and a Dutch Natural Language Dialogue system called DoNaLD (Claassen and Huls, 1990). One of the application domains involves a file system environment with documents, authors, a garbage container and so on. The user can interact with EDWARD by manipulating the graphical representation of the file system (a directed graph), by menus, by written natural or formal language, or by combinations of these.

Some work has been done on the generation of multimodal referring expressions by Neal and Shapiro (1988) and by Allgayer, Jansen-Winkeln, Reddig, and Reithinger (1989). The system described by Neal and Shapiro is a research prototype called CUBRICON. The application domain is military tactical air control. Neal

---

* This research was carried out within the framework of the research programme 'Human-Computer Communication using natural language' (MMC). The MMC-programme is sponsored by SPIN Stimuleringsprojectteam Informaticaonderzoek, BSO, Digital Equipment B.V.

and Shapiro use an attentional discourse focus space representation (adapted from Grosz, 1978; Sidner, 1979; Grosz and Sidner, 1985) and a display model to generate multimodal expressions. The conceptual content of these expressions is restricted to the basic level category the object at hand belongs to. The category which is expressed by a noun is preceded by a demonstrative pronoun e.g., *this air base* ↑[2]. CUBRICON 'points' to objects on the screen by blinking or highlighting icons.

Allgayer et al. describe XTRA, a German natural language interface to expert systems, currently applied to support the user's filling out an annual tax withholding adjustment form. The generation component of XTRA is called POPEL (Reithinger, 1992). It uses a dialogue memory and a so-called form hierarchy to generate multimodal expressions. Pointing is done using simulated pointing gestures. Much attention is being paid to the kind of pointing gesture that should accompany a particular utterance in a particular context. E.g., a dot, a hand containing a pencil, a hand pointing with a finger, etc.

Both CUBRICON and POPEL represent linguistic and non-linguistic influences on the dialogue context in two separate models. In this paper I will show how the framework presented by Alshawi (1987) is used in EDWARD to represent linguistic as well as non-linguistic effects on the dialogue context in one general context model, and how this context model is used to produce referring expressions.

2 Generating referring expressions in EDWARD

2.1 Three Types of Reference

EDWARD is capable of realizing referring actions in three ways. First, it can generate a pointing gesture, secondly it can utter (unimodal) referring expressions (e.g., uttering some proper noun), and thirdly, it can produce multimodal referring expressions which combine referring expressions with a pointing gesture e.g., *deze file* ↑ (this file ↑). The next sections deal with these three types of referring actions in turn.

Pointing Gestures

Some systems (e.g., CUBRICON) use marking (blinking, highlighting, or underlining) to direct the attention of the user to a particular object represented on the screen. Others, like POPEL, use simulated pointing gestures, which mimic human pointing behaviour in a more natural way. EDWARD applies a combination of these two techniques. This is illustrated in Figure 1.

From a fixed point on the screen (the location of the icon representing EDWARD) an arrow starts to grow towards the icon that represents the intended referent. This simulates the arm and hand movements which are very common in human pointing behaviour. As soon as the arrow reaches the icon, the icon is marked by several small arrows pointing at it, and subsequently the arrow shrinks again (animated). The small arrows around the icon remain visible until either the user moves the

---

[2] In this paper ↑ stands for a pointing gesture to the visual presentation of the referent of the preceding phrase.

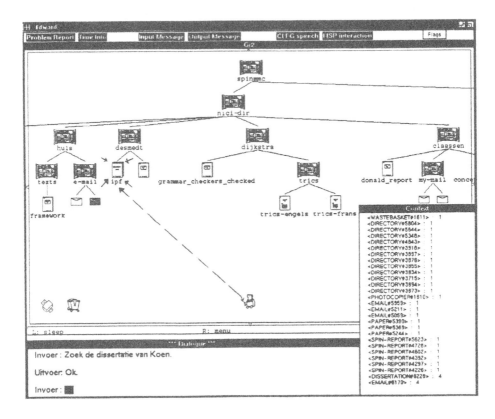

Fig. 1. A screen dump of EDWARD. The user has entered the command: Zoek de dissertatie van Koen. (Find Koen's Dissertation.). In response, the system points at the icon representing this file (post edited).

mouse cursor into the graphics display, or the next input sentence has been entered. So, whenever EDWARD consecutively points to several icons within one utterance, the marks stay, as a kind of trace to remind the user of what happened. Marking the indicated icons is important because pointing gestures and text output involve two different windows. This forces the user to shift his attention from one to the other. In future extensions, other kinds of marking could be used to realize pars-pro-toto pointing (i.e., pointing to a part of a referent) and vague pointing gestures. Note, that the *user* can point at an icon by selecting it, that is, by pressing the left mouse button while the mouse cursor is within the selection area of the icon. As a consequence, the user-indicated icon is marked using reverse video, and it can be manipulated, e.g., moved, by the user.

The only condition that triggers a unimodal pointing gesture is the input of a natural or formal language command, e.g., *Verwijder het rapport over parsing.*

(Remove the report about parsing.). Right after such a command has been interpreted, but before it is executed, the dialogue manager provides graphical feedback by producing a pointing gesture to the object at hand.

Referring Expressions

In principle, EDWARD is able to produce referring expressions of the following types:

- personal pronouns, e.g., *hij* (he);
- proper names, e.g., *Peter*;
- modified proper names, e.g., *Peter uit Nijmegen* (Peter from Nijmegen);
- definite NPs expressing a basic level category, e.g., *het rapport* (the report);
- definite modified NPs, e.g., *het rapport over parsing* (the report about parsing);
- indefinite NPs expressing a basic level category, e.g., *een rapport* (a report);
- indefinite modified NPs, e.g., *een rapport over parsing* (a report about parsing).

The NP modifiers produced by EDWARD presently involve only PPs and relative clauses, and no adjectives. Unimodal referring expressions appear in the answers to questions the user poses to the system, e.g., *Waar woont de auteur van dit artikel* ↑[3] *?*; *Hij woont in Amsterdam.* (Where does the author of this article ↑ live ?; He lives in Amsterdam.)

Multimodal Referring Expressions

Deictic expressions (e.g., *dit bestand/deze* (this file/this one)) in combination with the realization of an appropriate pointing gesture are common examples of multimodal referring expressions. Note, however, that deictic phrases are not necessarily accompanied by pointing gestures (they can be used anaphorically as well), and moreover, that pointing gestures can also be combined with other, non-deictic definite NPs, e.g., *Het rapport over EDWARD zit in Multi* ↑. (The report about EDWARD is in Multi ↑, where Multi is a directory name.). Within multimodal expressions we do not allow EDWARD to produce pointing gestures without some accompanying linguistic referring expression. So, for example, the expression *Het rapport zit in* ↑. (The report is in ↑.) will not be produced.

Multimodal referring expressions may occur in the answers EDWARD produces in response to user questions. E.g., the question/answer pair: *Bevat Multi een rapport?*; *Ja, het bevat het rapport* ↑ *van Gerard over parsing.* (Does Multi contain a report?; Yes, it contains Gerard's report ↑ about parsing.). Note that, in order to avoid confusion, the pointing gesture is produced right after the head of the NP has been uttered, and not after the complete NP has been realized (e.g., not right after *parsing*). The pointing gesture and the referring expression should preferably be initiated simultaneously, but this is not possible in the current implementation.

2.2 Knowledge Sources

In order to be able to decide the type and the conceptual content of referring expressions EDWARD's generator uses two knowledge sources: the knowledge base and the

---

[3] Here the ↑ means a pointing action by the user.

context model.[4] The knowledge base stores the permanent generic and specific world knowledge of the system, whereas the context model temporarily 'memorizes' which objects from the knowledge base have been referred to in the dialogue.

The Knowledge Base

The knowledge base, which is a semantic network somewhat similar to KL-ONE (Brachman and Schmolze, 1985), represents classes and instances of entities and relations. So the objects referred to in the dialogue are represented by objects in the knowledge base. Much like it is done in KL-ONE, relations[5] contain *role-filler type restrictions*, *cardinality information*, and *role-set restrictions*. E.g., the concept of 'sending an object to someone' is represented by a generic relation called <send>. With this relation three semantic (case) roles are associated called <agent>, <goal> and <recipient>. The role-filler type restrictions, then, specify for example that the fillers of the <agent> and <recipient> roles must be either persons or institutions and that the filler of the <goal> role (the object sent) can be any kind of concrete entity, excluding persons. The generation process uses these role-filler type restrictions in the pronominalisation rules described in section 2.3. The cardinality information of a relation specifies the maximum number of relations of that type that may be individuated for the filler of a particular role. For example, cardinality information is used to represent the fact that every husband has exactly one wife or that every person has his residence in maximally one town. In generation, cardinality information is of special importance when searching for a relation that is to distinguish a referent from an indefinite number of possible distractors (see section 2.4). The role-set restrictions, finally, specify for example that the filler of the <recipient> role in a <send> relation is not allowed to be identical to the filler of the <agent> role. The generator could use these restrictions use to exclude certain referents from the set of potential distractors (see section 2.3) but this has not been implemented yet.

The Context Model

In EDWARD the second knowledge source used to generate referring expressions (both multimodal and unimodal) is the context model. The central notion in this model is *salience*. The intuitive notion of salience has two important characteristics. In the first place, the salience of an instance at a given moment is determined by a rich diversity of factors, each of which plays a more, or less important role. In written language, recency of mention is known to be an important factor, as are syntactic and semantic parallelisms, the markedness of expressions and constructions used, and so on. Spoken language adds intonation, and when the situational context gets involved, various perceptual factors like visibility join in. The second notable characteristic of salience is that it is a graded notion. An individual entity may be more, or less salient, may gradually become less salient, and so on. This observation is important because it goes against predominant trends in the field of language comprehension. Focus, as it is employed in this field (see e.g., Grosz, 1978; Sidner, 1979; Grosz and

---

[4] Currently no user model is maintained.
[5] KL-ONE represents relations by 'roles' which correspond with two-placed predicates.

Sidner, 1985), is a rule based notion: it indicates the conditions under which this or that referent is (definitely) at the focus of attention.

Alshawi (1987) provides a general framework for modeling salience that does justice to both the characteristics mentioned above. The central constructs in this framework are so-called *context factors*. A context factor (CF) is defined by: (a) a' *scope*, which is a collection of individual entities; (b) a *significance weight*, represented by a numerical value; and (c) a *decay function*, which indicates in what manner the context factor's significance weight is to be decreased after it has been created.

The *salience value* of a concept at any given moment is obtained simply by adding the significance weights of the context factors that have that concept in their scope. The elegance of this particular notion of salience is that it allows for a unified measure of salience, which is determined by an indefinite number of independent factors which can be monitored separately. If a given circumstance contributes to a concept's salience, it does not do so directly, but acts via a context factor instead. It thus is possible to have not just more or less significant influences on a concept's salience, but also influences that are short-lived or long-lived, that decrease in more, or less complex ways, depending on all sorts of conditions and so on.

In EDWARD presently seven types of CFs are used (figure 2). Four to model linguistic context effects and three to model perceptual context effects. The linguistic CF types are called: *main term referent CF, subject referent CF, nested term referent CF*, and *relation CF*. Main-term referents are the referents of the subject, the direct object, the indirect object and the main modifiers of a sentence. They are the role-fillers of the relation expressed by the main clause. A main term referent CF has an initial significance weight of 3. Subject referent CFs model the observation that the referents of a subject clause are more salient than the referents of the other main terms. They have an initial significance weight of 2. Nested-term referents are the referents expressed by NP modifiers. These referents are mentioned in the sentence, but they are less prominent than the subject referents or main-term referents. Nested-term referent CFs have an initial significance weight of 1. Relation CFs are created for all the relations expressed by a sentence, e.g., by the main clause, or by NP-modifying PPs. They have a significance weight of 3. The decay function of the linguistic context factors subtracts 1 from a CF's weight at each successive update. If a CF's weight becomes 0 the CF is discarded.

The perceptual CF types are termed: *visible referent CF, selected referent CF*, and *indicated referent CF*. Visible referent CFs cause referents which are visible to be more salient than referents which are not visible. A visible referent CF has an initial significance weight of 1, so a referent which is visible will be a little more salient than a referent which is not. As soon as the graphical representations (icons) of the referents in the scope of a visible referent CF become invisible (e.g., as a result of a scroll action) the weight drops to 0 and the CF will be discarded. Selected CFs effectuate that selected referents are more salient than referents which are merely visible. A selected referent CF is created when an icon is selected. Its significance weight is initially 2, and it remains 2 for as long as the icon remains selected. As soon as the icon is deselected the weight becomes 0 and the CF will be discarded. An indicated referent CF, finally, causes a referent which is indicated by either the system or the user to be very salient for a short time. It has an initial significance weight of 30 to make sure that the referent in its scope will be most salient right after the pointing action occurred. After the first update it becomes 1, and the next update it becomes 0. Note the difference between pointing actions generated by the user, and pointing actions generated by EDWARD. The user points to an icon by selecting it whereas a pointing action produced by EDWARD has a more temporary effect. So, when the user points to an icon, two CFs are created: an indicated referent CF, and a selected referent CF.

linguistic context factor types	objects in scope	decay
main-term referents CF	referents of subject, direct object, indirect object and modifier	[3, 2, 1, 0]
subject referent CF	referents of the subject phrase	[2, 1, 0]
nested-term referent CF	referents of NP modifiers (e.g., PP, relative clause)	[1, 0]
relation CF	relations expressed by S, PP and relative clause	[3, 2, 1, 0]
perceptual context factors types		
visible referent CF	referents which are visible in the current view-port	[1, .., 1, 0]
selected referent CF	referents selected in the model world	[2, .., 2, 0]
indicated referent CF	referents indicated by a pointing gesture	[30, 1, 0]

Fig. 2. Context factor (CF) types and their significance weights after successive updates.

The present approach to context modeling has important advantages. First, the natural language analysis and generation modules can use the same model to handle reference. Secondly, entities as well as relations can be handled. Thirdly, it allows us to incorporate syntactic as well as perceptual influences on salience in one model. Fourthly, during generation, the salience value of an entity can be used to guide other decisions, for example, with respect to lexical selection and tactical linearisation (see Pattabhiraman and Cercone (1991) for a discussion of salience effects in natural language generation).

2.3 EDWARD's Algorithm for Generating Referring Expressions

I will now go into the pragmatic and semantic decisions involved in the generation of referring expressions by EDWARD. The syntactic formulation process will not be described in this paper. EDWARD's generator receives its input message from the dialogue manager. In the simplest case the message contains just a relation instance. A message may contain additional pragmatic information, e.g., that one of the case-role fillers of the relation instance is a *requested referent* (i.e., the referent requested by a question posed by the user). EDWARD's conceptual generator processes the input message and sends its output to the syntactic formulator and the graphics generator. Its basic task is (a) to determine the type and the conceptual content of the linguistic expressions that will be used to refer to the entity and relation instances in the input message, and (b) to decide which referents should be pointed at. It has been designed to produce referring expressions which are both concise and referentially unambiguous. Currently, the mode of the system output is not directly related to the mode of the user input. A related problem is that the system has no way to determine where the user is looking at. For instance, it may happen that a dialogue goes on for some time, but no pointing gestures occur at all. As a consequence, the user may no longer be attentive to the graphics display, and may not notice any pointing gestures produced by the system. It is this kind of problems that we are going to explore in our project, so I will not go into them here.

Figure 3 presents a slightly simplified[6] version of the decision tree used by ED-WARD's generator to produce referring expressions. The node numbers in the figure correspond with the decisions which are described below.

The first option considered is to pronominalise the referent (node 1). From a psycholinguistic point of view there are several reasons why pronominalisation should be considered first. If the decision is made to refer to an entity by a pronoun, the semantic and lexical search procedures will be simple and fast in comparison with the processing that needs to be done when generating full noun phrases. Furthermore, this model is in good keeping with the observation that corrections from pronouns to full noun phrases are more acceptable than vice versa.

There are three conditions in which pronominalisation of a referent is allowed. First, pronominalisation is allowed if the referent is the most salient referent in the context[7], and, at the same time, its salience value is bigger than 4. Secondly, pronominalisation is allowed if the referent is either the only <female> in the context, the only <set> in the context, or the only object in the context which is neither a <female> nor a <set>. In Dutch, a pronoun, used in this condition, will distinguish the referent from its potential distractors. This condition is rather language dependent though. Finally, pronominalisation is allowed if a referent has a salience value which is bigger than 2, and none of the other entities in the context satisfy the type restrictions belonging to the role that has been filled by the intended referent. The third condition requires additional explanation. Consider sentences (1), (2a) and (2b). Sentence (1) could be followed by either sentence (2a) or (2b).

(1)   *Het is Jan die de brief aan Peter heeft gegeven.*
      (It is Jan who has given the letter to Peter.)
(2a) *Maar hij heeft hem eerst gelezen.* (But he has read it first.)
(2b) *Hij heeft hem pas nog gesproken.* (He has recently talked to him.)

Let us assume that in all three sentences the agent refers to a person named Jan. According to the rules described above Jan may be pronominalised in both references. But, if it wasn't for the third condition, neither the letter, referred to in sentence (2a), nor Peter, referred to in sentence (2b), could be pronominalised. Note that in Dutch the same pronoun (*hem*) is used to refer to both the letter in

---

[6] The tree is simplified in the sense that plural reference is not represented.

[7] An entity is said to be *in the context* if its salience value is bigger than 0.

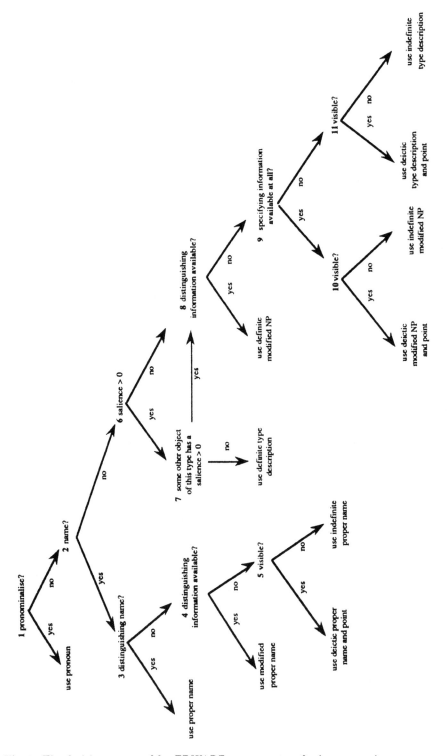

Fig. 3. The decision tree used by EDWARD to generate referring expressions.

sentence (2a), as to Peter in sentence (2b), but in neither sentence the reference is ambiguous. The reason for this is quite obvious. The object of a 'read' action will never be Peter, who is a person. Conversely, the recipient of a 'talking to' action will never be a letter.

EDWARD does not point at referents which are being pronominalised. If a referent can be pronominalised, it has been established in the context so well that a pointing gesture would hardly improve the quality of the reference. An important restriction with respect to pronominalisation is that requested referents are not allowed to be pronominalised, even if they are very salient. The dialogue manager has marked these referents with a flag. E.g., consider the following unacceptable question-answer pair: *Welk rapport gaat over parsing?*; *Het gaat over parsing.* (Which report is about parsing?; It is about parsing.).

If the referent cannot be pronominalised, the generator will check whether a proper name has been stored for it (node 2). Although proper names are merely properties, they tend to be pretty good specifiers of the objects they name. For this reason uttering a proper name is the second option in the tree. If a distinguishing name is known (node 3), it will be used to describe the referent. Otherwise, that is, if a name has been found, but some other entity in the context has the same name, the conceptual generator tries to collect additional information to distinguish the referent from the distractor(s) (node 4) to produce phrases like *Koen uit Nijmegen* (Koen from Nijmegen). In section 2.4 I will describe the rules applied by EDWARD to find distinguishing information. Note, that expressing a distinguishing relation may involve recursively generating referring expressions to specify the other role-fillers (if any) of the relation (*Nijmegen* in the example above). If no distinguishing information can be found the generator checks whether the referent is visible (node 5). If so, the generator will use a deictic phrase including a proper name, e.g., *deze directory die Multi heet* (this directory named Multi). If the referent is not visible, an indefinite phrase including the proper name will be used, e.g., *een directory die Multi heet* (a directory named Multi).

If the referent cannot be pronominalised and no proper name is known, the generator checks whether the referent is in the context (node 6). If this is the case and there are no other entities of the same concept type as the referent in the present context (node 7), the referent can be referred to with a definite NP that merely expresses its type, e.g., *de container* (the garbage container).

Otherwise, that is, either if the referent is in the context but there are several other entities in the context as well and these are of the same concept type as the referent, or if the referent is not in the context at all, information is sought that distinguishes the referent among the set of distractors (node 8). This set contains entities which are of the same concept type as the referent, but in the first case it contains only those which are in the context, and, in the second case, it contains all stored in the knowledge base. If distinguishing information has been found, it will be expressed using a definite modified NP, e.g., *de kopie van het rapport over parsing* (the copy of the report about parsing).

Otherwise, if there is some (ambiguous) specification available (node 9) but the referent is visible (node 10), a deictic modified NP will be produced, e.g., *dit rapport ↑ over parsing* (this report ↑ about parsing). If the referent is not visible (node 10), an indefinite modified NP will be produced, e.g., *een rapport over parsing* (a report about parsing). If there is no specifying information available at all (node 9) but the referent is visible (node 11), a deictic type description will be produced, e.g., *dit rapport ↑* (this report ↑). Finally, if there is no specifying information available at all (node 9) and the referent is not visible (node 11), an indefinite type description, e.g., *een rapport* (a report) will be used.

Apart from the rules above one additional rule is applied: If a referent is a requested referent and it can be visualised, a pointing gesture will be produced, even if this requires a scroll or 'open bookcase' action from the graphics generator. This is illustrated by the following question-answer pair: *In welke directory zit het rapport van Gerard?*; *Het zit in de container ↑.* (Which directory contains Gerard's report?; It's in the garbage container ↑.).

2.4 Searching for Distinguishing Information

During its search for distinguishing information, (see nodes 4 and 8 in figure 3) the natural language generator applies several rules to determine what information (i.e. which relation(s)) to use to specify the intended referent. The principal rules are presented below, in descending order of importance. They determine which relations are considered, and in what order. EDWARD does not consider combinations of relations to specify a referent, which might be a serious limitation in some domains. In a future extension this could be done, maybe using an adapted version of Dale and Haddock's (1991) algorithm. The decision whether a particular relation distinguishes a referent from a set of distractors will usually be simple: if the cardinality of the role filled by the intended referent equals 1, the relation is a distinguishing relation by definition, so there is no need to check any other relations. Consider, for instance: *de man van Wietske* (Wietske's husband). Else, that is, if the cardinality of the role filled by the intended referent is not equal to 1, the system has to determine whether none of the potential distractors fills the same role as the intended referent in any relation which is otherwise the same.

1. Do not use a relation with a salience value equal to or bigger than the initial weight of a relation CF (3) to specify some referent. This rule makes sure that relations cannot be used twice in one specification, which could yield infinite recursive specifications like the phrases: *de vrouw van de man van de vrouw ...* (the woman married to the man married to the woman ...) and *het rapport van de auteur van het rapport van de auteur...* (the report by the author of the report by the author...). In the conclusion of their paper Dale and Haddock (1991) propose a similar solution to this problem. In addition, this restriction prevents tautological sentences illustrated by the following question/answer pair: *Waar woont Gerard?*; *Hij woont in zijn woonplaats.* (Where does Gerard live?; He lives in his home town.).

2. Prefer relations in which the cardinality of the role filled by the intended referent equals 1. E.g., *de man van de secretaresse* (the secretary's husband). If such a relation exists, it is a distinguishing relation by definition. This rule will save the system a lot time, especially when the knowledge base contains many facts.

Note that, although the relation distinguishes the intended referent, it will only succeed to do so when its other role-fillers (if any) can be unambiguously referred to.

3. Prefer relations between the intended referent and referents that have a big salience value or a unique name. This rule makes it more likely that role fillers of the specifying relation can be uniquely referred to. In addition, this rule eases the realization of specifying information because references to objects like these can usually be generated faster and easier. E.g., *de secretaresse die HET kopieerde.* (the secretary who copied IT).

4. Prefer not to use visible relations with other visible objects to specify a referent which is both visible and in focus. For example, consider figure 1 again. In this context referring to the paper in the bookcase called *Desmedt* with a referring expression like: *het paper ↑ in Desmedt* (the paper ↑ in Desmedt) would be much less informative than: *het paper ↑ van Gerard* (Gerard's paper ↑). This would not be the case if the icon representing the directory named *Desmedt* would be outside the current view-port.

5. Prefer relations with relatively big salience values. This rule has two effects: First it contributes to the coherence of the discourse and, secondly, the case-role fillers of salient relations are likely to be salient as well, making them easier to refer to.

3 Example Dialogue

In this section I will illustrate some of the material presented in the previous sections, using screen dumps produced by EDWARD (see figure 4). Screen dumps are merely snapshots, so they have been post-edited in order to present EDWARD's pointing gestures. A dashed arrow pointing to an icon surrounded by several small arrows should be interpreted as follows: First, the pointing arrow starts to grow towards the icon, then the arrows surrounding the icon appear, subsequently the arrow disappears again, and finally the small arrows disappear, right after the next input sentence has been entered or the user has moved the mouse cursor into the graphics display (see section 2.1.1).

In figure 4, the input sentence: *Welke email stuurde Wietske aan Carla?* (Which email did Wietske send to Carla?) has just been entered. The output message will say something like: <WOMAN#5960> (in the text referred to by *Wietske*) sent <EMAIL#5959> (a particular email) to <WOMAN#1677> (in the text referred to by *Carla*). Let us first look at the salience values these referents got as a result of being referred to in the input sentence. The salience value of Wietske (<WOMAN#5960>) equals 3 (main term referent) + 2 (subject referent) = 5, whereas Carla (<WOMAN#1677>) has a salience value of 3 (main term referent). The referent of the email (<EMAIL#5959>) has a salience value of 1 (visible referent). Now Wietske can be pronominalised in the answer because it is the most salient entity with a salience value bigger than 3 (node 1). The referent of the email has a salience value of 1 so it cannot be pronominalised (node 1). There is no name stored for this referent (node 2), its salience value is bigger than 0 (node 6), other objects of

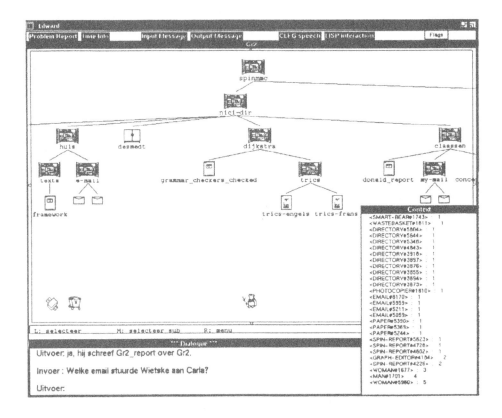

Fig. 4. A screen dump of EDWARD. The input sentence: *Welke email stuurde Wietske aan Carla?* (Which email did Wietske send to Carla?) has just been entered.

the same concept type (other emails) exist, and (node 7) some of these have salience values bigger than 0 (<EMAIL#6170>, <EMAIL#5211> and <EMAIL#5059> Therefore EDWARD decides to retrieve distinguishing information (node 8) to refer to this email.

Next to the relation representing the fact that the directory named *email* contains this email, there is just one other relation, representing the fact that the email is about <SPIN-REPORT#5623> (a report called *framework*). Although there exists some other email about <SPIN-REPORT#5623> in the knowledge base, specifying the email by expressing that it is about framework, is preferable over expressing that it is contained in the directory *email*. The referent is visible (node 10) so it will be described by a deictic modified NP: *deze email over framework* (this email about framework). Although Carla has a salience value of 3 this referent is not pronominalised because Wietske is in the context (see section 2.3 for more details). Note that the algorithm used is too cautious here. In Dutch (and in English as well) the reflexive pronoun would distinguish a reference to Wietske from a reference to Carla in this context. Moreover, the system could use role-set restrictions (section 2.1) here, to decide that it is very improbable that Wietske would send an email to herself, but we are still working on that. Figure 5 presents the answer: *Zij mailde deze email ↑ over framework aan Carla.* (She mailed this email ↑ about framework to Carla.).

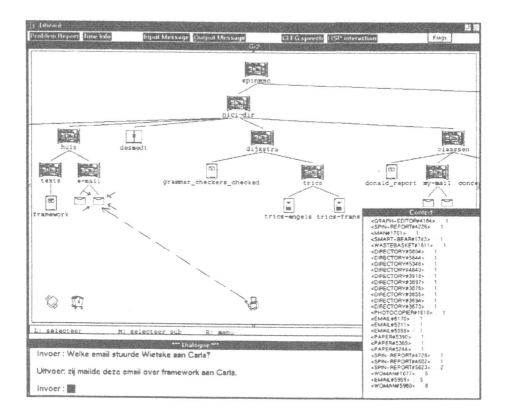

Fig. 5. A screen dump of EDWARD: EDWARD has produced the answer: *Zij mailde deze email ↑ over framework aan Carla.* (She mailed this email ↑ about framework to Carla.).

4 Concluding Remarks

I have described, in some detail, how EDWARD uses its context model in conjunction with its knowledge base to realize referring expressions. It must be emphasised here that these knowledge sources are used by the language interpretation component as well. The generation and interpretation components use the same CF types, with the same initial weights, and the same decay functions. In addition, they both use the role-filler type restrictions, the cardinality information, and the role-set restrictions from the knowledge base.

The current activation-based approach to context modeling has important advantage over a more rule-based approach like Sidner's (1979). The detailed algorithms she proposes combine lexical, syntactic, semantic, and pragmatic influences on the *stack of focus spaces* in a complex way. The focussing algorithms must take into account and combine all sorts of data from different levels of processing. In Alshawi's and our approach, on the other hand, influences originating from different levels and types of processing are modeled by individual CFs, which are created and managed locally, that is, by these processes themselves. As a result, the influences on an object's salience are represented distributively and independently, which is attractive from a psycholinguistic and computational point of view. The language interpretation and generation processes can use the general salience information provided by the context model, at all levels of processing, and for all kinds of purposes. In addition, taking into account new context factors, which would require explicit detailed changes in Sidner's rules, will be easier because the procedures that use the salience information could remain very much the same.

Of course, Sidner's treatment covers much more phenomena than can be handled using just the context factor types described in this paper. It would be interesting to explore how the insights of Sidner's work can be used to elaborate the present model. One could think of adding an association context factor to handle associative anaphora, a high level context factor to represent the salience of the global focus of multisentential texts, and additional syntactic CFs, for instance, to model the different context effects of reference by a pronoun versus reference by definite full NP.

There still are some problems, however. The present context factor types, their initial significance weights, and their decay functions have been established using a trial and error method. Although they worked fine in most of the dialogues so far, I do not claim that they are perfect. Getting the numbers right is an important empirical issue which we intend to concentrate on shortly.

Some aspects, although they are handled by EDWARD, could not be described here, e.g., plural and generic reference, the distinction between closed-world vs. open-world concepts, and the so-called Continuous Linguistic Feedback Generator (CLFG; De Smedt, Geurts and Desain, 1987), which optionally generates on-line natural language descriptions of the things the user is doing by manipulating graphical objects in the model world. Nonetheless, I hope that I have shown enough of the strength and elegance of the way reference is handled by EDWARD. I think that the present approach offers good opportunities for future extensions.

5 Acknowledgements

I wish to thank Edwin Bos and Carla Huls, who work with me on EDWARD, for their contributions to the work presented in this paper. In addition, I thank Alice

Dijkstra and Gerard Kempen for their comments on a preliminary version of this paper.

References

Allgayer, J., Jansen-Winkeln, R., Reddig, C., Reithinger, N.: Bidirectional use of knowledge in the multi-modal NL access system XTRA. Proceedings of the Eleventh International Joint Conference on Artificial Intelligence, Detroit, MI USA. 20-25 August 1989 (pp. 1492-1497).

Alshawi, H. (1987): Memory and Context for Language Interpretation. Cambridge (UK): Cambridge University Press.

Bos, E. (in press): A Graph-Editor. In L. Neal and G. Szwillus (Eds.). Syntax-Directed Editing. New York: Academic Press.

Brachman, R., Schmolze, J. (1985): An overview of the KL-ONE knowledge representation system. Cognitive Science, 9, 171-216.

Claassen, W., Huls, C. (1990): DoNaLD: A Dutch Natural Language Dialogue system (SPIN/MMC Research Report no. 11). Nijmegen, The Netherlands: NICI.

Claassen, W., Bos, E., Huls, C. (1990): The Pooh Way in Human-Computer Interaction: Towards Multimodal Interfaces (SPIN/MMC Research Report no. 5). Nijmegen, The Netherlands: NICI.

Dale, R., Haddock, N.: Generating Referring Expressions Involving Relations. Proceedings of the Fifth Meeting of the European Chapter of the Association for Computational Linguistics, Berlin, Germany, April 1991 (pp. 161-166).

De Smedt, K., Geurts, B., Desain, P.: Waiting for the gift of sound and vision: On natural-language sentence production in multimodal interfaces. ESPRIT Workshop on Natural Language Processing, Brussels, October 1987.

Grosz, B.J. (1978): Discourse Knowledge. In D. Walker (Ed.), Understanding Spoken Language. New York: North-Holland.

Grosz, B.J., Sidner, C.L. (1986): Attention, Intentions, and the Structure of Discourse. Computational Linguistics, 12(3):175-204, 1986.

Neal, J.G., Shapiro, S.C.: Intelligent Multi-media Interface Technology. Proceedings of the workshop on Architectures for Intelligent Interfaces: Elements and Prototypes, Lockhead AI Center, Monterrey, CA, 1988 (pp. 69-91).

Pattabhiraman, T., Cercone, N.: Salience in Natural Language Generation. Proceedings of the IJCAI-91 Workshop on Decision Making throughout the Generation Process, Sydney, Australia, August 1991 (pp. 34-41).

Reithinger, N.: The performance of an Incremental Generation Component for Multi-modal Dialogue Contributions. In: ????? (1992) ??????? Springer. These Proceedings.

Sidner, C.L. (1979): Towards a Computational Theory of Definite Anaphora Comprehension in English Discourse. Ph.D. Thesis, MIT, Cambridge, MA.

The Performance of an Incremental Generation Component for Multi-modal Dialog Contributions

*Norbert Reithinger**

SFB 314 – FB 14 Informatik IV, Universität des Saarlandes, D-W-6600 Saarbrücken 11, Germany (e-mail: bert@cs.uni-sb.de)

Abstract

In this paper, the performance of POPEL is demonstrated, an incremental and parallel natural language generation component for written German dialog contributions. The system's architectural approach is based on a cascaded model with feedback. It provides the flexibility essential for the integration into a dialog system. Furthermore, this architecture enables the seamless addition of the generation of multi-modal output to the decision flow of the generator. The rule-based gesture generator follows the simulation-oriented approach that mimics natural pointing gestures on a graphic. The analysis of the generation of a short text consisting of two sentences in different discourse contexts demonstrates POPEL's context-dependent mode of generation.

1 Introduction

The generation system POPEL[2] [14, 15] was developed as a part of XTRA, a natural language access system to expert systems (XPS) [2]. POPEL has to take into account the following major requirements:

flexibility with respect to two facts
- since XTRA is an access system to various XPSs, the structure of the conceptual knowledge depends on the actual XPS and will be exchanged if XTRA is connected to a new XPS.
- the range of utterances POPEL has to generate varies from ellipses to short explanatory texts.

multi-modality Both the user and the system can refer to a graphic presented on a screen by using pointing gestures.

---

* The work presented here is being supported by the German Science Foundation (DFG) in its Special Collaborative Program on AI and Knowledge-Based Systems (SFB 314), project N1 (XTRA/PRACMA). Thanks to Dagmar Schmauks who read this paper again and again and Alassane Ndiaye who rebooted XTRA.

[2] POPEL is an acronym for "Production Of {Perhaps, Possibly, P...} Eloquent Language".

In this article, I will first give an overview of POPEL's incremental and parallel approach to natural language generation. The generation of pointing gestures can be integrated into this architecture in quite a natural way as an extension of the decision process for referring actions. The main emphasis of this article is on the analysis of POPEL's performance with examples that show the generation of pointing gestures as well as the parallel and incremental generation of a short text consisting of two sentences in different discourse contexts.

2 The Architecture of POPEL

2.1 Constraints for the Design

Within XTRA, there are three different levels of knowledge: the *conceptual*, the *semantic*, and the *syntactic knowledge*. The domain dependent conceptual knowledge that is linked to the knowledge base of the connected XPS was separated from the domain independent linguistically based semantic knowledge. The rationale for this separation is that only the conceptual knowledge source has to be modified in major parts when the XPS is exchanged while the semantic knowledge can be kept.

The conceptual and the semantic knowledge is represented using SB-ONE, a KL-ONE like language [6]. The syntactic processing within both generation and analysis shares basic data structures and algorithms of the unification-based PATR formalism [19], but they are not completely bidirectional (cf. [11]). Transformation rules map the conceptual onto semantic knowledge, and a syntactic-semantic lexicon links the semantic and the syntactic level, and vice versa.

The shared contextual knowledge is represented in a *dialog memory*, a *user model*, and a so-called *form hierarchy*. The latter stores the information about the visual context, i.e., the graphic presented on a screen, especially the geometric features of the items the graphic consists of.

POPEL is part of the XTRA dialog system. Due to the competence required for analysis and generation, both components share the different knowledge sources of the overall system. This also avoids redundant and inconsistent knowledge sources (cf. [2]). Therefore, the knowledge base of the overall system and the division into the different knowledge levels is respected by the generator.

2.2 The Twofold Cascade of POPEL

In [15], I argued that the linguistic realization has to inform the planning processes about restrictions and additionally needed information caused by the realization processes, especially when the conceptual knowledge is encoded non-linguistically. The architecture of POPEL is based on a model which provides for a systematic way these interactions can be handled. It consists of a twofold cascade (see Fig. 1), where the outer parts are the "what-to-say" and the "how-to-say" components. The levels of the cascade run in parallel to one another – in the "how-to-say" even the single cascade levels are systems of cooperating processes –, so that different parts of the utterance are processed simultaneously in different levels. In this incremental and parallel processing cascade, requests for missing data are propagated "upward" from one level to another, until the request can be satisfied (cf. [14], p. 126 ff.). In parallel to the linguistic output, a gesture generation component visualizes pointing gestures, if they have been chosen for referent identification.

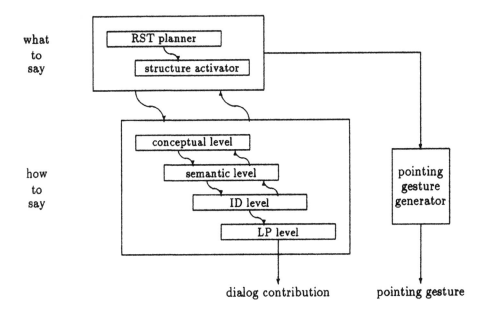

Fig. 1. The twofold cascade of POPEL

In the inner cascade of the "what-to-say" component, a planner and a so-called structure activator run in parallel. The planner is based on the operationalization of Rhetorical Structure Theory (RST) [9] developed by J. Moore [10]. It selects the contents of the utterance to be produced from the conceptual knowledge, but does not build a complete text plan which is then verbalized. Rather, incrementally selected elements of the conceptual knowledge are passed to the structure activator. Therefore, verbalization starts while planning is still in progress.

The structure activator works as the interface to the "how-to-say" component and passes the selected conceptual information on to the linguistic realization. Amongst other tasks, it also determines the propositional structure of the utterance by observing the structures that are built up in the "how-to-say" component and synchronizes the planning and realization processes. For example, the activator stops the planner if the latter proceeds too far ahead of the realization process.

The linguistic "how-to-say" component is a four-level cascade that receives parts of the conceptual knowledge. It is realized as a distributed, parallel system of cooperating processes (cf. [2, 12, 15] for further details). It incrementally builds the conceptual, semantic and syntactic structures of the utterances finally verbalized.

The knowledge sources for the conceptual and semantic levels are shared with the analysis component.

The syntactic processing is split up into two levels. In the immediate dominance (ID) level, dependencies between the phrases are built up and morpho-syntactic features are exchanged. The linear precedence (LP) level receives locally complete phrases, and inflects and linearizes them. It is a well known fact, that for a language with a relatively free word order like German, this separation facilitates syntactic processing and is a prerequisite for incremental verbalization [1, 12]. The last two levels of the "how-to-say" cascade correspond roughly to the system described in [1].

If a process cannot proceed in performing its task, i.e., building a correct syntactic structure in the ID level due to the lack of additionally required data, these data can be requested from the previous level of processing. If the request cannot be fulfilled, it is propagated further upward through the cascade until it reaches the "what-to-say" component. There, a request handler decides whether additional data is to be passed to the realization cascade.

2.3 The Integration of Pointing Gestures

In addition to the linguistic output, a gesture to an element of the graphic may be possible. The foundations for the treatment of pointing gestures are presented in [16].

There are two approaches for the processing of pointing gestures: the *simulation-oriented approach* which tries to model natural pointing and the *performance-oriented approach* which exploits all means the computer offers in order to direct the user's attention to an item on the screen, e.g., highlighting or inverting. The simulation-oriented approach has been chosen in XTRA because we think that it is more flexible, especially when using highly complex or scanned pictures. In these cases, the performance-oriented approach requires an extremely expensive description down to the last detail. Additionally, the simulation-oriented approach is more powerful because it allows complex pointing gestures like *pars-pro-toto deixis*, i.e., pointing to a part of the intended referent, and *shifted pointing*, where the pointing device is positioned beside or below the referent in order not to cover it. Both ways to point occur frequently when humans use gestures [18].

The decision when to use a pointing gesture fits seamlessly into the flow of decisions that are to be made in order to generate referring expressions. Figure 2 shows the data flow in POPEL during the generation of referring expressions. Again, there is feedback from the "how-to-say" to the "what-to-say" component. Remember, the conceptual knowledge is tied to the knowledge of the XPS and structured non-linguistically. Only when a conceptual element is mapped onto its semantic description it can be determined whether this element will be verbalized as a noun. This can be deduced from the type the semantic description gets in the terminological level of the semantic knowledge source.

In this case, a request is passed to the discourse-context handling, where three major tasks are performed that depend on the contextual knowledge sources:

- determination: is this concept (explicitly or implicitly) known or not? If true, how and when was it last mentioned in the discourse?

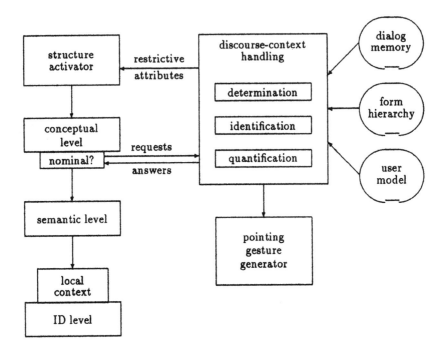

Fig. 2. The determination of referring expressions

- identification: do restrictive attributes have to be activated in order to identify it correctly (cf. [3] for the algorithm used in POPEL)?
- quantification: which quantifiers have to be selected?[3]

Currently, there are five different determination categories based on [13]: unknown, definite description with additional information required, short definite description required, unambiguous, and mentioned in the immediate context. The selection process is rule-based and utilizes the dialog memory, the user model and the form hierarchy.

A gesture can be generated if a link exists between the conceptual element under consideration and a node in the form hierarchy. The nodes represent the parts of the graphic and their geometric features. Gestures are generated preferably when new objects are introduced into discourse or when a complex description can be avoided. On the linguistic side, an appropriate description is selected which links the linguistic output to the gesture. This can vary from no linguistic output at all to a short text, when a concept is explained to the user and the corresponding items on the graphics are pointed at.

---

[3] Currently, the distinction is only made between 'one' and 'many'. The integration of the results of [1] is left to future work.

The gesture generator is a flexible, domain independent, rule-based system that selects and visualizes simulated pointing gestures by displaying an icon on the graphic, e.g., a hand holding a pencil [5]. In Fig. 3 a screen dump of the first application of XTRA is shown. XTRA is connected to an XPS which assists a user in filling out a German annual tax withholding adjustment form. The user's input

das kostet 35 dm im monat.
(*it is 35 dm per month.*)

causes the XPS to enter the yearly amount of money into the form, namely '420', The generator produces a gesture that underlines the number with no accompanying linguistic output. Later on in the dialog, after the user's question

was sind werbungskosten?
(*what is "werbungskosten"?*)

the system generates the definition

werbungskosten sind berufliche aufwendungen.
die können abgesetzt werden.
(*"werbungskosten" are job related costs. they can be deduced from the tax.*)

with a pointing gesture that underlines the caption "werbungskosten" several times. In Fig. 3, only the final position of the hand holding a pencil is shown.

The rules of the gesture generator classify the item on the graphic according to its geometric features, determine the application-dependent type, link the type to a gesture, and define the gestures by means of atomic actions, e.g., *move left*, *move right*, *draw circle*. This rule-based approach facilitates the adaption to different graphics. Two rules defining gestures at regions of the type FIELD using a *pencil* as pointing device are for example[4]

```
((FIELD ULC-X ULC-Y URC-X URC-Y LRC-X LRC-Y)
        (CIRCLE (+ ULC-X (/ (- URC-X ULC-X ) 30)) ULC-Y
                LRC-X (+ URC-Y (/ (- LRC-Y URC-Y ) 30)))
        *pencil* )
((FIELD LLC-X LLC-Y LRC-X LRC-Y)
        (MULTIPLE-LINE-ALONG
            (+ LLC-X 4) (+ LLC-Y 0) (- LRC-X 2) (+ LRC-Y 0))
        *pencil* )
```

From all possible gestures, the best fitting one is computed using an *anticipation feedback loop* [4]. In this loop, the possible gestures are processed by the analysis component for pointing gestures before the visualization in order to simulate the user's understanding of the gesture. The anticipation of the user's understanding allows for a correction of the gesture, if the intended item on the graphic was not recognized by the analysis which indicates that the reference might fail. For the

---

[4] The variables ULC-... etc. describe the coordinates of the rectangle: the first letter U stands for 'upper', L for lower, the second letters for left (L) or right (R). C stands for corner.

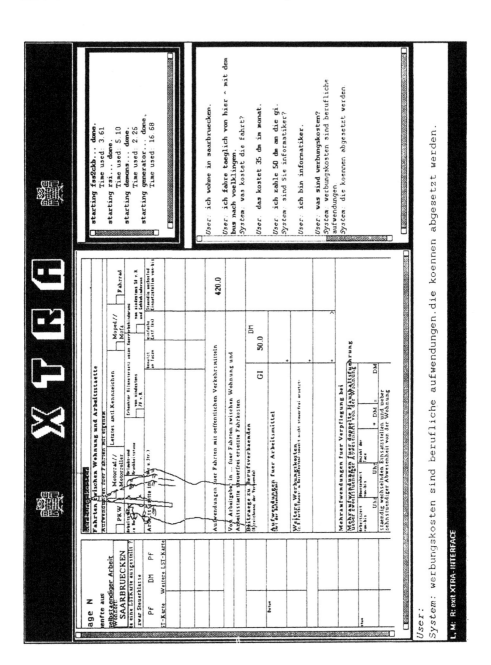

Fig. 3. A gesture generated by POPEL

gesture in Fig. 3, both gesture definitions shown above are possible. The second one
that defines the underlining gesture is selected and finally visualized because only
this one is unambiguously recognized by the analysis component.

The language-related features of the discourse-context handling are given back
to the requesting process and passed on through the mappings to the semantic
and syntactic levels. When creating the initial syntactic description in the ID level,
the syntactic features are determined with respect to the local context of the noun
phrase. For example, due to the incremental verbalization, the description category
might be changed because in the local syntactic context a certain category is no
longer appropriate (cf. [15], p. 190).

3 An Example of POPEL's Performance

3.1 The Input and Output

In order to demonstrate the performance of POPEL, I will analyze the performance
of the generation of a short text with two sentences. The core of POPEL consists of
about 860 Kbyte Lisp code, without the knowledge representation tools and knowledge sources. The example was computed on a Solbourne 5E/900 using LUCID
Common Lisp with incremental output enabled and an empty dialog memory:[5]

```
POPEL-WHAT>(popel '(swmb (know h (ic40 ic37))))
faehrt
ein mann faehrt
ein mann faehrt mit einem motorrad
ein mann faehrt mit einem motorrad von saarbruecken
ein mann faehrt mit einem motorrad von saarbruecken nach voelklingen
SAY: ein mann faehrt mit einem motorrad von saarbruecken
     nach voelklingen
     (a man drives with a motorcycle from saarbruecken to voelklingen)
dort
dort kauft er
dort kauft er einer frau
dort kauft er einer frau ein kochbuch
SAY: dort kauft er einer frau ein kochbuch
     (there buys he a woman a cookbook)
(11740000 614)
```

The input for the generator is an intentional goal "system wants that mutual
belief exists" (SWMB) that the hearer (h) knows the concepts with the internal de-
scriptors IC40 (BUY) and IC37 (DRIVE). The goal is the output of the user modeling
component BGP-MS [7] that stores the beliefs, wants, and goals of the user and those
of the system. Figure 4 shows the elements of the conceptual knowledge source that
are selected for verbalization during the selection process performed by the RST
planner.

---

[5] The English "translations" preserve the phrase order of the German sentences that contains important information about the thematic structure.

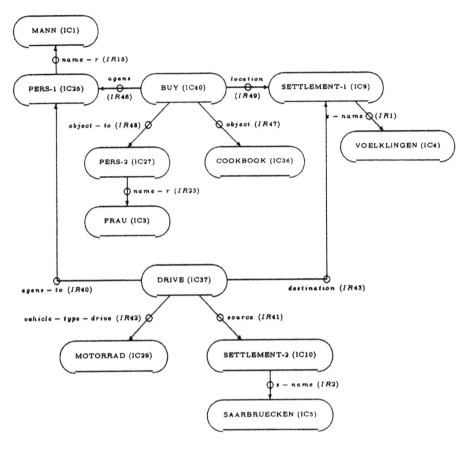

Fig. 4. The conceptual knowledge for the example

The lines in the example's output that begin with SAY are the sentences of the generated text. The first number of the list in the last line is the run-time in microseconds: the generator needs 11.74 seconds for the generation of the text.

3.2 The Activation Structure of the Processes

The timing diagram in figure 5 shows POPEL's processes and the flow of activation for the first sentence. Along the x-axis, the so-called scheduler steps are protracted. Since POPEL runs on a single processor machine, the parallel processing has to be simulated. Within one scheduler step, each process performs one uninterruptable step.

The processes are shown along the y-axis. In the top section there are the processes of the "what-to-say" component: the planner (RKS), the structure activator

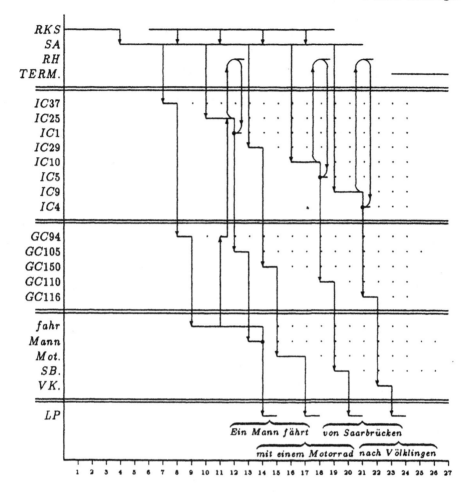

Fig. 5. Timing diagram for the first sentence

(SA), the request handler (RH) and the terminator which terminates the processes of the "how-to-say" component in a defined way.

Below are the processes of the "how-to-say" component with their internal names: first the processes of the conceptual level, followed by the semantic and syntactic processes. Each concept of the conceptual and semantic knowledge that is processed in the realization cascade and each syntactic phrase gets its own process. A process connects with the other processes in its level to build a correct structure according the underlying knowledge source. Then, it tries to map itself onto the next level. In addition, the processes in the syntactic level build the syntactic structures for the words and phrases. The process nearest to the x-axis is the LP process which inflects and orders the words. In the examples, only those processes are shown that map successfully through all levels. Alternatives which are processed but didn't succeed are omitted for clarity reasons.

The horizontal lines show the steps where a process is active and where it tries to map itself onto the next level. The punctuated lines show the steps when a process is looking for new information: due to POPEL's incremental way of processing, a process can never determine by itself whether its task is completed, since alternatives may arrive at any time and may lead to different process structures and different mappings. The processes in the "how-to-say" cascade have therefore to be terminated by a special process – the terminator – which is started by the structure activator. A process is waiting if the horizontal line is interrupted.

The downward arrows show the mappings between the levels. Two processes that can be mapped onto the next level only together have a dot at the mapping arrow. The arrows upwards show requests that are propagated through the levels

An example for a request is the one created by the process for the verb fahr (drive) at step 11. After the creation of the process and after the initialization of its syntactic structure, it cannot build up a locally complete syntactic description. Therefore, the syntactic features are analyzed: it needs a subject which will provide for the features for number and person. A request for a subject is passed upward to the semantic process that created the process for the verb. Since there is no appropriate process in the semantic level that will create the subject in the ID level, the request is reformulated and passed up to the conceptual level and from there further on to the request handler (cf. [14], p. 126 ff. for details).

Figure 6 shows the the diagram for the second sentence. In this sentence, the process for the verb creates the request for the subject twice (steps 37 and 42). The first request cannot be propagated beyond the conceptual level, because the process structure of this level contains no information about the role agens (IR46) at that scheduler step. The information asked for by the second request is already in the "how-to-say" cascade when the request arrives in the conceptual level and can therefore be ignored.

This diagram is a good example to demonstrate the incremental and parallel processing mode: the process for the verb cannot proceed until the process arrives that provides the information for the subject. Meanwhile, other processes arrived in the ID level and could build up their syntactic structures successfully.

3.3 The Influence of the Discourse Context

During the generation of the two sentences, the system updates the dialog memory. The generator has to react on the changed context that may be a result of its own output, or that may be caused by an input of the user.

If the generator is started anew with the same intentional goal as in the previous example, the changed context is taken into consideration. It influences the sequence of the sentences and the generation of the referring expressions:

```
POPEL-WHAT>(popel '(swmb (know h (ic40 ic37))))
das
das kauft er
das kauft er ihr
das kauft er ihr in voelklingen
```

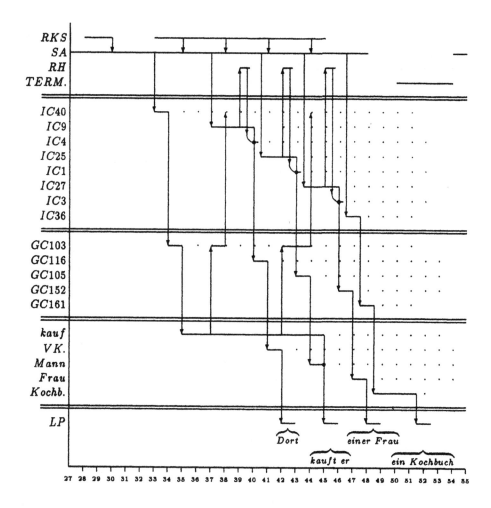

Fig. 6. Timing diagram for the second sentence

```
SAY: das kauft er ihr in voelklingen
     (that buys he her in voelklingen)
dorthin
dorthin faehrt er
dorthin faehrt er mit dem motorrad
dorthin faehrt er mit dem motorrad von saarbruecken
SAY: dorthin faehrt er mit dem motorrad von saarbruecken
     (there drives he with the motorcycle from saarbruecken)
(17070000 606)
```

The order of the two sentences has changed as well as the referring expressions. In the previous example run, the input concepts were sorted according to the

path-schema (cf., e.g., [8]). Now, the information is structured according to the requirements resulting from the changed dialog memory: a plan operator is selected
that tries to find a coherent connection to the previously uttered information. The
referring expression for 'the book', namely the demonstrative pronoun 'das', moves
to the front of the first sentence, and indicates by its form the close connection to
the previous sentence. If pro-words like 'dorthin' are unambiguous, they are used
instead of complete noun phrases. The higher complexity of the reasoning processes
results in a longer run-time, namely 17.07 seconds.

This example run demonstrates the flexibility necessary for a generator in a dialog
system, which must adapt itself to the changed discourse context.

4 Conclusions

POPEL has shown the feasibility of a flexible, incremental and parallel generation
system. The approach of a cascaded architecture facilitates the integration into a
dialog system and the bidirectional utilization of the knowledge sources by both
generation and analysis. The feedback in the cascade is especially important, if the
conceptual knowledge is linked to an AI-system whose knowledge is not structured
according to the needs of a language access system.

The approach chosen in POPEL also enables the integration of multi-modal
output in the decision flow of the generator in quite a natural way. The multi-modal
output is realized by simulated pointing gestures that complement, or replace, a
referring expression.

Despite the novel approach, POPEL uses state-of-the art knowledge representation methods and algorithms: a KL-ONE like knowledge representation language;
RST, the most widespread text structuring theory; and unification-based syntactic
processing. Parts of the generator can easily be separated and used by other modules, e.g., the generation of semantic paraphrases for a knowledge acquisition tool
[3].

Currently, POPEL needs from two to ten seconds per sentence. If the prototype is
optimized and implemented on a parallel processing computer, real time seems to be
within reaching distance. The parallel design, which is coarse-grained (compared to,
e.g., the fine-grained approach of FIG [20]), needs only 23 processors in the examples
presented, if each process runs on its own processor.

References

J. Allgayer and C. Reddig. What KL-ONE lookalikes need to cope with natural language.
In: K. Bläsius, U. Hedstück, and C.R. Rollinger. Sorts and Types in Artificial Intelligence. Springer (1990) 240–285

J. Allgayer, R.M. Jansen-Winkeln, C. Reddig, and N. Reithinger. Bidirectional use of
knowledge in the multi-modal NL access system XTRA. 11. IJCAI Detroit (1989)
1492–1497

R. Dale. Generating Referring Expressions in a Domain of Objects and Processes. PhD
thesis. Department of Artificial Intelligence, University of Edinburgh (1988)

K. DeSmedt and G. Kempen. The Representation of Grammatical Knowledge in a Model for Incremental Sentence Generation. In: C.L. Paris, W.R. Swartout, and W.C. Mann. Natural Language Generation in Artificial Intelligence and Computational Linguistics. Kluwer (1991) 329-349

W. Finkler and G. Neumann. POPEL-HOW – a distributed parallel model for incremental natural language production with feedback. 11. IJCAI Detroit (1989) 1518-1523

R.M. Jansen-Winkeln, A. Ndiaye, and N. Reithinger. FSS-WASTL – interactive knowledge acquisition for a semantic lexicon. In: E. Ardizzone, S. Gaglio, and F. Sorbello. Trends in Artificial Intelligence, 2nd AI*IA Congress. Palermo (1991) 108-116

A. Jameson and W. Wahlster. User Modeling in Anaphora Generation: Ellipsis and Definite Description. 6. ECAI Orsay (1982) 222-227

J. Jung, A. Kresse, N. Reithinger, and R. Schäfer. Das System ZORA – wissensbasierte Generierung von Zeigegesten. 13. GWAI Berlin (1989) 190-194

A. Kobsa. The SB-ONE representation workbench. In: Proc. of the workshop on formal aspects of semantic networks. Santa Catalina Island, CA. (1989)

A. Kobsa. Modeling the User's Conceptual Knowledge in BGP-MS, a User Modeling Shell System. Computational Intelligence 6 4 (1990)

G. Lakoff. Women, Fire, and Dangerous Things. Chicago University Press (1987)

W.C. Mann and S.A. Thompson. Rhetorical structure theory: A theory of text organisation. Technical Report ISI/RS-87-190. Information Sciences Institute, Marina del Rey (1987)

J.D. Moore. A Reactive Approach to Explanation. PhD thesis. Computer Science Department, University of California, Los Angeles (1989)

G. Neumann. A Bidirectional Model for Natural Language Processing. 5. EACL Berlin (1991) 245-250

G. Neumann and W. Finkler. A head-driven approach to incremental and parallel generation of syntactic structures. 13. COLING Helsinki (1990) 288-293

R. Reichman. Getting Computers to Talk Like You and Me. MIT Press (1985)

N. Reithinger. Eine parallele Architektur zur inkrementellen Generierung multimodaler Dialogbeiträge. Infix Verlag, St. Augustin (1992)

N. Reithinger. POPEL - an incremental and parallel natural language generation system. In: C.L. Paris, W.R. Swartout, and W.C. Mann. Natural Language Generation in Artificial Intelligence and Computational Linguistics. Kluwer (1991) 179-200

D. Schmauks. Deixis in der Mensch-Maschine Interaktion. Niemeyer (1991)

D. Schmauks and N. Reithinger. Generating multimodal output – conditions, advantages and problems. 12. COLING Budapest (1988) 584-588

D. Schmauks and M. Wille. Simulation of communicative hand movements in human-computer-interaction. Computers and the Humanities 25 (1991) 129-140

S.M. Shieber, H. Uszkoreit, F.C.N Pereira, J.J. Robinson, and M. Tyson. The formalism and implementation of PATR-II. In: Research on interactive acquisition and use of knowledge, SRI International Menlo Park, CA. (1983). 39-79

N. Ward. A Flexible, Parallel Model of Natural Language Generation. PhD thesis. Computer Science Department, University of California Berkeley (1991)

Panel:

Extending Language Generation
to Multiple Media

Communication by language is a specialized form of communication in general. As our theories of language generation — specifically, of communicative intentions, discourse structure, and text planning — grow more sophisticated, it is natural to wonder how many other modes of communication these theories encompass. Over the past several years, a number of projects have entered the area between language generation and multimedia communication, often focusing on a single specific functionality, such as nonlinguistic deictic reference by pointing or automated text formatting, and sometimes attempting significantly more, such as joint planning of text and diagrams.

Questions about the correspondences that seem to hold between language generation and communication generation include:

1. Can techniques for planning text be generalized to plan the structure and media-specific content of multimedia communications? How are the goals and plans affected?
2. What kinds of process negotiation is there between individual media specialists and the central communication planner, if any? How is this best effected?
3. How is consistent reference achieved across multiple media? How are the different presentations integrated in general? Are the text structures being produced by current text planners adequate to support multimedia requirements?

The following specialists, each representing a significant computational effort in this area, appear on the panel to discuss their thoughts on these and similar questions:

- Dr. Yigal Arens, Information Sciences Institute, Marina del Rey
- Dr. Robert Dale, University of Edinburgh, Edinburgh
- Dr. Stephan Kerpedjiev, Institute of Mathematics, Sofia
- Prof. Kathy McKeown, Columbia University, New York
- Dr. Oliviero Stock, IRST, Trento
- Prof. Wolfgang Wahlster, DFKI, Saarbrücken

Their statements follow.

Multimedia Presentation Planning as an Extension of Text Planning

Yigal Arens[1]
Information Sciences Institute of USC
4676 Admiralty Way
Marina del Rey, CA 90292-6695
U.S.A.
Email: ARENS@ISI.EDU

When communicating anything more complex than a simple message, people seldom use only a single modality. As computers' output requirements grow more sophisticated, an increasing need for integrated multimedia presentations is being felt. A central problem in multimedia communication systems is the allocation of information to the most appropriate medium and the coordination of media to best portray the information to be conveyed. This problem bears much resemblance to certain aspects of text planning, namely the selection of information to present and its structuring into a coherent text with appropriate cross-referencing.

This problem has surfaced and is begin dealt with in various ways; see [Feiner 88, Mackinlay 86, Neal 90, Wahlster et al. 91]. At ISI we have been engaged in work in the area of multimedia communication for several years now, starting with the Integrated Interfaces project, which automatically created displays of naval information using maps, icons, natural language text, forms and tables [Arens et al. 88]. We addressed the information-to-medium allocation and media coordination problems in a straightforward way, namely using fixed data-to-medium allocation rules.

Subsequently, we have been investigating ways of solving these problems in more sophisticated and powerful ways. Our ongoing work divides into two related directions of research.

A General Approach to Multimedia Presentation Planning

The sheer number of presentation possibilities available makes the task of producing and interpreting information with multiple media extremely complex. However, we have found that one can decompose the problem in such a way as to construct presentation rules that hold for several media at once and thereby simplify the problem. Instead of fixed information-to-medium allocation rules, we perform a two-step generalization process, first on the characteristics of the information and then on the characteristics of the presentation media available. In more detail, the first generalization is to assign a medium not to each data type, but instead to a combination of specific features that characterize data types (thus for example instead of saying *spatial locations must be presented on maps*, we write the rule *data duples (of which spatial locations are an example) are presented on maps, graphs, or tables*). The second generalization is to assign feature combinations not to specific media, but

---

[1] This work was done in collaboration with Eduard Hovy from ISI and two students from the University of Nijmegen, Mira Vossers and Susanne van Mulken.

instead to characteristics of media (thus for example the rule becomes *data duples are presented on planar media (which includes graphs, tables, and maps)*).

While this may sound like the opposite of simplifying matters, the identification and classification of such features as *dimensionality of data, dimensionality of media, permanence of data, transience of displays*, etc., is a necessary step in constructing presentation planning rules that hold no matter what new media are added to the system or what new types of information are defined. Extensive reading of literature on design, graphics, human-computer interaction, and some areas of cognitive science (for example [Bretin 83, Fleming and Levie 78, Larkin and Simon 86, Mayer 89, Roth and Mattis 90, Tufte 83] suggested to us that the factors pertaining to the planning and production of multimedia presentations can be classified into four general areas:

- features characterizing the presenter (incl. the system's communicative goals),
- features characterizing the audience,
- features characterizing the information to be displayed, and
- features characterizing the media available to the system.

We performed a series of studies to collect and categorize features relevant to information presentation [Arens and Hovy 90]; including an analysis of the use of graphics and text in instructional manuals such as those for sewing machines, motor cars, and electronic cooking utensils, which gave rise to a collection of interwoven features [Vossers 91]. To represent the features and their underlying interdependencies, we have found that the networks used in Systemic Linguistics [Halliday 85] provide a parsimonious and expressive formalism that, somewhat surprisingly, helps identify generalizations that reduce the complexity of the problem. Current work in our investigation includes two student projects to implement systems that use features of the data and the media to plan out multimedia presentations in different domains.

The Generation of Formatted Text

The second direction of our research involves the automated generation of formatted text, which we view as a part of the multimedia generation problem. Few texts longer than a paragraph are written without appropriate formatting. As argued also in Robert Dale's panel statement, to ensure readability, automated text generation programs must not only plan and generate their texts but be able to format them as well. This can be achieved by recognizing that each formatting device fulfills a specific communicative function in a text, and that many of these functions can be defined in terms of the text structure relations that govern the structure of coherent multisentence discourse.

The work at ISI on automated planning of multisentence text (see for example [Mann and Thompson 88, Hovy 88, Moore and Paris 89] has provided the necessary substrate of discourse structure relations and text planners to enable the definition of the communicative function of certain text formatting devices, such as footnotes, enumerations, and headings, in terms of known text structure plans. In an early experiment, a text was planned from a semantic representation to a final form that included English sentences and LaTeX formatting commands, intermingled as appropriate [Hovy & Arens 91]. Though this work is at an early stage, we believe that most text planners of the future will include some sort of text formatting facility, and that the extension of text structure planning to text formatting is one step on the way to full multimedia presentation planning.

References

[Arens et al. 88] Arens, Y., Miller, L., Shapiro, S.C. and Sondheimer, N.K. 1988. Automatic Construction of User-Interface Displays. In *Proceedings of the 7th AAAI Conference*, St. Paul, MN (808–813). Also available as USC/Information Sciences Institute Research Report RR-88-218.

[Arens and Hovy 90] Arens, Y. and Hovy, E.H. 1990. How to Describe What? Towards a Theory of Modality Utilization. In *Proceedings of the 12th Cognitive Science Conference*, Cambridge, MA.

[Bretin 83] Bretin, J. 1983. *Semiology of Graphics*, (trans. by J. Berg). Madison: University of Wisconsin Press.

[Feiner 88] Feiner, S. 1988. An Architecture for Knowledge-Based Graphical Interfaces. ACM/SIGCHI Workshop on *Architectures for Intelligent Interfaces: Elements and Prototypes*, Monterey, CA.

[Fleming and Levie 78] Fleming, M. and Levie, H.W. 1978. *Instructional Message Design: Principles from the Behavioral Sciences*. Educational Technology Publications.

[Halliday 85] Halliday, M.A.K. 1985. *An Introduction to Functional Grammar*. Baltimore: Edward Arnold Press.

[Hovy 88] Hovy, E.H. 1988. Planning Coherent Multisentential Text. In *Proceedings of the 26th ACL Conference*, Buffalo (163–169).

[Hovy and Arens 91] Hovy, E.H. and Arens, Y. 1991. Automatic Generation of Formatted Text. In *Proceedings of the 10th AAAI Conference*, Anaheim.

[Larkin and Simon 86] Larkin, J.H., and Simon, H.A. 1986. Why a Diagram is (Sometimes) Worth Ten Thousand Words. *Cognitive Science* 11 (65–99).

[Mackinlay 86] Mackinlay, J. 1986. *Automatic Design of Graphical Presentations*. Ph.D. dissertation, Stanford University.

[Mann and Thompson 88] Mann, W.C. and Thompson, S.A. 1988. Rhetorical Structure Theory: Toward a Functional Theory of Text Organization. *Text* 8(3) (243–281). Also available as USC/Information Sciences Institute Research Report RR-87-190.

[Mayer 89] Mayer, R.E. 1989. Systematic Thinking Fostered by Illustrations in Scientific Text. *Journal of Educational Psychology* 81 (240–246).

[Moore and Paris 89] Moore, J.D. and Paris, C.L. 1989. Planning Text for Advisory Dialogues. In *Proceedings of the 27th ACL Conference*, Vancouver (67–75).

[Neal 90] Neal, J.G. 1990. Intelligent Multi-Media Integrated Interface Project. SUNY Buffalo. RADC Technical Report TR-90-128.

[Roth and Mattis 90] Roth, S.F. and Mattis, J. 1990. Data Characterization for Intelligent Graphics Presentation. *CHI'90 Proceedings* (193–200).

[Tufte 83] Tufte, Edward R. 1983. *The Visual Display of Quantitative Information*. Cheshire, CT: Graphics Press.

[Vossers 91] Vossers, M. 1991. Automatic Generation of Formatted text and Line Drawings. Master's thesis, University of Nijmegen, The Netherlands.

[Wahlster et al. 91] Wahlster, W., André, E., Bandyopadhyay, S., Graf, W., Rist, T. 1991. WIP: The Coordinated Generation of Multimodal Presentations from a Common Representation. DFKI (University of Saarbrücken) Technical Report.

Visible Language:
Multimodal Constraints in Information Presentation

Robert Dale[1]
Centre for Cognitive Science
University of Edinburgh
2 Buccleuch Place
Edinburgh EH8 9LW
Scotland
Email: R.DALE@EDINBURGH.AC.UK

Ever since the very beginning of serious work in the field (at least since McDonald's Ph.D. work [McDonald 80]), a widely supported view of the natural language generation process is that it involves *decision making under constraints*: constraints imposed by the context of language production, and by the linguistic resources available to the language producer. Who could disagree? But, very surprisingly, this view is rarely taken to its logical conclusion. There have been a few pieces of research that have looked at the computer production of language in time-limited situations, with the effects this has on what can be said and how it can be said (see, for example, Hovy's Ph.D. work [Hovy 88], or some of the work now being carried out by Jean Carletta and Richard Caley at Edinburgh); but no current research takes account of the physical manifestation of the written word, and the constraints imposed by the *medium* of communication. There is research in multimedia generation that has started to address the apportioning of information between the graphical and the linguistic, and how the two interact — asking questions, for example, such as how forms of reference are affected when a picture is part of the message conveyed (as reported in the papers of Reithinger and Claassen in this volume). But, strangely, the result is still 'disembodied' text generators which take no real account of issues such as page layout and the use of space. We don't have a theory of these things — let's refer to them collectively as *the layout dimension* — and worse: we don't have a theory of how this layout dimension interacts with the language dimension.

But interact they do. Everyone is familiar with the situation: an eight page conference paper to write, and just a few lines of text end up on page nine. You start rewording the text to pull those renegades onto the previous page, looking for paragraphs which end in a line containing only one word; or you turn information presented in a bulleted list into body text, with appropriate use of punctuation marks to indicate the rhetorical structure previously carried by the layout. With a modern text processing system, and modulo some liberal interpretation of the layout guidelines, you have other alternatives: the line spacing can be changed, the column width changed, or the point size of the references reduced a little. All these possibilities interact; they are raw materials that copy-writers and graphic designers have been playing with for years. The layout is a resource just as the language itself is.

---

[1] My thanks to Jon Oberlander for many conversations that have made me think about the issues raised here.

It's also a communicative resource: as just mentioned, page layout can carry rhetorical force, indicating discourse structure; this is an avenue explored by some of the researchers at ISI [Hovy & Arens 91]. Some forms of layout are appropriate to some genres and not to others: you're unlikely to write a letter to your lover using the AAAI conference proceedings style. The parallels with the conditioning of lexical choice are clear. The notion of 'computer as author' has to keep up with the times: just as the traditional divisions of labour in publishing are being broken down by new tools, NLG systems need to take account of these more complicated alternatives. Perhaps the appropriate metaphor is 'computer as desktop publisher'.

There is a wealth of literature that addresses the ergonomic aspects of layout, but we in the generation community have pretty much ignored it so far. There is another literature that is concerned with the question of what makes 'good writing style': again, although some initial explorations have taken place here (see, for example, Scott and Souza's work [Scott & De Souza 90]), we've paid surprisingly little attention to what this work has to tell us about the generation process and what it means to generate good text. If we want to generate genuinely *embodied* language, it's time we started taking account of these different constraints — let's face it, a text generator which produces the text of an instruction manual without taking account of the physical layout of that manual is not going to be adequate. We need to be able to represent the textual constraints that determine coherence, cohesion and clarity by means of lexical, syntactic and punctuation choices; and we need to be able to represent the graphical constraints that determine the use of particular font sizes and styles and the use of white space and indentation. We need a multifaceted representation, just as recent approaches to language processing have found it useful to use representational languages that allow simultaneous expression of syntactic and semantic information and the constraints that hold between them (for example, Pollard and Sag's work on HPSG [Pollard and Sag 87]). This representation should allow simultaneous expression of information related to both language and layout, and the constraints and interactions that hold between these. We need to look towards systems that are capable of choosing between words and pictures, between the use of textual description and tables or charts, between straightforward linearisation of the text and the use of side bars or the generation of hypertext; and all the while these systems need to be aware of the consequences of these choices in both dimensions. Generating answers to questions is the easy bit; our systems shouldn't break the rules when they are asked for 'answers on a postcard, please'.

References

[Hovy & Arens 91] Hovy, E.H. and Arens, Y. 191. Automatic Generation of Formatted Text. In *Proceedings of the 8th AAAI Conference*, Anaheim.

[Hovy 90] Hovy, E.H. 1990. Pragmatics and Natural Language Generation. *Artificial Intelligence* 43 (153-197).

[McDonald 80] McDonald, D.D. 1980. *Natural Language Production as a Process of Decision Making Under Constraint*. Ph.D. dissertation, Massachusetts Institute of Technology, Cambridge.

[Pollard and Sag 87] Pollard, C. and Sag. I. 1987. *Information-Based Syntax and Semantics, Volume 1*. CSLI Lecture Notes.

[Scott & De Souza 90] Scott, D.R. and De Souza, C.S. 1990. Getting the Message across in RST-Based Text Generation. In R. Dale, C. Mellish, and M. Zock (eds), *Current Research in Natural Language Generation*. Boston: Academic Press (47-74).

Generation of Multimodal Weather Reports

Stephan M. Kerpedjiev
Institute of Mathematics
Bl. 8, Acad. G. Bonchev Street
1113 Sofia
Bulgaria

Overview of the Approach

The generation of multimodal weather reports, which is the subject of the present statement, manifests a more general problem, viz. how to present expressively and efficiently a dataset describing a given situation to a certain user group using different modes such as NL text or speech, graphics, tables, deictic expressions. This type of problem is observed in other spheres as well, such as economics marketing, ecology, sociology, demography.

Expressive and efficient presentation means the employment of the modes and languages that are best suited to the particular data and allow the user to perceive the information accurately, reliably and quickly. Specifically, expressiveness criteria identify the languages — verbal, graphical and tabular — that can express the desired information, while efficiency criteria identify which if these languages, for the current set of assertions, provide the information objects that require minimum perception time; cf. [Mackinlay 86, Bretin 83].

The basic principles and restrictions of our approach to generation are outlined below:

- We consider the generation of the multimodal products versus generation in multimodal interaction.
- We focus on the generation of informative texts, a particular subtype of narrative texts, rather than on the generation of descriptive, persuasive or instructional texts; cf. [Wilson 89].
- We place special emphasis on the generation of coordinated multimodal portions, and not only on the mechanical assembling of unimodal portions into a multimodal product.
- The generation is driven by the following information: the initial dataset, a specification by the user, and domain-specific knowledge of the individual languages.

Source Information and Target Product

The source information for the generator is a dataset which encodes a certain weather situation. The dataset is obtained through domain-specific routines and may contain both numerical and qualitative data. The weather attributes, defined as data types, and the relations existing between data items, constitute the weather model. Each data item specifies a certain aspect of the situation with respect to a given time period and location. Thus, associated with the weather model are a time and territory. As a rule, these model are created to support the research and practical work in the corresponding field and as such should be comprehensive.

The target product is a user-oriented multimodal document intended to convey weather information to users who may not be familiar with the models under which the dataset has been produced. These features of the final product call for the development of user oriented weather, territory, and time models that correspond to the user knowledge and to the communicative function of the report. So the user-oriented models are less comprehensive and deal with weather attributes, regions, and time periods whose granularity is rougher than that of the dataset models.

The modes under consideration are NL text, cartographical presentation, and tabular presentation. Along with stating his information needs in terms of weather attributes for a certain region and time period, the user has the right to request a specific mode of presentation. These two aspects of the query are specified by means of content and modal statements, respectively.

Content Extraction and Planning

Content extraction is the process of generating assertions (conformed with the user-oriented models) from the dataset. The relationship between the dataset models and the user-oriented models determines the content extraction as a summarizing process. Because of its summarizing nature, the process may produce imprecise or uncertain assertions. In our system, we employed weather forecast verification techniques to evaluate the precision of the assertions generated.

Planning is the process of assigning the consecutive assertions to one or more portions of the modal structure of the final document. Moreover, a sophisticated planner should be able to determine the modal structure that presents most efficiently the given set of assertions. In the current version of the system, the planning is oversimplified, because for each unimodal portion the user explicitly specifies the weather attributes that have to be presented in it. The only exception is the generation of a text comment to a distorted weather map.

Text Generation

Our approach to generation follows the basic steps as described by [McDonald 87], viz. selection of the content portions that are to be communicated to the user, planning the text by adoption of the most suitable rhetorical schemas, realizing the discourse plan as a surface structure, and rendering it as a text. The selection of content portions was discussed above. The following steps are based on rhetorical, grammatical, and lexical knowledge, respectively, and take into account certain stylistic features of the texts being produced.

Rhetorical knowledge is employed for ordering the assertions in a hierarchical structure of coherent chunks. This structure explicates the conversational moves that take place when the text passes from one chunk to another. Following [Enkvist 85], a chunk is considered coherent if its assertions are arranged according to a certain semantic relation defined in the user oriented model. We established seven types of rhetorical schemas observed in weather reports.

The grammatical knowledge consists of the syntactic structures that can absorb the assertions of the various types of chunks. The lexicon provides words and phrases to replace the terminals of the surface structure and produce the final text.

Because of the multitude of choices that occur at almost every step of the generation, we considered the concept of style as a possible factor that might help the system to select one or another alternative. [Karlgren 75] characterizes the style as a global text feature, a sort of trend. That is why it is very difficult to use the style for making local decisions. In our approach, the style is defined as a set of distributions of certain features - rhetorical, syntactical and/or lexical. Then the generation must be carried out in such a way that the same distributions are observed in the resulting text. Some possible features that can be considered in a style are type of the sentence (simple, compound, complex), length of the sentence, frequency of occurrence of the use of the members of a synonymous group, etc.

Map Generation

Our approach to map creation was strongly influenced by [Bretin 83]. A weather map is created for a given territory, time period, and a set of weather attributes.

Concluding Remarks

The progress made so far is encouraging; for more detail cf. [Kerpedjiev 92]. Most of the techniques has been tested. The only problem that has not been explored at all is the planning as a modal structure development process based on both the dataset and a user model. Much work has to be accomplished in order to obtain a more definite answer about the actual power of the style as a control mechanism. We believe that the approach presented can be applied in other fields where datasets are collected and multimodal reports have to be generated.

References

[Bretin 83] J. Bretin. *Semiology of Graphics*. The University of Wisconsin Press, 1983.

[Enkvist 85] N.E. Enkvist Introduction: Coherence, Composition and Text Linguistics. In N.E. Enkvist (ed), *Coherence and Composition* (11–26), Åbo Academy, 1985.

[Karlgren 75] H. Karlgren. Text Connexitivity and Word Frequency Distribution. In *Style and Text*, Skriptor, 1975.

[Kerpedjiev 92] S. Kerpedjiev. Automatic Generation of Multimodal Weather Reports from Datasets. In *Proceedings of the 3rd International Conference on Applied Natural Language Processing*, Trento, 1992.

[Mackinlay 86] J. Mackinlay. Automating the Design of Graphical Presentations of Relational Information. *ACM Transactions on Graphics* 5 (110–141), 1986.

[McDonald 87] D. McDonald. Natural Language Generation. In S.C. Shapiro (ed), *Encyclopedia of Artificial Intelligence* (642–655), 1987.

[Wilson 89] E. Wilson. Automating Text Typing. *Computers and the Humanities* 23 (429–442), 1989.

Steps Toward Hypergeneration

Oliviero Stock

IRST — Istituto per la Ricerca Scientifica e Tecnologica
38050 Povo
Trento
Italy
Email: STOCK@IRST.IT

When dealing with multiple media generation, often the first problem addressed is how to plan what medium to use when, and how to integrate the different media to produce the best communicative effect. The perspective discussed here is slightly different: the problem is how to best exploit the possibilities of generation, delivering a text that is also a layer of personalized access to a larger preexisting information space. This is particularly relevant when the information space contains things we are not able to represent in a detailed internal format such that it can be the starting point for further generation.

What is characteristic of present computer interfaces, and not of human-human biological interfaces, is that the transmitted things in the two directions are there, on the same medium, and unlike written paper-based communication, the physical medium can be made active. Things can be selected, changed, used for new input. With the concept of direct manipulation even the distinction between the notions of input medium and output medium is blurred.

Hypermedial systems promote a navigational, explorative access to multimodal information: the user, browsing around the network, is at the same time both exploring the network and searching for useful information; generally, information that could not be represented fully in an internal format. Hypertexts *per se* constitute a level of representation with a very limited number of entrypoints.

On the other hand, natural language processing yields the possibility, though with a lot of state of the art constraints, to make detailed sophisticated requests and to provide precise output oriented to the particular user and situation.

Often in answering a request for information in applied situations, a system should ideally satisfy two linked output aspects:

a) giving the right answer to the user punctually;
but also
b) providing further readily accessible optional information to the user.

The following situations are examples of this: 1) the user may want to see individually presented information as immersed in a more standard information base that can be directly explored if linked to the given presentation; 2) the user may want to see more specific details connected to the output presented by the system. There is no other vehicle than generated natural language if complex information is to be conveyed, tailored for the particular user in a dynamic context. Yet we would want the text to be produced dynamically connected to other preexisting and browsable text.

The NLP group at IRST has experimented these ideas developing a larger proto-typical dialog system that integrates natural language and hypermedia: ALFRESCO [Stock 91]. ALFRESCO is an interactive system for a user interested in frescoes. It runs on a SUN 4 connected to a videodisc unit and a touchscreen. The particu-lar videodisc in use includes images about Fourteenth Century Italian frescoes and monuments. The system, beside understanding and using natural language, shows images of masterpieces. Images are active in that the user may refer to items by com-bining pointing with the use of linguistic demonstratives; also the system's linguistic output includes buttons that allow the user to enter in a hypertextual modality. The dialog may cause zooming into details or changing the focus of attention onto other frescoes. The overall aim is not only to provide information, but also to promote other masterpieces that may attract the user.

Our generator [Carenini et al. 92] is supposed to intervene during a dialog in which the user is interested in obtaining information. The user is able both to make precise requests through language and browse around through a preexisting hyper-textual network. Also images are shown, linked to language and hypertext. At a certain point the user may want to receive some detailed information that is best conveyed by the system by generating a piece of text. This piece of text is produced by taking into account what seemed to be of interest for the user (in the previous portion of the interaction) and linked to the preexisting text. If a piece of generic text existed that was performing the same function, it is substituted by the more specific, generated text and the buttons in it link it in a new way to the rest of the hypertextual network. (In ALFRESCO the hypertextual network is concerned with what some art critics say about masterpieces and painters, and includes links to fresco images).

Interest for a given topic is assumed to be either a consequence of the activation of that topic in context (e.g. a specific request by the user) or of the anticipated ex-position of the user to an art work (remember that the system includes a videodisc from which images of frescoes are retrieved). The interest model, consisting an acti-vation/inhibition network whose nodes are associated with ordered sets of individual, concepts develops and becomes more focused in the course of the interaction between the user and the system.

The strategic generator chooses, in particular, what other instances (frescoes, tables etc.) to mention in the text, given its user's interest model. After the tactical generation part the whole text is enriched with the buttons that link it to the particular images and the particular pieces of hypertext that seem to be relevant for the user, thereby altering the preexisting hypertextual network.

As opposed to other recent work that combines hypertext and generation (see for example [Reiter et al. 92, Moore and Swartout 90]), here the emphasis is on allowing the user to browse around a preexisting net: the generator starts from an internal representation in our case as well, but the result is a text that permits access to other preexisting hypertext and images in a personalized way. Underlying this is the belief that the role of hypertext in a natural language centered interactive system is to allow the user to explore the surroundings of the focus of her attention. This provides a noncommitted mode of interaction, characterized by a fast turnaround that may result in some other stimulus for further requests .

References

[Carenini et al. 92] Carenini, G., Pianesi, F., Ponzi, M., and Stock, 0. (1992). Natural Language Generation and Hypertext Access. Submitted for publication to *Applied Artificial Intelligence*. Also *IRST-Technical Report* no. 9201-08, 1992.

[Moore and Swartout 90] Moore, J.D., and Swartout, W., (1990). Pointing: A Way toward Explanation Dialogue. *Proceedings of the 8th National Conference on Artificial Intelligence (AAAI)* (457–464).

[Reiter et al. 92] Reiter, E., Mellish, C., and Levine, J. (1992). Automatic Generation of On-Line Documentation in the IDAS Project. In *Proceedings of the 3rd Applied Natural Language Processing Conference (ANLP-92)*, 1992, Trento.

[Stock 91] Stock, O. (1991). Natural Language and Exploration of an Information Space: The AlFresco Interactive System. *Proceedings of the 12th International Joint Conference of Artificial Intelligence (IJCAI 91)*, 1991, Sydney.

WIP: Integrating Text and Graphics Design for Adaptive Information Presentation

Wolfgang Wahlster, Elisabeth André, Wolfgang Finkler, Winfried Graf,
Hans-Jürgen Profitlich, Thomas Rist, Anne Schauder
German Research Center for Artificial Intelligence (DFKI)
Stuhlsatzenhausweg 3
D-6600 Saarbrücken 11
Germany
Email: *last_name*@DFKI.UNI-SB.DE

When explaining how to use a technical device humans will often utilize a combination of language and graphics. It is a rare instruction manual that does not contain illustrations. Multimodal presentation systems combining natural language and graphics take advantage of both the individual strength of each communication mode and the fact that both modes can be employed in parallel. It is an important goal of this research not simply to merge the verbalization results of a natural language generator and the visualization results of a knowledge-based graphics design component, but to carefully coordinate natural language and graphics in such a way that they generate a multiplicative improvement in communication capabilities. Allowing all of the modalities to refer to and depend upon each other is a key to the richness of multimodal communication.

In the WIP system that plans and coordinates multimodal presentations in which all material is generated by the system, we have integrated multiple AI components such as planning, knowledge representation, natural language generation, and graphics generation. The current prototype of WIP generates multimodal explanations and instructions for assembling, using, maintaining or repairing physical devices. As we try to substantiate our results with cross-language and cross-application evidence WIP is currently able to generate simple German or English explanations for using an espresso-machine or assembling a lawn-mower.

In WIP we combined and extended only formalisms that have reached a certain level of maturity: in particular, terminological logics, RST-based planning, constraint processing techniques, and tree adjoining grammars with feature unification.

One of the important insights we gained from building the WIP system is that it is actually possible to extend and adapt many of the fundamental concepts developed to date in AI and computational linguistics for the generation of natural language in such a way that they become useful for the generation of graphics and text-picture combinations as well. This means that an interesting methodological transfer from the area of natural language processing to a much broader computational model of multimodal communication seems possible. In particular, semantic and pragmatic concepts like coherence, focus, communicative act, discourse model, reference, implicature, anaphora, or scope ambiguity take an extended meaning in the context of text-picture combinations.

A basic principle underlying the WIP model is that the various constituents of a multimodal presentation should be generated from a common representation of what is to be conveyed. This raises the question of how to decompose a given communicative goal into subgoals to be realized by the mode-specific generators, so that they complement each other. To address this problem, we explored computational models of the cognitive decision processes coping with questions such as what should go into text, what should go into graphics, and which kinds of links between the verbal and non-verbal fragments are necessary.

The task of the knowledge-based presentation system WIP is the context-sensitive generation of a variety of multimodal documents from an input including a presentation goal. The presentation goal is a formal representation of the communicative intent specified by the back-end application system. WIP is a highly adaptive interface, since all of its output is generated on the fly and customized for the intended target audience and situation. The quest for adaptation is based on the fact that is impossible to anticipate the needs and requirements of each potential user in an infinite number of presentation situations. We view the design of multimodal presentations including text and graphics design as a subarea of general communication design. We approximate the fact that communication is always situated by introducing generation parameters (see Fig. 1) in our model. The current system includes a choice between user stereotypes (e.g. novice, expert), target languages, layout formats (e.g. hardcopy of instruction manual, screen display), and output modes (incremental output vs. complete output only). The set of generation parameters is used to specify design constraints that must be satisfied by the final presentation.

The technical knowledge to be presented by WIP is encoded in RAT (Representation of Actions in Terminological Logics). In addition to this propositional representation, WIP has access to an analogical representation of the geometry of the machine in the form of a wireframe model (see Fig. 1). Note that the incrementality

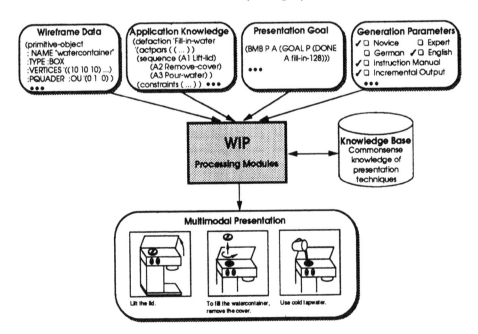

Fig. 1. A Functional View of the WIP system

mentioned above as one of the options for the generation of multimodal output, characterizes a likely application scenario for systems like WIP, since the intended use includes intelligent control panels and active help systems, where the timeliness and fluency of output is critical, e.g. when generating a warning. In such a situation, the presentation system must be able to start with an incremental output although it has not yet received all the information to be conveyed from the back-end system.

References: Selected Papers from the WIP Project

[André and Rist 90a] André, E. and Rist, T. 1990. Towards a Plan-Based Synthesis of Illustrated Documents. In *Proceedings of the 9th ECAI* (25–30).

[André and Rist 90b] André, E. and Rist, T. 1990. Synthesizing Illustrated Documents: A Plan-Based Approach. In *Proceedings of InfoJapan '90* Vol. 2 (163–170).

[André and Rist 92] André, E. and Rist, T. 1992. The Design of Illustrated Documents as a Planning Task. German Research Center for Artificial Intelligence, DFKI Research Report.

[André et al. 92] André, E., Finkler, W., Graf, W., Rist, T., Schauder, A., and Wahlster, W. 1992. WIP: The Automatic Synthesis of Multimodal Presentations. German Research Center for Artificial Intelligence, DFKI Research Report.

[Finkler and Schauder 92] Finkler, W. and Schauder, A. 1992. Effects of Incremental Output on Incremental Natural Language Generation. German Research Center for Artificial Intelligence, DFKI Research.

[Graf 92] Graf, W. 1992. Constraint-Based Graphical Layout of Multimodal Presentations. German Research Center for Artificial Intelligence, DFKI Research Report.

[Harbusch 90] Harbusch, K. 1990. Constraining Tree Adjoining Grammars by Unification. in *Proceedings of the 13th COLING* (167–172).

[Harbusch et al. 91] Harbusch, K., Finkler, W. and Schauder, A. 1991. Incremental Syntax Generation with Tree Adjoining Grammars. In Brauer, W. and Hernández, D. (eds.) *Proceedings of the 4th International GI Conference on Knowledge-based Systems*. Berlin: Springer-Verlag (363–374).

[Rist and André 92] Rist, T. and André, E. 1992. From Presentation Tasks to Pictures: Towards an Approach to Automatic Graphics Design. German Research Center for Artificial Intelligence, DFKI Research Report.

[Schauder 92] Schauder, A. 1992. Incremental Syntactic Generation of Natural Language with Tree Adjoining Grammars. German Research Center for Artificial Intelligence, DFKI Research Report.

[Wahlster et al. 89] Wahlster, W., André, E., Hecking, M., and Rist, T. 1989. WIP: Knowledge-based Presentation of Information. German Research Center for Artificial Intelligence, DFKI Research Report.

[Wahlster et al. 91] Wahlster, W., André, E., Graf, W., and Rist, T. 1991. Designing Illustrated Texts: How Language Production Is Influenced by Graphics Generation. In *Proceedings of the 5th Conference of the European Chapter of the ACL* (8–14).

[Wahlster et al. 92a] Wahlster, W., André, E., Bandyopadhyay, S., Graf, W., and Rist, T. 1992. WIP: The Coordinated Generation of Multimodal Presentations from a Common Representation. In Ortony, A., Slack, J., and Stock, O. (eds.), *Computational Theories of Communication and their Applications*. Berlin: Springer-Verlag.

[Wahlster et al. 92b] Wahlster, W., André, E., Finkler, W., Profitlich, H.-J., and Rist, T. 1992. Plan-based Integration of Natural Language and Graphics Generation. German Research Center for Artificial Intelligence, DFKI Research Report.

[Wazinski 92] Wazinski, P. 1992. Generating Spatial Descriptions for Cross-modal References. In *Proceedings of the 3rd ACL Conference on Applied Natural Language Processing*.

Panel:

Multilinguality and Generation

In line with good software development practise, more generators are being constructed in a modular fashion, with the syntactic and other knowledge resources represented declaratively and separated from the process control. This fact, coupled with the increasing expressive richness of more recent grammars and semantic representation systems, invites the question of multilingual generation by a single system. To date, several generators have demonstrated this ability with a greater or lesser degree of success. The following questions seem to play a central role:

1. What is required of grammatical and lexical formalisms to be adequately language-independent? What work has been done in this regard?
2. How can input representations be made language-independent? Do the particularities of inputs for generation have general consequences for Interlinguas or Transfer Rules in machine translation systems?
3. How can language-specific grammars and other knowledge resources be integrated into a single generator?
4. What aspects of generation procedures — planning, realization, lexical choice, etc. — impact on language-independence? Are these aspects necessary?

The following members of the generator community were invited to share their experience in multilingual generation.

- Dr. Eduard Hovy, Information Sciences Institute, Marina del Rey
- Prof. Richard Kittredge, University of Montreal, Montreal
- Prof. Christian Matthiessen, University of Sydney, Sydney
- Dr. Sergei Nirenburg, Carnegie Mellon University, Pittsburgh
- Dr. Dietmar Rösner, FAW, University of Ulm, Ulm

Their statements follow.

Constructing an Interlingua Using Generator Resources

Eduard Hovy[1]
Information Sciences Institute of USC
4676 Admiralty Way
Marina del Rey, CA 90292-6695
U.S.A.
Email: HOVY@ISI.EDU

In Interlingual Machine Translation, the representational power of the interlingua is central to the success of the translation. In this talk, an interlingua consists of three parts: the notation, the terms used to represent individual aspects of meaning, and the substrate knowledge representation system in which terms are defined and composed to represent texts.

Building a truly language-neutral set of interlingua terms is a daunting prospect; indeed, from practical experience with representation building, I believe it is an ideal to be approached at best asymptotically. Term selection, definition, and taxonomization into an ontology is always performed by people, and is therefore always open to being influenced by the distinctions made in the languages they speak. Consider, for example, the problem of representing the colors: how many are there, and how are they organized? Even the basic distinction into the three primary colors, so natural to any westerner, is unlikely to occur to the Dani people of New Guinea, who have only two color terms (*mili* = dark-cool and *mola* = light-warm) and have proven difficulty in learning names for nonfocal colors [Rosch 73]. Though I do not want to take a position here on what has been called Whorf's postulate (i.e., on whether or not language *necessarily* influences conceptualization [Whorf 56]), I believe that it is extremely difficult in practise to conceive of ontologizations alien to the languages you speak. Furthermore, since there are few clearly established methods for constructing ontologies, most ontologies to date seem to have been assembled on rather intuitive and *ad hoc* grounds, often reflecting the idiosyncrasies of the builders more than the requirements of the translation task.

Given these problems, and accepting that any given ontology will inevitably be "closer to" some languages than to others, one wonders: can one exploit this fact to facilitate the construction of a powerful interlingual MT system? The "closer" the ontology is to the source and target languages, the less work the parser and generator have to do to bridge the gap between interlingua texts and source and target language texts. To find the point of "minimal distance" from all source and target languages, one can formulate the

Basic criterion underlying terminology creation and taxonomization: *The ontology must be just sufficiently powerful to represent the distinctions required to analyze the source languages and generate the target languages in the given domains.*

---

[1] I would like to acknowledge the PANGLOSS machine translation system Interlingua Committee, Lynn Carlson, David Farwell, and especially Sergei Nirenburg, for their discussions and help.

I would like to outline a methodology for building the ontology of an interlingua in a somewhat more principled way by using the criterion to provide answers to the following basic questions:

- What terms must be included in the ontology?
- How should the terms be organized in the ontology?
- What level of detail should the representation reach?
- How close can the ontology terms be to the particular words and phrases of any single natural language?

To make the criterion more precise, here is a description of how to define the distinctions needed to support the languages. We start with a list of linguistic phenomena to be covered in a language, for example for English the fact that nouns pattern into mass and count, the fact that adjectives and adverbs pattern differently than do verbs, or the fact that many different forms of possession (to have an arm, to have a spouse, to have a car) are expressed similarly. We create a taxonomy of the linguistic abstractions required to generate these phenomena in the language. This taxonomy would, for these examples, contain nodes for *MassObj* and *CountObj* under *Obj* to help handle nouns, nodes *Quality* and *Process* as high-level taxonomic separators of adjectival/adverbial modifiers from verbal actions, and *Generalized-Possession* as a high-level organizational point for the various types of possession. Any proposed term is accepted only if it captures a distinct linguistic phenomenon of the language not yet handled in the taxonomy[2]. We then use the taxonomy as the upper region to categorize all terms representing domain entities, processes, and the like (though this is not the only way, it is the most straightforward way to use the taxonomy as a guide). By such a taxonomization, each domain term is located so as to inherit precisely the representational distinctions required to support its generation in the target language (a more specific example appears below). We call this taxonomy the Language Base (LB) of the language.

Using abstractions for any particular language means giving up the basic goal of language neutrality. Therefore we need a method of progressively making a taxonomy more language-neutral. This process involves merging the LB for a second language with the LB for the first to form a hybrid taxonomy we call the Ontology Base (OB), and then repeating the process for additional languages, according to the following procedure:

1. Construct the LB taxonomy for language 1. This is the ontology base (OB).
2. For each subsequent language,
   (a) construct the LB for its phenomena,
   (b) merge it with the existing OB, ensuring that the lower-level OB terms remain properly taxonomized.

---

[2] It must be understood that there is no claim that one must (or even can) perform exhaustive decomposition of all the facets of meaning of a concept to place it in the ontology. The Basic Criterion argues that just enough must be represented to enable the generation of the languages in question. Thus for example we do not need a term *Pink* for *Pale Red* unless the domain is such that there are implicative effects to saying "pale red" instead of "pink" (the former being a noncentral meaning in some contexts; see [McCawley 78] and [Jackendoff 85], p. 115).

As discussed in [Whorf 56] and [Lakoff 87], conceptual systems (like OBs and LBs) can be commensurable in several different ways; Lakoff lists five types (p. 322).

Given the OB and an LB for a new language, the merging process involves for each item in the LB one of three alternative operations:

- **Identity**: the LB item and its relative organization is identical to a (corresponding) item and portion of the OB. In this case, no further work is required beyond a name change to the OB item name. For related languages, especially in the more abstract regions of the OB, identity of OB and LB items is frequent.

- **Extension**: the LB item is more specific than the appropriate OB item(s); that is, it straightforwardly subcategorizes some OB item(s). In this case, the OB is grown by including the LB item as a child of the OB item. For example, if the OB were initially constructed from English, its system of honorifics would probably contain only two items, one for *FormalSuperordinate* and the other for *EqualAndSubordinate*; a Japanese LB would cause this system to be fleshed out to include a more elaborate substructure along the lines described in [Bateman 88].

- **Cross-classification**: the LB item represents aspects of more than one OB items. This is the case the new language partitions the phenomenon under consideration in a different way to the previous language(s) studied. Typically, several parallel LB items represent one partitioning of the phenomenon and several OB items represent a different partitioning. In this case, a cross-classification is required: the LB items must be entered into the OB as a parallel but distinct taxonomization of the phenomenon, and all their descendants must be added as well, unless items representing the same descendants are already in the OB, in which case these items must be linked up also to the appropriate LB item(s).

An example of the abstractions that can be used as major organization of the LB for English is the Penman Upper Model [Bateman et al. 88], a taxonomy that has been used to support the generation of English text in numerous domains.

References

[Bateman et al. 88] Bateman, J.A., Kasper, R.T., Moore, J.D., and Whitney, R.A. 1989. The PENMAN Upper Model — 1989. USC/Information Sciences Institute Development Note.

[Bateman 88] Bateman, J.A. 1988. Aspects of Clause Politeness in Japanese: An Extended Inquiry Semantics Treatment. In *Proceedings of the 26th Annual Conference of the ACL*, Buffalo (147-154).

[Jackendoff 85] Jackendoff, R. 1985. *Semantics and Cognition*. Cambridge: MIT Press.

[Lakoff 87] Lakoff, G. 1987. *Women, Fire, and Dangerous Things*. Chicago: University of Chicago Press.

[McCawley 78] McCawley, J.D. 1978. Conversation Implicature and the Lexicon. In P. Cole, ed. *Syntax and Semantics* vol. 9. New York: Academic Press (245-259).

[Rosch 73] Rosch, E. 1973. Natural Categories. *Cognitive Psychology* 4 (328-350).

[Whorf 56] Whorf, B.L. 1956. *Language, Thought, and Reality: Selected writings of Benjamin Lee Whorf*, ed. John B. Carroll, Cambridge: MIT Press.

Bilingual Report Generation: Experience with Interlingae

Richard Kittredge
Department of Linguistics[1]
Université de Montréal
Montreal, QC
Canada
Email: KITTREDG@IRO.UMONTREAL.CA

Background

The current Montreal work in bilingual text generation has its historical roots in the University's TAUM translation project of the 1970s. Thanks to Alain Colmerauer's Q-system language (a precursor to Prolog), we were able to develop systems for English-to-French translation in two limited domains, weather forecasting and aircraft maintenance. By 1976 the TAUM-METEO system was headed towards daily service for the Canadian government, while TAUM-AVIATION was showing promise on much more difficult hydraulics manuals. Somewhat surprised by our success considering the state of the art at the time, I became intrigued at how technical sublanguages of English and French seemed to show greater resemblance than the two languages did in general. After looking at a number of cases I concluded that whereas some of the resemblance might be illusory, due to comparing translation twin texts, a large part was really due to the commonality of domain, text purpose, and hence sublanguage. It really did look a lot easier to write an English-French contrastive grammar (or transfer rules, if one was building MT systems) for technical sublanguages, than for "unrestricted text". At that time, my interest was in getting sublanguage texts into "information formats" of the kind being used by Naomi Sager at New York University for information retrieval. One of the most interesting sublanguages was in stock market reporting, where, by adding a few extra steps to the discourse analysis techniques of Harris and Sager, one could work the information format into a relational database that contained the "core" information of the text. Hearing of this in 1981, Karen Kukich decided to generate stock reports from the database forms for her Ph.D. thesis (1983). One of Montreal's M.A. students in linguistics, Chantal Contant, then managed to get Karen's generator to output French (1986).

English and French weather forecasts

By 1985 the Canadian environment ministry began funding research in generating English weather forecasts. Using a shallow linguistic model, only a bit more articulated than Kukich's phrasal lexicon, we built RAREAS at the Université de

---

[1] Since early 1990, the author and colleagues have been working on bilingual generation at CoGenTex, Inc. in Montreal. The support of Communications Canada for research and development of the LFS system, and of Environment Canada for further development of the FoG system, is gratefully acknowledged.

Montréal [Kittredge et al. 86]. RAREAS produced Arctic marine forecasts from a formatted data set. Part of the problem in getting started was deciding on a reasonable data input format. Environment Canada had no initial notion of what form might be needed, nor how to get from raw forecast data to the selected set of " salient weather facts" that gets encoded linguistically in a forecast. As our sponsor became more involved in representing meteorological knowledge to carry out fact selection, we improved the language model. In 1987 RAREAS was extended to produce French marine forecasts.

However, at this point we were forced to develop an interlingua if we did not want to bias the text planner towards one language. It was here that Meaning–Text models (MTMs) became useful, because word order, and other major differences between English and French forecasts, were abstracted away at the DSyntR (deep syntactic) representation level. This allowed us to use a single DSyntR-style interlingua as the output of the text planner, and then use parallel MTM-based sentence realizers for deriving correct word strings in each language. The now bilingual MTM-based system was baptised FoG (Forecast Generator) and made its bureaucratic way through the testing process until, by the autumn of 1990, it entered daily service in three Eastern Canadian weather centres [Bourbeau et al. 90]. FoG is currently being extended to produce official public forecasts, where information priorities are different. The linguistic models for the two languages, however, seem to require very little change except in the lexicons. More significant changes are required to adapt the text planning component to the new conceptual distinctions and priorities.

Bilingual statistical reporting

Since early 1990, researchers at CoGenTex have been applying a more complete Meaning–Text modelling to the problem of generating English and French summaries of employment data [Iordanskaja et al. 91]. The first aim is to reproduce published reports, using tables of employment data as the starting point. The linguistic model for English was already partially developed under the Gossip project [Iordanskaja et al. 90], devoted to reporting on the activity of computer operating systems. As in Gossip, sentence realization begins at the level of semantic networks. The many grammatical choices made possible within MTMs are somewhat constrained by theme and rheme markings built into the network during the text planning process.

In the case of statistical reports, the problem of establishing an interlingua is more problematic, because each language makes broader use of its grammatical and lexical resources. Published bilingual reports in our domain occasionally exhibit deep differences between corresponding English and French sentences such as in:

(1) *Employment remained virtually unchanged.*

(2) *L'emploi a peu varié.* ["Employment changed little."]

Not only can the surface syntactic structures be incomparable, but they cannot easily be related on the level of linguistic semantics, because the semantic primes used in corresponding sentences may be dissimilar. We have therefore built a text planner which outputs a **conceptual** interlingua, a representation which might be appropriate for domain-based reasoning, but which does not favor the semantic primes in either language. From the conceptual network, separate semantic representations are derived and sent to separate realizers for generating sentences in each language. Thus the two sentences above are derived from non-isomorphic Meaning–Text semantic networks, which permit each language to take a separate "viewpoint" on the same conceptual material. Needless to say, the limited data from this one domain are hardly enough to justify this pre-semantic interlingua in general. Moreover, any serious attempt to formalize a conceptual interlingua should deal with the fact that a single sentence in one language may be expressed as two or more sentences in another. Our "application-oriented" approach is limited to "sentential interlinguae" (cf. [Polguère 91]), since Meaning-Text theory has not really addressed the problem of semantic representation of longer stretches of text.

Meaning-Text models and interlingual representation

Our limited application experience to date has shown Meaning-Text theory to provide an interesting basis for interlingual modelling. Despite the neglect of extrasentential representations at the semantic level (a repairable defect), one can cite a few factors in favor of MTMs:

- multiple levels of representation (semantic, deep-syntactic, surface-syntactic, etc.) provide an engineering basis for creating an efficient interlingua for a particular application, as well as for experimenting with general, theoretically satisfying, interlingual representations;
- MTMs provide for declarative grammars and lexica for a variety of language in a uniform metalanguage; also, many languages have been described in MTMs;
- the dependency formalism used for both levels of syntactic representation has simplified the comparison between telegraphic sublanguages and more "normal" varieties of English and French.

References

[Bourbeau et al. 90] Bourbeau, L., D. Carcagno, E. Goldberg, R. Kittredge and A. Polguère 1990. Bilingual Generation of Weather Forecasts in an Operations Environment. *Proc. of COLING-90*, vol.3, pp. 318–320.

[Iordanskaja et al. 90] Iordanskaja, L., R. Kittredge and A. Polguère 1990. Lexical Selection and Paraphrase in a Meaning-Text Generation Model. in *Natural Language Generation in Artificial Intelligence and Computational Linguistics* (C. Paris, W. Swartout and W. Mann, eds.), Kluwer, pp.293–312.

[Iordanskaja et al. 91] Iordanskaja, L., M. Kim, R. Kittredge, B. Lavoie and A. Polguère 1991. Generation of Extended Bilingual Statistical Reports. submitted to COLING-92.

[Kittredge et al. 86] Kittredge, R., A. Polguère and E. Goldbe rg 1986. Synthesizing Weather Forecasts from Formatted Data. *Proc. of COLING-86*, Bo nn, pp.563–565.

[Kittredge and Polguère 91] Kittredge, R. and A. Polguère 1991 . Dependency Grammars for Bilingual Text Generation: Inside FoG's Statificational Models. *Proc. of ICCICL*, Penang, pp.318–330.

[Polguère 91] Polguère, A. 1991. Everything has not been said about interlinguae: the case of multi-lingual text generation systems. *Proc. of Natural Language Processing Pacific Rim Symposium*, Singapore.

Multilingual Generation: Dimensions of Organization and Forms of Representation

Christian Matthiessen, Keizo Nanri and Zeng Licheng[1]
Department of Linguistics
University of Sydney
Sydney, NSW
Australia
Email: XIAN@BRUTUS.EE.SU.OZ.AU, LICHENG@BRUTUS.EE.SU.OZ.AU

Representation and Multilinguality

The themes of grammatical representation and multilinguality come together very centrally in the multilingual version of the Penman generation system [Mann 82, Mann and Matthiessen 83] being developed at the University of Sydney as part of the collaboration in the use and extension of the Penman system at ISI/USC, GMD/IPSI, and the University of Sydney [Bateman et al. 91, Matthiessen et al. 91]. On the one hand, the question of what form of representation is appropriate for a grammar can only be answered relative to some task (cf. [Kay 85]) and multilingual processing outside of MT is emerging as an important one. On the other hand, we need forms of representation that will support the specification of true multilingual grammars (going beyond mere collections of grammars of different languages) and multilingual processing. Though we base our discussion on the multilingual Penman, we introduce the principles in a sufficiently abstract, implementation-independent form that they can be explored in other generation systems as well.

We take as a base Systemic-Functional theory, which is designed to be general across languages, and extend it in a multilingual direction. The new contribution is to bring out the consequences of existing theory for a multilingual account and to extend it to support demands that are specifically multilingual (cf. the discussion of the exchange between theory and research application in [Matthiessen and Bateman 91]).

The distinction we maintain between resources and processes, while fully justified from the point of view of monolingual processing, enables us to adopt a very powerful working hypothesis: we treat the processes as general — as common across all the languages — and locate language-particular information *entirely* within the resources.

In this paper, we are concerned only with representing multilingual specifications; for the full architecture see [Bateman et al.]. The most basic requirement we place on these resources is that they should have the complementary properties of integration and integrity.

Integration of the different languages to allow commonality across grammars to be factored out and re-used: Our basic position is that the commonality must be factored out on *functional* grounds. For instance, it is well-known

---

[1] We are grateful to John Bateman for substantial contributions in the collaborative development of the multilingual Penman system. The research at the University of Sydney is supported by the Australian Research Council.

that although for example English, German, and French all have what we can call passive verb morphology, the functional scopes of these passive constructions are different, and what has to be kept 'constant' across the languages is the functional sentence perspective (i.e., the textual distribution of information) and the agency. Since commonality across languages is functional in the first instance, not structural or realizational, functionality has to be preserved across languages, while structural realizations may differ. The common functionality is based on text in communicative context, and it is realized stratum by stratum in a given linguistic system (semantics, lexicogrammar, phonology/graphology).

Integrity of each individual language so that it can be used separately: It should be possible to view the resources both from the point of view of their multilinguality and from the point of view of the individual languages. This requirement stands in direct contrast with approaches that neutralize language-specific information in some form of "language-free" representation such as Conceptual Dependency; cross-language generalizations arise out of the integration of language-particular specifications.

Implementation Example

To add the ability to define multilingual grammar components, we have extended the grammar definition notation used in the Penman generator. We illustrate the extended notation with the grammatical system 'declarative/interrogative' of the MOOD systems:

```
(system
 :name (:L1 :L2 MULTILINGUAL-SYSTEM-EG1 :L3 EG-SYSTEM)
 :inputs (and a b :L3 c))
 :outputs ( (x (insert F1))
             :L1 :L2 (y (insert F2) :L1 (order F1 F2))
             (z :L3 (insert F3)) )
 :chooser (:L1 :L2 MULTILINGUAL-SYSTEM-EG1-chooser-L1L2
              :L3 MULTILINGUAL-SYSTEM-EG1-chooser-L3) )
```

This defines a system called MULTILINGUAL-SYSTEM-EG1 that is applicable to three languages L1, L2 and L3. For L1 and L2, it is named MULTILINGUAL-SYSTEM-EG1, for L3 it is named EG-SYSTEM. This system is invisible to languages other than L1, L2 and L3. The entry conditions for this system are, for languages L1 and L2, the simple conjunction of features a and b, and for language L3, the slightly more complex conjunction of features a, b, and c. The output features of the system are, for language L3, x and z, and for languages L1 and L2, the features x, y and z. Furthermore, only for language L3 does the feature z have a structural realization, while for feature y occurring in languages L1 and L2, both languages call for the structural realization of 'inserting a grammatical function F2', while language L1 goes further and calls additionally for the structural realization that the function F1 be ordered before the function F2. Finally, the semantic decision procedure that chooses the grammatical feature that is appropriate for the current communicative goal is also conditionalized: a chooser with name MULTILINGUAL-SYSTEM-EG1-chooser-L1L2 is used for languages

L1 and L2, while a chooser with name `MULTILINGUAL-SYSTEM-EG1-chooser-L3` is used for language L3. The figure below shows the internal definitions required for the Chinese and English MOOD system `INDICATIVE-TYPE`, which is applicable to all languages covered, but has structural consequences only at this level of delicacy in English and Japanese.

```
(system :name INDICATIVE-TYPE
        :inputs indicative
        :outputs ( (interrogative
                      :japanese ((insert Interrogator)
                                 (lexify Interrogator ka)
                                 (conflate Finite Process)
                                 (order Finite Interrogator)))
                   (declarative
                      :english (order Subject Finite)) ) )
```

In an analogous manner, Penman's chooser-inquiry formalism is extended to include language-sensitive specifications.

The semantic environment (Penman's ideation base) is also extended in the multilingual system (for details of the description of English with references to Chinese and multilinguality in general, see [Halliday and Matthiessen]). The ideation base is modelled in the LOOM knowledge representation system, whose conceptual inheritance feature facilitates the definition of a multilingual ideation base.

References

[Bateman et al. 91] Bateman, J., C. Matthiessen, K. Nanri and L. Zeng. 1991b. The rapid prototyping of natural language generation components: an application of functional typology. In *Proceedings of the IJCAI*, Sydney.

[Bateman et al.] Bateman, J., C. Matthiessen, K. Nanri, and L. Zeng. in prep. Multilinguality in natural language processing.

[Halliday and Matthiessen] Halliday, M.A.K. and C. Matthiessen. forthcoming. *Construing experience through meaning: a language-based approach to cognition*. Berlin: de Gruyter.

[Kay 85] Kay, M. 1985. Parsing with Functional Unification Grammar. Reprinted in K. Sparck-Jones and B. Webber (eds) *Readings in Natural Language Processing*.

[Mann 82] Mann, W. 1982. An Overview of the Penman Text Generation System. ISI/RR-83-114.

[Mann and Matthiessen 83] Mann, W. and C. Matthiessen. 1983. Nigel: a systemic grammar for text generation. Three chapters in J. Benson and W. Greaves (eds, 1985) *Systemic Perspectives on Discourse*, Volume 1. Norwood: Ablex.

[Matthiessen and Bateman 91] Matthiessen, C. and J. Bateman. 1991. *Systemic Linguistics and Text Generation: Experiences from Japanese and English*. Frances Pinter.

[Matthiessen et al. 91] Matthiessen, C., K. Nanri, and L. Zeng. 1991. Multilingual resources: ideational focus. In *Proceedings of the 2nd Japan-Australia Joint Symposium on Natural Language Process*, Kyushu Institute of Technology, October 1991.

On Language-Independent Inputs
for Multilingual Generation

Sergei Nirenburg
Center for Machine Translation
Carnegie Mellon University
Pittsburgh, PA 15213-3890
U.S.A.
Email: SERGEI@NL.CS.CMU.EDU

I would like to comment on only one of the questions offered for the panel, namely, "How can input representations be made language-independent?" The answer, in a nutshell, is — by making sure that no language-dependent information is included. This requirement imposes different extra costs on different types of generators. For example, in the case of generators built specifically as modules of multilingual knowledge-based MT (KBMT) systems the extra costs are zero, due to the nature of the application.

The basic underlying assumption of knowledge-based MT as a scientific and technological enterprise is the interlingua hypothesis, which could be formulated as follows. *Meanings encoded in a natural language[1] can be made explicit and recorded in one of a class of artificial languages called* **interlinguas**; *the syntax and semantics of interlinguas are explicitly defined in such a way that they are not attuned to any particular natural language; the resulting interlingua texts can be used as inputs to generation modules for any natural language.* In the KBMT paradigm the following practical constraint on the above hypothesis is universally agreed upon: automatic translation is applicable only in such subject areas and among such languages for which there is a single global economic, political and sociological substrate. The interlingua hypothesis can be viewed alternatively as a statement about human cognitive processes associated with translation ("strong" interlinguality) or as a structural device facilitating the design and efficiency of computational systems which, if successful, parallel human capabilities ("weak" interlinguality). While it may often be useful to make practical generation systems informed by data or hypotheses about human language generation mechanisms, most of the work in our field follows a "functional equivalence" tradition in AI and aims at producing systems whose outputs are as close to those of human language generators as possible. The weak interlinguality hypothesis conforms to this pattern.

It follows from the above that

- there is no single "canonical" interlingua waiting to be "discovered."
- particular interlingua specimens can (and must be expected to) contain errors, just as, say, specimens of formal grammars for any particular language.

---

[1] The set of meanings to be encoded in a modern KBMT-related interlingua includes all of propositional, pragmatic, discourse-related, rhetorical and stylistic facets of text meaning, so that the boundary between semantics and pragmatics is thoroughly blurred and, in fact, discarded as spurious.

– in practice the complexity of generating language A from a given interlingua may be greater than that of generating language B.

Still, none of the above contradicts the basic interlingua hypothesis. What *would* contradict it is an alternative hypothesis to the effect that meaning is by nature language-dependent. The reverberations of this hypothesis in theoretical linguistics and philosophy of language very quickly lead to the Quinean position that translation among languages (not only *machine* translation!) is impossible. However intellectually entertaining this hypothesis is, it runs against significant empirical evidence. But even if one does not extend the corollaries of this hypothesis that far, its adoption means discarding the possibility of a single language-independent input to multilingual generation. Instead, one would have to rely on conversions among language-dependent meaning representations. From the point of view of system building this is inefficient (the standard numerical criticism of multilingual transfer-based MT environments applies here). Empirically, it seems quite redundant, too — a number of experiments in KBMT (e.g., the KBMT-89 system at CMU or Ultra at New Mexico State University) showed that non-toy ontologies and domain models can be developed and applied in a language-independent fashion.

Architecturally, adopting the interlinguality hypothesis for multilingual generation makes the step of text planning necessary even if, as in an MT environment, there is no need in the "what to say" component of the generation process. A number of text planners have been developed primarily for the latter purpose. But many of them, such as, for instance, Spokesman [Meteer 89], already have a lot of machinery required for text planning in the multilingual set-up. The output of such text planners can vary depending on the amount of work it is designed to perform. But in practice it seems appropriate to posit an intermediate stage of the overall generation process which marks the end of the planning stage and the beginning of the realization stage. The results of the planning stage must then be encoded in a special formalism which would serve as the input formalism to the realization stage. The SPL language used in the Penman generator is an example of such formalism [Kasper 89].

The difference between the two intermediate languages — the interlingua and the text plan language — is essentially the fact that the former does not depend on the target language whereas the latter overtly does. Among these types of target language-dependent facts which belong in a text plan language and don't belong in an interlingua are sentence boundaries; order of sentences in the output text; nature of dependence among target language clauses; lexical realizations of underlying meanings; decisions on pronominalization and ellipsis as options of lexical selection; etc.

An example of such generator architecture can be found in the DIOGENES generator [Leavitt et al. 91]. The input language to DIOGENES is the interlingua language TAMERLAN [Nirenburg and Defrise 92]. The meaning of a text, as represented in TAMERLAN, includes information about the speech situation (the identity of the speaker and hearer and the time and location of the speech situation) and additional "pragmatic factors" such as *force, directness,* or *respect,* in addition to text meaning "proper." Text meaning in TAMERLAN is represented as a set of TAMERLAN clauses, relations, attitudes, and producer intentions.

A text plan is an intermediate data structure which is the output of the DIO-GENES text planning module and the input to the semantics-to-syntax mapping module that produce LFG-like syntactic structures which in turn serve as input to the final realization module. While the input to DIOGENES, written in TAMERLAN, gives no indication as to the boundaries or order of sentences in the output text, the ways of treating co-reference, or the selection of the appropriate lexical units (both open-class items and such closed-class ones as realizations of producer attitudes and discourse cohesion markers, connectives) for the target text, the text plan structure already contains such information. Additionally, the text planning stage also produces values for such features as definiteness, tense and mood. Due to space constraints, we do not give examples of TAMERLAN structures, opting instead to illustrate the text plan language.

In summary, we believe that language-independent inputs to multilingual generation are both possible and desirable. A small-scale illustration of one such approach has been suggested.

References

[Kasper 89] Kasper, R.T. 1989. A Flexible Interface for Linking Applications to Penman's Sentence Generator. In *Proceedings of the DARPA Speech and Natural Language Workshop*, Philadelphia.

[Leavitt et al. 91] Leavitt, J., E. Nyberg, S. Nirenburg, D. Gates, and C. Defrise. 1991. DIOGENES-90. Technical Report CMU-CMT-91-123. Center for Machine Translation, Carnegie Mellon University, Pittsburgh.

[Meteer 89] Meteer, M. 1989. The SPOKESMAN Natural Language Generation System. Technical Report 7090. Bolt, Beranek, and Newman, Cambridge.

[Nirenburg and Defrise 92] Nirenburg, S. and C. Defrise. 1992. Application-Oriented Computational Semantics. In R. Johnson and M. Rosner (eds.), **Computational Linguistics and Formal Semantics**. Cambridge University Press.

Remarks on Multilinguality and Generation

Dietmar Rösner
FAW Ulm
P.O. Box 2060
D-7900 Ulm
Germany
Email: ROESNER@DULFAW1A.BITNET

Multilinguality: Why We Should Care

There seem to be three main motives for work in multilingual generation: Practical needs, linguistic motivation, and generator design issues.

In a variety of domains, multilingual generation of documents could be an alternative to human or machine translation of those documents. In the near future, generation technology could help to overcome some of the intrinsic problems of documentation, e.g., the problems of updating and keeping documentation consistent with changes in the respective product, the sheer mass of documentation needed and the time pressure and lack of experienced technical writers.

From a linguistic point, work in multilingual generation is an interesting exercise in contrastive linguistics. The generation perspective differs significantly from other approaches because the central question is: Given a common content, how do the languages under consideration express this content?

For generator design, steps towards multilingualism always give an impetus to separate more clearly between generator machinery and language-specific data.

Multilinguality in Generation Systems

Although multilinguality has never been a central topic of discussion in the natural language generation community, it has been already an issue in very early generators. Goldman's BABEL program delivered outputs not only in English, but in a variety of languages, including Spanish, Mandarin, and German. BABEL started from Conceptual Dependency graphs, a semantic representation that was designed to be as universal as possible.

Recent work with respect to multilinguality may roughly be classified as:
- attempts to address multilinguality in the design from the very beginning
- experiments to transfer a tactical generator to another language
- experiments to let text generators produce their texts in different languages

The first category is represented by the POLYGLOSS project at Stuttgart University and the multilingual PENMAN project at the University of Sydney (see the panel statement of Matthiessen).

Experiments to adapt a tactical generator to another language have often been carried out more for pedagogical reasons than with the goal of a real working version in mind. Not too much is reported about such experiments. The discussion of experiences from the attempt to transfer MUMBLE to German by [Jacob and Maier 88] is a rare exception.

In the third category are report generators that got a version in another language. FRANA for example is a French version of Kukich's ANA program [Kukich 83] delivering stock market reports from Dow Jones data [Contant 86]. Both SEMTEX and GEOTEX, text generators based on the SEMSYN tactical component [Rösner 86], have an English version: SEMTEX-E produces English versions of reports on labour market developments [Rambow 88]. For GEOTEX the German and English versions have been combined into a programme that simultaneously describes geometric constructions in both languages [Kehl 89]. In addition to the questions of ease or difficulty of the creation of the capability to produce output in an additional language, a very interesting question is what parts of the overall text generation system could be left untouched, and from what step of the overall procedure on language-dependent changes had to be carried out. This opens a window as well on the question of how input representations can be made language-independent.

How can Input Representations be Language-Independent?

There are some obvious requirements that are sometimes hard to fulfill in real applications. Language-independent input representations cannot contain words nor should they contain syntactic features. They have to be on a purely conceptual level. On the other hand, all information that will be needed for syntactic decisions in the languages concerned has to be available. Even closely related languages like English, German and French differ significantly with respect to, e.g., the tense system, rules for using definite, indefinite or zero determiners, pronominalization rules etc.

Do the particularities of inputs for generation have any consequences for interlinguas for machine translation systems? Ideally spoken, machine translation systems should have no interlinguas as they are employed nowadays, but should be based on "deep semantics". As long as the problems of analysis are not sufficiently solved, the pressure to use "shallow" interlinguas will be hard to overcome.

How can Language-Specific Grammars and Other Knowledge Resources be Integrated into a Single Generator?

The term "single generator" seems to allow two readings:

- Strong multilinguality: There is a single generation programme, and all language-specific information is put into declarative knowledge sources: Grammar rules, lexicalization rules, etc. There is some doubt about how feasible such an approach is for the near future. I will therefore opt for a more engineering-like, "weaker" approach.
- Weak multilinguality: For practical purposes, it could be sufficient to start from a shared knowledge basis and language-independent representations of the content and structure (i.e., structural relations between the propositions involved) of

the intended texts. These representations could then be the basis for language-specific generators producing texts in their respective target language. These generators could be "close relatives" or quite distinct in their internal working, the only commitment would be that they can work from the common input representation and exploit the related knowledge basis.

References

[Contant 86] Contant, C. 1986. *Génération automatique de texte: Application au sous-language boursier.* M.A. dissertation, Dépt. de Linguistique, Université de Montréal.

[Jacob and Maier 88] Jacob, D. and Maier, E. 1988. Die Übertragung des MUMBLE-Generators für die Generierung von Deutsch. In Trost, H. (ed.), *4. Österreichische Artificial-Intelligence-Tagung Proceedings*, Informatik-Fachberichte 176, Springer-Verlag.

[Kehl 89] Kehl, W. 1989. GEOTEX-E: Generierung zweisprachiger Konstruktionstexte. In Endres-Niggemeyer, B. et al. (eds.) *Interaktion und Kommunikation mit dem Computer*, GLDV-Jahrestagung Proceedings, Informatik-Fachberichte 238, Springer-Verlag.

[Kukich 83] Kukich, K. 1983. Design and Implementation of a Knowledge-Based Report Generator, *Proceedings of the Annual Meeting of the ACL.*

[Rambow 88] Rambow, O. 1988. Teaching a Second Language to a Computer: A Programmer's View. In Trost, H. (ed.), *4. Österreichische Artificial-Intelligence-Tagung Proceedings*, Informatik-Fachberichte 176, Springer-Verlag.

[Rösner 86] Rösner, D. 1986. *Ein System zur Generierung von deutschen Texten aus semantischen Repräsentationen.* Ph.D. dissertation, Institut für Informatik, Universität Stuttgart.

List of Contributors

Claassen, Wim – NICI, University of Nijmegen, Montessorilaan 3, P.O.Box 9104, 6500 HE Nijmegen, The Netherlands
email: `claassen@nici.kun.nl`

Cumming, Susanna – Department of Linguistics, Institute of Cognitive Science, University of Colorado, Boulder CO 80309-0430, USA
email: `scumming@clipr.colorado.edu`

Elhadad, Michael – Department of Computer Science, Columbia University, New York, NY 10027, USA
email: `elhadad@mermaid.cs.columbia.edu`

Horacek, Helmut – Fakultät für Linguistik und Literaturwissenschaft, Universität Bielefeld, P.O.Box 8640, 4800 Bielefeld 1, Germany
email: `horacek@techfak.uni-bielefeld.de`

Hovy, Eduard – USC/Information Sciences Institute, 4676 Admiralty Way, Marina del Rey, CA 90292, USA
email: `hovy@isi.edu`

Hozumi, Tanaka – Department of Computer Science, Tokyo Institute of Technology, 2-12-1 Ôokayama Meguro Tokyo 152, Japan
email: `tanaka@cs.titech.ac.jp`

Ishizaki, Masato – Human Communication Research Centre, University of Edinburgh, 2 Buccleuch Place, Edinburgh EH8 9LW, Scotland, UK
email: `masato@cogsci.ed.ac.uk`

Jones, Mark A. – Computer and Information Sciences, University of Delaware, Newark DE 19716, USA
email: `jones@udel.edu`

Kalra, Prem – MIRALab, CUI, University of Geneva, 12 rue du Lac, 1207 Geneva, Switzerland
email: `kalra@cui.unige.ch`

Kentaro, Inui – Department of Computer Science, Tokyo Institute of Technology, 2-12-1 Ôokayama Meguro Tokyo 152, Japan
email: `inui@cs.titech.ac.jp`

Lascarides, Alex – Centre for Cognitive Science, Human Communication Research Centre, University of Edinburgh, 2, Buccleuch Place, Edinburgh EH8 9LW, Scotland, UK
email: `alex@cogsci.ed.ac.uk`

Lavid, Julia – Departaménto de Filologia Inglesa, Universidad Complutense de Madrid, 280040 Madrid, Spain
email: `lavid@isi.edu`

Linden, Keith Vander – Department of Computer Science, Institute of Cognitive Science, University of Colorado, Boulder CO 80309-0430, USA
email: `linden@cs.colorado.edu`

Oberlander, Jon – Centre for Cognitive Science, Human Communication Research Centre, University of Edinburgh, 2, Buccleuch Place, Edinburgh EH8 9LW, Scotland, UK
email: `jon@cogsci.ed.ac.uk`

Magnenat-Thalmann, Nadia – MIRALab, CUI, University of Geneva, 12 rue du Lac, 1207 Geneva, Switzerland
email: `thalmann@cgeuge51.bitnet`

Maier, Elisabeth – Projekt KOMET, GMD-IPSI, Dolivostr. 15, 6100 Darmstadt, Germany
email: `maier@ipsi.darmstadt.gmd.de`

Martin, James – Department of Computer Science, Institute of Cognitive Science, University of Colorado, Boulder CO 80309-0430, USA
email: `martin@cs.colorado.edu`

McCoy, Kathleen F. – Computer and Information Sciences, University of Delaware, Newark DE 19716, USA
email: `mccoy@udel.edu`

McDonald, David D. – 14 Brantwood Road, Arlington MA 02174, USA
email: `mcdonald@brandeis.edu`

McGlashan, Scott – Social and Computer Sciences Research Group, Department of Sociology, University of Surrey, Guildford, UK
email: `Scott.McGlashan@soc.surrey.ac.uk`

Mittal, Vibhu – Department of Computer Science, University of Southern California, Los Angeles, CA 90089, USA
email: `mittal@isi.edu`

Paris, Cécile – USC/Information Sciences Institute, 4676 Admiralty Way, Marina del Rey, CA 90292, USA
email: `paris@isi.edu`

Reithinger, Norbert – SFB 314 – FB 14 Informatik IV, Universität des Saarlandes, 6600 Saarbrücken, Germany
email: `bert@cs.uni-sb.de`

Robin, Jacques – Department of Computer Science, Columbia University, New York, NY 10027, USA
email: `robin@beach.cs.columbia.edu`

Rösner, Dietmar – FAW, P.O.Box 2060, 7900 Ulm, Germany
email: `roesner@dulfaw1a.bitnet`

Rubinoff, Robert – Institute for Research in Cognitive Science, 3401-4C Walnut St., University of Pennsylvania, Philadelphia, PA 19104, USA
email: `rubinoff@linc.cis.upenn.edu`

Saint-Dizier, Patrick – IRIT University Paul Sabatier, 118 route de Narbonne, 31062 Toulouse (Cedex), France
email: `stdizier@irit.irit.fr`

Stede, Manfred – Dept. of Computer Science, University of Toronto, Toronto M5S 1A4, Canada
email: `mstede@cs.toronto.edu`

Takenobu, Tokunaga – Department of Computer Science, Tokyo Institute of Technology, 2-12-1 Ôokayama Meguro Tokyo 152, Japan
email: `take@cs.titech.ac.jp`

Youd, Nick J. – Logica Cambridge Ltd, Betjeman House, 104 Hills Road, Cambridge, UK
email: `nick@logcam.uucp`

Lecture Notes in Artificial Intelligence (LNAI)

Lecture Notes in Computer Science